Implementing Cisco VPNs: A Hands-On Guide

Implementing Cisco VPNs: A Hands-On Guide

Adam Quiggle

McGraw-Hill
New York • Chicago • San Francisco • Lisbon
London • Madrid • Mexico City • Milan • New Delhi
San Juan • Seoul • Singapore • Sydney • Toronto

Osborne/**McGraw-Hill**
2600 Tenth Street
Berkeley, California 94710
U.S.A.

To arrange bulk purchase discounts for sales promotions, premiums, or fund-raisers, please contact Osborne/**McGraw-Hill** at the above address. For information on translations or book distributors outside the U.S.A., please see the International Contact Information page immediately following the index of this book.

Implementing Cisco VPNs: A Hands-On Guide

1234567890 CUS CUS 01987654321

ISBN 0-07-213048-2

Publisher
Brandon A. Nordin

**Vice President &
Associate Publisher**
Scott Rogers

Acquisitions Editor
Francis Kelly

Acquisitions Coordinator
Alex Corona

Project Manager
Dave Nash

Technical Editor
Mark Newcomb

Cover Design
William Chan

Production
MacAllister Publishing Services, LLC

Dedication

To my wife and best friend, Meg, the smartest, funniest, most inspiring person I know. You are the source of all my joy.

Contents at a Glance

Contents

Acknowledgments

First and most importantly, I want to thank my wife for her endless ideas and encouragement throughout this writing process and all other aspects of our lives. It is amazing to me the clarity with which she sees everything from the straightforward to the most multifaceted and the ease with which she can then explain it to me. Meg, it's time to hang up the proverbial typewriter and get back to filling our lives with fun!

I'd like to thank Franny Kelly, Acquisition Editor, McGraw-Hill, who successfully maintained the role of "fearless leader," effectively coordinating this project from beginning to end, while never losing his "nice guy" hat. Once again, it was a pleasure to work with such a talented and patient man.

As with Franny Kelly, this is the second opportunity I've had to work with Beth Brown, project manager at MacAllister Publishing Services. And, once again, Beth proved to be a gracious and obliging editor who put forth the extra effort to ensure that my vision for this book was not lost.

I'd like to thank Mark Newcomb, my technical editor, whose insight and candor regarding the subject matter aspects of this book I trusted implicitly. It's my goal to ensure that we actually meet in person before we take on one more project together!

Andrew Mason cheerfully offered keen insight into some of the finer points of PIX Firewall deployments and also volunteered access to an incredible lab for testing configurations. Many thanks!

Finally, thanks to Dave Dini of Cisco Systems, who also tendered access to extensive lab facilities, an incredible advantage during the final stages of writing.

About the Author

Adam Quiggle is a Senior Network Engineer at the MCI Worldcom Network Operations Center in Cary, NC. He is responsible for transitioning the network management of an international Fortune 100 company to MCI Worldcom. He has designed, implemented and supported complex networks in numerous enterprise environments. He is a CCNA, a Master CNE, an MCSE and a Spectrum Administrator and he holds a Bachelor of Science in Electrical Engineering. In addition, he is the author or co-author of several previously published books (*Building Cisco Remote Access Networks* and *Interconnecting Cisco Network Devices* with McGraw-Hill and *Windows 2000 Server System Administration Handbook* with Syngress Media).

About the Reviewer

Mark J. Newcomb, CCNP (Security), CCDP, MCSE is a consulting network engineer working for Aurora Consulting Group (www.auroracg.com), where he provides network design, security and implementation services throughout the Pacific Northwest. He has more than 20 years experience in the Microcomputer industry. His other publications include co-authorship of McGraw-Hill's *Cisco Internetwork Troubleshooting* and contributing author on McGraw-Hill's *Interconnecting Cisco Network Devices*.

CHAPTER 1

Introduction to Cisco VPNs

In today's world, exchanging information is a fact of life. In order for computers to exchange information, they need to be connected by networks. Over the last ten years, the computing industry has seen a tremendous increase in the number of networking products in *Local Area Networks* (LANs) and *Wide Area Networks* (WANs).

Organizations are no longer confined to information available on their own corporate networks. Instead, they can access a virtually inexhaustible source of information on the Internet; thus, the Internet has become a very large extension of the corporate network. Now that businesses have become comfortable with the idea of using the Internet to exchange non-confidential data, they are looking at using the Internet to carry their own internal, highly confidential data. Why? As with any business, they want to stay competitive. By leveraging the vast infrastructure of the Internet, a business can eliminate the costs associated with dedicated circuits to a remote site or even to a business partner.

Unfortunately for businesses, the protocols that run on the Internet are generally considered insecure. Remember that the biggest users of the Internet, prior to the commercialization of the Internet, were universities where information and ideas were freely exchanged. A need for security like large corporations require did not exist.

In this chapter we will provide a brief definition of *Virtual Private Networks* (VPNs), show the fundamental aspects of any VPN, and define the terminology that we will use throughout the rest of this book. These three important tasks need to be accomplished before you read this book. Otherwise, you could find yourself disagreeing when, in fact, you agree.

1.1 Who Should Read This Book?

The primary audience for this book is network designers and network engineers who need to implement a VPN. However, with the recent inclusion of IPSec in the *Cisco Certified Internetwork Expert* (CCIE) routing and switching lab, and L2TP in the CCIE service provider lab we expect that CCIE candidates will use this book as a resource as well.

If you've picked up this book, you no doubt already understand the importance of security. Therefore, you won't be regaled with tales of security breaches or business cases discussing why you need to have a VPN. This does not mean that you don't need to do your homework before implementing a VPN. As a matter of fact, before implementing any VPN, you should have a complete business case for your solution, which should include a good security policy defining acceptable risks as well as a documented understanding of the traffic flows that need to be kept private.

This book is not about building a justification for a VPN or determining a good security policy. It is assumed that you have already done your homework and know what problem you are trying to solve, and now you want to know the "how." This book has been written as a "where the rubber meets the road" type of book. You will look at the different types of VPNs and what types of problems they are used to solve.

So, you may be asking yourself, "What do I need to know before reading this book?" Early on in the writing of this book, the decision was made to discuss only VPN-related topics and leave out the OSI model, Cisco configuration basics, TCP/IP fundamentals, and IP routing. Many fine books are available out there that cover these topics in depth, so it is unnecessary to cover what should be the fundamentals of any networking professional. Instead, the focus of this book is on just the implementation aspects and considerations for VPNs. However, if you do need to brush up on a few of these topics, take a look at the bibliography for a list of excellent reference material.

Note:
For those of you familiar with Cisco's certification track, a Cisco Certified Network Professional (CCNP)—specifically the objectives outlined in the Building Cisco Remote Access Networks exam—will provide you with an excellent background for reading this book. This does not mean you must have passed Building Cisco Remote Access Networks *(BCRAN) to understand this book; this material is suggested only as a primer to this book.*

1.2 Overview of Chapters

To facilitate a greater understanding of VPNs as a whole, this book is broken down into two sections:

- VPN Primer
- VPN Case Studies

The VPN Primer section is designed to provide an understanding of the fundamentals of building a Cisco VPN, such as basic encryption principles, and configuring dialup services on Cisco hardware and various Windows platforms. The VPN Case Studies section is designed to introduce the various VPN protocols to the reader, give detailed explanations on their format, show how to configure them on Cisco hardware, and then provide a case study for the reader to actually try out his new found knowledge.

1.2.1 VPN Briefing

These chapters are designed to help you understand the components that go into supporting a VPN. Although it is assumed that you know how to configure an IP address on a Cisco router, it isn't assumed that you know how to configure ISDN on a Cisco router or that you understand the difference between cryptography and encryption. These chapters will give you the knowledge required to understand the VPN Case Studies.

1.2.1.1 Chapter 1—Introduction to Implementing Cisco VPNs

This chapter has been written to provide the reader with the terminology used throughout the book. All the hype and the eagerness by vendors to claim that their products are VPNs has created a lot of confusion in the marketplace. Therefore, Chapter 1 covers the following:

- VPN definition
- What is not considered to be a VPN
- Categories of the different VPN types
- VPN basic components
- When not to deploy a VPN

Although the first chapter of any book is not normally considered all that important, in this book Chapter 1 is a must-read for those not familiar with VPN terminology.

1.2.1.2 Chapter 2—Windows Support for Dialup

VPN compulsory tunnels frequently require the configuration of the client machine to support standard PPP connections. The focus of this chapter is on three different Microsoft operating systems: Windows 95, Windows NT, and Windows 2000. Each section focuses on configuring the *Point-to-Point Protocol* (PPP) aspects of each operating system. Those of you who are familiar with MS-Windows may consider skipping this section.

1.2.1.3 Chapter 3—Dialup over Cisco Routers

This chapter is designed to review dialup material. Similar to Chapter 2, since VPN voluntary tunnels utilize a significant portion of the dialup features, you need to know how to configure a Cisco router to support dialup (POTS and ISDN).

1.2.1.4 Chapter 4—VPN Security Primer

This chapter focuses primarily on the concepts and configuration commands required for the case studies. Encryption, cryptography, authentication, and AAA are discussed in depth so that you understand the information provided in the later chapters.

1.2.2 VPN Case Studies

These chapters get to the heart of the material. In addition to a solid foundation of information, an in-depth explanation of the technology is provided. Each chapter has a technology overview that covers the basic principles, Internet standards, and concepts behind each of the technologies. You then see how to implement them with Cisco equipment. Finally, for greater comprehension of the knowledge just acquired, up to three case studies are provided.

1.2.2.1 Chapter 5—GRE and CET

Even though this is not generally considered to be a VPN, you can create a pseudo-VPN using a *Generic Routing Encapsulation* (GRE) tunnel with Payload Encryption on a Cisco router. In addition, understanding the basic principles of tunneling provides a better understanding of these fundamentals. This allows for quicker digestion of the other chapters.

1.2.2.2 Chapter 6—IPSec

This chapter covers the history of IPSec and explains what makes it fundamentally different from other VPN protocols. It capitalizes on the knowledge acquired in Chapter 4 so that you can understand its fundamental components. In addition, this chapter explains the how and why of each command used when configuring IPSec.

1.2.2.3 Chapter 7—PPTP

This chapter focuses on the VPN protocol PPTP, developed by a consortium (led by Microsoft). Chapter 7 discusses its many advantages and disadvantages. Although you won't learn how to configure a traditional PPTP VPN network using Microsoft Windows NT Server as the VPN server, you will read about one of Cisco's latest additions to their VPN line and how to configure a Cisco Router to be a PPTP VPN server.

1.2.2.4 Chapter 8—L2TP

The last VPN protocol covered is L2TP. L2TP utilizes the best technology from L2F as well as PPTP to provide this very functional VPN protocol. We will show you how to configure Cisco hardware to work with L2TP.

1.2.2.5 Chapter 9—PIX Firewall VPNs

In this chapter, we will not explore any new VPN protocols, but we will learn how to configure PPTP and IPSec on a PIX firewall. In addition, we will learn a handful of PIX commands so we can configure IPSec and PPTP on a PIX firewall. This chapter will not teach you all of the aspects of configuring a PIX firewall—the commands necessary to configure a PIX firewall to support a VPN.

1.3 What Is a VPN?

For the last several years, the phrase VPN has been tossed around as one of the latest buzzwords, and many companies are trying to associate themselves with this latest and greatest technology. Unfortunately, the effect of this is to confuse or mislead those who make the decisions.

A VPN tries to extract the advantages of both the public and private networking worlds. The advantage of a public network is that it is a shared environment and thus its cost is low compared to building a private international network. The advantage of a private network is security; because it is your network, you control access to it.

1.3.1 VPN Definition

To understand the definition of VPN used in this book, the acronym is broken down into its basic components. The first word, "virtual," is defined by Webster's as "possessing certain physical virtues." In this case, the "virtual" defines a dynamic connection between two remote nodes through a public internetwork, as seen in Figure 1-1. This "virtual" connection gives the routers a logical connection to each other.

The second word, "private," is defined by Webster's as "intended for or restricted to the use of a particular person or group." This aspect of a VPN is usually accomplished through the use of two components: authentication and encryption.

Authentication is the process in which an individual or node is identified. It is typically imposed prior to accessing a network and the available services provided by the network. Encryption is a method of transforming a body of information in order to conceal its original meaning. Figure 1-2 shows that without data encryption applied to the message, it is sent in

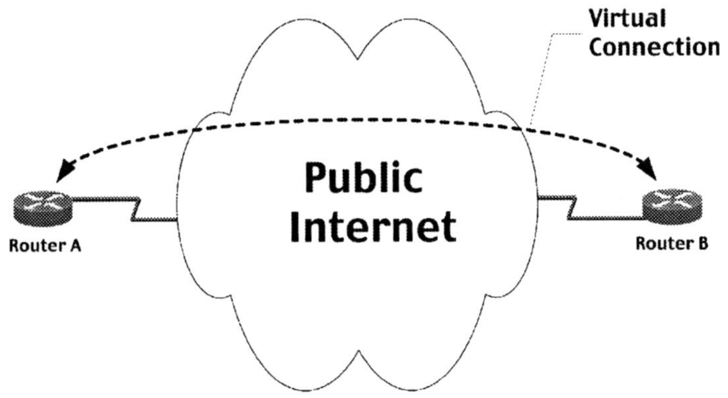

Figure 1-1

Virtual connection through an internetwork

Virtual Connection

Public Internet

Router A

Router B

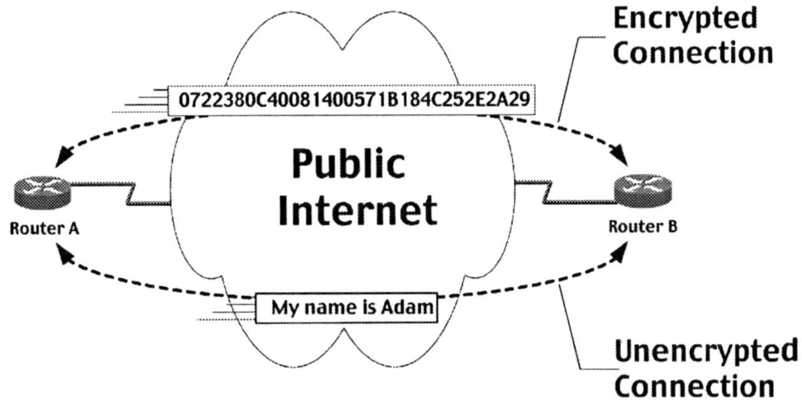

Figure 1-2

Example of encrypted and unencrypted data through an internetwork

Encrypted Connection

0722380C4008140057 1B184C252E2A29

Public Internet

Router A

Router B

My name is Adam

Unencrypted Connection

clear text. With data encryption applied to the message, it is unreadable, unless you know how to decrypt it.

The last word, "network," is defined by Webster's as "a system of computers, terminals, and databases connected by communications lines." This is the most fundamental aspect of a VPN and the most obvious. The network enables computers to communicate through various media.

1.3.2 What Isn't a VPN?

Given these fairly liberal definitions, the following is what a VPN isn't, or at the very least what isn't considered to be a VPN solution for the purposes of this book.

Point-to-Point Connections: Some people argue that dedicated point-to-point connections can be considered a VPN. Consider the fact that a leased line infrastructure uses multiplexers to combine multiple customers' physical layer data for transmission over common long-haul circuits. A customer's physical layer signal is then demuxed and sent over the customer's local loop to the customer's router. Although you can definitely consider this paradigm as using a shared public infrastructure for your data, there is nothing virtual about it.

Packet Switched Connections: Others will argue that Frame Relay should be considered a VPN. After all, a Frame Relay cloud can be considered a public infrastructure. And when using Frame Relay the customer's data link layer frames are encapsulated into a cell-switched service and sent across a Frame Relay cloud. Once the cell reaches the remote frame switch, the cells are recombined to form the original frame, which is then delivered to the customer's local loop. Although these types of services have been used to build private intranets, they lack one of the components identified earlier to make a VPN private: encryption. In addition, because this involves the data link layer and not the network layer, a firewall is not required to protect one Frame Relay customer's data network against possible attacks from another customer's connection.

1.4 VPN Categories

Now that you know the definition of a VPN used in this book, let's take a look at the various categories that VPNs fall into. It is important to remember that these classifications are general definitions. The infrastructure you have and the problem you are trying to solve will define the type of VPN you choose.

Note:

Although no attempt has been made to define business terminology in this section, one goal is to get you thinking about the type of problems that can be solved with VPNs.

Five generally accepted categories of VPNs are: Remote Access VPNs, Intranet VPNs, Extranet VPNs, Enhanced Voice/IP VPNs, and Enterprise VPNs.

1.4.1 Remote Access VPNs

Remote Access VPNs provide connectivity for remote users whose primary access to the company network is through an *Internet Service Provider* (ISP). A business can realize savings by outsourcing the remote access infrastructure to an ISP. Both telecommuters and road warriors can benefit from these types of VPNs.

1.4.2 Intranet VPNs

By providing site-to-site connections for an organization's remote sites through the Internet, a company can reduce its WAN costs. The advantage of using Intranet VPNs is that they are easy to set up; the disadvantage is that service levels are not guaranteed when using the Internet.

1.4.3 Extranet VPNs

An extranet is fundamentally the same as an intranet, but the tunneling nodes are generally business partners and do not belong to the same organization. Although technically the solution is the same, the main difference between an Intranet VPN and Extranet VPN is security. For example, although it may be OK to have your employees browse for network resources, you wouldn't want to let your business partners have this type of access.

1.4.4 Enhanced Voice/IP VPNs

Enhanced Voice/IP VPNs support secure Internet telephony. Think of this as similar to an Intranet VPN except that, instead of tunneling encrypted data, encrypted voice is tunneling across the Internet.

1.4.5 Enterprise VPNs

Enterprise VPNs are used to support the convergence of voice and data applications securely over the public Internet. They combine data VPNs (generally just Intranet VPNs) with Voice VPNs.

   This book does not address any voice technology and, as such, does not address Enhanced Voice/IP VPNs or Enterprise VPNs. However, for more information about these types of VPNs, an excellent reference is *Cisco Packetized Voice & Data Integration* by Robert Caputo.

1.5 VPN Tunnel Type

Figure 1-1 showed a logical connection between two devices. This logical connection, called a tunnel, provides the "virtual" component of a VPN. The phrase "VPN tunnel type" refers to the paradigm between three devices: the VPN user, the VPN initiator, and the VPN server.

Note:

This section defines the terminology that is used throughout the book. In some cases, the terms that are used are not necessarily well-accepted terms. However, for descriptions to be more accurate, they need to be more specific so that the ideas are clearer. In the previous paragraph, the term VPN client could have been used to describe the VPN initiator and VPN user. Under certain instances this would be fine, but this lack of clarity can lead to confusion about what role is being discussed. For example, when the duties of the VPN client are split up like they are in the compulsory tunnel (see the section on compulsory tunnels later in this chapter), it would be difficult for the reader to understand exactly which device is being discussed.

The following is a look at the architecture of these three devices using two different VPN tunnel types: voluntary and compulsory.

1.5.1 Voluntary Tunnels

Voluntary tunnels require clients to have the ability to manage their own VPN tunnel, as seen in Figure 1-3. In this scenario, when data is destined for the corporate network, it is routed through the tunnel established by the client.

Figure 1-3

Virtual Private Dialup Network using a voluntary tunnel

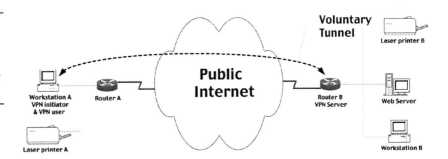

The beauty of this paradigm is that a VPN user is also the VPN initiator, thus allowing the VPN user to establish a VPN as long as it is connected somehow to the Internet. This Internet connection can be through a multitude of different services such as a local dialup ISP, *x-Type Digital Subscriber Line* (xDSL) service, cable modem connection, or even from a business partner. This configuration is particularly advantageous with a mobile workforce. Another advantage is that the VPN server does not necessarily have to be a router, as shown in Figure 1-3. The VPN server could have easily been Web Server B or Workstation B.

Note:
Having an Internet connection may not always be enough. If there is a firewall between you and your corporate network, you may have to reconfigure the firewall to allow your connection through it.

Because these tunnels are dynamic, once the VPN server has been set up by the administrator, the VPN initiators are responsible for setting up the tunnels. You can think of this paradigm as similar to a *Remote Access Server* (RAS), in which clients will dial up to your network. The only thing the VPN server administrator has to be concerned about, aside from troubleshooting connections with the VPN initiator, is making sure that the hardware for the VPN server is of adequate size.

Note:

Many Cisco routers can be used as a VPN server. In this book, any reference to a VPN server includes those that support VPNs through Cisco's IOS; however, a reference to a Cisco router does not necessarily mean a VPN server. This is a subtle, but important, distinction to clarify.

As with every advantage there is always a disadvantage, and with voluntary tunnels that disadvantage is that the user's computer must have special software installed so that it can manage its own VPNs. This can make deployment cumbersome, especially when you are just adding this service to a laptop that has already been deployed. This is because the VPN client needs to be nestled deep in the operating system, which can conflict with pre-existing services on the client's machine. Combine this with the inability to test all the variations before deployment and you have a recipe for a delayed or, worse, a stalled rollout. You should consider the deployment of new client machines when deploying a voluntary tunnel. This will give your IT group the opportunity to thoroughly test the configurations before deployment, allowing you to reduce the support calls of a VPN using voluntary tunnels rollout.

Voluntary tunnels are most often used with Remote Access VPNs. With a mobile workforce, it is particularly useful because your roaming users will never know what is the source of their network connections. Voluntary tunnels are also useful for telecommuters, especially if they aren't physically located within the same geographic region. By allowing your telecommuters to use any ISP, you can avoid the long distance charges associated with dialing directly to the corporate network. Although voluntary tunnels are not generally deployed with any other type of VPN, a case can be made for deploying a voluntary tunnel as an Extranet VPN.

Another distinct advantage of using voluntary tunnels is that they can generally be deployed fairly quickly. In situations that are driven top-down by an application or business need, as seen in Figure 1-4, it may be better to set up a voluntary tunnel.

Figure 1-4

Business layers from a technical perspective

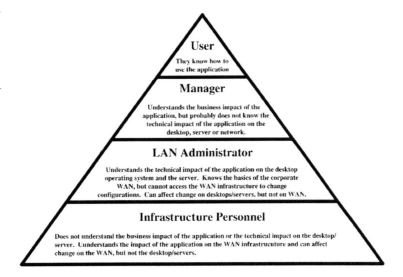

This is not because you can set up the components required for a voluntary tunnel more quickly (this is rarely the case), but because it reduces the number of people that need to be involved. Voluntary tunnels might be the most appropriate solution for short-term projects in an Extranet VPN or in cases in which your infrastructure group will not support VPNs.

1.5.2 Compulsory Tunnels

Compulsory tunnels, frequently known as mandatory tunnels, are completely transparent to the end user. Figure 1-5 shows an example of a VPN using a compulsory tunnel. In this example, the resources connected to Router A (Workstation A, email server, and laser printer A) are required to use the tunnel to access resources connected to Router B (Workstation B, Web server, and laser printer B). This type of tunnel requires a coordination of efforts between the administrators of both Router A and Router B.

Figure 1-5

VPN using a
compulsory
tunnel

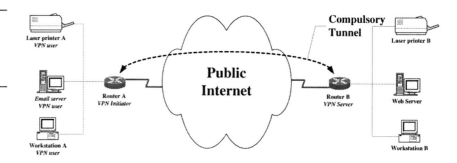

The advantage of this type of tunnel is that none of the devices on both networks require any reconfiguration or special software to use this VPN. This is a tremendous advantage for those devices in which VPN software is not available, such as printers or older operating systems. The disadvantage of this type of scenario is that it requires more time to deploy new tunnels, because each new tunnel must be configured, as opposed to a voluntary tunnel.

This type of tunnel is frequently used with all five different types of VPNs: Remote Access, Intranet, Extranet, Voice, and Enterprise VPNs. However, with Remote Access VPNs the architecture is slightly different. When using a compulsory tunnel with a Remote Access VPN, efforts must be coordinated between the ISP and the corporate office. As seen in Figure 1-6, the VPN user connects to his local ISP and the local ISP tunnels his connection from Router A (VPN initiator) to Router B (VPN server).

At this point, Router B is responsible for allocating an IP address and all of the other attributes that are required to support that dialup connection. Then, the VPN user thinks he or she has dialed directly into Router B.

The advantage to this method is that there is no client configuration. This can be a major advantage as long as the clients can use the same ISP with minimal telecommunication charges.

Unlike other tunnels, multiple dial-up clients can share remote access compulsory tunnels. When a second client dials into the ISP in Figure 1-6, there is no need to create a new instance of the tunnel. Instead, the new client's data traffic is carried over the existing tunnel. Since multiple clients can simultaneously use a single tunnel, the tunnel is not terminated until the last user of the tunnel disconnects.

Figure 1-6

Remote Access VPN using a compulsory tunnel

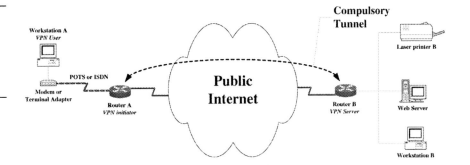

Potential drawbacks to widespread use of such a compulsory tunnel are that all communications are indiscriminately tunneled (which can create significant overhead). Figure 1-7 provides a worse case scenario in which Workstation A wants to Telnet to Router A.

Figure 1-7

Example of poor VPN design

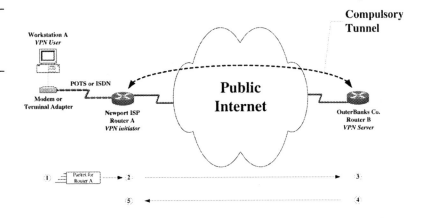

1. Workstation A wants to Telnet to Router A and sends a packet over its dialup connection.

2. The VPN initiator (Router A) encapsulates the data from Workstation A and sends it off across the Internet to the VPN server (Router B).

3. The VPN server (Router B) unencapsulates the data and looks through its route table to see where to send it.

4. Router B sends the data across the Internet to Router A.

For Router A to send data back to Workstation A, the above process must be reversed. Although this is an extreme circumstance, it does reinforce the need to understand the problem to be solved to prevent misuse of the available bandwidth.

1.6 Security

The second keyword in VPN, "private," is provided through the use of two security features: authentication and encryption. Authentication is the process that identifies an individual, while encryption is what keeps the data secret as it is transmitted over the network.

1.6.1 Authentication Protocols

Authentication is typically used prior to being allowed access to a network and the available services provided by the network. Authentication is typically based upon something you know, such as a password, or have, such as a token card. Environments that require the tightest level of security use both for authentication purposes.

Two commonly used authentication protocols are the *Password Authentication Protocol* (PAP) and the *Challenge Handshake Authentication Protocol* (CHAP). PAP is the simplest authentication protocol commonly used with PPP. CHAP can be used to improve security because it is a more secure authentication method. CHAP is recognized as more secure because it never passes the password in clear text over the network. In addition, CHAP, by default, will repeatedly challenge a host every two minutes to limit the exposure of a hijacked session.

There are other forms of authentication that we will explore in Chapter 4.

1.6.2 Security Protocols

Authentication is one of the first topics that should be resolved when an organization starts to increase the number of services available to its customer base. The primary defense against any unauthorized use of a service is authentication, and the best way to handle most passwords is through the use of a *Terminal Access Controller Access Control System* (TACACS+) or *Remote Access Dial-In User Service* (RADIUS) authentication server.

Note:

The use of the term "security" in this book refers to all of the components that make up a secure environment: encryption, authentication, and security protocols. "Security protocol" refers specifically to RADIUS or TACACS+.

By moving the username/password database from the Cisco VPN server to another device, you can centralize the storage of this information for use by multiple devices on the network. In addition, you can use this information for purposes other than authentication in a Cisco VPN server. For example, this username/password database can be used to authenticate network administrators who Telnet into a Cisco router or switch. This minimizes the number of usernames and passwords that network technicians have to remember (because everything is centralized) and it also allows network administrators to centrally control the username database, instead of having to create a username on every Cisco router so a technician may access the device. To better understand how the authentication protocols and management protocols come together to form a complete security solution, see Figure 1-8.

Figure 1-8

Multiple protocols being used for authentication

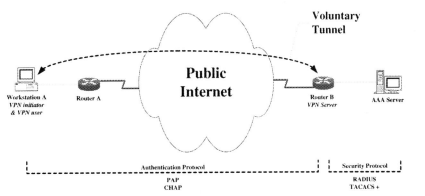

In Figure 1-8, it looks like the authentication protocols used are independent of the security protocols. Although this is generally the case, unexpected consequences of selecting two of these protocols to work together may occur. For example, suppose you want to use CHAP and RADIUS as authentication mechanisms for your remote access solution. In addition, you want the RADIUS server to use a pre-existing username database, thus minimizing the number of usernames and passwords your end users have to remember. However, several RADIUS servers require the use of a different password in order to authenticate the user with CHAP. Think of this as a second password for the same user. Typically, this stems from the algorithms used to provide the authentication. A good example of this is Novell's BorderManager. Not all implementations of RADIUS are subject to this situation, but it is something to keep in mind when evaluating potential security servers.

1.6.3 Encryption Protocols

Encryption is the process of transforming a message into an unreadable form known as ciphertext. To restore ciphertext back to its original form, it must undergo a process called decryption. The algorithm used to turn a message into ciphertext is known as cryptography. Think of cryptography as what makes a message secret, while encryption is the standard formula used to create the ciphertext. Figure 1-9 shows how encryption becomes useful for keeping information private.

Figure 1-9

How encryption protects data

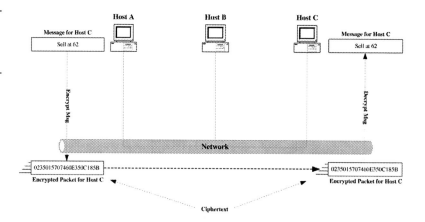

In Figure 1-9, Host A has data to send to Host C. Before sending the data to Host C, Host A encrypts the message using a simple cipher, which makes the message intelligible. This encryption enables Host A and Host C to communicate securely over the network though even the Host B has "seen" the transmission.

Note:

In a switched environment, it is possible to keep Host B from "seeing" that data transmission; however, the attempt here is to illustrate a fundamental aspect of encryption.

A suitably encrypted packet will be unintelligible to any attacker. Unfortunately, many encryption schemes can be hacked. This is the reason for having a good security document in which you define "acceptable risks," as well as an understanding of the problem you are solving that will allow you to select the appropriate encryption protocol. When developing a security policy you should evaluate the following points:

- Who would want your data?
- How hard would they work to get it?
- What would be the cost if it were exploited?

Many times a simple encryption scheme is enough to keep roaming eyes out, such as if you are sending your Aunt Betty Jane's secret recipe for her famous potato salad. Other times you will need to have the most advanced encryption available when sending messages during military actions, in which human life is at stake. It is important to remember that all of this encryption comes at a price and you want to develop a policy that recognizes a cost-benefit analysis. Why spend a million dollars protecting a $100 investment?

Two components to any encryption scheme are the algorithm and the key. All encryption algorithms rely on cryptography. Cryptography is the mathematical process used to make the data secret. These are some of the different types of cryptography:

- *Data Encryption Standard* (DES)
- *Triple-DES* (3DES)

- Blowfish Algorithm

- *International Data Encryption Algorithm* (IDEA)

- RC2

- RC4

- RC5 Block Cipher

- Skipjack

- Vernam Cipher

- *Message Digest 2, 4, and 5* (MD2, MD4, and MD5)

- Secure Hash Algorithm

These different types of cryptography use fundamentally different principles to create their ciphertext. The basic components of encryption are explored in Chapter 4, "VPN Security Primer."

In many cryptography methods, there is a key used to encrypt and decrypt a message. Two different strategies for the key are available: symmetric cryptography and public-key cryptography. Symmetric cryptography is when both devices use the same key for encrypting and decrypting the message. Public-key encryption works completely differently than symmetric cryptography. Instead of using a single key for encryption, public-key uses a pair of keys, a public key and a private key. In this methodology, everyone knows the public key, whereas the private key is kept secret. The distinct advantages for using this type of methodology are elaborated on in Chapter 4.

Depending upon your security policy, you might have to consider when and where to encrypt a message. For those of you familiar with the OSI model, encryption is generally specified as being a function of the presentation layer, as seen in Figure 1-10.

This means that it is the application's responsibility to determine when a message should be encrypted and when it shouldn't. In Figure 1-11, Application ABC has chosen to encrypt the data before sending it on the wire, while application XYZ has chosen not to encrypt it.

When using a VPN, the privacy of the data is not dependent upon whether the application programmer chooses to encrypt his data. VPNs by their very nature relieve the application from this responsibility. Instead, VPNs encrypt the data at the network layer. This means that all data gets encrypted, regardless of whether the application programmer chooses to encrypt the data or not.

Figure 1-10

The OSI model

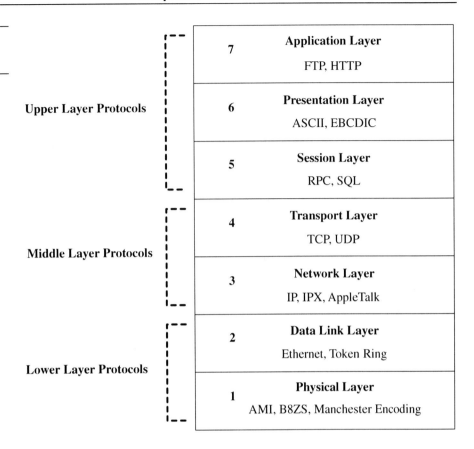

Upper Layer Protocols	7	**Application Layer** FTP, HTTP
	6	**Presentation Layer** ASCII, EBCDIC
	5	**Session Layer** RPC, SQL
Middle Layer Protocols	4	**Transport Layer** TCP, UDP
	3	**Network Layer** IP, IPX, AppleTalk
Lower Layer Protocols	2	**Data Link Layer** Ethernet, Token Ring
	1	**Physical Layer** AMI, B8ZS, Manchester Encoding

Figure 1-11

Encryption according to the OSI model

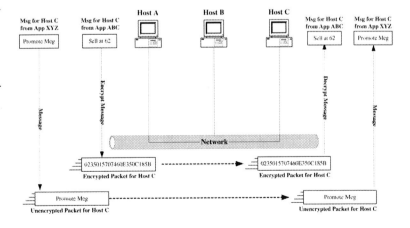

1.6.3.1 Considerations for VPN Tunnel Types

When selecting a VPN, it may be necessary to choose an appropriate VPN tunnel type based upon your security policy. In Figure 1-3, an example of using a voluntary tunnel is shown. By definition, in a voluntary tunnel the data is encrypted by the local VPN user. When the VPN server receives the data, it then decrypts the data. When using a compulsory tunnel, the VPN user has no idea that the data is being encrypted and then tunneled to the VPN server; therefore, data sent by the VPN user to the VPN initiator is unencrypted. If this local segment between the VPN user and VPN initiator is considered a public network, you should reconsider your selection of VPN tunnel type depending upon your security policy.

1.7 When Not to Deploy a VPN

Certain instances do occur in which a VPN is not suitable for your solution. When entertaining VPNs as a technical solution, it is important to understand the complete problem you are trying to solve.

1.7.1 Latency

If latency is an issue for your network application, then a VPN may not be suitable. Latency is generally accepted as the amount of time required to send a packet to its destination. The more hops a packet has to take and the more operations that have to be performed for a packet to make it through a router, the more latency that is introduced to the packet. Some protocols are not latency-sensitive; others are very latency-sensitive, such as voice. Two reasons explain why latency is introduced into a packet stream.

The most obvious reason latency is introduced to a packet is there is congestion which can happen frequently on the Internet. There will be times will arise when the Internet becomes congested or network paths will not be optimal, thus introducing latency into your packet stream.

The not-so-obvious reason latency is introduced to a packet is that extra headers must be generated to properly build the packet for its destination. In addition, the time required to encrypt/decrypt the packet can add significant latency to a data stream. Remember that one device will have to encrypt the packet and another will have to decrypt it before the destination can read the packet. This is where selecting the appropriate hardware will be critical to the success of your VPN solution.

1.7.2 Performance

Similar to latency, if performance is an issue for your application then you probably shouldn't use a VPN to solve your problem. From an application perspective, the performance of the network is based upon throughput of the data. *How much data can be sent through the network during a specified time period?*

Just like the Internet can introduce latency to a data stream, it also can impact the throughput of your data stream when it experiences congestion or network outages. Because additional headers are added to each packet, it effectively reduces the amount of user data that can be sent through to your ISP.

1.7.3 Additional Support Forums

In addition to this book, a network professional can venture to many avenues for additional peer support. This support comes in many forms and takes on several different variations. If you are interested in pursuing a Cisco certification, two listservs run from `http://www.group-study.com` that can provide an additional viewpoint on the technologies covered within this book. This is a great place to listen to other people's questions and answers (lurking), ask your own questions, or impart the wisdom you've found after reading this book to others. Although the last method may not seem worthwhile, remember that by explaining a topic to someone else you gain a greater understanding of the topic. This not only enables you to solidify the knowledge you have, but also maybe helps you gain a friend who can assist you in understanding a difficult topic one day.

These are definitely exciting times; the industry is young and growing by leaps and bounds every day. By working hard now to study and learn these concepts, you are on your way to understanding the fundamentals required to comprehend new technologies as they are developed. Now let's get started with *Implementing Cisco Virtual Private Networks*. Enjoy.

Education is not the filling of the pail, but the lighting of the fire.
William Butler Yeats

CHAPTER 2

Windows Support for Dialup

In the last chapter we discussed the definition of VPN. In this chapter, we will look at configuring the telecommuter/mobile user's computer to use the standard tools provided by Microsoft to create a dialup connection. Those of you familiar with how to configure Microsoft's three main operating systems (95/98, NT, and 2000) for dialup might consider skipping this chapter.

Microsoft's Windows 95/98 and Windows NT Workstation have become the premiere operating system for today's business user. With the recent release of Windows 2000 and its advanced Virtual Private Networking features, we expect it to become a very popular operating system for busienss users.

2.1 Objectives to be Covered in This Chapter

- Configure Windows 95 dialup networking
- Configure Windows NT Workstation remote access service
- Configure Windows 2000 dialup connections

Although all three operating systems listed previously reference a different name for their remote access component, they do refer to the dialup components of their respective operating system. Although the newer operating systems tend to provide more functionality than the older ones, they all have one thing in common, the capability to connect using PPP.

So where do you learn how to configure Windows to support the various voluntary tunnel VPN protocols such as *Point-to-Point Tunneling Protocol* (PPTP), *IP Security* (IPSec), and *Layer Two Tunneling Protocol* (L2TP)? In the Case Study section where the various VPN protocols are covered, you will be shown how to configure Windows to support the respective protocol. This chapter has been included so that you would know how to configure the VPN user machine in a Remote Access compulsory tunnel VPN.

2.2 Overview of Client Side Dialup

Before an operating system can be configured to support a *Point-to-Point Protocol* (PPP) connection, you must first make sure that the appropriate hardware is in place. The hardware needs to not only be installed, but also configured correctly. In this section, some of the aspects of configuring the hardware are covered.

2.2.1 Hardware

In order to get any modem working properly, the device must not have any hardware conflicts with any system resources. Many different types of system resources exist, but only the two that are typically pertinent to a modem are discussed in this chapter: Interrupt (IRQ) and port address (I/O).

Two different types of modems are available: internal and external. External modems typically connect to the serial port of the computer, while an internal modem is installed inside the computer and connects directly to the computer's bus.

If you are using an external modem, no configuration of IRQs or port addresses exist because the serial port (such as COM1, COM2, and so on) handles communication with the computer (for example, IRQ and port address). Internal modems, on the other hand, communicate directly with the computer and must therefore have the capability to set the IRQ and port address of the modem device. By changing the IRQ and the port address, an internal modem can integrate with any system as long as system resources are available.

External modems communicate with the computer through the serial port. This means that the serial port controls the IRQ and port address. The two ports frequently used by the serial port are COM1 and COM2. Any physical serial port can be assigned to the logical COM1 or COM2. Typically the assignment of a predefined IRQ and port address designate a port as COM1 or COM2 (see Table 6-1).

Table 6-1

Standard IRQ and port address for serial ports

Serial Port	IRQ	Port Address
COM1	4	3F8h
COM2	3	2F8h

When configuring a PC for any new hardware, it is important that no system resource conflicts. With the advent of plug-and-play, hardware conflicts are typically a thing of the past. However, if you are trying to use hardware that is not plug-and-play-aware in a plug-and-play environment, things can get difficult. This is because any system resources that the non-plug-and-play aware device is using inside the plug-and-play environment need to be reserved. For more information about the configuration of COM ports, see the following URLs:

```
http://www.byterunner.com/tech.html
http://www.comminfo.com/
```

2.2.2 UART

The heart of any serial port is the *Universal Asynchronous Receiver/ Transmitter* (UART) chip. In order to understand the purpose of the UART, the internal computer communication must be discussed. All data paths inside of a computer run in parallel. A UART chip assembles this information sent to it in parallel and converts it to serial communications and vice versa.

Several different types of UART chips are available on the market. However, several different UART chips have been around for a long time. For example, the 8250 UART can still be found in many low-priced serial cards. It was originally developed for use on the original IBM PC and IBM

XT. The next generation of the UART was the 16450, which is better suited for high-speed communication but still does not provide any remarkable functionality over the 8250.

The 16550 was developed for use in the PS/2 line of computers produced by IBM. The chip had a 16-byte buffer that aids in faster communication and enables multiple DMA channel access. However, some bugs affected its first implementation, and the 16550A was released shortly afterwards, which corrected these bugs.

The latest generation of high-speed UARTs are the 16650 and 16750, which offer 32-byte and 64-byte buffers respectively. This enables them to support data transfer rates from 115,200 bps to 230,400 bps. The 16650 is an enhanced version of the 16550A but is not fully compatible with the 16550A, so, it may not work properly with some software and drivers. The 16750 provides a 64-byte buffer and is fully compatible with the 16550A. To take advantage of 16750 UART, you need a driver or software that supports it.

2.2.3 Port Settings

The port settings used on your COM ports are very important. As shown in Figure 2-1, they define the speed of the connection between the modem and the serial port.

Figure 2-1

Speed of a port

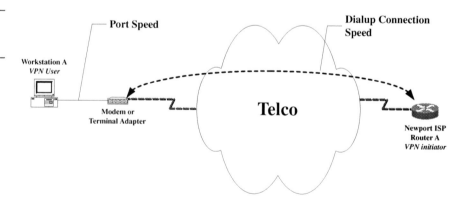

If not set properly, you might limit the throughput. The COM port speed should be set to the highest supported speed by both the serial port and the device it is connected to, no matter if it is an external modem or the console port on a Cisco Router.

When connecting a serial port to the console port on any Cisco device, the default speed is 9600 bps; however, today's newer modems can handle port speeds up to 115,200 bps. Therefore, if you are using the same serial port to connect to both the console port on a Cisco Router and to a newer modem, you need to make sure that you adjust the speed accordingly when using either one. If you leave the port speed to 9600 bps, you limit your throughput when using the modem. If you leave the port speed to 115,200 bps, you are not able to communicate with the console port on any Cisco Router.

2.3 Windows 95

Windows 95 was designed as a transitional operating system. The intention was to provide an operating system that could bridge the old 16-bit environment to the new 32-bit environment. In addition, it provided backward compatibility for real-mode drivers but enabled vendors to develop drivers that ran in protected mode, an option that has been available since the introduction of the 386.

One of the additional features that Microsoft provided in Windows 95 over previous versions of Windows was the inclusion of dialup networking. Before Windows 95, getting a PPP connection was more of an art form than a task-driven process. This was because previous versions of Windows (3.1 and lower) did not have the native capability to connect to a network, let alone use a modem. The introduction of Windows for Workgroups was also the beginning of networking with Windows, which has culminated to the Windows 95's networking paradigm.

Dialup networking provides Windows 95 the capability to establish network connections through a modem. Dialup networking is a very simple-to-use tool (once you understand all of the components involved) to establish dialup connections. Windows 95's dialup networking can be broken down into two different areas:

- Dialup networking
  Components that enable Windows 95 to use a modem
- Creating dialup scripts
  Scripts that utilize dialup network to establish a PPP connection

2.3.1 Install and Configure Dialup Networking Software

When preparing to install dialup networking, make sure you know which network protocols are required to support the functionality needed. For example, if you need to connect to a NetWare server running *Internetwork Packet Exchange* (IPX)/*Sequenced Packet Exchange* (SPX), make sure that you have already installed IPX/SPX. This prevents you from having to do it after the installation of dialup networking.

Installation of dialup networking can be performed in five steps:

1. Open **Control Panels** under **My Computer**.
2. Open **Add/Remove Programs**.
3. Select **Windows Setup** tab, as shown in Figure 2-2.
4. Select the **Communications** option and click on **Details**.
5. Select **Dialup Networking,** as shown in Figure 2-3 (if it is already selected, you can skip this step).

If you do not have a modem configured in your system, Windows 95 asks you if you would like to install a modem, as shown in Figure 2-4.

You may be prompted to find the installation media. Make sure that you have it ready if Windows 95 needs it. In the next section, you will learn how to create dialup scripts so that you can connect to the central site.

2.3.2 Creating Dialup Scripts

Dialup scripts specify all the attributes necessary to connect to an *Internet service provider* (ISP). Each script specifies the connection requirements for a particular ISP. Creating a dialup networking script in Windows 95 using the Make New Connection Wizard involves three steps:

Figure 2-2

Windows setup tab

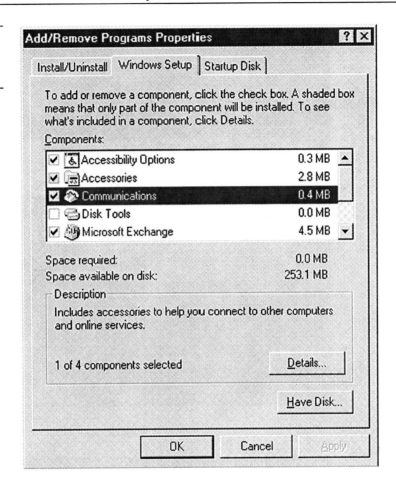

1. Open **Dialup Networking** under **My Computer**.

2. Open **Make New Connection**.

3. Enter the name of the connection script, as shown in Figure 2-5, and select **Next**.

4. Enter the phone number and area code of the Central Site PPP connection and select **Next**.

5. Select **Finish** to complete the creation of the dialup script.

6. Open the new connection script and enter your username and password in the appropriate fields, as shown in Figure 2-6.

   The script is ready to dial the central office.

Figure 2-3

Windows 95
communications
window

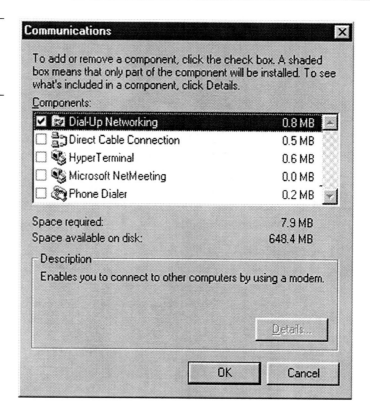

Figure 2-4

Windows 95
modem
installation
wizard

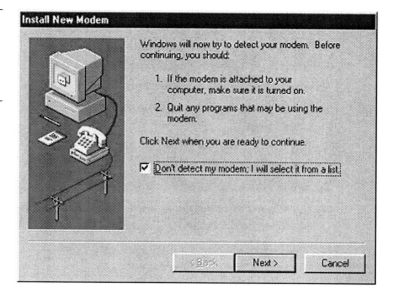

Figure 2-5

Make new
connection
window

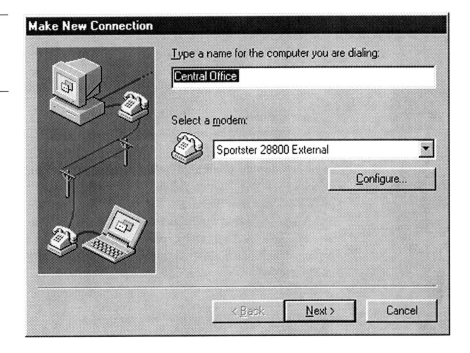

Figure 2-6

Windows 95
connection script

Note:

The "Save password" check box only saves the password after a successful logon connection.

Your dialup connection script is now complete. Several other attributes can be customized on the connection script. Once the creation of the connection script has been completed, modify those additional attributes by right-clicking on the script and selecting properties. This displays a window, as shown in Figure 2-7.

You can see from Figure 2-7 that once a script has been created, you can select what modem you want to use for that script. This is useful if you install a new modem into your computer. Figure 2-8 shows that the server types tab has additional configuration that most administrators will want to customize.

Figure 2-7

Dialup script attributes: general tab

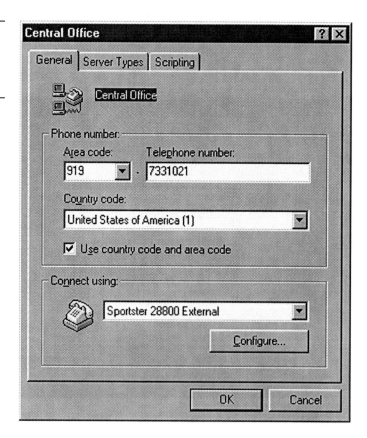

Figure 2-8

Dialup script attributes: server type tab

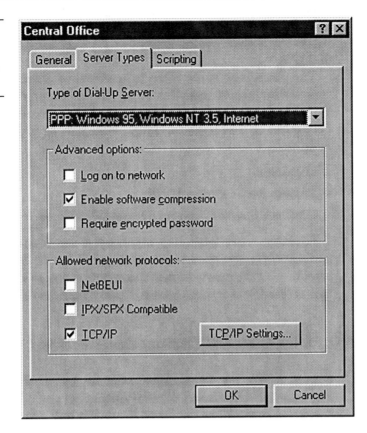

Using the options on this tab enables the selection of the type of dialup connection you would like to make. Windows 95 not only supports PPP connections, but several others as listed here:

- *Point to Point Protocol* (PPP) - DEFAULT
- *Serial Line Internet Protocol* (SLIP)
- *NetWare Remote Node* (NRN); NetWare Connect's original encapsulation method
- *Compressed Serial Line Internet Protocol* (CSLIP)

The three options in the advanced options section provide the dialup script with a great deal of flexibility. For example, when connecting to the network, you can have Windows attempt to authenticate to its primary logon network. You can also enable software compression. Lastly, you can require an encrypted password. This option is how an administrator specifies that the user should authenticate only with CHAP. Windows 95, by default, uses either *Challenge Handshake Authentication Protocol* (CHAP) or *Password Authentication Protocol* (PAP) to authenticate to a dialup server.

The last section enables you to specify the network protocols you want your dialup script to negotiate. The TCP/IP button enables you to specify TCP/IP-related information every time that connection connects to a dialup server. The following information can be predefined for the local machine:

- IP address
- *Domain Name System* (DNS)
- *Windows Internet Naming Service* (WINS)

Situations occur when it is necessary to set these attributes when connecting to other dialup servers (non-Cisco). However, Cisco access servers can provide all of the information to the remote client, so it is best to leave these options blank and assign these attributes by the *Remote Access Server* (RAS).

2.3.3 Verifying Windows 95 Dialup Connections

Once your Windows 95 machine has connected, verify that the connection was successful because a window displaying your connection speed and connected time will be displayed, as shown in Figure 2-9.

Figure 2-9

Example of the connection status window

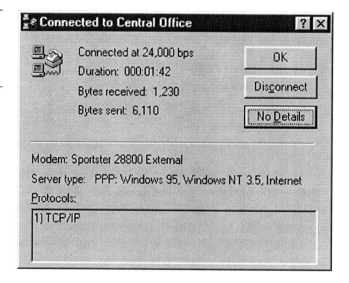

Modem: Sportster 28800 External

Server type: PPP: Windows 95, Windows NT 3.5, Internet

Protocols:

1) TCP/IP

2.3.3.1 Fine-Tuning Windows 95 Dialup Networking Connections

Now that your Windows 95 machine can connect to the central site, several attributes can be fine-tuned to simplify life for the end user. By right-clicking on the dialup script, you will bring up the window shown in Figure 2-10.

Some of the settings that dictate how Windows 95 dialup networking operates can be modified. For example, you can set the number of times to attempt to redial a connection and how long to wait in between attempts.

Windows 95 is one of the most deployed operating systems in the business world today. Its configuration and operation in a remote environment already have been discussed. Now, we will focus on Microsoft's pure 32-bit platforms.

Figure 2-10

Fine-tuning the properties of a Windows 95 dialup script

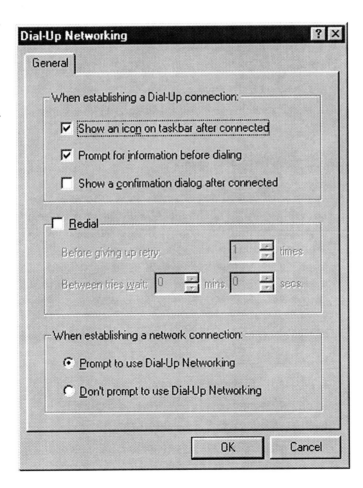

2.4 Windows NT

Windows NT's underlying structure is very different than Windows 95's. It removes the capability of the software to talk directly to the hardware by inserting the *Hardware Abstraction Layer* (HAL). This gives Windows NT a level of stability not known by Windows 95. On the other hand, it lends a layer of complexity that can make it difficult to get configured correctly.

In order to perform any of the tasks from here on out, you must be logged in as an administrator. A handful of functions can be performed as a power user, but very few functions can be performed as just a user (for example, using a dialup connection).

Setting up Windows NT's RAS is very similar to any other types of network-related services that can be installed. Similar to Windows 95, installation can be broken down into two areas:

▓ Install and configure RAS

Components that enable Windows NT to use a modem

▓ Create dialup scripts

Scripts enable RAS to establish a PPP connection

2.4.1 Install and Configure RAS

In order to install any services in Windows NT, you must be logged in as an administrator of the local machine, or if the machine is a member of a domain, as a domain administrator. Without administrator privileges, you are not be able to add the necessary services. In addition, you need to know which network protocols need to be used. For example, if you only need access to TCP/IP, you don't want to be subjected to the *Routing Information Protocol* (RIP)/*Service Advertisement Protocol* (SAP) updates associated with IPX/SPX.

Installation of RAS can be performed in six steps:

1. Open **Control Panels** under **My Computer**.

2. Open the **Network** control panel.

3. Select **Services** tab, as shown in Figure 2-11.

4. Click Add to add a new service.

5. Select **Remote Access Service**, as shown in Figure 2-12. You may be prompted to find the installation directory (that is, C:\I386).

Figure 2-11

Services tab in
the network
control panel

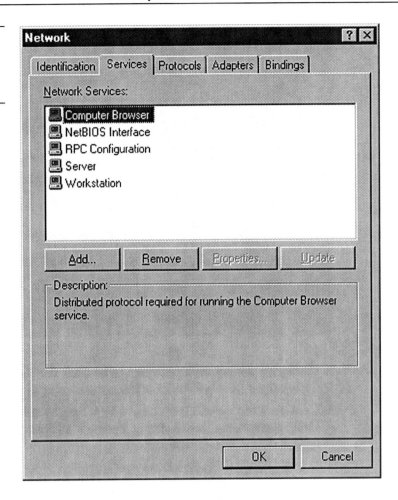

6. If you do not have a modem installed, you will be asked to install a
   modem so that RAS can bind to the interface. If you do not have a
   modem installed in the operating system, you cannot continue this
   installation.

Note:

*You do not necessarily need a modem in the machine to install a modem.
Just remember that the service won't be operational until the modem is
attached to the machine with the correct system resources.*

Figure 2-12

Adding RAS to
Windows NT

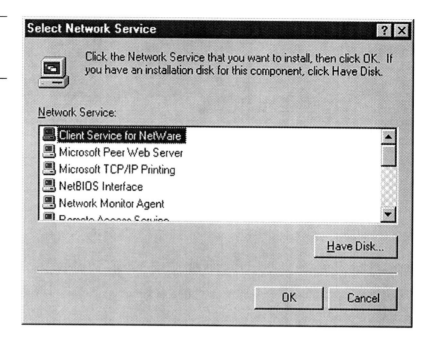

7. Configure the network protocols to be used during any RAS session by selecting the **Network** button, as shown in Figure 2-13.

8. Configure the direction of calls to be placed by selecting the **Configure** button, as shown in Figure 2-13 (you must select an option that allows for dialout calls).

9. Select **Continue** to finish the configuration of RAS.

Figure 2-13

Remote access
setup properties

Note:

If during installation you needed to access the installation media, the service packs must be reapplied.

RAS has now been installed into Windows NT, but scripts that use this service still need to be created.

2.4.2 Create Dialup Scripts

Similar to Windows 95, a wizard is available to help create dialup scripts. The process for creating these dialup scripts is as follows:

1. Open **Dialup Networking** under **My Computer**.

2a. If Windows NT informs you that no scripts are available and asks if you would like to create a new script, select OK.

   Or

2b. If scripts are available, Windows NT brings you to the phonebook. Select **new** to start the Dialup Script Creation Wizard.

3. Name the dialup script and click **next**.

4. Select "I am calling the Internet" and click **next**.

5. Enter the phone number of the central office dialup server.

6. Click **finished** to end the Dialup Script Creation Wizard.

You will now be presented with a screen that looks like Figure 2-14.

2.4.2.1 Fine-Tuning Windows NT Dialup Connection Scripts

Once the dialup script has been created, you can make minor changes to it. Those features that can be modified include:

- Dialup protocol (PPP, SLIP, or Windows for Workgroups)
- Network protocol (TCP/IP, IPX/SPX, and NetBEUI)
- Authentication protocol (PAP and/or CHAP)
- Callback
- Redial attributes

Figure 2-14

Editing a dialup script

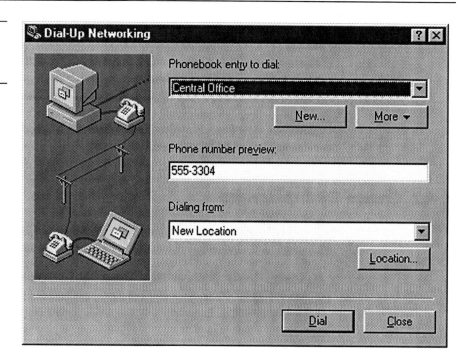

By selecting the **More** button on the dialup script entry in Figure 2-14 and selecting "Edit entry and modem properties," you can edit the dialup protocol, network protocol, and authentication protocol. If you want to edit the callback and redial attributes, you need to select "User Preferences."

Microsoft does not make reference to PAP, CHAP, and the *Microsoft Challenge Handshake Authentication Protocol* (MSCHAP), in the Security tab, for authentication protocols. Instead the three following entries are used to represent those authentication protocols:

- Accept any authentication including clear text (PAP, CHAP, or MSCHAP)
- Accept only encrypted authentication (CHAP or MSCHAP)
- Accept only Microsoft-encrypted authentication (MSCHAP only)

When using this newly created dialup script, a dialog box is presented, as shown in Figure 2-15.

Figure 2-15

Example of
dialup connection
script

This is where you will put your username and password. However, do
not enter a domain name in the box provided (even if you are primarily an
NT shop). This is only for Windows NT dial-in RAS.

Remember that the "Save password" check box only works if you successfully complete a dial-in connection. If the connection fails on the first
connect attempt, Windows NT acts as though the password used was
incorrect and will fail to save the password.

2.4.3 Verifying Windows NT Dialup Connections

Verifying a Windows NT dialup connection can be done through the Monitor Status window. You can active the Monitor Status window by selecting **More** from the Windows NT phonebook, and selecting **Monitor
status**. Figure 2-16 displays the Monitor status window and can tell you
many different aspects of your dialup connection.

Figure 2-16

Example of dialup networking monitor

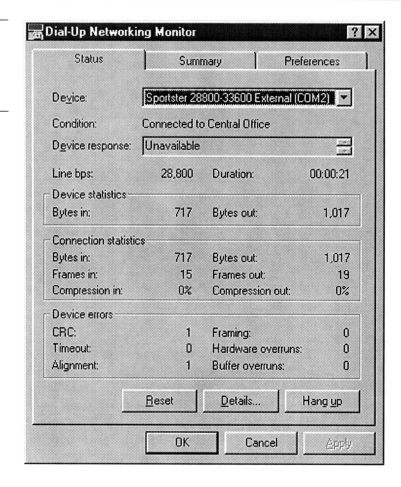

Here is a sampling of the information that can be seen from the Monitor status window:

- Connection speed
- Connection duration
- Bytes in/out
- Frames in/out
- Compression in/out
- CRC errors
- Alignment errors
- Framing errors

Unlike Windows 95, not everyone can make modifications to the system. This cuts down on the number of support calls because users accidentally change their configuration. However, it also requires an administrator to make any changes to the system. Users can still create and modify scripts, but they can't change the configuration of the services running on their Windows NT machine.

2.5 Windows 2000

The recently released Windows 2000 is the next version of Windows NT (not Windows 98, which is a very common misconception). Although many components have undergone a serious metamorphosis from Windows NT, only those that are relevant to dialup connections are be addressed.

As shown in Figure 2-17, Microsoft now addresses LAN interfaces, modem connections, and VPN connections similarly. This change in paradigm actually makes life easier for the end user because his or her connections can be categorized from the same perspective (such as Ethernet, LAN, dialup, and so on).

2.5.1 Creating Dialup Scripts

With a major change in architecture, Windows 2000 does not have a service to install to activate RAS. It is now available by default. Instead, you only have to create your dialup scripts using the following process:

1. Open **Network and Dialup Connections** in the Control Panel window.
2. Select **Make New Connection**.
3. Select **Dialup to private network**, as shown in Figure 2-18.

Note:
You can select Dialup to the Internet, but a number of different screens must be answered. The easiest is Dialup to private network.

Figure 2-17

Windows 2000
network and
dialup
connections

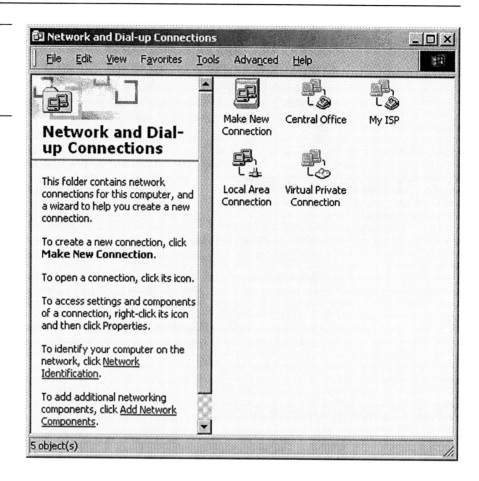

4. Enter the phone number of your ISP.

5. Select whether this connection is for **all users** or **only for myself**.

6. Name the Dialup script and click **finish**.

Just like Windows 95 and Windows NT, you have the opportunity to modify the connection attributes. By opening the dialup script, you get a window, as shown in Figure 2-19.

Windows 2000 supports multiple authentication types, which can be configured under the properties of the login script. Those authentication protocols are:

- PAP

- *Shiva Password Authentication Protocol* (SPAP)

Figure 2-18

Network
connection
wizard

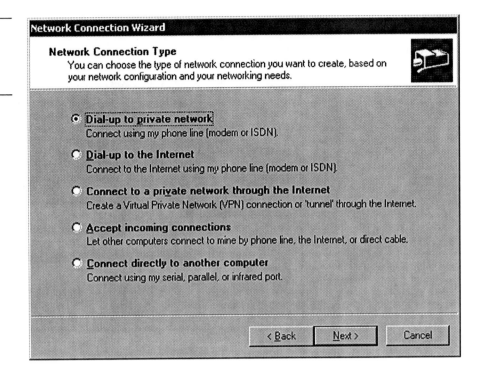

- CHAP
- MSCHAP
- Microsoft Challenge Handshake Authentication Protocol version 2 (MS-CHAPv2)

Many of the attributes that can be configured in a dialup script are only supported by a Windows 2000 RAS server. Keep this in mind when exploring the Windows 2000 Dialup Networking and Connections.

2.5.2 Verifying Windows 2000 Dialup Connections

Once connected, the status of the connection can be viewed by opening the connection script in the Dialup Networking Connections window. Figure 2-20 shows an example of the Dialup Connection Status window.

Figure 2-19

Dialup connection
script

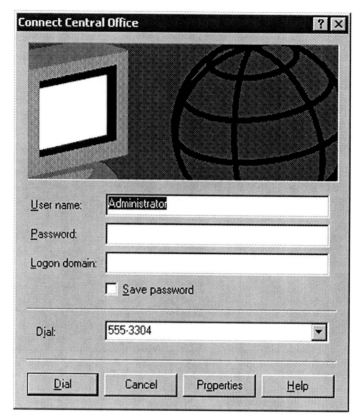

If details page of the Dialup Connection Status window are displayed,
you can see various other information, such as:

- Dialup protocol
- Successfully negotiated network protocols
- Compression
- PPP multilink framing
- IP address

Windows 2000 has provided many tools to ease the configuration and
installation of RAS.

Figure 2-20

Dialup
Connection
Status window on
successful login

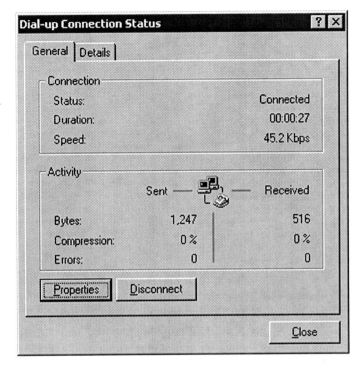

2.6 VPNs and Windows

A VPN can take on many different topologies. The effect a VPN has on the performance of a machine running Microsoft Windows (95/98/ME/NT/2000) is directly dependent upon the type of VPN deployed. The type of VPN chosen also depends upon the components that are under your control as you will see later in this section.

2.6.1 VPN Performance and Windows

As discussed in length in Chapter 1, "Introduction to Implementing Cisco VPNs," a compulsory tunnel hides the VPN from the Windows user. The computer acts as though it is directly connected to the remote site. The user's computer makes no special considerations when using the VPN because the VPN initiator takes on the burden of building the specialized packets. Because of this paradigm, as shown in Figure 2-21, when using a

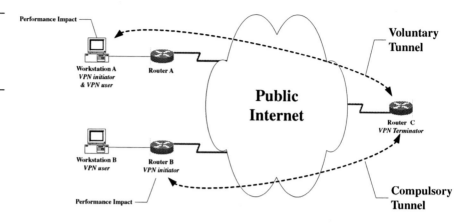

Figure 2-21

Compulsory
tunnel versus
voluntary tunnel

compulsory tunnel, no performance degradation occurs on your Windows machine no matter what type of encryption is used on your VPN.

On the other hand, when using a voluntary VPN tunnel, the performance of your local Windows machine is impacted. The stronger the encryption, the bigger the performance hit to your local computer. This is because your local computer is performing the encryption of the data, as well as building the headers not just once (those for the ultimate destination of the packet), but twice (header for the destination of the VPN terminator).

2.6.2 VPN Design Considerations and Windows

One of the design considerations that must be taken into account when determining the type of VPN to build is which devices are best equipped to perform the calculations required to encrypt the data in a VPN. Although these calculations might seem trivial, they are not. This is shown in Chapter 4, "VPN Security Primer," when the various encryption techniques used in VPNs are explored.

In addition to taking performance into account, the reliability of the local machine needs to be taken into account. One of the methods used by network administrators to keep a corporate machine running without incident is installing the minimum number of applications required for the computer to perform its task. Using voluntary tunnels presents the potential for VPN software to conflict with another piece of software required for the machine to operate. Using compulsory tunnels eliminates the need to install any special software on your Windows machine, which can make the rollout of a VPN especially easy.

The type of VPN topology you choose to rollout is very dependent upon the location of your users and the access you have to their devices. Voluntary tunnels are very flexible and enable the user to connect from any location, including dialup ISPs, cable modems, and xDSL. In order for a voluntary tunnel to work, they must have network visibility to your VPN terminator. The downside to voluntary tunnels is that they require configuration of the local PC. On the other hand, compulsory tunnels are very easy to rollout for entire organizations because it only requires the configuration of two routers: the VPN initiator and the VPN terminator. However, this paradigm is extremely limiting because that equipment is not always accessible.

2.7 Summary

In this chapter, you learned how to connect Windows 95, Windows NT, and Windows 2000 to an ISP using PPP over analog communications. You've also been shown how to support the various network protocols, authentication protocols, and dialup protocols. In the next chapter, we will focus on configuring a Cisco access server to support dialup connections, a critical component for the support of compulsory tunnels.

CHAPTER 3

Dialup over Cisco Routers

In the last chapter, we looked at how to configure Microsoft Windows (95/98, NT, and 2000) to support dialup. In this chapter, we will be covering the circuit-switched technologies (physical layer) and encapsulation methods (data link layer) used to support a dialup environment. An understanding of this technology, and how to improve it, is critical when dealing with both compulsory and voluntary remote access *Virtual Private Network* (VPN) tunnels.

It is important to remember that the chapters in this section are here solely as a primer to the case studies found in later chapters. If you are comfortable with configuring and troubleshooting dialup connections, then you should consider glancing through this chapter and move on to Chapter 4, where we start learning the fundamentals of encryption and authentication.

3.1 Objectives to be Covered in This Chapter

- Understand and configure analog dialup
- Understand and configure an *Integrated Services Dialup Network* (ISDN) dialup
- Understand and configure the *Point-to-Point Protocol* (PPP)

Two different types of circuit-switched connections are in use today: analog and ISDN. Analog connections, frequently called the *Plain Old Telephone System* (POTS), was originally designed to carry the human voice. Because computers use digital signals to communicate, the telephone system is not a natural choice of communication media. However, by converting digital signals to analog and then back again, POTS can be used as a transmission media between two hosts. As you will see later in this chapter, it isn't the most efficient method of communication available, but nevertheless, it does enable computers to communicate using standard phone lines.

Although both analog and ISDN connections have the same objective, which is to use circuit-switched networks to create dynamic paths from one site to another, they use fundamentally different technologies to achieve that goal.

If you look at Figure 3-1, you can see that both technologies provide access to the Telco cloud, but the signal used to get to the Telco cloud is different.

In Figure 3-1, the modem serving Host X must convert the digital signal to analog before sending it to the Telco, where it is then converted back to digital by the Telco. Host Y's transmission starts as a digital transmission and remains a digital signal as it is sent to the Telco, thereby providing a more efficient transmission medium for data.

Figure 3-1

The difference between analog and ISDN communications

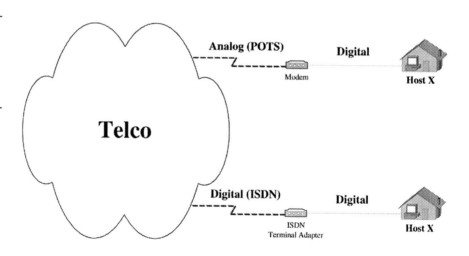

3.2 Overview of Dialup Protocols

In this section, we will discuss the main components that make up a standard dialup connection. We will first look at the physical layer options (analog and ISDN) and then at the data link layer options: the *High-Level Data Link Control* (HDLC) and PPP. Although HDLC is not an option for analog connections, it is an option for ISDN. HDLC is also the default encapsulation for an ISDN interface, but it is generally not used because of HDLC's limited security and propriety (remember that HDLC is vendor-specific).

3.3 Analog

Analog connections are the most prevalent circuit-switched connections available today and have been around for more than 50 years. With so many years of constant deployment, it is easy to see why POTS is the largest network in the world. Although the dedicated serial connection is designed to move binary data from one point to another, the telephone system is designed to move analog data from one point to another.

Data can be represented in one of two schemes: analog or digital. Data transmissions using analog signals are typical human forms of communication. For example, as we speak, the sounds we create vary in frequency and amplitude. This type of signal can carry large amounts of information, because it can easily represent different values, such as high, medium, low, and none. The most basic representation of data in a computer is binary (1's and 0's). Data transmissions using binary signals can represent one of two states: on or off.

So what does this mean? It means that in order to utilize POTS as a network connection, we must use a system created for carrying analog signals to transmit binary signals. This is done through the use of a modem, more formally known as a *Modulator/Demodulator*. This enables computers to send binary data over a medium that is designed for analog communications. However, the algorithms used to represent digital data in an analog medium are inefficient and translate into slower connection speeds.

In order for Host X to communicate with Host Y, three different segments must be transversed: two digital segments and one analog segment (see Figure 3-2).

Both segments A and C in Figure 3-2 are where the computer sends digital information to the modem. The modem takes those digital signals and modulates them to a series of audible tones and sends the signal to the Telco cloud. The Telco cloud then forwards the analog signal to the remote modem (segment C in Figure 3-2). In the last step of this process, the modem converts the signal from analog back to a digital format so that Host Y can interpret the data. This enables Host X and Host Y to communicate over an analog network.

Figure 3-2

Modem-to-modem communications through a Telco

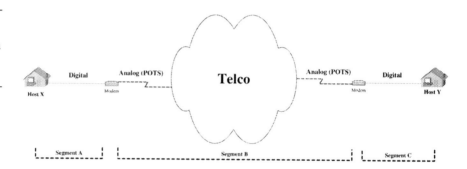

3.3.1 Analog Versus Asynchronous

The confusion over analog and asynchronous is very common, and people tend to use them synonymously. Although they aren't synonymous, they are typically used together, which is why people use them interchangeably.

As previously discussed, analog communication is a series of waves that varies in amplitude (how high), frequency (how quick), and phase (the relationship to a standing wave). These different variations enable a large number of combinations to represent data. The best example of analog communication is speech. On the other hand, asynchronous communication is a method of digital communication that does not use a precise form of clocking. Instead of having a regularly defined time in which bits are sent, as in synchronous communications, a start bit and stop bit are utilized to indicate the beginning of a byte and the end of the byte respectively.

3.3.2 Cables and Signaling

In order for two devices to communicate over a synchronous serial interface, one end must be the *Data Circuit-Terminating Equipment* (DCE), while the other end must be the *Data Terminal Equipment* (DTE). In all cases, the DCE end always provides the clocking on the *Wide Area Network* (WAN) link. In most situations, the Telco provides clocking on the circuit, as shown in Figure 3-3.

There will be times when the Telco doesn't provide clocking on the WAN link, such as when the run is very short. In such instances, it is possible to turn the DTE interface on a Cisco Router to a DCE interface by indicating the speed of the link using the command clock.

Figure 3-3

Clocking provided by Telco

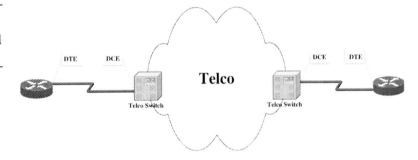

Note:

When setting up a home lab, it is customary to use a back-to-back cable to connect two routers together. However, by using a back-to-back cable, no Telco can provide clocking on the WAN circuit, and thus the clock command must be used in a home lab. This is a common problem for many beginners using back-to-back cables. The telltale sign of clocking missing from a serial link is the interface going up and down.

In order for a DCE and a DTE device to communicate, they must have a common method of signaling to each other. Many different signaling standards exist, and several of them are listed here:

- *Electronics Industry Association* (EIA)/*Telecommunications Industry Association* (TIA)-232
- *High-Speed Serial Interface* (HSSI)
- X.21
- V.35
- EIA/TIA-449
- EIA-530

Each standard defines the signaling used on the wire and sometimes even the physical interface.

3.3.2.1 EIA/TIA-232

The standard for EIA/TIA-232 was defined first in 1962, under the name RS-232-C. Although the DB-25 connector is common for EIA/TIA-232, it is not the only connector created for this type of connection. DB-9 and RJ-45 are two connectors that are commonly used with the EIA/TIA-232 specification. This is because the original specification does not specify a DB-25 pin connector.

Of the 25 pins on an EIA/TIA-232 DB-25 pin connector, only eight are utilized (2-8 and 20). These eight pins can be categorized into three distinct classifications:

- Data transfer
- Hardware flow control
- Modem control

Note:
Pin 1 provides a protective ground.

The data transfer pins are responsible for the flow of data between the DTE and DCE devices. The three pins that make up this category are used for receiving, transmitting, and grounding. See Table 3-1.

Table 3-1

Data transfer
pins

Pin	Signal	Meaning
2	TxD	DTE transmits data to the DCE
3	RxD	DTE receives data from the DCE
7	GRD	Ground, which provides reference voltage

The hardware flow control pins are used to determine when data can be sent. When a DTE device wants to send data, it must indicate to the DCE that it has data to send. This is accomplished through the use of *Ready to Send* (RTS). Typically, the data path the DCE is trying to send data to (POTS) is much slower than the data path between the DTE and DCE devices. This leads us to the potential problem of the DTE device sending too much data too fast for the DCE to keep up. To fix this problem, use *Clear to Send* (CTS) to tell the DTE device when you are ready to receive data and when it needs to stop sending data. Table 3-2 shows a summary of the pins, the signals, and their meanings.

Table 3-2

Hardware flow
control pins

Pin	Signal	Meaning
4	RTS	DTE is ready to send data
5	CTS	DCE is ready to receive data

The last category of pins, modem control, determines when to initiate, terminate, and monitor the connection. The *Data Terminal Ready* (DTR) pin tells the DCE that the DTE is ready to start receiving data. This is different than RTS in that DTR tells the modem it is there and ready to start communicating, while RTS indicates when it is ready to actually send data. When a call is being set up, the modem first determines whether or not a physical connection exists to the POTS line.

The Carrier Detect pin indicates whether or not a valid POTS connection exists to the DCE. Times will occur when a physical connection leads to the POTS line, but the modem can't detect the signal. This can happen when using a modem on a phone system that uses a series of beeps to indicate you have voice messages on your company's internal voice mail.

The last pin is *Data Set Ready* (DSR) and is not used on modem connections. Table 3-3 lists a summary of pins, signals, and their corresponding meanings.

Table 3-3	Pin	Signal	Meaning
Modem control pins	20	DTR	DTE ready to start sending data
	8	CD	Carrier Detect; there is a physical connection
	6	DSR	Data Set Ready, which is not used with modems

3.3.3 Pulse Code Modulation

One of the problems inherent with analog communication is that the farther you need to send that analog signal, the worse the signal gets. Physical limitations exist on how far a signal can be sent over any type of media and still be recognizable at the receiving end. This is because the electrical properties of the materials you use have resistance.

Resistance, measured in ohms, is the property that determines how poorly a specific material enables electricity to flow. Although good conductors have values that are very low, none actually have a value of zero (except superconductors). The higher the resistance, the quicker the signal is degraded.

Note:

Superconductors are created through a combination of exotic materials and super cold temperatures. If a material is ever found that operates as a superconductor at room temperature, a whole plethora of new devices will operate with extremely low power consumption.

In order to combat the effects of resistance, repeaters are used. They listen to a signal (analog or digital), amplify the signal, and forward it to the next segment. Without a repeater, two devices that are relatively far apart would not be able to communicate. This is because the signal on the wire would have degraded so much that it would be impossible to distinguish between the highs and lows on the receiving end.

As a signal travels over a relatively long distance, not only does the signal degrade, but also noise is introduced from other sources. These sources can be introduced by many different sources, such as the sun and high-powered voltage lines.

Depending upon the type of signal, repeaters amplify not only the intended signal, but also the noise picked up by external sources. Because an analog signal is by definition a series of waves that varies their frequency and strength in a continuous fashion, when noise is introduced to the line, you can do nothing but amplify the noise as well as the intended signal. However, a digital signal is by definition a zero or a one. When noise is introduced into the line, it can be removed by the repeater. This is because the repeater only needs to regenerate a one or a zero and can remove the noise that has been introduced into the line. This is why digital cellular phone signals are so much clearer than their analog counterpart. Figure 3-4 shows the difference between amplifying an analog signal and repeating a digital signal.

Figure 3-4

The effects of noise on a digital signal versus an analog signal

A long time ago, the Telcos understood this and adapted their internal Telco network to take advantage of digital communication. This meant that they could send an analog signal a long way, with little signal degradation. In order to convert the analog signal to digital, the Telcos use *Pulse Code Modulation* (PCM).

PCM uses the Nyquist theorem to represent analog data in a digital format. The theorem states that to precisely reconstruct an analog signal, the number of sample points must equal twice the maximum frequency of the signal. A voice channel has a bandwidth of approximately zero to 4,000hz; using the Nyquist theorem, the sampling rate must be 8,000 samples per second. Each sample is then encoded into eight bits. Therefore, in order for the Telco to represent a single voice channel, it needs to transmit 8,000 samples per second at eight bits per sample, or 64,000 bits per second (64Kbps). This is why DS0 trunk lines are 64Kbps. It is this technology, PCM, which makes 56K dialup connections possible.

3.3.4 Configuration of Analog Connections

We should now have a basic understanding of modems and the underlying technology used by them. The focus of this chapter will change from discussing concepts to implementing them.

3.3.4.1 Line Types and Numbering

Configuring a modem requires a discussion about several different subtopics. For instance, you need to know where to physically connect a modem and then how to address it in the Cisco *internetworking operating system* (IOS). You also need to know the characteristics of the physical connection, such as the speed of the communication, the flowcontrol method to be used, and so on.

Four different types of lines are available in a Cisco Access server. Those four types are *Console* (CON or CTY), *Auxiliary* (AUX), *Asynchronous* (TTY) and *Virtual Terminal* (VTY).

Note:

Although not all Cisco routers have an AUX or TTY line type, they all do have CON and VTY lines. Those who do not have access to a Cisco Access server (2509, 2511, and so on) can make do with a Cisco router that has both a console and an auxiliary port.

The CON or CTY line references the console port. As you may already know, the console port is used to configure the router. It does not require that any of the other interfaces be configured to administer the Cisco Access server. This is because the console port communication settings default to the following:

- 9600 bps
- Eight data bits
- No parity
- One-stop bit
- No flow control

These provide access to the IOS as long as you have physical access to the console port and a terminal access program (such as HyperTerminal or Tera Term Pro). When configuring the console port, it is always addressed as line 0.

The next series of lines is the asynchronous devices. Devices like the Cisco 2509 have eight physical asynchronous ports. An external modem can be attached to each of these ports. Cisco's Access server products, the AS5x00 line, are capable of handling an ISDN *Primary Rate Interface* (PRI), but in order to support connections from POTS lines, they still require modems. This is because they need to convert the incoming analog signal to digital. Therefore, Cisco has built network modules that can hold many modems (up to 120 on some modules). These modems, known as *MICA modems*, are considered an asynchronous connection just like the physical asynchronous connections on the 2509. The only difference is that these asynchronous lines already have a modem attached. In both a Cisco 2509/2511 and a Cisco AS5x00, each asynchronous line can be configured independently of the others if necessary (in case you have different modems connected to each of the lines). However, generally they are grouped together and configured as a single unit. The number of TTY lines available in the Cisco IOS depends upon how many internal MICA modems and/or asynchronous ports are in your Cisco Access server.

If an auxiliary port is available, it will be displayed immediately after the asynchronous lines. An auxiliary port is not just a second console port, but it can be considered an additional asynchronous port that can be used to route protocols.

Note:

IP over PPP using the async port for routing data can cause unusually high central processing unit *(CPU) utilization.*

The last sets of lines in a Cisco Access server are the VTY lines, better known as the *telnet lines*. These lines do not correlate to any physical interface. Instead, they are created dynamically in the router through the config file. For as many VTY lines as there are, you can establish that many Telnet sessions to the Cisco Access server.

To determine which lines are currently available, use the IOS command show lines at the global configuration mode. Using this command in Figure 3-5, you can see one console port (line 0), 12 asynchronous interfaces (lines 1-16), one auxiliary port (line 17), and five virtual terminal lines (lines 18-22).

In the Cisco IOS, when addressing the four different types of lines (CON, TTY, AUX, VTY), use relative line numbering or absolute line numbering to identify a line. The absolute line number of any line can be identified by finding its TTY value in the show line command. In Figure 3-5,

Figure 3-5

Output from the show line command on a Cisco 2511

```
Router>show line
 Tty Typ Tx/Rx    A Modem Roty AccO AccI Uses Noise Overruns
*  0 CTY  - - - - - - 0 0 0/0
A  1 TTY 9600/9600  - - - - - 0 0 0/0
   2 TTY 9600/9600  - - - - - 0 0 0/0
   3 TTY 9600/9600  - - - - - 0 0 0/0
   4 TTY 9600/9600  - - - - - 0 0 0/0
   5 TTY 9600/9600  - - - - - 0 0 0/0
   6 TTY 9600/9600  - - - - - 0 0 0/0
   7 TTY 9600/9600  - - - - - 0 0 0/0
   8 TTY 9600/9600  - - - - - 0 0 0/0
   9 TTY 9600/9600  - - - - - 0 0 0/0
  10 TTY 9600/9600  - - - - - 0 0 0/0
  11 TTY 9600/9600  - - - - - 0 0 0/0
  12 TTY 9600/9600  - - - - - 0 0 0/0
  13 TTY 9600/9600  - - - - - 0 0 0/0
  14 TTY 9600/9600  - - - - - 0 0 0/0
  15 TTY 9600/9600  - - - - - 0 0 0/0
  16 TTY 9600/9600  - - - - - 0 0 0/0
  17 AUX 9600/9600  - - - - - 0 0 0/0
  18 VTY  - - - - - 0 0 0/0
  19 VTY  - - - - - 0 0 0/0
  20 VTY  - - - - - 0 0 0/0
  21 VTY  - - - - - 0 0 0/0
  22 VTY  - - - - - 0 0 0/0
```

you can see that the absolute line number for the AUX port is 17. However, at times, it may not be convenient to know the exact line number you want to configure. Therefore, relative addressing can help a network administrator remember which line it is he or she wants to configure. Using Table 3-4, you can see the correlation between the absolute line numbering and the relative line numbering from Figure 3-5.

Table 3-4

The correlation between absolute and relative line numbering from Figure 3-5

Absolute Line Number	Relative Line Number
Line 0	CON 1
Line 17	AUX 0
Line 18	VTY 0
Line 19	VTY 1
Line 20	VTY 2
Line 21	VTY 3
Line 22	VTY 4

In Figure 3-5, lines 18 through 22 support Telnet sessions that can be addressed absolutely (line 18 - line 22) or relatively (vty 0 - vty 4). To configure a line on a Cisco router using relative addressing, use the following command:

```
Router (config)#line line-type
```

line-type	con	0	Configure console
	aux	0	Configure auxiliary
	tty	x - y	Configure the relative TTY line, x is the starting number of the TTY lines, and y is the last TTY line available
	vty	0 - z	Configure the relative Telnet session line where 0 is the first line and z is the number of VTY lines available

To configure a line on a Cisco router using absolute addressing, use the following command:

```
Router (config)#line line-number
```

line-number	x	The absolute line to be configured

In addition, we can also configure multiple lines simultaneously by using a variant of the previous commands, as shown here:

```
Router (config)#line first-line last-line
```

first-line	x	The absolute line to be configured
last-line	x	The absolute line to be configured

If you want to determine ahead of time the relative line numbering for a specific interface when using fixed configuration routers, you can use this simple formula displayed in Table 3-5.

In Figure 3-6, you can see that this particular router has 16 asynchronous interfaces. The exact line numbering scheme varies from router to router when using modular routers. For example, when using a Cisco 3640, the line numbering becomes a bit convoluted. For example, in Figure 3-6, you can see that your MICA modems (asynchronous interfaces) are using lines 65 to 76. This is because the Cisco 3600 series router reserves 32 line numbers for each network module slot.

Table 3-5

Calculating line numbers for a fixed configuration router

Interface	Keyword	Number of Lines	Line Number
Console	CON	1	Line 0
Asynchronous devices	TTY	x	Lines 1 through x
Auxiliary	AUX	1	Line x+1
Virtual Terminal	VTY	y	Line x+2 through

Figure 3-6

Example of show lines command on a Cisco 3640

```
Router#show line
  Tty Typ Tx/Rx A Modem Roty AccO AccI Uses Noise Overruns Int
*  0 CTY - - - - - 0 0 0/0 -
I 65 TTY - inout - - - 0 0 0/0 -
I 66 TTY - inout - - - 0 0 0/0 -
I 67 TTY - inout - - - 0 0 0/0 -
I 68 TTY - inout - - - 0 0 0/0 -
I 69 TTY - inout - - - 0 0 0/0 -
I 70 TTY - inout - - - 0 0 0/0 -
I 71 TTY - inout - - - 0 0 0/0 -
I 72 TTY - inout - - - 0 0 0/0 -
I 73 TTY - inout - - - 0 0 0/0 -
I 74 TTY - inout - - - 0 0 0/0 -
I 75 TTY - inout - - - 0 0 0/0 -
I 76 TTY - inout - - - 0 0 0/0 -
  129 AUX 9600/9600 - - - - - 0 0 0/0 -
  130 VTY - - - - - 0 0 0/0 -
  131 VTY - - - - - 0 0 0/0 -
  132 VTY - - - - - 0 0 0/0 -
  133 VTY - - - - - 0 0 0/0 -
  134 VTY - - - - - 0 0 0/0 -

Line(s) not in async mode -or- with no hardware support:
1-64, 77-128
```

To calculate the line numbers associated with a slot, use the following formula:

$$\text{First line number} = \text{Slot number} * 32 + 1$$

$$\text{Last line number} = (\text{Slot number} + 1) * 32$$

After applying the previous formula to Slot 3 of a Cisco 3640 router, the following line numbers are reserved for potential asynchronous lines. These asynchronous lines could be MICA modems or 60 Pin serial ports.

First line number = 3 * 32 + 1 = 97

Last line number v (3 + 1) * 32 = 128

By manipulating the First Line Number formula, as shown previously, you can determine that the MICA modem module in your Cisco 3640 in Figure 3-6 is in slot 2.

Slot number = (First line number − 1)/−32

Slot number = (65 − 1)/32 = 2

3.3.4.2 Reverse Telnet

Cisco Access Servers support incoming and outgoing asynchronous connections. An example of an incoming connection is a user dialing into a Cisco Access server. Incoming connections are the easiest type of connection to understand. Figure 3-7 shows two modems and one Cisco 2501 connected to the asynchronous ports of a Cisco 2509.

Using an outgoing asynchronous connection, you can modify the configuration of the modem, or you can connect to the console port of the Cisco 2501 so that you can configure it even when all of the physical interfaces on the 2501 do not support a Telnet session. Consider it a backdoor to the router. This type of connection is called a *Reverse Telnet*.

Figure 3-7

Cisco 2509 connected to two modems and the console of a 2501

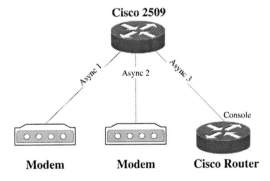

Cisco 2509

Async 1   Async 2   Async 3

Console

Modem   Modem   Cisco Router

Note:

A common misconception for beginners is the term Reverse Telnet. Reverse Telnet is only similar to Telnet in that they both send character-based data back to the application for viewing by the end user. The difference between the two lies in the methods used to send the data to the application. Frequently when configuring a Cisco router, a network engineer connects the serial port on his or her computer to the console of the router and uses an application like HyperTerminal to access the console port. Reverse Telnet is similar to this paradigm, in that once a connection with the router has been established (through whatever means), you can use the router's asynchronous ports (which are identical to the console port on a computer) to Reverse Telnet to the consoles of other devices. This out-of-band management is useful when the traditional network interfaces won't support a Telnet session.

In order to Reverse Telnet, you must perform the following two commands on the lines where you want to Reverse Telnet out of. These commands are *transport input all* and *modem inout*. Figure 3-8 shows these two commands being executed.

Figure 3-8

Configuring 48 lines on a Cisco access server for reverse telnet

```
Router#configure terminal
Enter configuration commands, one per line. End with CNTL/Z.
Router(config)#line 1 48
Router(config-line)#transport input all
Router(config-line)#modem inout
```

Now that the Cisco Access server supports Reverse Telnet, you only need to Telnet to the address you are interested in. This is done by using the command *telnet ipaddress port*. To determine the address we are interested in, let's look at Figure 3-9.

Figure 3-9 shows us Telneting to IP address 192.168.12.1 and Port 2001. The IP address used is the IP address of the Cisco Access server (192.168.12.1). The second number in the Telnet command is the port. Port 20xx defines that we want to Telnet to an asynchronous line, while xx01 specifies which asynchronous line. In this case, it's line 1 or AUX 0 on a Cisco 2501.

Figure 3-9

An example of
Reverse Telnet

```
Router#telnet 192.168.12.1 2001
Trying 192.168.12.1, 2001 ... Open
*****************************************
*Welcome to the Test Router *
*****************************************


User Access Verification

Password:
```

It is recommended though that you set an unregistered IP address in a loopback interface and use that IP address to perform a Reverse Telnet (this address does not need to be routable). You may ask, why can't I just use the IP address on one of my real interfaces? You can, but if, for whatever reason, that interface were to go down (because of the network being physically disconnected or a network card failure), the IP address would no longer be valid. You also would not be able to Reverse Telnet or, worse, you would lose your connection while you are configuring a modem.

Different port addresses are also available for accessing a different type of service. Table 3-6 shows the list of services available.

Table 3-6

Ports used for
Reverse Telnet

Service	Base TCP Port
Telnet	2000
Raw TCP protocol	4000
Telnet protocol, binary mode	6000
Xremote protocol	9000

Note:

If you have difficulty establishing Reverse Telnet sessions out of an asynchronous port, you may want to use the command **no-exec** *in addition to* **transport input all** *and* **modem inout**.

Terminating a Reverse Telnet session is a two-step process. First, suspend your Reverse Telnet session and then terminate it at the Global Configuration mode. To suspend your reverse client session, use the key sequence, ctrl-shift-6 and x. This can be tricky because it isn't all four keys simultaneously. Instead, you press the first three keys (ctrl-shift-6), let go, and then you type the x. To terminate the Reverse Telnet session, you must issue the *disconnect [session number]* command. The session number can be found by using the command *show sessions*. Figure 3-10 shows the use of the show sessions and disconnect commands to terminate a Reverse Telnet session.

Figure 3-10

Disconnecting a session

```
Router#show sessions
Conn Host Address Byte Idle Conn Name
* 1 192.168.12.1 192.168.12.1 0 0 192.168.12.1

Router#disconnect 1
Closing connection to 192.168.12.1 [confirm]
```

For frequent Reverse Telnet connections, the *ip host* command can simplify these connections. This can be done using the following command:

```
Router (config)# ip host hostname port ip-address-of-route
```

hostname	**WORD**	The name used to represent the shortcut
port	**20XX**	The port address of an asynchronous port; XX is the absolute line number
ip-address-of-router	**a.b.c.d**	IP address of the router

Figure 3-11 shows an example of this command being configured and then used for the purposes of a Reverse Telnet.

Figure 3-11

Use of the IP host command to simplify reverse telnet sessions

```
Router(config)#ip host RouterA 2001 192.168.12.1
Router(config)#end
Router#
Router#RouterA
Trying modem (192.168.12.1, 2001)... Open
****************************************
*Welcome to Router A *
****************************************


User Access Verification

Password:
```

3.3.4.3 Line Configuration

In order to successfully make an asynchronous connection to a Cisco Access server, make sure that both the modem and the line are configured correctly. Remember that you can configure each line individually or all of the lines as a group. In Figure 3-12, all of the lines are configured simultaneously.

Figure 3-12

Configuring all lines simultaneously

```
Router#config t
Enter configuration commands, one per line. End with CNTL/Z.
Router(config)#line 65 76
Router(config-line)#speed 115200
Router(config-line)#flowcontrol hardware
Router(config-line)#transport input all
Router(config-line)#modem inout
Router(config-line)#stopbits 1
Router(config-line)#end
Router#
```

Various commands are used to configure the lines on an asynchronous port. In order to use them effectively, you need to know their purpose.

The *speed* command is used to determine line speed. This is not the speed of a dialup connection, but the speed of the DTE-to-DCE communication (the router to the asynchronous port). It is important to keep in mind that in order for any effective compression to take place, youneed to keep the line speed higher than the dialup connection. Otherwise, you will starve the modem for data and waste bandwidth.

The typical *flowcontrol* method for asynchronous ports is hardware. It is the equivalent of the RTS and CTS, as described in Table 3-2, which controls the flow of data. The modem tells the router when its buffers are full and to back off from sending any more data.

Because Cisco routers do not accept incoming network connections on an asynchronous port by default, you need to identify which type of protocol you will allow on that asynchronous connection. Multiple types of protocols can be used (lat, mop, pad, rlogin, telnet, and v120). The *transport* command enables you to define which protocols can be used. The *transport input all* command enables all types of traffic to pass on the line:

To configure which protocols should be allowed over a line, use the following command:

```
Router (config-line)#transport direction-preference protocol
```

direction-preference	**input**	Protocols that can connect to the Cisco Access server
	output	Protocols that can be used on outgoing connections
	preference	Preferred protocol
protocol	**all**	All protocols
	pad	X.3 PAD
	rlogin	Unix rlogin protocol
	telnet	TCP/IP Telnet protocol
	v120	Async over ISDN

When setting up a Cisco Access server, so many options are available. One of the options that lends great flexibility to your Cisco Access servers is the *modem* command. This command determines which direction of asynchronous connections you will support. To specify the direction of communication, use the following command:

```
Router (config-line)#modem direction-preference
```

direction-preference	**dialin**	Protocols that can connect to the Cisco Access server
	inout	Preferred protocol

Figure 3-13

Configuring an asynchronous line to support an incoming connection

```
Router(config)#line 65 76
Router(config-line)#modem dialin
```

Figure 3-13 shows an example of lines 65 through 76 being configured to support dial-in.

Cisco's Access server supports many asynchronous protocols, such as *AppleTalk Remote Access* (ARA), *Serial Line Internet Protocol* (SLIP) and the *Point-to-Point Protocol* (PPP). The *autoselect* command enables the Cisco IOS to start detecting the protocol being used. To configure an asynchronous line to support the various protocols, use the following command:

```
Router (config-line)#autoselect protocol
```

protocol	arap	Support ARA protocol connections
	during-login	Support character-based connections
	ppp	Support PPP connections
	slip	Support SLIP connections

Unlike other commands where the choice is one protocol or another, here it is not unusual to see the command multiple times to support the protocol(s) you are interested in. For example, Figure 3-14 shows three instances of the autoselect command.

Figure 3-14

Example commands to configure PPP, ARAP, and during login

```
Router(config)#line 65 76
Router(config-line)#autoselect ppp
Router(config-line)#autoselect arap
Router(config-line)#autoselect during-login
Router(config-line)#end
Router#
```

The second and third lines enable lines 65 through 76 to support PPP and ARA. The last autoselect command is a bit different. Historically when using bulleting board type systems and after two modems are connected, you would hit Return a few times to bring up the username/password prompt. These types of terminal connections are normal with programs like HyperTerminal or Kermit. Using the *autoselect during-login* command enables the Cisco Access server to display a prompt as soon as you establish a connection with the receiving modem, without hitting Return. If you are using a terminal program like HyperTerminal to establish a connection, you will be presented with a login screen. However, if you are connecting with PPP, you can start sending packets as soon as you are connected.

3.3.4.4 AT Commands and Initialization Strings

In order for a modem to work properly, it must be configured. Modems are not the dumb devices that most people think they are. This is because operating systems like Windows 95 and Windows NT typically hide all the modem configuration commands. It is important to understand the basics of configuring a modem, so that when problems occur within initialization strings or chat scripts, you can interpret their commands.

The basic commands used to configure and troubleshoot a modem originate from the AT command set. The AT command set was originally developed by Hayes to work with their Smartmodem 300.

The AT command set can be broken down into two different kinds of instructions: configuration commands and operation commands (usually called the *S-Registers*). Table 3-7 shows the different types of attributes that can be configured on a modem.

Table 3-7	**Configuration Commands**	**Operation Commands**
Various attributes that may need to be configured on a modem	Define flow control	Dial a phone number
	Set modulation	Hang up the phone
	Set data compression	Test the modem
	Define RS-232 signaling characteristics	Inquire the modem

In order to send commands to most modems, you must start with the AT command. From there, you can configure different attributes about the modem using a series of commands appended to each other. For example, in Table 3-8, you may want to configure Cisco's MICA modems to use the following attributes.

Table 3-8	**Desired Effect**	**Command**
Various MICA AT commands	Set to factory defaults	&F
	Answer the phone	S0=1
	Enable echoing of commands to workstation	E1
	Use V.90 modulation	S29=6

The end result of these commands would be as follows:

`AT&FS0=1E1S29=6`

Note:

This is a limited set of commands and would not necessarily initialize a modem the way you want it.

One of the important things to do when creating a modem script is to set the modem back to the factory defaults (see line 1 in Table 3-8). Because so many different variables can be set in a modem, you'll want to make sure that you start from a known state.

When several commands are placed together, as you saw in the previous example, it is called an *initialization string*. Although many of the commands used to configure the initialization strings are similar, they aren't identical from vendor to vendor, or even from model to model. In order to know the commands used to configure a particular modem, you will have to refer to the documentation that came with the modem. For more information on the AT commands used to configure Cisco's MICA modems, see the following URL:

> `http://www.cisco.com/univercd/cc/td/doc/product/acces/`
> `acs_serv/5300/mod_info/at/atcmnds.htm.`

Because the initialization commands need to be used on the modem every time the Cisco Access server is booted or after a user disconnects a session, you need a way to automate these initialization strings.

3.3.4.5 Modem Auto-Configuration

Modem auto-configuration is used to automate the configuration of modems attached to a Cisco Access server. Cisco Access servers come with a number of preconfigured initialization strings for some of the most commonly used modems. These preconfigured initialization strings are stored in the modemcap database. Here are some of the entries in the modemcap database that come with Cisco IOS 11.3:

- codex_3260
- usr_courier
- usr_sportster
- hayes_optima

- global_village

- viva

- telebit_t3000

- microcom_hdms

- microcom_server

- nec_v34

- nec_v110

- nec_piafs

- cisco_v110

- mica

In addition to these entries, you can create your own initialization strings, which will be covered later in this chapter. The need to create your own initialization strings could stem from one of two different areas: you aren't using any of the modems listed or you need to modify the pre-configured scripts.

Each modemcap database entry uses the specific vendor's own unique set of commands. At times, you may need to view the settings for particular modemcap entries. This can be done using the command *show modemcap*. As shown in Figure 3-15, a list of configuration parameters that the usr_courier modemcap entry knows about is displayed.

Figure 3-15

The contents of usr_courier modemcap entry attributes

```
Router#show modemcap usr_courier
Modemcap values for usr_courier
Factory Defaults (FD): &F
Autoanswer (AA): S0=1
Carrier detect (CD): &C1
Drop with DTR (DTR): &D2
Hardware Flowcontrol (HFL): &H1&R2
Lock DTE speed (SPD): &B1
DTE locking speed (DTE): [not set]
Best Error Control (BER): &M4
Best Compression (BCP): &K1
No Error Control (NER): &M0
No Compression (NCP): &K0
No Echo (NEC): E0
No Result Codes (NRS): Q1
Software Flowcontrol (SFL): [not set]
Caller ID (CID): [not set]
On-hook (ONH): H0
Off-hook (OFH): H1
Miscellaneous (MSC): [not set]
Template entry (TPL): default
Modem entry is built-in.
```

In Figure 3-15, you can see that the settings used by the current usr_courier modem entry are the vendor-specific commands you first learned about at the beginning of this chapter.

3.3.4.6 Creating New modemcap Database Entries

If the entries in the modemcap database do not fill your needs, you can always create a new entry to the database. Creating a new entry has two parts: knowing the attributes that need to be modified and their corresponding command, and the name of the new modem entry. The attributes that can be modified are as follows:

- autoanswer
- best compression
- best error control
- caller ID
- carrier-detect
- DTR
- factory default
- hardware flowcontrol
- miscellaneous commands
- no compression
- no echo
- no error control
- no results
- software flowcontrol
- lock modem speed

Using the command modemcap edit, you can create and edit new modem cap entries. The format of the modemcap edit command is as follows:

```
Router (config)#modemcap edit entry-name attribute-name setting
```

entry-name	**WORD**	Name for the new modemcap entry
attribute-name	**autoanswer**	Edit entry for autoanswer
	best-compression	Edit entry for best compression
	best-error-control	Edit entry for best error control
	caller-id	Edit entry for caller ID
	carrier-detect	Edit entry for carrier-detect
	dtr	Edit entry for DTR
	factory-default	Edit entry for factory default
	hardware-flowcontrol	Edit entry for hardware flowcontrol
	miscellaneous	Edit entry for miscellaneous commands
	no-compression	Edit entry for no compression
	no-echo	Edit entry for no echo
	no-error-control	Edit entry for no error control
	no-results	Edit entry for no results (quiet mode)
	software-flowcontrol	Edit entry for software flowcontrol
	speed	Edit entries for locking modem speed
	setting	This is attribute-dependent

Figure 3-16 shows an example of a modemcap entry being created.

Figure 3-16

Creating a new modemcap entry

```
Router#configure terminal
Router(config)#modemcap edit TestModem autoanswer AA
```

In Figure 3-16, the autoanswer for your fictitious modem TestModem is modified. Most likely, you would want to modify numerous attributes. Thus, you would have to enter this command for each attribute that needs to be configured.

Note:

The modemcap database entries are case-sensitive. If you are not careful, you can accidentally create multiple entries with the same name but different capitalization.

Times may occur when you want to extend the functionality of an entry in the modemcap database. Unfortunately, you can't modify any of the predefined modemcap entries, so you must create a modemcap entry similar to the one that is already defined. Creating a modemcap database entry can be quite a bit of work and can be error-prone because the commands are cryptic values such as &F.

Cisco has provided a way, however, to use a predefined modemcap entry as a template for creating a new modemcap entry. This cuts down on the number of errors possible because you are creating an entry from a known good state and modifying it from there. The command to copy a predefined modemcap entry is as follows:

```
Router (config)# modemcap edit new-modemcap-entry template predefined-
modemcap-entry
```

new-modemcap-entry	*WORD*	Name for the new modemcap entry
predefined-modemcap-entry	*WORD*	Name of the modemcap entry to copy

This command needs to be executed from the global configuration mode. From here, you can modify your new modemcap entry using the modemcap edit command, as shown in Figure 3-16. This entry is stored in the config file stored in *Non-Volatile Random Access Memory* (NVRAM).

3.3.4.7 Configure Modem Attached to Cisco Access Server with Modemcap Entry

You have assembled a lot of information throughout this section, but you still need to apply it to the lines on your Cisco Access Server. To apply a MICA modemcap entry to the lines in our Cisco Access Server, use the commands shown in Figure 3-17.

Figure 3-17

Configure Cisco
Access server to
use a MICA
modemcap entry

```
Router(config)#line 65 76
Router(config-line)#modem autoconfigure type mica
```

3.3.4.8 Modem Auto-Discovery

Cisco has provided a way to auto-discover the modems attached to your
Cisco Access server. The Cisco IOS starts with the first entry in the
modemcap database and tries to initialize the attached modem. If it is
successful, then the IOS searches no further. If the modem fails to initialize properly, the IOS goes to the next entry in the modemcap database.
The IOS repeats this process until the modem successfully initializes or it
runs out of database entries. If the modem fails to initialize after going
through all the modemcap entries, then the administrator must create a
modemcap entry to support the modem.

The modem auto-discovery command is useful when you know one of
the entries will configure the modem but don't know which one will. However, in practical terms, a penalty exists for having the modem initialized
using the auto-discovery mode: time. In environments that have a heavy
demand for dial-in lines, the extra time required by the IOS to run
through all the modemcap entries is the time the modem is unavailable
for use by your users. In small environments, this may not be a problem,
but with several hundred modems, you could lose 10 minutes or more
waiting for the modems to initialize. In addition, only so many threads in
the router kernel are for initializing modems. If a lot of modems exist, it
may take a lot of time in order for the router to configure all of its
modems.

3.3.4.9 Chat Scripts

Chat scripts can be used to direct a modem to initialize, dial out, and log
in to a remote system. A chat script works by receiving some expected
input and sending some predefined data as a result of that input. The
command used to create a chat script is as follows:

```
Router (config)# chat-script chat-script-name expect-string send-string
```

chat-script-name	***WORD***	Name for the new chat script
expect-string	***WORD***	Expected string
send-string	***WORD***	Response string

Chat scripts work around expected input and send pairs. For example, if you were to execute the command AT, you would expect to see an OK from the modem. This tells you that the modem is functioning. Thus, you can then send another command such as ATDT to dial a phone number.

Using the command *start-chat,* you can start a chat-script on any asynchronous line that is not in use. The format is as follows:

```
Router (config)# start-chat chat-script-name line-type line-number
```

chat-script-name	***WORD***	Name of the chat script
line-type	**con**	Apply to the console line
	aux	Apply to the auxiliary line
	tty	Apply to the asynchronous line
	vty	Apply to the Telnet line
line-number	*x*	Apply to this absolute line number

Now that you've explored the basics of analog communication, let's explore the counterpart to analog: ISDN.

3.4 ISDN

The first discussions surrounding *Integrated Services Digital Network* (ISDN) started in 1968. It was envisioned that this new technology would integrate access to a broad range of services, including voice, networking, packet switching, and cable television.

Although ISDN is fundamentally different than analog communications, it has been designed to enable end-to-end compatibility for analog communications (such as standard telephone). ISDN has several advantages over analog communications:

- Extremely fast call setup
- Less expensive than leased lines
- Faster transmission speeds than analog lines

ISDN comes in several different variants: *Basic Rate Interface* (BRI), *U.S. Primary Rate Interface* (PRI), and *European Primary Rate Interface* (PRI). Although they are all based upon the same technology, the differentiating aspects are the number of channels, as shown in Table 3-9.

Table 3-9

Comparison of BRI, T1, and E1 channels

ISDN Variant	Useable B-channels	Transmission Rate of B-channel	Number of D-channels	Transmission Rate of D-channel
BRI	2	64Kbps	1	16Kbps
T1 - PRI	23	64Kbps	1	64Kbps
E1 - PRI	30	64Kbps	1	64Kbps

Although ISDN BRI can come in variations other than 2B + 1D, such as 1B + 1D and 0B + 1D, this chapter will focus primarily on 2B+D, T1 PRI, and E1 PRI. 0B+1D is primarily used for credit card terminals, while 1B + 1D is generally deployed when only a single B-channel is required.

3.4.1 Channelized T1/E1

A channelized T1 multiplexes a line to logically create multiple channels on the same physical media. This creates the perception that multiple physical lines exist, but really only one physical wire is present. Many methods are available for creating these logical channels. Two examples are *Time Division Multiplexing* (TDM) and *Frequency Division Multiplexing* (FDM).

A radio is a good example of FDM. All the radio transmissions travel over the same media (air), and at the same time, but each radio station uses its own frequency to broadcast.

TDM works by logically dividing the channel up into time slices. This type of multiplexing works well with digital signals. ISDN uses a TDM method called PCM to represent multiple channels on a single wire. Defined by ITU-T I.431, PCM creates timeslots on a physical wire in which each timeslot is used to represent data for its channel, as shown in Figure 3-18.

Figure 3-18

The channelized
T1 frame format

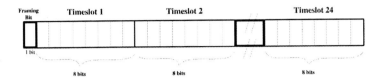

The end result is that each frame contains 24 timeslots, with eight bits in each timeslot, plus one bit for framing, for a total of 193 bits in each frame. Earlier in this chapter, using Nyquist's theorem, you learned the need for 8,000 samples (frames) per second to accurately represent an analog signal. Using a combination of Nyquist's theorem and the timeslots created by PCM for a T1, you can calculate the bandwidth of a T1.

T1 B-channel:

(8 bits/channel × 23 channels) × 8000 samples per second
= 1,472,000 bps

T1 D-channel:

(8 bits/channel × 1 channel) × 8000 samples per second = 64,000 bps

T1 framing:

1 bit/frame × 8000 frames per second = 8000 bps

T1 overall bit rate:

1,472,000 bits per second + 64,000 bits per second + 8,000 bits per second = 1,544,000 bps

Europe and many other locations around the world use channelized E1s that use 32 timeslots instead of 24 timeslots per frame, as shown in Figure 3-19. However, instead of using one bit inside the frame for frame synchronization, an E1 provides an entire B-channel for framing, typically timeslot 15.

Figure 3-19

Channelized E1
frame format

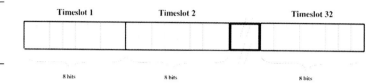

Once again, using Nyquist's theorem and the frame format of an E1, you can calculate the bandwidth available on an E1.

E1 B-channel:

$$(8 \text{ bits/channel} \times 30 \text{ channels}) \times 8000 \text{ samples per second} = 1,920,000 \text{ bps}$$

E1 D-channel:

$$(1 \text{ bits/channel} \times 1 \text{ channels}) \times 8000 \text{ samples per second} = 64,000 \text{ bps}$$

E1 framing:

$$(8 \text{ bits/channel} \times 1 \text{ channel}) \times 8000 \text{ samples per second} = 64,000 \text{ bps}$$

E1 overall bit rate:

$$1,920,000 \text{ bps} + 64,000 \text{ bps} + 64,000 \text{ bps} = 2,048,000 \text{ bps}$$

Even though the total throughput of a T1 is 1,544,000 bps and an E1 is 2,048,000 bps, not all of this is available for data communications. Anything that has to do with framing must be removed from your overall calculations. In addition, most of the time you must remove the D-channel from your overall throughput calculations, because the D-channel is only used for signaling and not user data.

3.4.2 ISDN BRI

An ISDN BRI line typically has two B-channels and one 16Kbps D-channel. Defined by ITU-T I.430, Figure 3-20 shows the frame format of an ISDN BRI line.

An interesting note is that the frame format is different depending upon its direction.

Figure 3-20

The ISDN frame
format BRI

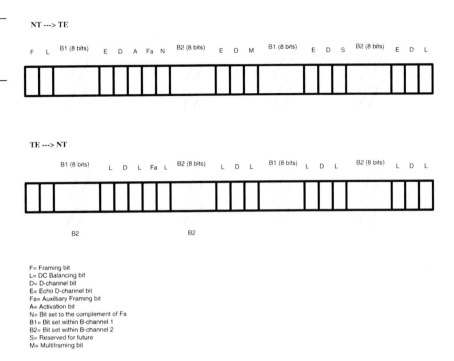

F= Framing bit
L= DC Balancing bit
D= D-channel bit
E= Echo D-channel bit
Fa= Auxilliary Framing bit
A= Activation bit
N= Bit set to the complement of Fa
B1= Bit set within B-channel 1
B2= Bit set within B-channel 2
S= Reserved for future
M= Multiframing bit

If you exclude all the bits related to B1, B2, and D, 12 bits per frame are
related to the framing and synchronization. Unlike a channelized T1/E1,
an ISDN BRI frame contains 16 bits of data for each B-channel (refer to
Figure 3-20), while a T1/E1 frame only carries eight bits of data for a each
B-channel (refer to Figure 3-18 and 3-19). This means that your equipment only needs to sample the ISDN BRI line half as many times as compared to an ISDN PRI line. Therefore, in order for a Cisco router to keep
from violating the Nyquist theorem, your equipment only needs to sample
the ISDN BRI line 4,000 times a second, instead of 8,000 times a second.

Once again, using Nyquist's theorem and the frame format of a BRI,
the bandwidth of a standard BRI can be calculated:

BRI B-channel:

(16 bits per frame/channel $\times$ 2 channels) $\times$ 4000 samples per second
= 128,000 bps

BRI D-channel:

(4 bits per frame) $\times$ 4000 samples per second = 16,000 bps

BRI framing and synchronization:

(12 bits/channel per frame) $\times$ 4000 samples per second = 48,000 bps

BRI overall bit rate:

128,000 bps + 16,000 bps + 48,000 bps = 192,000 bps

In order to calculate your true data throughput rate, remove the bit rate for framing and synchronization as well as the D-channel. Remember these are used in support of the B-channels.

3.4.3 Reference Points

Reference points are used to define the signaling standards between the different devices. Figure 3-21 shows the four reference points and how they are related to each other.

As shown in Figure 3-21, the Japanese and U.S. Telcos provide an interface up to the U reference point, while in Europe the Telcos provide a connection to the S/T reference point. Figure 3-22 shows how all these reference points come together.

The S/T reference point is a passive bus network with four wires. This architecture enables multiple devices to connect to the reference point,

Figure 3-21

IDSN reference points

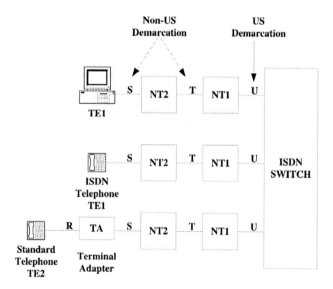

Figure 3-22

The relationship of ISDN reference points and physical equipment

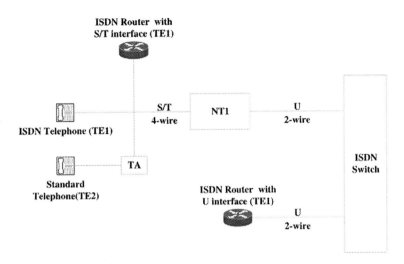

similar to connecting multiple telephones to a standard POTS line, while the U reference point can only have a single device attached to it.

Most Cisco ISDN routers, offered in the U.S., have an NT1 interface and can connect to the U reference point. This removes the need for an NT1 device but doesn't allow for an S/T interface in order to connect additional ISDN-compliant devices. The protocol ANSI T1.601 has been defined to specify signaling characteristics across the U interface in the U.S.

3.4.4 ISDN Protocols

The ITU-T has organized the ISDN protocols into three different types of protocols: Q, E, and I.

Q-Series

The Q-series of protocols defined by the ITU-T specifies the switching and signaling protocols used between devices. Examples include the following:

- **Q.921**: The ISDN user-network interface data link layer for general aspects
- **Q.931**: The ISDN user-network interface network layer specification for basic call control

I-Series

The I-series of protocols is used to define the concepts and interfaces associated with ISDN:

- **I.430**: The basic user-network interface for physical layer specifications
- **I.431**:The primary rate user-network interface for physical layer specifications

E-Series

Lastly, the E-series of protocols is used to define telephone network standards:

- **E.164**: The numbering plan for the ISDN era
- **E.172**: The call routing in the ISDN era

It is important to note that some protocols have been defined in multiple categories. Here are some examples:

- **Q.921** is also I.441, the ISDN user-network interface data link layer specification.
- **Q.931** is also I.451, the ISDN user-network interface network layer specification.

For a more complete list of ISDN protocols, go to the following URL: `http://www.cisco.com/warp/public/84/6.html`

To better understand how these protocols come together, Figure 3-23 shows us how each channel's protocols relate to the OSI model.

This is an important diagram to understand so that you can better understand the context of all the protocols and how they relate to each other.

3.4.5 D-channel

The primary purpose of the D-channel is to provide signaling and control for the ISDN line. Several protocols are used to set up and tear down calls on an ISDN line. Their relationship can better help you understand how to troubleshoot them when you are having problems.

D-channel's primary functions are setting up and tearing down calls for the B-channels. The signaling required to set up and tear down the B-

Figure 3-23

ISDN protocols
and the OSI
model

	B-Channel	D-Channel
Network Layer	IP/IPX/AT	Q.931
Data Link Layer	HDLC/PPP	Q.921 LAPD
Physical Layer	ANSI T1.606 I.430 BRI I.431 PRI	

channels will most likely not consume the bandwidth available on the D-channel. Subsequently, excess bandwidth on the D-channel can be used for user data. Although any signaling information gets priority over any data flow, the D-channel can be used for data flow rates up to 9.6Kbps. This type of data flow, also known as X.25 over a D-channel, is only available on a BRI.

3.4.6 B-channel

The B-channel is responsible for user services such as sending digital data and voice for phone calls that the D-channel has set up. B-channels can be used on demand or on a permanent basis. If a B-channel is provisioned as a permanent service, no D-channel signaling is required for the operation of the B-channel.

The B-channel has been designed to carry 64,000 bps, but in some cases the B-channel will only carry 56Kbps. This is usually due to legacy Telco equipment, which uses a signaling method called *robbed-bit signaling* (RBS). Instead of using the D-channel for call setup and teardown, RBS steals the low-order bit of every sixth sample inside the B-channel for signaling information. Because of the robbed bit in the B-channel, all bits are not available for data. This limits the number of useable bits to seven.

Subsequently, the data rate drops to 56,000 bps (7 bits * 8000 samples/sec = 56,000bps).

3.4.7 Configuration of ISDN PRI

As complicated as ISDN is, the configuration of an ISDN PRI is not difficult once the concepts are understood. Seven components need to be addressed in order to configure an ISDN PRI line to accept incoming analog and ISDN calls:

- Controller type (T1/E1)
- Framing and linecoding
- Clocking
- Switch type
- Identify timeslots
- Configuration of B-channels
- Accept analog calls

3.4.7.1 Controller Type (T1/E1)

Two different types of ISDN PRI controllers are available: T1 and E1. The controller you purchase will be dictated by the local Telco that provides your ISDN PRI service. As a general rule of thumb, T1s can be purchased in North America and Japan, while E1's are typically available in Europe.

Unlike other interfaces, to configure a T1 controller, you do not preface the command with an interface (such as interface Ethernet 0/0). Use the following command to select the controller's interface for configuration:

```
Router (config)#controller controller-type slot-number
```

controller-type	**T1**	Configure T1 controller
	E1	Configure E1 controller
slot-number	*x*	Controller unit number

3.4.7.2 Framing and Linecoding

Framing and linecoding are attributes that are provided by your ISP. If you are using the wrong framing and linecoding, your PRI line will not come up.

In a normal T1 frame, 193 bits are available, of which 192 bits are used for data and one bit is used for framing. Unfortunately, the single bit in a T1 frame cannot easily convey the signaling information required to keep a T1 line synchronized.

In an effort to deal with this problem, the superframe has been created. The *superframe format* (SF, and also known as D4) is composed of 12 T1 frames in which the 12 framing bits go through the following 12-bit pattern: 100011011100. That is, the framing bit from the first frame is a 1, then 0 for the next three frames, 1 for the next two frames, and so on until the end of the 12-bit pattern is reached. Once the end is reached, it starts over. By looking for this specific pattern in every 193rd bit of 12 frames, the receiver can establish frame synchronization.

In the late 1970s, a new method of framing called *T1 extended super-frame format* (ESF) was developed. With ESF, a block of 24 frames is grouped together, creating a block of 24 framing bits. These framing bits are broken down into three functions:

- Frame alignment sequence (FAS), six bits

- Frame check sequence (FCS), six bits

- Maintenance channel, 12-bits

FAS uses a repeating pattern (001011) from its six bits to ensure that the frames are correctly synchronized. If the receiver loses synchronization (a slip), it will find the appropriate bit pattern in the next five ESF frames (24 T1 Frames per ESF Frame * 5 ESF Frames = 120 frames).

FCS uses a six-bit *cyclic redundancy check* (CRC) to determine if bit errors occurred in the previous multi-frame. FCS is used only for error detection and not correction.

The maintenance channel, also called the *Facilities Data Link* (FDL), forms a 4Kbps-side channel that can be used for network maintenance and operations. However, a PRI does not have a specific operation for this channel.

Other framing methods such as HDB3, CRC4, and NO-CRC4 are only available when using an E1. The CRC and NO-CRC4 versions have different algorithms depending upon whether it is an E1 in Europe or an E1 in Australia.

One of the requirements of a T1 circuit is to maintain one's density level. This enables repeaters to maintain the timing. If a long string of binary zeros is transmitted, a repeater could easily lose its timing. Thus, there must be a way of ensuring that a binary one or marker pulse occurs every so often. Three methods are used today and they are typically dependent upon the type of linecoding that is used. Table 3-10 shows examples of the most commonly used framing and linecoding formats.

Table 3-10	Framing	Linecoding
Typical Framing and Linecoding pairs	Superframe (SF)	Alternate Mark Inversion (AMI)
	Extended Super Frame (ESF)	Binary 8-zero Substitution (B8ZS)
	Cyclic Redundancy Check 4 (CRC4)	High-Density Bipolar 3 (HDB3)

Framing and linecoding configuration are performed on the controller. Different framing and linecoding can be used on different controllers. The format of the framing command is as follows:

```
Router (config-controller)#framing frame-type
```

frame-type   **sf**   Configure T1 controller for SF format

esf   Configure T1 controller for ESF format

crc4   Configure E1 controller for CRC 4

To configure the linecoding on a controller, use the following command:

```
Router (config-controller)#linecode linecoding-type
```

linecoding   **ami**   Configure T1 controller for alternate mark

-type   **b8zs**   Configure T1 controller for ESF format

hdb3   Configure E1 controller for CRC 4

Figure 3-24 shows an example of these two commands being executed:

Figure 3-24

Framing and linecoding commands example

```
Router#config t
Router(config)#controller t1 0
Router(config-controller)#framing esf
Router(config-controller)#linecode b8zs
```

3.4.7.3 Clocking

In order to send data to the ISDN switch, you must use a clock so that you can time your transmissions correctly. Therefore, a clock is defined on the T1/E1 controller. The Cisco Access Server you have will determine the command used to specify the T1 clock source. The AS5x000 series of routers has a different command set than the Cisco 3600 series, 4000 series, and 7000 series of routers. The AS5x000 series of routers enables you to configure one of the T1s as the primary source for clocking and the others as secondary. The command is as follows:

```
Router (config-controller)#clock source line clock-source
```

clock-source	**primary**	Configure the T1 interface as the primary TDM clock source
	secondary	Configure the T1 interface as the secondary TDM clock source

You should only configure one of the T1 controllers as the primary, and all other T1 controllers get configured as secondary. The other Cisco routers (3600, 4000, and 7000) use the following command to configure the clocking:

```
Router (config-controller)#clock source source-type
```

source-type	**line**	Will use clocking received from the T1
	internal	Will use its own internal clock

3.4.7.4 Switch Type

The type of switch to select is dependent upon the Telco you get your ISDN PRI from. After the installation of the ISDN PRI line, your Telco should indicate the switch type they are using.

Cisco's IOS can support seven different switch types:

- AT&T 4ESS switch
- AT&T 5ESS switch
- Northern Telecom switch
- European switch type for NET5
- National ISDN switch
- Japan switch
- Australia switch

Prior to IOS 11.3, the selection of the ISDN switch type was only available at the global configuration mode. Starting with 11.3 and later, the selection of your switch type can be handled in one of two ways: globally or on a specific interface. If you select your switch type globally, you only have to set it once for all of your interfaces. However, if you select your switch type on the interface, you can support different switch types on different interfaces. To configure the switch type globally use the following command:

```
Router (config)#isdn switch-type telco-switch-type
```

telco-switch-type	primary-4ess	AT&T 4ESS switch type for the U.S.
	primary-5ess	AT&T 5ESS switch type for the U.S.
	primary-dms100	Northern Telecom switch type for the U.S.
	primary-net5	European switch type for NET5
	primary-ni	National ISDN switch type
	primary-ntt	Japan switch type
	primary-ts014	Australia switch type

If you configure the switch type on the interface, the command and syntax are identical. However, do not configure the T1 controller interface, but the D channel of the ISDN line, which modifies the command prompt to the following command:

```
Router (config-if)#isdn switch-type telco-switch-type
```

Note:

In order for the configuration change to be effective, you must reload the router.

3.4.7.5 Identify Timeslots

When configuring your ISDN PRI line, you must specify the number of fixed timeslots that have been allocated by the provider's ISDN switch. To do so, the following command must be applied to the controller's interface:

```
Router (config-controller)#pri-group timeslots-range
```

timeslots-range	1-24	For use with a T1
	1-31	For use with a E1

3.4.7.6 Configuring the D-Channel

Now that you have defined the number of timeslots, you need to identify which channel will be the D-channel. Once the D-channel's timeslot is identified, other attributes need to be configured. Configuring the D-channel is not difficult, because all T1 lines use the last channel as the D-channel, while E1 lines use channel 15 as the D-channel. The command is as follows:

```
Router (config)#interface serial timeslot
```

timeslots	x:23	x is the slot of the T1 network module
	x:15	x is the slot of the E1 network module

3.4.7.7 Accepting Analog Calls

Because ISDN calls use the D-channel for call setup and teardown, you must make special provisions for standard analog calls. This is because they use in-band signaling to establish a call, whereas ISDN uses out-of-band signaling. During an incoming call, the Cisco IOS examines the data on the D-channel to see if the call is a voice call (remember that an analog modem call looks just like a call placed with a standard phone). If it is a voice call (as opposed to an ISDN device placing the call), the Cisco IOS routes the call to the internal modem for processing. The command that enables this behavior is as follows:

```
Router (config-if)#isdn incoming-voice source-type
```

source-type	**modem**	Voice calls are handled as modems
	data 56	Voice calls are handled as data at 56Kbps
	data 64	Voice calls are handled as data at 64Kbps

Remember that this command is applied to the D-channel of your ISDN line. If you have multiple D-channels (because you have multiple ISDN PRI lines), then it must be applied to all of them.

3.4.8 Configuration of ISDN BRI

Although an ISDN BRI can support both dial-in and dial-out, the main focus in this section is on supporting dial-in connections (modem over BRI). Starting with Cisco's IOS 12.0, a Cisco router with ISDN BRI can support not just incoming ISDN BRI dial-in connections, but incoming analog connections as well.

Configuring an ISDN BRI line is not as difficult as configuring an ISDN PRI line. However, a few things are different when configuring a BRI, while some aren't. Three components need to be configured to make an ISDN BRI line support incoming calls:

- Switch type
- Service provider identifiers (SPID)
- Accept analog calls

3.4.8.1 Switch Type

Just like an ISDN PRI interface, you must configure the switch type on an ISDN BRI interface. The selection of the switch type is dependent upon the version of IOS you are running. Also similar to an ISDN PRI, prior to IOS 11.3, switch type selection has been limited to the global configuration, but with IOS 11.3 and later, the switch type selection can be configured in two ways: globally or on the interface. By configuring the switch type on the interface, you can support multiple switch types (assuming you have multiple BRI interfaces).

The format of the command used to configure the switch type of an ISDN BRI interface is identical, but the options to configure an ISDN BRI line are slightly different. The code is as follows:

```
Router (config)#isdn switch-type telco-switch-type
```

telco-switch-type		
	basic-1tr6	1TR6 switch type for Germany
	basic -5ess	AT&T 5ESS switch type for the U.S.
	basic -dms100	Northern DMS-100 switch type
	basic -net3	NET3 switch type for UK and Europe
	basic-ni	National ISDN switch type
	basic -qsig	QSIG switch type
	basic -ts013	TS013 switch type for Australia
	ntt	NTT switch type for Japan
	vn3	VN3 and VN4 switch types for France

3.4.8.2 Service Profile Identifier (SPID)

A *Service Profile Identifier* (SPID) is typically a 13-digit numeric number that enables service providers to associate the terminal with a terminal service profile. This allows the service provider to assign service characteristics to your equipment (such as call forwarding, caller ID, call waiting, and so on).

Not all switch types require a SPID. Currently, only DMS-100 and NI1 require SPIDs. Similar to a DLCI for Frame Relay, it is only locally significant. Configuration of the SPID is performed on the ISDN BRI interface. To configure an ISDN BRI SPID, use the following command:

```
Router (config-if)#isdn B-channel-number spid-number phone-number
```

B-channel-number	**spid1**	Specify SPID for first B-channel
	spid2	Specify SPID for second B-channel
spid-number	*xxxxxxxxxxxxx*	Thirteen-digit SPID assigned by service provider
phone-number	*xxxxxxx*	Phone number associated with the SPID

3.4.8.3 Accept Analog Calls

Modem over BRI enables small offices to support 56K dial-in connections without the need for an expensive PRI or an extra dialup line, thus saving monthly recurring costs. In order to support Modem over BRI, we need a method to interpret the in-band signaling as well as demodulate the analog signal. The command to support analog calls is as follows:

```
Router (config-if)#isdn incoming-voice source-type
```

source-type	**modem 56**	B-channel bandwidth of 56Kb/s
	modem 64	B-channel bandwidth of 64Kb/s
	data 56	Voice calls are handled as data at 56Kbps
	data 64	Voice calls are handled as data at 64Kbps

When configuring encapsulation and authentication, care needs to be taken when issuing these commands. Although both the encapsulation and authentication commands are supported on all interfaces, you must know where to place those commands so that you achieve the effect you desire. For instance, when you need to support Modem over BRI, configure your BRI interface to support the physical layer attributes, but use the group-async interface to configure your data link and network layer characteristics.

3.5 PPP

This section will cover the most prevalent asynchronous protocol in use today: the *Point-to-Point Protocol* (PPP). This is a method for transporting datagrams over a point-to-point link. The only requirement imposed by PPP is that it must operate in full-duplex mode, as specified in RFC 1662. PPP has the capability to run in an asynchronous- or synchronous-dedicated connection or circuit-switched connection. In synchronous environments, it can provide interoperability between Cisco routers and non-Cisco routers (remember HDLCs between different vendors' routers is rarely compatible).

PPP consists of three major components:

- Encapsulation method (HDLC-like framing)
- Link Control Protocol (LCP)
- Network Control Protocol (NCP)

Figure 3-25 shows us the relationship between NCP, LCP, and HDLC.

Figure 3-25

The structure of a PPP packet

PPP Frame	OSI Layer
TCP/IP IPX/SPX AppleTalk	Network Layer
Network Control Protocol (NCP) - - - - - - - - - - - - - Link Control Protocol (LCP) - - - - - - - - - - - - - HDLC	Data-Link Layer
ISDN, EIA/TIA-232, V.35	Physical Layer

Once you understand the fundamentals of these three protocols, we will then look at how to configure them. It is important to understand these crucial components so that when troubleshooting your PPP connections you know where to look first.

PPP is a bit-oriented protocol that can run over synchronous or asynchronous links. It uses a variant of HDLC as the foundation for encapsulation. This encapsulation provides for the multiplexing of multiple network-layer protocols simultaneously over the same link.

LCP gives PPP its versatility, allowing for the negotiation of packet formats, packet sizes, and authentication. It also gives PPP the capability to determine when the line is failing or functioning properly.

NCP is actually a suite of protocols. Each subprotocol is designed to handle the configuration intricacies required by its respective network layer protocol.

These three components have enabled PPP to become the dialup protocol of choice for business and personal use. Let's now take an in-depth look at each of these protocols and how they operate.

3.5.1 HDLC-Like Framing

The PPP encapsulation protocol, while based upon ISO HDLC, is not Cisco's proprietary HDLC protocol. As shown in Figure 3-26, PPP encapsulation is made up of six distinct fields:

Figure 3-26

PPP frame format

Flag	Address	Control	Protocol	Data	FCS
1 Byte	1 Byte	1 Byte	1 or 2 Byte(s)	up to 1500 Bytes	1 Byte

- **Flag**: All Frames start and end with the same binary sequence 01111110 (7Eh).

- **Address**: Because PPP does not assign a data link layer address (the equivalent of a *Media Access Control* [MAC] address in Ethernet), the HDLC broadcast address of 11111111 is used.

- **Control**: The value of this field is always set to 03 Hex. If a PPP frame contains any other value, it is discarded. If compression is used, the address and control fields are omitted.

- **Protocol**: This is a two-byte field that identifies the encapsulated protocol. Table 3-11 shows a list of currently assigned data link layer protocol numbers. Note that all protocol numbers must be odd.

* **Data**: This consists of upper-layer protocol data. The data field may be padded with an arbitrary number of octets. It is the protocol's responsibility to distinguish between padding and real information.

* **Frame Check Sequence**: Normally, this is a two-byte or four-byte field that contains the frame checksum calculation. PPP verifies the FCS upon receipt of the packet.

In order to give dialin access to your Cisco Access server, you must configure two components: asynchronous lines and asynchronous interfaces. You have already seen the commands used to set the line speed, flow control, and other physical layer attributes that are configured on an asynchronous line. Now let's look at how to the commands to configure data-link layer and network layer protocols as performed on the asynchronous interface.

3.5.2 Configuration of PPP

Configuring PPP encapsulation is a straightforward task, but where to apply the encapsulation can be confusing. Encapsulation for PPP is not applied to the asynchronous lines in your Cisco Access server (line tty 1 12) such as when you are configuring the dialin direction or when specifying the flow control (refer to Figure 3-8). Instead, you address each line from the global configuration mode as an interface using the *interface async* command:

```
Router (config)#interface async line-number
```

line-number	*x*	the line number used to address the asynchronous interface

Configuring the encapsulation is identical to the process of setting the encapsulation on an Ethernet interface, as in the following code:

```
Router (config-if)#encapsulation encapsulation-type
```

encapsulation-type	**ppp**	Point-to-Point Protocol
	slip	Serial Line Internet Protocol
	bstun	Block Serial Tunneling

Point-to-Point Data Link Layer ID	Assigned Protocol Assigned Protocol
0021	Internet protocol
0023	OSI Network layer
0025	Xerox NS IDP
0027	DECnet Phase IV
0029	AppleTalk
002b	Novell IPX
002d	Van Jacobson Compressed TCP/IP
002f	Van Jacobson Uncompressed TCP/IP
0031	Bridging PDU
0033	Stream Protocol (ST-II)
0035	Banyan Vines
0201	802.1d Hello packets
0231	Luxcom
0233	Sigma Network Systems
8021	Internet Protocol Control Protocol
8023	OSI Network Layer Control Protocol
8025	Xerox NS IDP Control Protocol
8027	DECnet Phase IV Control Protocol
8029	AppleTalk Control Protocol
802b	Novell IPX Control Protocol
8031	Bridging NCP
8033	Stream Protocol Control Protocol
8035	Banyan Vines Control Protocol
c021	Link Control Protocol
c023	Password Authentication Protocol
c025	Link Quality Report
c223	Challenge Handshake Authentication Protocol

Table 3-11

Sampling of the assigned point-to-point data link layer protocol IDs

If you have multiple asynchronous interfaces that need to be configured identically, you could easily see where individually defining the characteristics of each interface would be a repetitive task and not necessarily conducive to keeping your configuration error-free. Cisco has seen this and given you a way to address a logic unit of asynchronous interfaces simultaneously using the *group-async* command. This command enables you to create a virtual group of asynchronous interfaces. The format of the command is as follows:

```
Router (config)#group-async group-number
```

group-number *x*   the logical number used to describe a group of asynchronous interfaces

Once configuring that interface, you can specify which asynchronous lines you want to include using the following command :

```
Router (config-if)#group-range start-line end-line
```

start-line   *x*   the first asynchronous absolute line to use in your Cisco Access server

end-line   *x*   the last asynchronous absolute line to use in your Cisco Access server

You can now specify the encapsulation of all your asynchronous lines simultaneously, as shown in Figure 3-27.

Figure 3-27

Configuring multiple lines for PPP encapsulation simultaneously

```
Router#config terminal
Router(config)#interface group-Async 1
Router(config-if)#group-range 65 76
Router(config-if)#encapsulation ppp
```

3.5.2.1 Link Control Protocol (LCP)

Before any network layer protocols can be routed, such as TCP/IP and IPX/SPX, LCP must open a connection and negotiate the configuration. LCP has four main components:

▓ Authentication

▓ Callback

- Compression
- Multilink PPP

PPP Authentication PPP authentication is the very first protocol to be negotiated within the LCP suite of protocols after a client has connected and successfully negotiated a modulation method. If authentication fails, the Cisco Access server immediately terminates the connection.

Two authentication protocols are commonly used: the *Password Authentication Protocol* (PAP) and the *Challenge Handshake Authentication Protocol* (CHAP).

Note:

Although authentication is not necessary to connect using PPP, it is definitely an integral part of any security strategy.

Password Authentication Protocol (PAP) PAP is the simplest authentication protocol. Once a client connects to the Cisco Access server, PPP has the option to authenticate. During this period, the username/password pair is repeatedly sent to the Cisco Access server until the authentication is accepted or rejected. Rejection of the authentication is usually in the form of connection termination.

When the username/password is sent using PAP, no encryption scheme is used to hide the username or password, as shown in Figure 3-28.

Because the data sent is just the username and password, it is subject to a *playback attack*. A playback attack is when an intruder "listens" to the line during the authentication process, intercepts, and records the authentication process. An intruder would then be able to use that recorded authentication process to gain access to your system. Although this is not an easy process, it can be done.

The configuration of authentication on a Cisco Access server is performed on an interface, similar to PPP encapsulation. The format of the command is as follows:

```
Router (config-if)#ppp authentication pap
```

Challenge Handshake Protocol (CHAP) To improve security, you can use a more secure authentication method: CHAP. During a CHAP authentication, the Cisco Access server sends a challenge to the connecting host, as shown in Figure 3-29.

Figure 3-28

The PAP
authentication
process

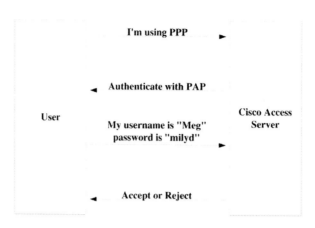

**PAP Authentication between
Dial-Up User and Cisco Access Server**

Figure 3-29

The CHAP
authentication
process

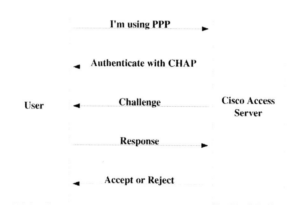

**CHAP Authentication between
Dial-Up User and Cisco Access Server**

The challenge is in the form of a random number. This number, called an *encryption key*, is generated by the Cisco Access server and must be unique and unpredictable. The host then encrypts the username and password using a one-way hash function, MD5. This newly encrypted message sent by the host is called the *response*. When the Cisco Access server receives the response, it generates a hash using the password it has for the user and then compares the newly created hash with the response received from the user to authenticate the user.

Note:
The different encryption methods such as MD5 will be discussed in Chapter 4.

These security features in CHAP make it more secure than PAP. Because the random number sent in the challenge is unique and unpredictable, CHAP protects against playback. Because the host uses the encryption key to encrypt the username and password, neither the password nor the username is sent over the wire in clear text form. In addition, CHAP provides additional protection by repeatedly challenging the host every two minutes. These repeated challenges limit your exposure to any single attack. Configuration of your Cisco Access server to use CHAP is almost identical to that of PAP. The format of the command is as follows:

```
Router (config-if)#ppp authentication chap
```

Note:
When a host is trying to authenticate, it is the receiving access router that determines the authentication method. As an administrator, you must specify PAP, CHAP, or both authentication protocols.

Creating User Accounts   Now that you have a basic understanding of PAP and CHAP authentication, it is important to know how to create a user account so that you have something to compare the authentication requests against.

Cisco routers have the capability to create a local user account database. Creating a username on the local Cisco Access server is a straightforward process. Adding the username command in the global configuration mode, you use the following syntax:

```
Router (config)#username user-account-name encryption-type password
```

user-account-name	**WORD**	The name of the user (such as jquiggle)
encryption-type	**0, 7**	(Optional) The level of encryption used to encrypt the password for the user; this keeps the password from being displayed clear text in the configuration file
password	**WORD**	The password

Two different encryption types are available when creating a user account on a local Cisco router. It is important to understand the distinction between the two different levels and how to make passwords unreadable in the configuration file. The first encryption type is *0*, which specifies that the password that is about to be entered is unencrypted. This enables plain text passwords to be entered during the creation of a user account The second encryption type is *7*, which specifies that a Cisco router has already encrypted the password that is about to be entered. Although it may not be apparent why this is important, it should become clear in just a moment.

If a user account is created using the encryption type 0, you may not necessarily want everyone with access to the configuration file to know everyone else's password. In order to encrypt user passwords in a configuration file, the *service password-encryption* must be turned on. This is easily accomplished using the following command:

```
Router (config)#service password-encryption
```

Once password encryption has been enabled, all passwords in the configuration file are encrypted. Once a user's password has been encrypted, disabling the password encryption does not decrypt the user's password. It still remains encrypted.

Figure 3-30 shows us that service password-encryption is disabled and you can view the password for user Suzy.

Figure 3-30

The user's password before password-encryption is enabled

```
RouterA#show running-config
Building configuration...

Current configuration:
!
version 11.3
service timestamps debug uptime
service timestamps log uptime
no service password-encryption
service udp-small-servers
service tcp-small-servers
!
hostname RouterA
!
username suzy password 0 suzy
!
```

In Figure 3-31, you can see that after password-encryption has been enabled you can no longer see the password for Suzy's account.

Figure 3-31

The user's password before password-encryption is disabled

```
RouterA#show running-config
Building configuration...

Current configuration:
!
version 11.3
service timestamps debug uptime
service timestamps log uptime
service password-encryption
service udp-small-servers
service tcp-small-servers
!
hostname RouterA
!
username suzy password 7 1404071115
!
```

Now, if you wanted to copy Suzy's user account from RouterA to Router B, as shown in Figure 3-32, you can use the encryption type of 7 to create the user's account and password without actually knowing the value of the password.

Figure 3-32

Creating a user account with encryption-type 7

```
Router(config)#username suzy password 7 1404071115
```

For various reasons that will be covered in Chapter 4, it is possible to locate user accounts not on the local router, but on a centralized server. In order to use this user accounting paradigm, you must use Cisco's *Authentication, Authorization, and Accounting* (AAA). In order to enable Cisco's advanced AAA security facility in Cisco's IOS, you must use the *aaa new-model* command.

Note:

The encryption algorithm used to encrypt a password at level 7 is not considered a strong encryption and can readily be broken. Many password crackers out there can easily convert a level-7 password to plain text. This level of encryption should only be used for casual security. For a more secure environment, username passwords should be located on an AAA server.

This *aaa new-model* command changes the way authentication and authorization is handled. Once this command is executed, every line on the Cisco Access server receives the implicit *login authentication default*.

Note:

The CON, AUX, TTY, and VTY are all considered lines. It is very easy to accidentally lock yourself out once you have issued this command. For example, if you Telnet to the Cisco Access server using the VTY login password and then during your session, you are issuing the aaa new-model. Subsequently, you log off without creating any user accounts. This locks you out of the Cisco Access server, thus requiring you to connect to the console port and use the password recovery techniques found in the appendices of this book.

The format of the aaa new-model command is as follows:

```
Router (config)#aaa new-model
```

Now that you are using Cisco's advanced AAA security model, you need to understand some of the basics. Authentication is the process used to determine who you are, while authorization determines what rights a user has. This is an important distinction, because it gives you more control over your security.

Cisco's advanced security model provides for several authentication mechanisms. You can store the usernames in the local configuration file, a *Remote Authentication Dial-in User Service* (RADIUS) server, a *Terminal Access Controller Access Control System* (TACACS+) server, or any combination. (RADIUS and TACACS will be discussed further in Chapter 4). The following command enables you to specify the security model you want to use:

```
Router (config)#aaa authentication service-type authentication-list
security-model
```

service-type	**ppp**	An authentication mechanism for ppp
	arap	An authentication mechanism for arap
	nasi	An authentication mechanism for nasi
	login	An authentication mechanism for exec logins
	enable	An authentication mechanism for enable mode
authentication-list	**default**	Make this the default list
	WORD	Create a list with this name
security-model	**local**	Use the usernames in the config file
	local-case	Use the usernames in the config file with case-sensitive passwords
	radius	Store passwords in a RADIUS server
	tacacs	Store passwords in a TACACS server
none	**No authentication**	

Figure 3-33 shows an example of this command being executed.

Figure 3-33

A command used to create a local account

```
Router(config)#aaa authentication login default tacacs
```

3.5.2.2 Network Control Protocol (NCP)

NCP is a collection of independently defined protocols that are responsible for negotiating a network layer's attributes during call setup and then encapsulating the network layer protocol for transport in a PPP packet. In order for the NCP protocols to start their job, LCP negotiations must have been completed successfully.

Each NCP protocol is defined in a separate RFC. Table 3-12 shows a sample of the current NCP protocols.

Table 3-12

NCP RFCs

NCP Protocol	Network Layer Protocol	RFC
IPCP	IP	1332
IPV6CP	IP v6	2023
IPXCP	IPX	1552
ATCP	AppleTalk	1378

Although the NCP suite of protocols is critical to the operation of PPP, all NCP attributes are modified through the configurations of their corresponding network layer protocols. This section will focus on three of the most commonly used network protocols: TCP/IP, IPX/SPX, and *NetBIOS Extended User Interface* (NetBEUI).

Network Layer Configuration of TCP/IP   Although discussing how TCP/IP works is not within the scope of this book, getting your Cisco Access server to issue the appropriate TCP/IP attributes is. For more information about TCP/IP fundamentals, access the following URL:

`http://www.cisco.com/univercd/cc/td/doc/cisintwk/ito_doc/ip.htm`

When configuring TCP/IP for the Central Access server, you must follow three basic steps to configure the central office to accept incoming PPP connections:

1. Configure dynamically assigned IP addresses.
2. Configure IP-related services (such as the *Domain Name System* [DNS], the *Windows Internet Naming Service* [WINS], and so on).
3. Use IP unnumbered for routing purposes.

Dynamic IP address assignments can be performed on a Cisco Access server for PPP connections. This is important because a PPP client dialing into the Central Access server typically does not have an IP address and will subsequently need one upon successfully authenticating to the Cisco Access server. The first step for accomplishing this task is to define the range of IP addresses to be assigned. Use the following command to assign a block of IP addresses to hand out when clients dial-in:

```
Router (config)#ip local pool address-pool-name first-ip-address last-
ip-address
```

address-pool-name	**default**	Default IP address block
	WORD	Named IP address block
first-ip-address	*a.b.c.d*	The first IP address in the block of IP addresses
last-ip-address	*a.b.c.d*	The last IP address in the block of IP addresses

Having just a TCP/IP address and no other attributes makes using TCP/IP difficult at best. Therefore, you also need to provide your dialup client TCP/IP information. By using the following command, you can hand out a variety of information:

```
Router (config)#async-bootp ip-attribute a.b.c.d
```

ip-attribute	**dns-server**	*a.b.c.d*	Set the DNS server for the remote client to use
	lpr-server	*a.b.c.d*	Set the LPR server for the remote client to use
	nbns-server	*a.b.c.d*	Set the WINS server for the remote client to use
	time-server	*a.b.c.d*	Set the time server for the remote client to use

In order to focus on the next topic, you need to perform a brief analysis on TCP/IP network numbering.

Every network segment in a TCP/IP network has a unique IP network number. In order to adhere to standard IP numbering, every interface on a network must have a unique host number (IP address). The subnet mask enables Host A to determine whether or not the IP address of Host B is on the local IP network or is on a different network. As shown in Figure 3-34, Host B (192.168.2.10/24) is not on the same network as Host A (192.168.1.10/24). At this point, the basic rules of TCP/IP state that it must forward the packet to its default gateway (192.168.1.1/24).

Router A then uses its routing table to determine where to send the packet destined for Host B. Router A sends the packet, destined for Host B, out of its serial interface (192.168.3.1/24) to Router B's serial interface (192.168.3.2/24). Router B's Ethernet interface (192.168.2.1/24) shares a network segment with Host B (192.168.2.10/24) and can send the packet directly to Host B.

Figure 3-34

Typical IP
communications

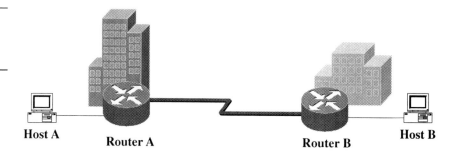

Host A   Router A   Router B   Host B

STEP 1: Packet sent from Host A to Router A
STEP 2: Router A forwards packet to Router B
STEP 3: Router B forwards packet to Host B

HOST A	192.168.1.10 / 24
HOST B	192.168.2.10 / 24
ROUTER A E0	192.168.1.1 / 24
ROUTER A S0	192.168.3.1 / 24
ROUTER B E0	192.168.2.1 / 24
ROUTER B S0	192.168.3.2 / 24

From this example, it is apparent that you need three different TCP/IP networks to get a packet from Host A to Host B. Unfortunately for your WAN link, you waste 252 IP addresses on this serial line. This is where the command *ip unnumbered* can be useful. IP unnumbered lets you use the IP address of one of your LAN interfaces to use as an IP address for WAN packet flow. This eliminates the need for an additional network and saves on IP addressing.

Note:

Although you can reduce the number of IP addresses wasted in the previous scenario by changing the subnet mask, the point is that some of your IP addresses are wasted, and using ip unnumbered *wastes no IP addresses.*

Normally, the routing table shows which local IP address and local interface that the router should use to get to the next hop, as shown in Figure 3-35.

However, using *ip unnumbered,* the routing table updates are entered into the routing table using the IP address of the remote router's Ethernet interface and the serial interface of the local router, as shown in Figure 3-36.

Figure 3-35

A routing table without IP unnumbered

```
Router A Routing Table
C 192.168.1.0/24 is directly connected, Ethernet0
R 192.168.2.0/24 [120/1] via 192.168.3.2, 00:00:20, Serial0
C 192.168.3.0/24 is directly connected, Serial0

Router B Routing Table
R 192.168.1.0/24 [120/1] via 192.168.3.2, 00:00:10, Serial0
C 192.168.2.0/24 is directly connected, Ethernet0
C 192.168.3.0/24 is directly connected, Serial0
```

Figure 3-36

A routing table with IP unnumbered

```
Router A Routing Table
C 192.168.1.0/24 is directly connected, Ethernet0
R 192.168.2.0/24 [120/1] via 192.168.3.2, 00:00:05, Serial0
S* 0.0.0.0/0 is directly connected, Serial0

Router B Routing Table
R 192.168.1.0/24 [120/1] via 192.168.3.2, 00:00:06, Serial0
C 192.168.2.0/24 is directly connected, Ethernet0
S* 0.0.0.0/0 is directly connected, Serial0
```

Because of this fundamental aspect, ip unnumbered only works on point-to-point links. This is identical to the situation in which a client connects to your Cisco Access server. The client needs to send all TCP/IP traffic out its asynchronous connection. Therefore, you can use the ip unnumbered command on your group-async interface. This keeps you from having to assign a point-to-point network between each of our dial-in hosts. The format of the command is

```
Router (config-if)#ip unnumbered interface
```

interface	**Ethernet** *slot/port*	Use this Ethernet interface for IP unnumbered
	Async *slot/port*	Use this async interface for IP unnumbered
	Loopback *slot/port*	Use this Ethernet interface for IP unnumbered
	Serial *slot/port*	Use this Ethernet interface for IP unnumbered

The ports you can use are directly related to the type of hardware found in your router. It is recommended that you create a loopback adapter and assign that loopback adapter routable IP address that is not used on your network (preferably from the private IP range).

Let's look at an example of a network in which the Cisco Access server has three interfaces: one Ethernet, one Frame Relay, and one asynchronous connection. If you were to reference your Ethernet interface for your ip unnumbered connection on your group-async interface, then whenever your Ethernet connection goes down, your asynchronous clients would not be able to access the Frame Relay connection until the Ethernet connection is back up. Remember that when an interface goes down, the IP address becomes deactivated and the router does not respond to requests to that IP address.

However, if you create a loopback interface and assign an IP address (which, by definition, never goes down unless you manually shut it down), then your asynchronous clients would still be able to access all the networks that were up, even when other interfaces are down.

Network Layer Configuration of IPX/SPX   Historically, IPX/SPX has been the default protocol for Novell's NetWare. The initiative behind IPX/SPX is to provide an easy-to-setup routable network protocol. Configuring a Cisco Access server for use with IPX/SPX is not as straightforward as TCP/IP. Configuring IPX/SPX on your PPP network has four steps:

1. Enable IPX routing.
2. Create a loopback interface.
3. Configure a loopback interface with an IPX network number.
4. Associate a loopback interface with an asynchronous interface.

Unlike TCP/IP, the default for a Cisco Access server is not to route IPX. You must manually turn IPX routing on. You can then use the following command to enable IPX routing:

```
Router (config)#ipx routing mac-address
```

mac-address   *xxxx.xxxx.xxxx*   (Optional) Use a non-duplicate MAC address

When deciding on which MAC address to use, it is advisable not to use the MAC address of an existing interface, but to choose a MAC address that represents that router. For example, if you are configuring IPX routing on router 4, use the MAC address 0004.0004.0004. By correlating the MAC address to something specific on the router, you simplify things like IPX pings because the node ID of the router is 0004.0004.0004. If you fail to indicate a MAC address when enabling IPX routing, the Cisco IOS will put its first Ethernet MAC address in place.

In order for a Cisco Access server to route IPX/SPX packets from an asynchronous interface, it must be associated with a loopback interface that has been configured with a valid IPX network number. Think of this loopback interface as being a virtual network that has a cable segment of all the remote clients connecting, as shown in Figure 3-37.

Figure 3-37

An IPX network
with PPP clients

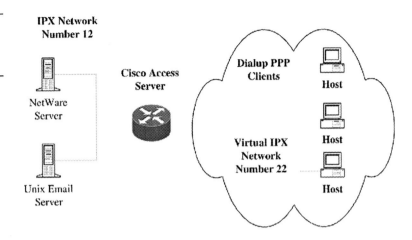

Loopback interfaces are imaginary interfaces and do not connect to any physical device. The purpose of a loopback interface is to provide an interface that never goes down. Many different options require a network layer address, such as an IP address to be referenced in order for the protocol to work correctly. Take, for instance, *Open Shortest Path First* (OSPF), which uses the highest IP address of an active interface as its *Router ID* (RID). If a real interface were to go down, then OSPF would have to create a new RID and propagate that new RID to the other routers, thus forcing them to recalculate their OSPF databases. This would have to happen every time an interface goes down. By using a loopback interface, you can assure that the RID will not change unless you administratively shutdown the loopback interface.

Creating a loopback adapter is a simple process. In global configuration mode, simply use the following command where the loopback-number is a loopback interface not previously defined in the router. Simply enter the command *interface loopback N* where N is a loopback interface not previously defined in the router configuration. To start adding loopback interfaces, use the command *interface loopback 0*. By selecting a loopback address that previously didn't exist, the Cisco IOS dynamically creates a loopback interface.

```
Router (config)#interface loopback loopback-number
```

loopback-number   *x*   Any whole number between 1 and 9,999,999,999

When the loopback interface is created, it automatically changes to an up state, as shown in Figure 3-38.

Figure 3-38

A loopback interface automatically changing to an upstate upon creation

```
Router(config)#interface loopback 3
01:10:18: %LINEPROTO-5-UPDOWN: Line protocol on Interface
Loopback3, changed state to up
```

Now that the loopback adapter has been created, you can configure the IPX network number that your PPP remote clients will use:

```
Router (config)#ipx network ipx-network-number
```

ipx-network-number   *xxxxxxxx* Any hexadecimal number between
                                    00000001 and FFFFFFFE

Once the loopback interface is configured, you must associate the loopback interface with your asynchronous interface. Typically, you will be associated with the group-async interface:

```
Router (config-if)#ipx ppp-client loopback loopback-number
```

loopback-number   *x*   This is the loopback number used to
                                 define your IPX address

Figure 3-39 shows the association of an asynchronous interface to the loopback interface for use with IPX over PPP.

Figure 3-39

The association of a loopback interface with a group-async interface to provide IPX over PPP

```
Router(config)#interface group-async 1
Router(config-if)#ipx ppp-client loopback 1
```

Network Layer Configuration of NetBEUI *NetBIOS Extended User Interface* (NetBEUI) is a network protocol designed for PCs on a single LAN environment, but NetBEUI lacks the capability to carry a network address, thus making NetBEUI non-routable. However, NetBEUI can be bridged. Remember that routing occurs at the network layer of the OSI model, while bridging occurs at the data link layer of the OSI model.

To enable remote clients using NetBEUI to connect through a Cisco Access server router, you must configure the asynchronous interface to accept NetBEUI services, so use the following command:

```
Router (config-if)#netbios nbf
```

To view NetBEUI connection information, use the following command:

```
Router#show nbf sessions
```

3.6 Dial on Demand Routing (DDR)

Dial on Demand Routing (DDR) is a very useful feature when using ISDN as your connectivity solution. Unlike dedicated connections that typically charge a flat rate per month, circuit switched connections charges can be based upon a number of different attributes including:

- Time connected
- Long distance charges
- Tariffs

Although some aspects of these charges may be different depending upon the proximity of the two sites, your state's tariff's, and other various attributes, one thing is for certain: The less time you stay connected, the less expensive your ISDN charges. The exception to this rule is Centrex service, which is a fixed cost, flat rate distance sensitive ISDN service. It enables you to leave your connection up 24 hours a day without worrying about your per month connections charges.

The basic concept of DDR is to enable an Access Router to set up a connection with a remote site when "interesting traffic" is destined for that remote network. The type of service that we need to access characterizes "interesting traffic." For example, if we need to retrieve mail from our mail server, we can classify SMTP packets as "interesting traffic" and have the ISDN line call the central site when SMTP packets are needed to go to the remote site. We can also classify certain traffic as "uninteresting" and not allow it to bring up a connection. An example of "uninteresting traffic" would be when a Windows 95/98/NT/2000 computer boots up, it tries to contact the WINS server to tell the WINS server its IP address. We don't want to bring up the ISDN line every time we reboot a computer.

However, some services require that we see their periodic updates so that we can establish communication with them. For example, NetWare servers broadcast a SAP every 60 seconds to indicate its availability, as shown in Figure 3-40.

Figure 3-40

NetWare SAP bringing up ISDN line

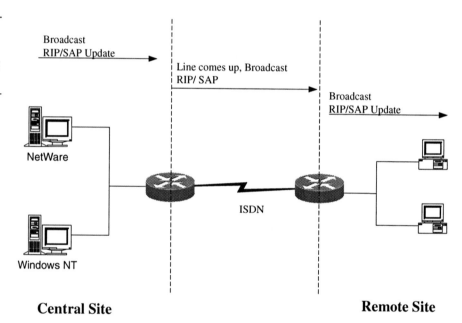

However, we don't want our ISDN line to come online every 60 seconds so that we can hear about its availability. This is where we can use some of the DDR features to overcome this limitation and help minimize WAN costs, as seen in Figure 3-41.

Figure 3-41

Example of DDR
feature
minimizing cost

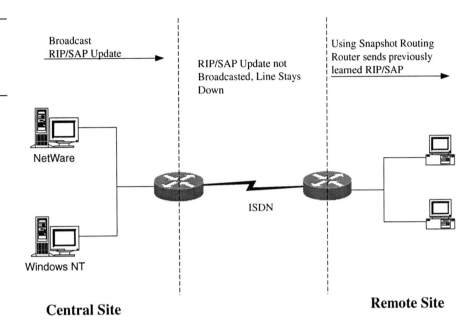

Broadcast
RIP/SAP Update

RIP/SAP Update not
Broadcasted, Line Stays
Down

Using Snapshot Routing
Router sends previously
learned RIP/SAP

NetWare

Windows NT

ISDN

Central Site

Remote Site

Now that we have a basic understanding of *Dial on Demand Routing* (DDR), the next section will focus on the configuration of Dial on Demand Routing in a Cisco environment

3.6.1 Configuring DDR using ISDN

Cisco has provided us with many options to configure DDR. We can use DDR for basic connectivity or we can use it to back up our WAN connection. In this section we will concentrate on using DDR for basic connectivity.

When configuring DDR, three main components must be determined:

Table 3-13

DDR Commands
and Their
Function

Topic	Function
dialer-list	What is "interesting traffic"
dialer-group	Which interface should we use
dialer-map	Where is the traffic going

3.6.1.1 Dialer-list

As previously mentioned, the **dialer-list** command is used to specify what traffic should bring the line up. This is important because of the need to keep uninteresting traffic from bringing the line up, but still allow the line to come up when we need it to as shown in Figure 3-42.

Figure 3-42

Examples of interesting and uninteresting traffic on a DDR link

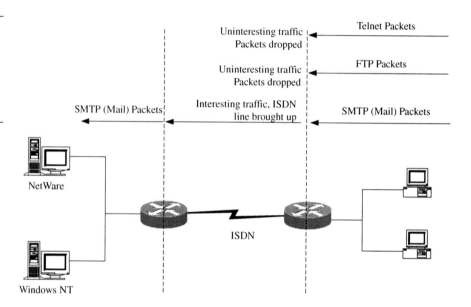

Central Site   **Remote Site**

When defining a dialer-list we can use the simple form and allow/deny an entire protocol; or we can use access lists for a more refined control over what traffic we want to block or pass.

To specify which protocols are interesting and/or uninteresting use the following command:

```
Router (config)#dialer-list list-number protocol protocol-type
permission
```

list-number	**1-10**	Specify which dialer-group this list applies to
protocol-type	**appletalk**	Appletalk
	decnet	DECnet
	ip	IP
	ipx	Novell IPX
	vines	Banyan Vines
	xns	XNS
permission	**deny**	Deny specified protocol (simple form)
	list	Add access list to dialer list
	permit	Permit specified protocol (simple form)

Note:

The protocol type listed previously is only a partial list.

Access Control Lists enable an administrator to be more selective about which protocols are allowed to bring the line up. Before you can start using access lists to specify which protocols can pass or will be blocked, you must understand the environment you are working in. Otherwise, you could inadvertently block protocols that are required for the operation of the remote office.

You can specify protocol selection when using access lists to define interesting traffic with the following command:

```
Router (config)#access-list list-number permission protocol-option
```

list-number	**1-99**	IP standard access list
	100-199	IP extended access list
	200-299	Protocol type-code access list
	300-399	DECnet access list
	600-699	Appletalk access list
	700-799	48-bit MAC address access list
	800-899	IPX standard access list
	900-999	IPX extended access list
	1000-1099	IPX SAP access list

	1100-1199	Extended 48-bit MAC address access list
	1200-1299	IPX summary address access list
permission	deny	Reject packets
	list	Allow packets
protocol-option		Attribute that is specific to the protocol selected in the access-list.

Note:

You can only use one access-list to define interesting traffic.

You need to be careful about what is defined as interesting traffic and what types of traffic are allowed to flow. Once the line comes up, any traffic is enabled to flow across the line. This can potentially cause problems. Take the situation in which we only allow SMTP (email) traffic to bring our line up. It is possible for SMTP traffic to legitimately bring the line up, and once up, a host could establish a telnet session with an outside host. Because the timeout timers only reset when they see interesting traffic, the expiration of a timer will drop the line even though an active Telnet session is there. In this scenario, it is important that we block potentially problematic protocols using Access Control Lists instead of allowing the definition of interesting traffic to keep from establishing a connection. Although this particular situation is not likely to occur, it does represent the types of problems that might occur using DDR.

For a complete list of options on access lists see the following URL: http://www.cisco.com/univercd/cc/td/doc/product/software/ios120/12 cgcr/secur_c/scprt3/scacls.htm

3.6.1.2 Dialer-group

The **dialer-group** command is used to associate a dialer-list to an interface, as shown in Figure 3-43.

Because we are associating a command that is executed at the global configuration mode (dialer-list) with an interface, we need to execute this command on the interface we want associated with this traffic. The format of the dialer-group command is:

```
Router (config-if)#dialer-group group-number
```

| *group-number* | 1-10 | Dialer-group number assigned in dialer-list statement |

Figure 3-43

Dialer-Group
directing which
interface an
interesting packet
should use

Cisco Router

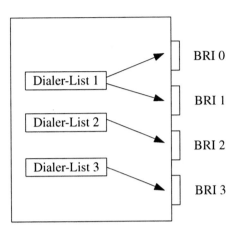

BRI 0

Dialer-List 1

BRI 1

Dialer-List 2

BRI 2

Dialer-List 3

BRI 3

3.6.1.3 Dialer-map

At this point we have defined "interesting traffic" and the interface responsible for handling those packets. We now need to specify a destination for those packets. Figure 3.44 shows us how the dialer-map command can make decisions on what number to call based upon the destination IP address.

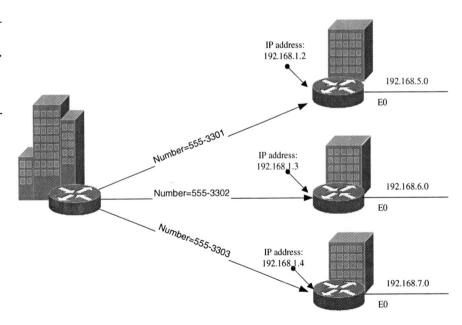

To assign a phone number to a next-hop address use the following command:

```
Router (config-if)#dialer map protocol next-hop-address name host
broadcast dial-string
```

protocol	ip	IP
	bridge	Bridging
	llc2	LLC2
	netbios	NetBIOS
next-hop-address	a.b.c.d	Protocol specific address
host	WORD	Name of the remote system
dial-string	xxxxxxx	The phone number to dial to reach this IP address

---

Note:

Any references to Legacy DDR are in reference to the Dialer-Map statements.

A **dialer map** command enables us to manually map a layer 2 address to a network address. Think of the **dialer map** command as a manual form of *Address Resolution Protocol* (ARP).

3.6.1.4 DDR Summary

We have seen the three main components of configuring DDR and should have an understanding of how they operate. The flow chart in Figure 3-45 gives us an overview of how these commands come together to establish a link with a remote site.

Even though the router has set the call up for us, it does not mean that it knows how to route packets.

3.7 Advanced DDR

In the last section, we saw that only three commands are needed to set up a DDR environment: dialer-list, dialer-group, and dialer map. However many more attributes are used in support of DDR environments, such as:

- Authentication
- Multilink capabilities

Figure 3-45

Flowchart of DDR
establishing a
connection

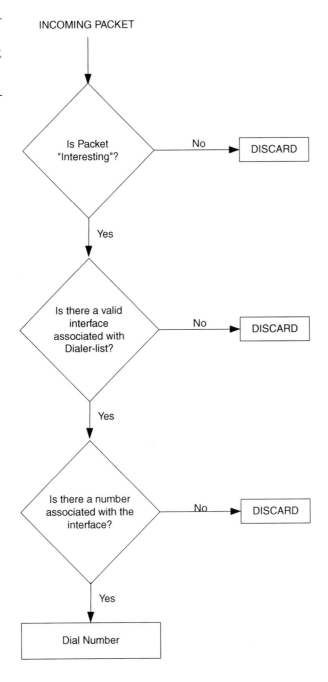

- Rate adaptation
- Network protocols
- Various timers

When multiple sites are needed to be accessed from the same site, we can use multiple dialer map, dialer-list, and dialer-group statements to support multiple locations as shown in Figure 3-46a.

Figure 3-46a

Central Site connecting to multiple remote sites

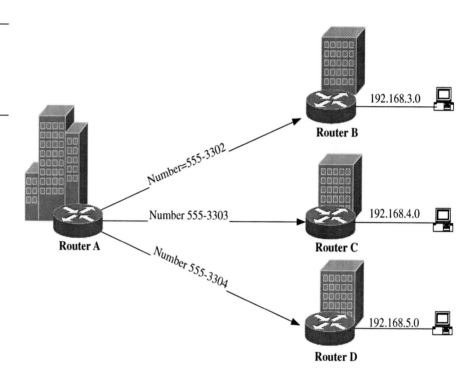

To support a scenario as given in Figure 3-46a, we can use the following configuration on the central office router.

Figure 3-46b

Configuration on the central office router

```
hostname RouterA
!
username RouterB password cisco
username RouterC password cisco
username RouterD password cisco
isdn switch-type basic-dms100
!
interface Ethernet0
ip address 192.168.2.0 255.255.255.0
!
interface BRI0
description Central Office ISDN BRI interface
ip address 192.168.1.1 255.255.255.0
encapsulation ppp
ppp authentication chap
dialer map ip 192.168.1.2 name RouterB 5553302
dialer map ip 192.168.1.3 name RouterC 5553303
dialer map ip 192.168.1.4 name RouterD 5553304
dialer-group 1
dialer fast-idle 40
dialer idle-timeout 180
!
router igrp 10
redistribute static
network 192.168.2.0
no auto-summary
!
ip route 192.168.3.0 255.255.255.0 192.168.1.2
ip route 192.168.4.0 255.255.255.0 192.168.1.3
ip route 192.168.5.0 255.255.255.0 192.168.1.4
!
dialer-list 1 protocol ip permit
```

Although we can support multiple sites from this configuration file, all of the remote sites must use the following attributes:

- PPP encapsulation
- CHAP authentication
- Fast-idle timeout of 40 seconds
- Idle-timeout of 180 seconds
- WAN IP network 192.168.1.0/24

What happens if we have multiple sites to connect to that are not in our complete control and aren't identical? For example, we may have one remote site that requires both IP and IPX while another remote site should only have IP. Without any special features we would have to purchase a router with multiple BRI interfaces and a corresponding number of ISDN BRI lines to support such a configuration.

We need a mechanism that doesn't lock the physical interface into a set configuration, but enables it to assume a specific configuration as needed. We will look at those mechanisms throughout this chapter.

3.7.1 Dialer Interfaces

Dialer interfaces are the crux for creating complicated DDR environments. Dialer interfaces enable us to specify various sets of configurations that can be used based upon the destination of an outgoing call or the starting point of an incoming call. The dialer interface is not a physical interface within the Cisco Router, but a logical interface that can be applied to any dial-out interface.

When establishing a call to a remote site, the physical interface inherits the properties of the dialer interface that we have defined for that remote site as seen in Figure 3-47.

One of the attributes that is conspicuously missing from Figure 3-47 are commands that are generally associated with the data-link layer, such as encapsulation, authentication, and so on. Depending upon the configuration, you use both the encapsulation and authentication command under the dialer interface or both the dialer interface and the physical interface. Both rotary groups and dialer profiles handle this aspect differently and we will cover it in the appropriate section.

The dialer interface, just like the loopback interface and the group-async, are all virtual interfaces that are dynamically created when we specify them. These virtual interfaces can be created using the following command:

```
Router (config)#interface dialer group-number
```

group-number   **0-255**   Specify the number of the logical dialer interface

Once created we have access to all of the configuration attributes available to any other dial interface.

Figure 3-47

Example of a
Dialer Interface
using an ISDN
BRI interface

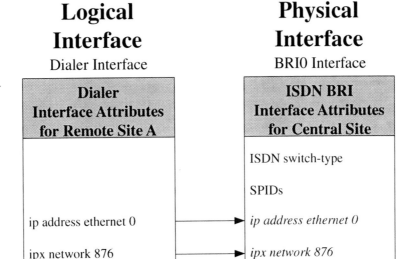

Logical Interface

Dialer Interface

Dialer Interface Attributes for Remote Site A
ip address ethernet 0
ipx network 876
dialer idle-timeout 360
no cdp enable

Physical Interface

BRI0 Interface

ISDN BRI Interface Attributes for Central Site
ISDN switch-type
SPIDs
ip address ethernet 0
ipx network 876
dialer idle-timeout 360
no cdp enable

Dialer interfaces are used in two distinct methods to provide different levels of sophistication: rotary groups and dialer profiles. Both rotary groups and dialer profiles take advantage of dialer interfaces, but the rationale behind each is different.

3.7.2 Rotary Groups

A rotary group is a single dialer interface that can be applied to multiple physical interfaces. This enables us to centrally define the configuration of multiple physical interfaces for incoming and outgoing connections.

Rotary groups are typically used on the hub of a "hub and spoke" environment, as shown in Figure 3-48. Typically the hub is considered a router that accepts calls and/or places calls to more than one other router, while a spoke is a router that accepts calls and/or places calls to only one router.

Figure 3-48

Example of the
logical layout of a
hub and spoke
environment

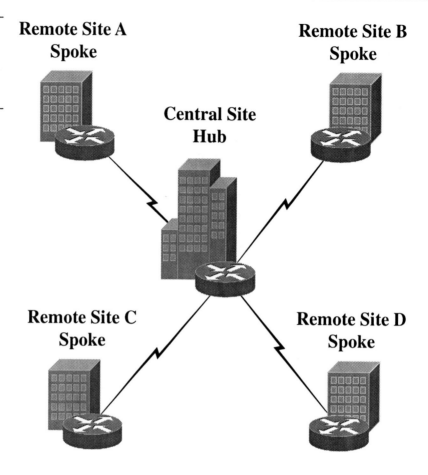

In a "hub and spoke" environment, spokes only dial into the hub. If they need to access resources within another spoke, they must do it through the hub.

Two distinct components to Rotary Groups exist:

■ Physical interface
■ Dialer interface

In addition to these two components, we will look at how a Telco feature called Hunt Groups helps alleviate some of the problems associated with rotary groups.

3.7.2.1 Physical Interface

Up until now all of the configurations commands used in support of a DDR environment have been on the physical interface. However, when using rotary groups, our physical interface will only be configured with the physical characteristics required to connect it to the network (such as ISDN switch type, SPIDs, and so on). All of the data-link layer and network layer attributes will be applied by a dialer interface. In addition, our physical interface can only be associated to one dialer interface. Although this limits our ability to have multiple physical interfaces performing different duties, it does provide a single point of configuration for multiple physical interfaces. This can eliminate human errors when entering the same configuration multiple times on different interfaces.

When using rotary groups we can specify which dialer interface a physical interface should inherit its data-link layer and network layer configuration as shown in Figure 3-49.

In order to associate a physical interface with a rotary group we must first be in interface configuration mode of the interface we wish to associate with the rotary group. Once we have selected the interface to modify, we can use the following command to associate the physical interface with a logical dialer interface:

```
Router (config-if)#dialer rotary-group group-number
```

group-number   **0-255**   The number of the logical dialer interface

If during the assignment of the rotary group to a physical interface, the dialer interface does not exist, it is dynamically created. In addition, any dialer map statements, encapsulation, and authentication commands that were on the physical interface are removed from the physical interface configuration. This is done because we now have a separation of the physical configuration with the data-link layer and network layer configuration. For example, in Figure 3-50, we can see that BRI0 is being configured as a member of the rotary-group 10.

Next we will attempt to configure the encapsulation on the physical interface, but the Cisco Router does not let us perform this task because the physical interface is now a member of a rotary group and those commands are reserved for the dialer interface.

We will now look at the dialer interface and how to use it in relationship to rotary groups.

Figure 3-49

Multiple Dialer
Interfaces used to
configure
multiple physical
interfaces

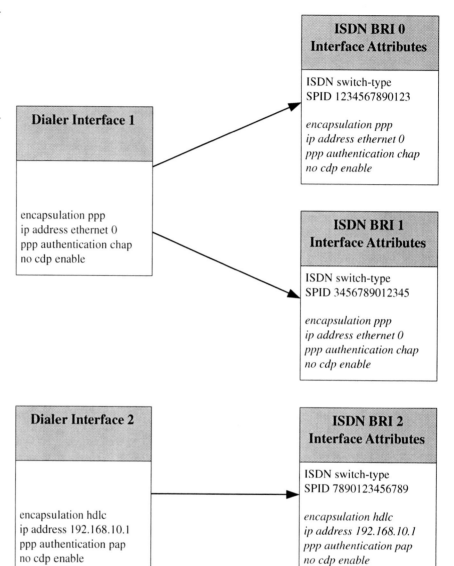

Figure 3-50

Attempt to
configure data-
link layer
attributes on a
physical interface
associated to a
rotary group

```
Router#config t
Enter configuration commands, one per line.   End with CNTL/Z.
Router(config)#interface bri0
Router(config-if)#dialer rotary-group 10
Router(config-if)#encapsulation ppp
percent Cannot change encapsulation of hunt group member
```

3.7.2.2 Dialer interface

In the last section we saw how to associate a physical interface to a rotary group using the **dialer rotary-group** command. When this command is used, it associates the physical interface to a dialer interface whose number is determined by the dialer rotary-group command. For example, in Example 3-51, we can see that interface BRI0 is now associated to dialer interface 10.

The command set available to a dialer interface is almost identical to the command set available to any dial interface. However, one of the commands missing from the dialer interface are those that start with ISDN (such as ISDN switch-type, ISDN spid1, and so on). Remember that because we have separated the physical configuration from the logical configuration, we do not need any of the commands used to configure the physical aspects of our BRI interface.

In order to get a dialer interface to dial, the **dialer in-band** command must be used on the dialer interface. This enables DDR and V.25bis dialing on dialer and async interfaces. V.25bis is an ITU-T standard for in-band signaling to bit synchronous devices. The format of the command to enable DDR dialing on a dialer interface is:

```
Router (config-if)#dialer in-band
```

Let's now look at how we can use rotary groups in a DDR environment. Figure 3-51 is an example of a hub and spoke DDR environment.

Figure 3-52, 3-53, and 3-54 are configuration files for Router A (Hub), Router B (spoke), and Router C (spoke).

Figure 3-51

Example of a hub
and spoke DDR
configuration
using rotary
groups

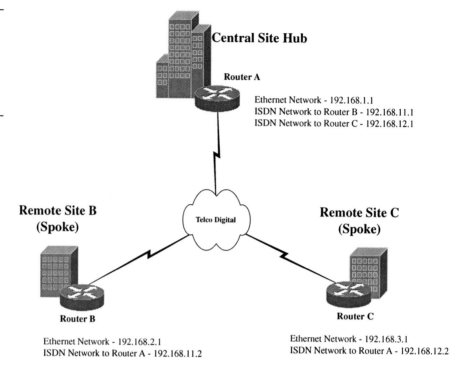

Central Site Hub

Router A

Ethernet Network - 192.168.1.1
ISDN Network to Router B - 192.168.11.1
ISDN Network to Router C - 192.168.12.1

Remote Site B
(Spoke)

Telco Digital

Remote Site C
(Spoke)

Router B

Ethernet Network - 192.168.2.1
ISDN Network to Router A - 192.168.11.2

Router C

Ethernet Network - 192.168.3.1
ISDN Network to Router A - 192.168.12.2

In Figure 3-53, the command **dialer rotary-group 1** indicates that the
BRI1/0 and BRI1/1 should use the attributes from interface dialer 1 for
their configuration.

3.7.2.3 Hunt Group

One of the problems with the configurations in Figures 3-52–3-54 is that
both remote sites (Routers B-C) are calling the same number. In this situation, both routers could potentially be trying to dial the BRI1/0 on the
central site and not attempting to use BRI1/1 interface. The way to overcome this is not through any special IOS configuration commands, but by
contacting your Telco and requesting a hunt group for the two ISDN BRIs.

Figure 3-52

Router A
configuration file
for Figure 3-51

```
Router A (DDR Hub)
!
hostname RouterA
!
interface ethernet 0/0
 ip address 192.168.1.1 255.255.255.0
!
interface BRI1/0
 dialer rotary-group 1
 isdn switch-type basic-dms100
 isdn spid1 3840200001 3840200
 isdn spid2 3840300001 3840300
!
interface BRI1/1
 dialer rotary-group 1
 isdn switch-type basic-dms100
 isdn spid1 3840400001 3840400
 isdn spid2 3840500002 3840500
!
interface dialer 1
 ip address 192.168.11.1 255.255.255.0
 ip address 192.168.12.1 255.255.255.0 secondary
 encapsulation ppp
 dialer in-band
 description this dialer map goes to Router B
 dialer map ip 192.168.11.2 3840600
 description this dialer map goes to Router C
 dialer map ip 192.168.12.2 3840800
 dialer-group 1
!
ip route 192.168.2.0 255.255.255.0 192.168.11.2
ip route 192.168.3.0 255.255.255.0 192.168.12.2
!
dialer-list 1 protocol ip permit
!
router eigrp 10
 network 192.168.1.0
 network 192.168.11.0
 network 192.168.12.0
 redistribute static
!
end
```

A hunt group is a cluster of telephone lines that are programmed by the telco to try the second line if the first line is busy, third line if the first and second line are busy, and so on. Figure 3-55 shows an example of the logic behind a hunt group.

In Figure 3-55, we can see an incoming call for 555-3301, but 555-3301 is busy; so the Telco dynamically routes the call to a free line (555-3303) within the hunt group.

Figure 3-53

Router B standard legacy DDR configuration file for Figure 3-51

```
Router B (DDR Spoke)
!
hostname RouterB
!
interface ethernet 0
ip address 192.168.2.1 255.255.255.0
!
interface BRI0
isdn switch-type basic-dms100
isdn spid1 3840600001 3840600
isdn spid2 3840700001 3840700
ip address 192.168.11.2 255.255.255.0
encapsulation ppp
description this dialer map goes to Router A
dialer map ip 192.168.11.1 3840200
dialer-group 1
!
ip route 0.0.0.0 0.0.0.0 192.168.11.1
dialer-list 1 protocol ip permit
!
end
!
```

Figure 3-54

Router C standard Legacy DDR configuration for Figure 3-51

```
Router C (DDR Spoke)
!
hostname RouterC
!
interface ethernet 0
ip address 192.168.3.1 255.255.255.0
!
interface BRI0
isdn switch-type basic-dms100
isdn spid1 3840800001 3840800
isdn spid2 3840900001 3840900
ip address 192.168.12.2 255.255.255.0
encapsulation ppp
description this dialer map goes to Router A
dialer map ip 192.168.12.1 3840200
dialer-group 1
no shutdown
!
ip route 0.0.0.0 0.0.0.0 192.168.12.1
dialer-list 1 protocol ip permit
!
end
!
```

Figure 3-55

Example of a
hunt group in
operation

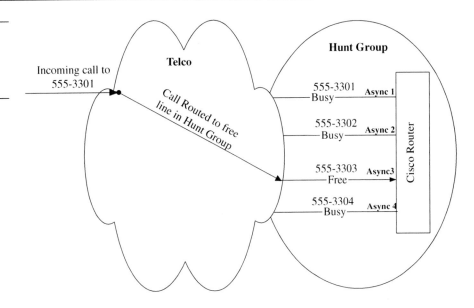

A hunt group can be set up for any number of lines, and is a requirement for the central site to support DDR rotary-group connections. When setting up a hunt group, you should thoroughly test the hunt group to make sure that it works correctly before deployment, because it is frequently not configured correctly the first time.

As with previous DDR configurations, we shouldn't forget that we still have to define "interesting traffic" with our **dialer-list** and then apply them to our dialer interfaces with the **dialer-group** command.

In this section, we looked at using dialer interfaces to centralize the configuration of multiple physical interfaces. In the next section, we will see how to allow any physical interface to use any dialer interface using dialer profiles.

3.7.3 Dialer Profiles

When using rotary groups, we can only associate a physical interface to a single dialer interface. This paradigm is very limiting when dealing with large heterogeneous environments. For example, let's look at an example in which we have 100 remote sites and 24 interfaces. In order to maximize the number of physical interfaces that could be available to the remote sites, we would want to make the configuration for each remote site identical (same encapsulation, authentication, timers, and so on), thus allowing us to have one rotary group for all of our physical interfaces.

What would happen if we only wanted to route IP with half of our sites and only wanted to route IPX with the other half of our remote sites? In this case, we would have two rotary-groups (that is, dialer interfaces) in which we would have to divide the physical interfaces into two distinct groups; those that supported dialer interface 1 and those that supported dialer interface 2, as seen in Figure 3-56.

In Figure 3-56, we can see that Remote Site A and Remote Site B can only use the physical interface BRI0/0; while Remote Site C and Remote D can only use the physical interface BRI0/1.

Figure 3-56

Division of physical interfaces based upon the need for different characteristics using rotary groups

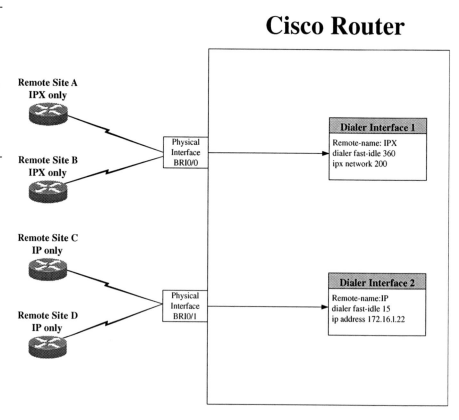

This division of physical interfaces reduces the effectiveness of our current resources. For example, if the physical interface that supported dialer interface 2 were being used by Remote site C then Remote Site D could not connect because the interface is being used by Remote Site C. Meanwhile, the physical interfaces supporting dialer interface 1 (rotary-group 1) could be idle.

In order to overcome this problem, we need to assign a dialer interface on a per call basis. This would enable us to have multiple dialer interfaces (multiple configurations) that all of our physical interfaces could use, instead of allocating physical interfaces to support a particular configuration through rotary groups. Dialer profiles give us the ability to dynamically assign any dialer interfaces to any physical interface based upon the call requirements, as seen in Figure 3-57.

Figure 3-57

Example of physical interfaces being dynamically assigned characteristics based upon information about the incoming connection

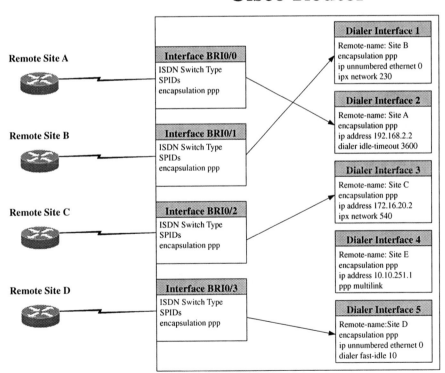

In Figure 3-57, we can see that the incoming connection to BRI0/0 from Remote Site A is dynamically assigned to dialer interface 2. From this perspective, it is obvious that dialer profiles enable us to configure a dialer interface for each specific location that we want to support.

Four components to Dialer Profiles exist

- Physical interface
- Dialer interface
- Dialer pool
- Dialer map-class (optional)

Figure 3-58 shows us the relationship between the physical interfaces, the dialer pool, and the dialer interface.

As we can see from Figure 3-58, the dialer pool concept is the way to associate a physical interface (ISDN or async interface) with a logical interface (dialer interface). We will now look at how to configure the interfaces using dialer profiles.

Figure 3-58

Relationship between physical interface, dialer pool, and dialer interface

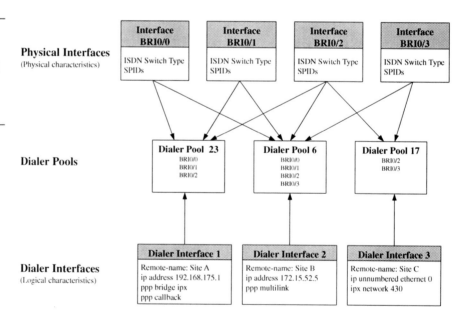

3.7.4 Physical Interfaces

When using rotary groups in the previous section, we left the data-link layer configuration to the dialer interface. This was possible because a physical interface could belong to only one dialer interface. However, the ability to dynamically assign a dialer interface configuration to a physical interface creates a new set of problems.

Because the binding of the dialer interface to a physical interface only occurs after we've identified the incoming call, we must define the encapsulation method on the physical interface. If we failed to specify an encapsulation type on the physical interface, we would never be able to communicate with the remote site to determine who they are and subsequently which dialer interface to bind to the physical interface. Therefore, when using dialer profiles, we must configure the encapsulation method and authentication method on both the dialer interface and the physical interface. Additionally, the parameters revolving around encapsulation must match between the dialer interface and the physical interface. If they do not match your connection, attempts will fail.

Note:

Remember that for ISDN connections, you can use either PPP or HDLC for your encapsulation protocol. Therefore, if you need to support multiple encapsulation types with Dialer Profiles, you will need to split the interfaces into two pools: those that support ppp encapsulations and those that support HDLC encapsulation.

To configure a physical interface using dialer profiles we can use the following task list:

- Specify encapsulation method
- Specify dialer pools to participate

We have already seen in the previous chapters how to specify encapsulation with **ppp encapsulation** and authentication with **ppp authentication**, so we will focus on the association of a physical interface with a dialer pool.

In order to bind a physical interface with a dialer pool, we must use the **dialer pool-member** command on the physical interface. The format of the command is seen in the following:

```
Router (config-if)#dialer pool-member group-number priority num-of-
channels
```

group-number	**1-255**	Specify the number of the dialer pool
priority	**1-255**	Specify the priority of the physical interface
num-of-channels	**min-link 1-255**	Min number of B channels reserved for dialer pool
	max-link 1-255	Max number of B channels to be used for dialer pool

The **priority** option is only used when dialing out. Its purpose is to determine which interface should be used first within a dialer pool. The lower the number, the higher the priority.

The **min-link** option defines the minimum number of ISDN B-channels reserved for a dialer pool; while the **max-link** option sets the maximum number of ISDN B-channels reserved for the dialer pool.

3.7.4.1 Dialer Interface

When using dialer profiles, we typically configure a dialer interface on a per site basis. This enables us to customize each dialer interface to the characteristics required by a site.

Each dialer interface contains the configuration information required to support a specific configuration. To configure a dialer interface using dialer profiles, we can use the following task list:

- Specify encapsulation method and authentication protocol
- Specify network protocols
- Specify remote router name
- Specify the dialing pool to use
- Specify remote destination call string (optional)

We have already seen how to specify the encapsulation of a dialer interface using either the **encapsulation ppp** or **encapsulation hdlc** command as well as how to specify the IP address or IPX network numbers associated with the network protocols. We will now focus only on the attributes we haven't covered.

When a remote site dials into the central site, the central site router must determine which remote site is dialing in and what dialer interface to bind to the physical interface. Figure 3-59 shows the process in which a physical interface is bound to a dialer interface.

Figure 3-59

Dynamic binding of a dialer interface to a physical interface

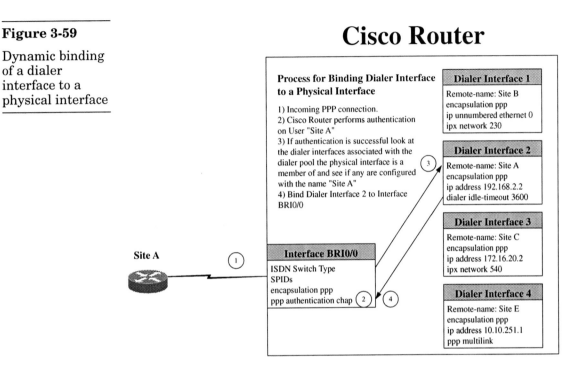

Cisco Router

When using dialer profiles, a remote site dials in and provides a username. This username is used for more than authentication. Assuming that the username and password combination supplied by the remote sites passes, the Cisco Router looks for a dialer interface within the dialer pool in which the dialer profile has the name given by the remote site. The command used for this task is very simple and must be executed within the dialer interface configuration mode.

```
Router (config-if)#dialer remote-name name
```

name WORD Use the name of the remote router

When using dialer profiles, a dialer interface can only belong to a single dialer pool; although multiple physical interfaces can belong to the same dialer pool. To associate a dialer interface with a dialer pool, we use the following the same command:

```
Router (config-if)#dialer pool pool-number
```

pool-number   **0-255**   Specify the number of the dialer pool to participate in.

When using rotary groups, we used the dialer map statement to indicate the phone number of the next hop. However, when using dialer profiles, we use the **dial string** command to specify the remote destination to call. Because we can be more granular with our dialer interfaces (that is, build a dialer interface on a per destination basis) we don't need to map the IP address to a phone number; we can just specify the destination phone number.

```
Router (config-if)#dialer string string class map-class-name
```

string   **WORD**   The number used to dial the remote site.

map-class-name **WORD**   Name used for defining more specific attributes. See section on map-class.

When using dialer profiles, don't forget that we still need to specify interesting traffic as well as associate it to the dialer interface.

3.8 Chapter Summary

In this chapter, we learned how to configure a Cisco Access Server to handle incoming dialup connections. The reason that we have covered this material in such detail is that Remote Access VPNs require extensive knowledge of how dialup works. Understanding these key components will enable you to more quickly grasp the concepts that will be covered in the Case Study section, specifically PPTP and L2TP. In the next chapter, we will focus on the fundamentals of encryption, authentication, and AAA protocols. An understanding of these aspects is required so that you can more easily troubleshoot problems that occur, as well as learn how protocol selection can affect the performance of your router.

CHAPTER 4

VPN Security Primer

In the last two chapters, we have shown how to configure the various dial-up technologies (dial-up client and dial-up server) required for remote access *Virtual Private Networks* (VPNs). In this chapter, we will discuss the elements required to make data secure and the more common types of attacks that we are trying to prevent. In addition, we will cover the technologies used to keep data secure as it traverses the Internet.

4.1 Objectives to be Covered in This Chapter

- Security concerns (authentication, confidentiality, and data integrity)
- Security threats (spoofing, man-in-the-middle, and sniffing)
- Security solutions (authentication and encryption)

The bulk of this chapter focuses on security solutions. To accurately communicate the ideas presented in the security solutions section, we need to review the items that comprise a secure solution and the types of attacks that we are protecting ourselves from.

The in-depth analysis of each protocol provides a better understanding of the strengths and weaknesses of the different VPN protocols. This will allow you to better select the appropriate VPN protocols for your solution.

4.2 Security Concerns

A network's purpose is to enable computers to communicate. The fundamental truth of every network is that no network is completely secure. However, in most cases, the benefit of keeping a system on the network is higher than the cost of not having the system on the network.

Determining how much security a solution requires can be a difficult task. The Internet community uses the following standard to determine whether a system is secure enough:

- Is the cost of breaking into the system more expensive than the information is worth?

Various aspects with regard to security should be addressed. Once a transaction has been authenticated, authorized, and accounted, we need to make sure that the data received is sent by the intended source, kept confidential, and arrives unaltered. These three elements, which can be found in many VPN protocols, can be summarized as the following:

- Authentication
- Confidentiality
- Data integrity

4.2.1 Authentication

Authentication is a relatively straightforward concept to understand. It is the process of determining with whom you are communicating. It is not just the identification of an individual, but the verification of that identification through some other independent means. For example, when you go to the bank and fill out a withdrawal slip, you will write down your identity. This only indicates who you are; it does not verify your identity. When you present that withdrawal slip to the bank teller, he or she will ask for verification of your identity (for example, driver's license, passport, and so on). The process of the bank teller looking at your driver's license picture and then looking at you is the authentication process. Once your identity has been authenticated you can proceed, assuming you have authorization of course!

When data is sent through the Internet, we want to make sure that the person we want to communicate with sends it. We need a method of verifying who sent us the data. Take for instance a scenario in which our bank calls us and asks questions about a bank account. Has this transaction been authenticated? No. Unless we have independently verified who that individual is at the other end, we do not know with whom we are talking. It is not enough for individuals to tell us who they are; we need to identify them some other way, like recognizing their voice. In cases where you cannot independently verify the calling entity, it is best to call the bank back using their published telephone number. By using the bank's published number, we have independently verified that we are talking to the right entity.

Note:
One popular technique by scam-artists is to call an individual, claiming to be your credit card company just to verify your credit card number and expiration date. If you do not independently verify a person's identity, you could easily be the victim of credit card fraud.

4.2.2 Confidentiality

Confidentiality is the process of making sure that no one else can read your data even if it is intercepted. Because our data is traversing the public Internet, we must assume that an attacker can easily intercept the data stream. By using ciphertext (a message that has been encrypted), we can make it more difficult for an attacker to gain access to a message. It is important to note that three components are used to generate ciphertext, as seen in Figure 4-1.

Although the combination of a cryptography algorithm and a key determines the type of encryption that is used, they can still be regarded as individual mechanisms that generate ciphertext. We will explore the many different methods that cryptographic techniques can be used for encryption later in this chapter.

Figure 4-1

Components used
in encryption

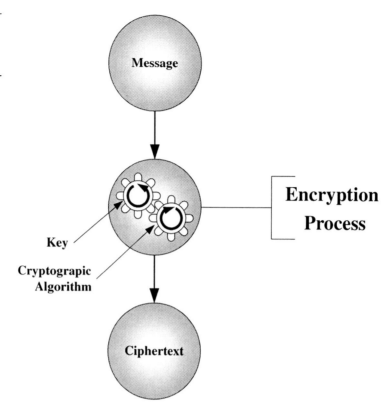

4.2.3 Data Integrity

Data integrity is used to ensure that no third party has altered the data.
At first, the distinction between data integrity and confidentiality might
seem a little blurred. However, confidentiality can be thought of as not
allowing anyone to "see" your data, whereas data integrity means that you
know when someone has "modified" your data. This is because an attacker
does not necessarily need to view the data in order to modify it.

Now that we understand the three basic components of providing a
secure solution, we will take a brief look at the most common types of
security attacks.

4.3 Security Threats

In order to maintain some modicum of security in any networked environment, the methods of communication must be scrutinized. To better understand where the potential threats exist, we will discuss some of the more conventional types of security threats that network engineers might have to deal with when evaluating their environment for possible security holes.

4.3.1 Spoofing

The most basic nature of IP is to provide devices with the ability to communicate even though many different networks separate them. This is accomplished through the use of a source IP address and a destination IP address. The destination IP address indicates where the packet is headed, whereas the source IP address indicates where the packet came from, as seen in Figure 4-2.

This is important from the perspective of a receiving device because the receiving device will use the source IP address to determine the destination IP address for all communication with that particular device. Spoofing takes advantage of the fact that an attacker can insert someone else's IP address into a packet and pretend to be someone else.

Figure 4-2

Basics of IP addressing

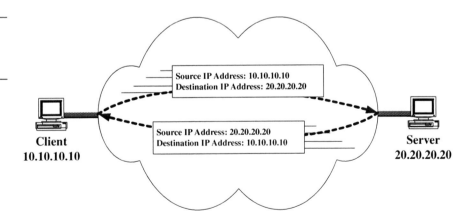

Source IP Address: 10.10.10.10
Destination IP Address: 20.20.20.20

Source IP Address: 20.20.20.20
Destination IP Address: 10.10.10.10

Client
10.10.10.10

Server
20.20.20.20

Once an attacker has identified a pair of computers that are communicating, he or she can attempt to establish a connection with the server in such a way that the server believes it is communicating with the client, but it is really conversing with the attacker's computer, as seen in Figure 4-3.

Figure 4-3

Spoofing an IP address

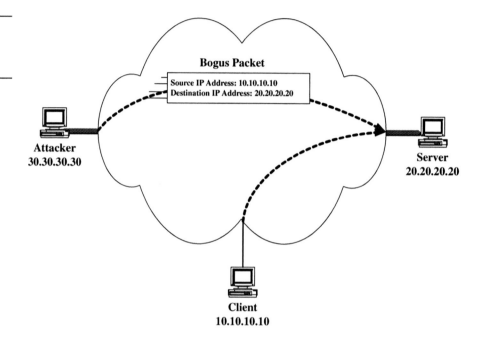

This type of attack is generally limited to the insertion of data or commands into an existing stream of data passed between two hosts. This insertion of data can have two effects between two hosts. First, the attacker could destroy the integrity of a data stream between two hosts. If the attacker were clever enough, he or she could actually insert his or her own data into the data stream. Secondly, if the attacker is not worried about receiving any response from the host, they could send messages telling the host to perform some other task such as emailing a sensitive file to the attacker.

In this type of scenario, the attacker is concerned about two problems. The first is preventing the client from responding to any packets from the server. A moderately sophisticated attacker can resolve this problem quite easily by overflowing the client's buffer with a large number of packets preventing the client from responding to any messages from the server.

In order for the attacker (who is impersonating the client) to complete the sessions setup with Server B, the server is expecting the client to acknowledge its sequence number in order to proceed. In certain instances, guessing the sequence numbers is not difficult, which would allow the attacker to send the server transactions.

4.3.2 Session Hijacking

Session hijacking takes spoofing one step further. Instead of just inserting packets into a data stream, session hijacking allows the attacker to assume the identity of a currently logged in user. Session hijacking can be accomplished by using a combination of spoofing and denial of service or by modifying routing tables so that an attacker can redirect packets.

When an attacker attempts to hijack a session using spoofing and denial of service, he or she must first take control of a network device such as a router, firewall, or computer on that network. This allows the attacker to monitor the conversations for the sequence numbers being used by two communicating computers. Once the attacker has obtained the sequence numbers, the attacker can flood traffic to the client, while simultaneously communicating with the server, as seen in Figure 4-4.

Note:

You should note that the flooding of packets to the client does not have to be performed by the same device hijacking the session. However, the attacker might have to compromise two devices. This is because the attacker might not be able to generate a data stream large enough through a wide area network (WAN) to keep the client busy enough to drop packets from the server.

Figure 4-4

Session hijacking

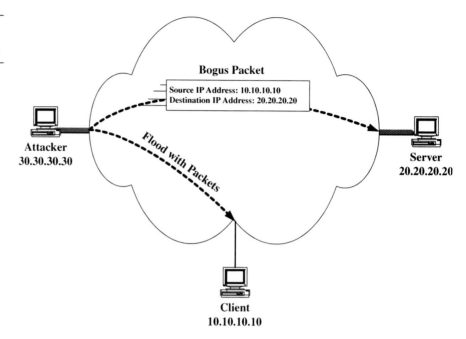

Another approach to this problem would be to change all the routing tables to point the spoofed IP address back to the attacker. This would enable bi-directional communication, allowing the attacker to act as any trusted user. The attacker would still have to be concerned about knowing the sequencing numbers, but this would eliminate the need to flood packets to the client and would provide for a more interactive session.

4.3.3 Sniffing

The basic design of almost every *local area network* (LAN) technology, such as Ethernet and Token Ring, is to provide all computers with access to the same media. This allows all computers to listen for packets whose MAC address is either destined for them or is a broadcast address.

Note:

Switches get away from the basic premise of allowing all computers to hear the conversations taking place on the network. However, mechanisms are available that allow one port to hear the conversations of another port (span port).

By using what is called "promiscuous mode," a computer's *network interface card* (NIC) can access all of the transmissions that pass on the wire. In this situation, it is impossible to know that someone is listening to your network because the "sniffing" device is not doing anything out of the ordinary except collecting the data for analysis by the would-be hacker.

Sniffers are an extremely important tool in a network engineer's arsenal. They allow network engineers to listen to the conversations that are taking place and find errant behavior between computers. Unfortunately, a sniffer put in the hands of an attacker quickly becomes a different tool. For example, attackers with a sniffer on the victim's network cannot only see the different conversations, but also can look inside those packets at the data that is being sent back and forth.

As seen in Figure 4-5, the objective is generally to snoop for passwords in login traffic, specifically in those systems that allow clear text passwords to be sent. By knowing the passwords, one can gain access to systems that he or she is not allowed to access. However, an attacker could

Figure 4-5

Sniffing the network

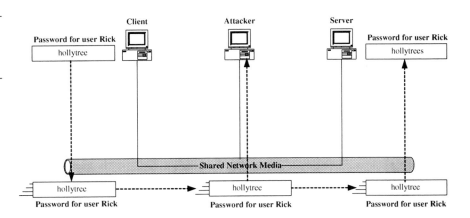

potentially be looking for other types of communication, such as who is communicating with whom, whereas this activity may not seem important, consider communications with secret partners or merger talks.

Although most sniffers are LAN-based, WAN-based sniffers are available, but are significantly more expensive. However, we can circumvent the need for these expensive WAN sniffers with some creative engineering. For example, an ingenious attacker could dual-home his or her network to two *Internet Service Providers* (ISPs) using *Border Gateway Protocol* (BGP). Then, he could advertise to the first ISP that the best route for the attacked network is through his network. Now, all the data going to the victim's network, which goes through the first ISP, will go through his network, at which point he could forward the packets out to the second ISP. Although any good ISP will prevent this, it only takes one ISP to make a network vulnerable. In addition, this type of attack can go undetected by the customer for a long time.

4.3.4 Man-in-the-Middle Attacks

Although it may seem obvious that encryption can be used to conceal the data passed in an IP packet, many threats to IP security exist. If these threats are not carefully managed, an encryption system could be vulnerable to man-in-the-middle attacks.

In order to use encryption, you have to exchange encryption keys. How this exchange actually takes place could be one of a couple of different methods, including sneaker-net.

Note:

"Sneaker-net" is a jargon term used for a method of exchanging information by personally carrying it from one place (one floppy disk) to another computer. The idea is that someone is using his or her feet (probably wearing sneakers) to move data around, rather than using the network.

Exchanging unprotected keys over the network defeats the purpose of using keys in the first place because a would-be attacker could intercept those keys and have access to your data. However, some methods are used to securely exchange keys over the network so that an attacker sniffing the network would be unable to figure out the key. Unfortunately, some circumstances occur in which an attacker can place his or herself in the middle of a key exchange and plant his or her own key early in the process. This would let the end devices think they have successfully traded keys with each other, when in fact they have given their keys to the man-in-the-middle!

4.3.5 Replay Attack

A replay attack is exactly what it sounds like it would be. An attacker, sniffing the network, records an encrypted transmission from A to B. Although the attacker might not be able to read the data in the message, he or she could replay the message at a later time to gain access to a system, as seen in Figure 4-6.

As we can see from Figure 4-6, the attacker never knew the password; however, he is able to replay the message to the server, fooling the system

Figure 4-6

Replay attack

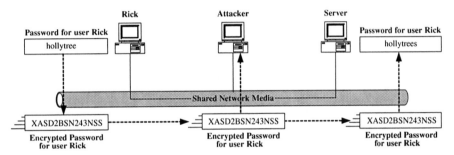

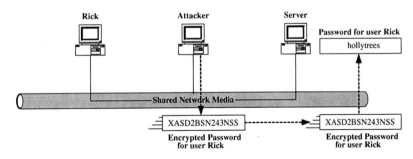

into thinking the attacker is user Rick. This type of attack is particularly useful to an attacker when the system he or she is trying to gain access to does not send clear text passwords. These types of attacks are sometimes used in conjunction with IP spoofing or man-in-the middle.

Now that we have covered the most basic security threats, we will look at the solutions that can be used to prevent unscrupulous individuals from gaining access to data.

4.4 Security Solutions

As we send data through a public network, we need to make sure that that we know with whom we are communicating (authentication), that the data is only read by the intended recipient (confidential), and that the data is intact when it arrives to the intended recipient (data integrity). Two elements are used in order to secure data:

- Encryption (symmetric or asymmetric)
- Authentication

Two fundamentally different types of encryption techniques exist: symmetric and asymmetric. Symmetric, sometimes known as single key encryption, is by far the most widely used type of encryption. In this section, we will discuss the basics of cryptography and the differences between symmetric and asymmetric encryption. In addition, we will cover the various authentication protocols and how to configure them on a Cisco router.

4.4.1 Encryption

Encryption is the process of taking an intelligible message, converting it to an unreadable message, and converting it back to a readable message. This concept is relatively straightforward, but the implementation is not. Two different types of encryption can be used depending on the goal of the encryption.

- Lossless encryption
- Lossy encryption

In addition to lossless and lossy encryption, some encryption processes utilize a key and others do not. We will now take a look at the advantages and disadvantages of each approach.

4.4.1.1 Lossless Encryption versus Lossy Encryption

Lossless encryption is generally the type of encryption that most people think of when they think of encryption. Lossless encryption is exactly as its name implies; no loss of information occurs, thus ciphertext can be computationally reversed to see the original message before it was encrypted. Lossy encryption is just the opposite of lossless encryption in that some of the pertinent information in the ciphertext is missing and one cannot recreate the original message from the ciphertext. Most cryptographic algorithms use both an algorithm and a secret value known as a key to generate ciphertext. However, not all algorithms require the use of a key, but algorithms that use a key display a different set of characteristics than those that do not. Now we will take a look at the properties that are displayed by the combination of lossless algorithms versus lossy algorithms and keyed algorithms versus keyless algorithms.

4.4.1.2 Keyed Algorithms with Lossless Encryption

Information that needs to be kept confidential until such time that it is needed necessitates the use of an algorithm that can encrypt data, making it confidential, and then decrypt it, when one is ready for it. Under ideal circumstances, anyone should be able to look at lossless ciphertext and not make any sense of it or easily reverse it. By using an encryption algorithm that uses a key, we can unlock the ciphertext by reversing the encryption process, but only if we have the key. Although the encryption algorithm gives us some protection, the use of a key provides additional protection because an attacker would need to know not only the algorithm, but the key as well. Because an attacker may know the types of transactions that are being passed, it is important to use a key when encrypting data.

4.4.1.3 Keyless Algorithms with Lossless Encryption

Algorithms that do not utilize a key can be reversed by anyone who knows the algorithm. Thus, algorithms that are lossless and do not utilize a key provide minimal protection. However, they do provide a modicum of protection from the casual observer. A good example of lossless encryption that does not utilize a key is the *enable password* used in Cisco IOS. Literally hundreds of programs on the Internet, even Excel spreadsheets, are available that can reverse the enable password in Cisco's IOS because the encryption algorithm does not employ a key. Thus, if we know the algorithm, we can reverse the process because reversing the encryption process is an integral part of lossless compression.

4.4.1.4 Keyless Algorithms with Lossy Encryption

So, when do we use encryption algorithms that do not require a key? In the previous paragraphs, we discussed scenarios in which we needed the ability to see the exact message. However, lossy encryption algorithms, also known as one-way hash functions, do not need to be reversed because the primary motivation for using them is to compare one hash value with another. Unlike lossless encryption, a hash should use an algorithm that is irreversible. So, why would we want to use an algorithm we cannot reverse?

The perfect place for this type of algorithm is authentication. By using hashed passwords, we can make it impossible for a system to display the value of a person's password, but the system knows how to calculate the hash based on the value entered by the end user. The system can then compare the output from the recently calculated hash to the hash value stored in its local database. If the two hash values match, the person has been successfully authenticated. A good example of this kind of encryption is the *enable secret password* used in Cisco's IOS. This type of encryption is useful because we do not have to worry about people knowing the password, even though they can see the hash value.

4.4.1.5 Keyed Algorithms with Lossy Encryption

The next logical question to the previous paragraph is, can we have hash functions that utilize a key and if so, what are they good for? Yes, some hash functions do utilize an asymmetric key (public key) infrastructure, which is routinely used for digital signatures. We will examine how they operate a bit later in this chapter after we describe how asymmetric keys work.

To summarize these differences, Table 4-1 illustrates how these differing approaches can be used for different security functions.

Table 4-1

Encryption
Comparisons of
Fundamentally
Different
Encryption
Paradigms

	Lossy Encryption	Lossless Encryption
Keyed Algorithms	Digital Signatures	Strong Encryption
Keyless Algorithms	Authentication	Weak Encryption

Now that we understand the basic building blocks of encryption and how keys can be utilized or not utilized to provide a specific function, let us take a look at the different types of keys that are available. In order to understand the strengths and weaknesses of the various encryption methods available, we need to have a firm understanding of the types of keys that can be used with those encryption methods.

4.4.1.6 Symmetric versus Asymmetric Keys

Today's modern encryption algorithms that utilize a key in combination with an algorithm are ideal for sending encrypting messages that need to be decrypted. Depending on the type of key used, we must keep it secure (that is, not share it with anyone) or we may need to share it with others. How you utilize your key depends on the type of algorithm being used. Now we will look at the two different types of keys that are used within cryptography:

- Symmetric
- Asymmetric

Symmetric key encryption uses a common key that both devices use to encrypt and decrypt the message. Because they use the same key, they also use the same algorithm to generate ciphertext. Figure 4-7 illustrates how users Jim and Morgan would communicate securely using a symmetric key.

Communicating securely over the network requires Jim and Morgan to agree on a cryptographic algorithm and a common key to encrypt/decrypt the message. In Figure 4-7, the following steps must occur in order for Jim and Morgan to communicate securely:

Figure 4-7

Secure
communication
using a
symmetric key

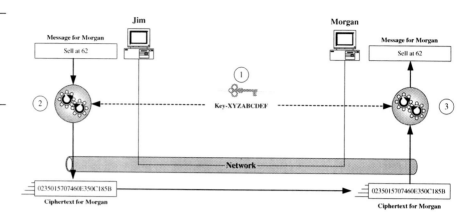

1. Jim and Morgan agree on an encryption method and a common key.

2. Jim encrypts the confidential message "Sell at 62" and sends the ciphertext to Morgan.

3. Morgan receives the ciphertext, and decrypts the ciphertext using the same key and encryption method used by Jim.

4. Morgan then reads the confidential message.

Anyone intercepting this message as it is transmitted across the network cannot read the original message without knowing the key used by Jim and Morgan as well as the encryption algorithm. This type of communication is the simplest form of encrypted communication. Because of this simplicity, the following challenges arise with secret key encryption:

▪ Securely generating secret keys

▪ Securely distributing the secret keys

▪ Changing secret keys frequently to avoid the risk of compromising the data

Asymmetric encryption, commonly referred to as public key encryption, uses a pair of keys to scramble and unscramble messages. This type of encryption is a radical departure from the standard substitution and permutation provided by symmetric key algorithms. Asymmetric key encryption is based on mathematical functions rather than substitution and permutation, but more importantly, they involve the use of two separate keys. The use of two keys has a profound consequence in the areas of confidentiality and key distribution, as we will see later in this chapter.

In asymmetric key encryption, two keys are created. One of those keys is a public key and the other is a private key. As their names indicate, the public key is distributed to the world, whereas only the user knows the private key. Most public/private keys are based on a mathematical truth where it does not matter which key is shared. However, it is extremely important that once you decide which key is public and which is private, you never share your private key, otherwise the whole public/private key paradigm falls apart. In Figure 4-8, we can see how users Meg and Morgan could communicate securely using asymmetric key encryption.

Figure 4-8

Data confidentiality and integrity using asymmetric keys

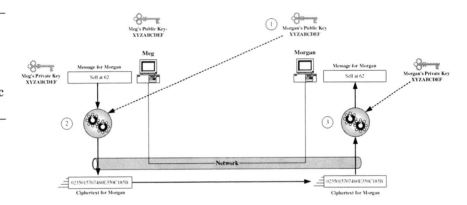

1. Meg gets Morgan's public key using any means necessary without the worry of compromising the confidential message.

2. Meg encrypts the confidential message "Sell at 62" using Morgan's public key and sends the ciphertext to Morgan.

3. Morgan receives the ciphertext and decrypts it using her private key and complimentary encryption method.

4. Morgan then reads the confidential message.

When sending a message in the opposite direction, the process is reversed. Morgan uses Meg's public key to encrypt and Meg will decrypt using her private key.

In this encryption paradigm, data confidentiality can be ensured because only the receiver knows the private key and he or she is the only one who can decrypt the message. Data integrity is also preserved because a malicious attacker would need to know the receiver's public key (the receiver's private key to decrypt the message). In addition, Meg and Morgan can freely exchange their public keys without worrying about compromising their message. Unfortunately, anyone can generate a message to Meg pretending to be Morgan because everyone has access to Morgan's public key.

By modifying the encryption paradigm, we can provide sender authentication. This is useful if we want to be reasonably certain that a message came from Meg. Using the steps listed below, we show how this could be done (shown in Figure 4-9).

Figure 4-9

Authenticated communication using asymmetric keys

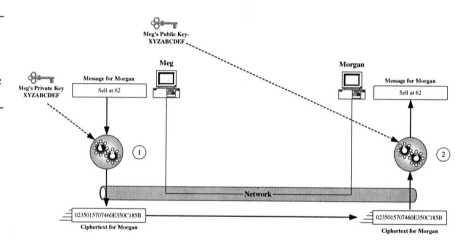

1. Meg encrypts the confidential message "Sell at 62" using her private key and sends the ciphertext to Morgan.

2. Morgan receives the ciphertext and decrypts it using Meg's public key and complimentary encryption algorithm, and then reads the confidential message.

In this encryption paradigm, only Meg could have encrypted the message; thus, we can conclude that only Meg could have sent the message. Unfortunately, anyone intercepting the encrypted message could decrypt the message because Meg's public key is available to everyone. However, anyone receiving this message would know for certain that it came from Meg.

Until now, we have shown you how to make sure only the intended recipient can read the message (confidentiality) and how to verify who sent the message (authentication). Regrettably, neither paradigm allows us to do both. However, by combining the two key paradigms, we can obtain both confidentiality and authentication of the message, as seen in Figure 4-10.

Figure 4-10

Authenticated, data confidentiality, and data integrity using asymmetric keys

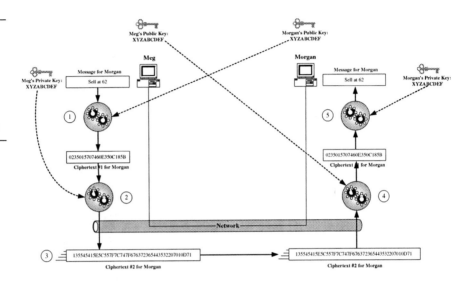

1. Meg encrypts the confidential message "Sell at 62" using Morgan's private key to generate the first ciphertext message.

2. Meg then encrypts the first ciphertext message using his private key, which generates the second ciphertext message.

3. Meg sends the twice-encrypted message to Morgan.

4. Morgan decrypts the ciphertext using Meg's public key to regenerate the first ciphertext message.

5. Morgan decrypts the first ciphertext message using her own private key to generate the confidential message "Sell at 62."

   In this encryption paradigm, only Jim can read the message, which could have only come from Morgan. This scenario is called non-repudiation. It means that neither party can later deny having sent the message, unless one party claims that his or her private key has been compromised.

4.4.1.7 Digital Signatures

Digital signatures are based on asymmetric key encryption and one-way secure hash function algorithms. Instead of encrypting the entire document using an asymmetric key, giving us authenticated communication, a hash value is calculated based on the original message and then appended to the document. Figure 4-11 shows the steps involved with digital signatures.

Figure 4-11

Digital signatures

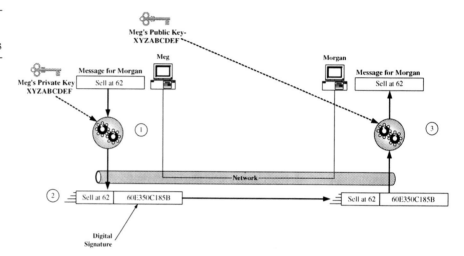

1. Meg's computer calculates a hash value of the message "Sell at 62" using her private key and appends the hash to the message.

2. Meg's computer sends the message with a digital signature to Morgan.

3. Morgan receives the message with the digital signature and then calculates the hash value using Meg's public key and the contents of the message. If the newly calculated hash and the hash that was received in the message match, we have authenticated the message. At this point, Morgan can then read the non-confidential authenticated message.

In this encryption paradigm, everyone can read the message, so it should not be confidential. In addition, we can verify quickly who sent the message through the digital signature. The advantage of a digital signature over the steps outlined in Figure 4-9 is speed. A hash value can be calculated quickly compared to calculating an encrypted message.

Symmetric Encryption Advantages   One of the distinct advantages that symmetric encryption has over asymmetric encryption is the speed of encryption. Symmetric encryption is significantly faster than any currently available asymmetric encryption method. In addition, because of the fundamental nature of the algorithms used, symmetric cryptography requires a smaller key for an equivalent level of security when compared to asymmetric keys, as seen in Table 4-2.

Table 4-2

Equivalent level of security key lengths for symmetric and asymmetric encryption

Symmetric Key Length	Equivalent Asymmetric Key Length
56 bits	384 bits
64 bits	512 bits
80 bits	768 bits
112 bits	1,792 bits
128 bits	2,304 bits

Asymmetric Encryption Advantages   Asymmetric encryption has a distinct advantage over symmetric encryption in that it makes key management possible. With asymmetric encryption, everyone has a single set of public/private keys they can use to communicate with anyone, whereas symmetric encryption requires a different private key between each two discrete users. For example, let us look at a system that has 100 users who must communicate securely. Using asymmetric encryption, we only need 100 different public/private key pairs, whereas symmetric encryption requires almost 5,000 different private keys, as seen in Figure 4-12.

Figure 4-12

Number of keys required in a symmetric encryption paradigm

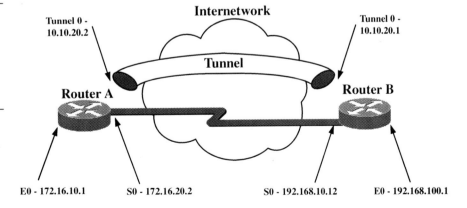

As we can see from Figure 4-12, this type of paradigm does not scale well for an enterprise. It does not even begin to mention the hurdles that must be overcome when attempting to distribute 5,000 keys. Although asymmetric cryptography may seem weak, it is generally regarded as having increased security and convenience because the private keys are never transmitted or revealed to anyone. Contrast that with symmetric cryptography in which the secret key must be revealed through some transmission channel where the attacker could discover it.

In any environment, trade-offs exist between different fundamental approaches to the same problem, and encryption is no different. In general, symmetric encryption is best when used in small environments or single user environments, such as keeping your files secure or setting up a single VPN. On the other hand, asymmetric encryption is best suited for an open, multi-user environment and can scale to meet the needs of large-scale VPN projects.

The one common aspect that can be found throughout this section and cannot be stressed enough is that regardless of whether we are using asymmetric encryption or symmetric encryption, the key must be protected. Although asymmetric encryption makes this an easier prospect than symmetric encryption, they both still have their weaknesses.

4.4.1.8 Cryptography

As previously discussed, cryptography can use both an algorithm and a secret key to generate ciphertext or just an algorithm. The algorithms used by a cryptographic mechanism are subject to scrutiny by the world's best cryptographers, who validate the strength of the algorithm. Assuming no shortcuts exist to decrypting ciphertext within the algorithm itself, the ciphertext is still subject to a brute force cryptanalysis.

Note:

Cryptanalysis is the science of creating and breaking cryptographic algorithms.

To better understand the concept of a brute force attack, let us look at one of the easiest and oldest encryption processes in existence: the Caesar Cipher. The Caesar Cipher works by replacing every letter in the message with a letter X number of places further down the alphabet. The key in this situation would be the number X. For example, in Figure 4-13, the key is 6.

Figure 4-13

Example of
Caesar Cipher

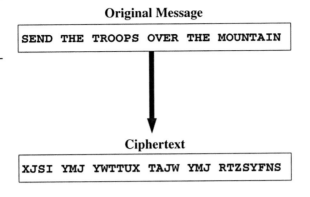

Original Message

SEND THE TROOPS OVER THE MOUNTAIN

Ciphertext

XJSI YMJ YWTTUX TAJW YMJ RTZSYFNS

KEY = 6

A -> F   N -> S
B -> G   O -> T
C -> H   P -> U
D -> I   Q -> V
E -> J   R -> W
F -> K   S -> X
G -> L   T -> Y
H -> M   U -> Z
I -> N   V -> A
J -> O   W -> B
K -> P   X -> C
L -> Q   Y -> D
M -> R   Z -> E

Using the letter six places further along in the alphabet, we would replace *a* with *f*, *b* with *g*, *c* with *h*, and so on. In this particular example, an attacker would need to know both the algorithm (replace each letter with the one six letters away) as well as the key, otherwise the message would be useless.

However, if the attacker knew which algorithm was used, he or she could decode the message using brute force fairly quickly because only 26 permutations are possible (1-26). Although this key space is weak, it does emphasize one important aspect of cryptography, which is to guard the cryptography algorithm you are using. If an attacker has to guess at what type of algorithm you are using, it increases the difficulty of a brute force attack by several orders of magnitude.

Assuming that an attacker has determined the algorithm you are using, the only thing left standing between your confidential message and the attacker is the length of the key. The longer the key, the more permutations that must be tried before the solution can be found during a brute force attack. In Table 4-3, we can see the number of possible keys based on the size (length) of the key.

As we start to look at more sophisticated algorithms that use longer keys, a trade-off occurs between being mathematically secure from a brute force attack and the amount of computation power required to provide minimal latency when generating the ciphertext.

Table 4-3	Length of Key (bits)	Number of Possible Keys
Number of Possible Keys Based on Length of Key	32	4,294,967,296
	40	10,99,511,627,776
	56	72,057,594,037,927,936
	64	18,446,744,073,709,551,616
	112	~5,192,296,858,534,827,628,530,496,329,200,000
	128	~340,282,366,920,938,463,463,374,607,430,000,000,000

Quite a bit of controversy over the years surrounding brute force attacks, specifically against *Digital Encryption Standard* (DES) (we will discuss DES later in this chapter). It has been alleged by many that DES was deliberately sabotaged by the *National Security Agency* (NSA). This is because the computations required to attempt a brute force attack on a 56-bit encrypted message is small enough that a major government or large corporation could afford to build a system capable of trying all 72 quadrillion keys in a reasonable period of time.

A book has recently been published that outlines the steps required to crack 56-bit DES encryption for under $200,000. This book outlines the theory and gives schematics on how to build such a machine! Although few network engineers have to deal with attackers who have $200,000 at their disposal to build such a machine, it does highlight an important fact; as computational horsepower increases, the length of time any message can stay encrypted is finite. For more information about cracking DES, see *Cracking DES: Secrets of Encryption Research, Wiretap Politics & Chip Design* by the Electronic Frontier Foundation, John Gilmore (Editor).

We will now discuss the different types of encryption algorithms used to generate ciphertext. Although many look like they were made for protecting network data, others are only marginally suitable for encryption.

Cipher Modes of Operation   In our previous example using Caesar Cipher, the amount of data encrypted at any single time was a single character. It is obvious that attempting to decrypt a single character at a time becomes a trivial exercise. In order to provide a more secure system for encrypting data, two basic types of cipher methodologies are used to encrypt data:

- Block cipher
- Steam cipher

Block Cipher   A block cipher works by encrypting data in blocks of a fixed size. This allows the algorithm to treat the entire block of plain text as a whole and is used to generate a ciphertext of equal length. In order to create a message of random length, several techniques are used called "modes of operation." Four different modes are used with block ciphers.

- *Electronic Code Book Mode* (ECB)
- *Cipher Block Chaining Mode* (CBC)
- *Cipher Feedback Mode* (CFB)
- *Output Feedback Mode* (OFB)

When using ECB, each plain text block is encrypted independently of the others. Although this mode secures the data, it is possible to find patterns within the ciphertext that can give away the contents of the ciphertext. However, one of the advantages of this type of mode is that it can be encrypted in parallel, which can yield higher performance on optimized machines.

CBC mode uses the mathematical operation of exclusive OR operator (XOR) with the previous ciphertext block to conceal patterns within the current ciphertext block. Because the algorithm uses the previous text block as a seed for encrypting the next block, it is difficult to put in a parallel process; thus, it is difficult to optimize the encryption process. In order to start the process, because no previous ciphertext block is available to XOR with, an initialization vector is used to seed the process. This seed can be transmitted with the ciphertext.

CFB is similar to CBC mode in that the previous ciphertext block is XORed with the current ciphertext block. This also hides patterns within a ciphertext message. However, in certain instances, it is possible for the plain text blocks to leak through. Like CBC, the process is difficult to put in parallel, and once again it is difficult to optimize the encryption process.

OFB is similar to CFB mode except for the quantity XORed with each plain text block. The advantage of OFB mode is that any bit errors that occur during transmission are not propagated through subsequent encryption/decryption of the blocks. Like CBC and CFB, OFB cannot be parallelized easily; however, we can save time by generating the keystream (a sequence of bits used as a key) before the data is available for encryption.

Stream Cipher   Stream ciphers are designed to be exceptionally fast. This is because a block cipher is designed to operate on large blocks of data. A stream cipher typically operates on a much smaller unit of plain text. A stream cipher generates a keystream, and encryption is accomplished by performing a bitwise XOR. Classic examples of stream ciphers are Vigenere cipher and the Vername cipher.

4.4.1.9 Hash Functions

Hash functions work by using a message of variable length as input and then producing a fixed length string, usually 128 bits or more, commonly referred to as a "hash." It should be obvious that if we take any variable length message and produce a fixed length string, some of the information would be lost during the computation of the hash. This is why hash functions are frequently known as lossy encryption.

Hash functions have the following properties:

- Must be consistent
- Must give the appearance of being random
- Output must be unique
- Cannot be reversed

Message Digest 2 (MD2)   In the late 1980's, Ron Rivest of *Rivest-Shamir-Adleman* (RSA) Labs developed *Message Digest 2* (MD2). This hash function takes a string of variable length and produces a fixed-length output of 128-bits. It was optimized for 8-bit microprocessors and is described in *Request for Comments* (RFC) 1319. Due to some weaknesses found in the message field, if some calculations are not performed, MD2 is considered weak and no longer deployed.

Message Digest 4 (MD4)   In the early 1990's, Ron Rivest designed *Message Digest 4* (MD4) as an improvement over MD2. It utilizes a 512-bit block message and is optimized for 32-bit architectures. Based on three rounds to implement, a flaw was found relatively quickly when leaving off the first or third round. Using a typical PC, it has been shown that a reduced version of MD4 can be reversed, which means it is no longer one-way. MD4 is no longer considered secure for general use.

Message Digest 5 (MD5)   In 1991, Ron Rivest developed *Message Digest 5* (MD5), and it is considerably stronger than any of the previous algorithms. MD5 processes the hash in 512-bit blocks and has an output of

128-bits, which is similar to MD4, but more secure and slightly slower than MD4 due to the increased number of rounds.

Although MD5 enjoys widespread popularity, including deployment in Cisco's enable secret hash, reports of its weakness have appeared. From a cryptanalytic point of view, Dobbertin has developed the most serious attack on MD5. Without getting into the details, this is clearly a significant step in the breaking of MD5, and it should now be considered vulnerable.

Secure Hash Algorithm (SHA and SHA-1) Developed by the *National Institute of Standards and Technology* (NIST) and published as a federal standard in 1993, *Secure Hash Algorithm* (SHA) is based on the MD4 algorithm. SHA-1 is basically an update to SHA, which corrected an unpublished flaw in SHA, and was published in 1994. This algorithm produces a 160-bit message digest and is slightly slower than MD5; however, it is considered more secure against brute force attacks and inversion attacks.

4.4.1.10 Shared Key Algorithms

Shared key algorithms, also known as symmetric key algorithms, are much more secure and faster than their public key algorithm counterparts. However, key distribution tends to be a real problem with shared key algorithms, which makes it difficult to scale these types of solutions.

DES In the 1950's, the National Security Agency of the United States of America in conjunction with IBM developed the *Digital Encryption Standard* (DES). Originally called "Lucifer" by IBM, it was endorsed by the U.S. government in 1977 as an official standard. It also forms the basis of UNIX password programs and Automatic Teller Machines' PIN authentication.

The DES algorithm, a block cipher, works on 64-bit blocks with a 56-bit key. Although technically 64 bits exist in the key, eight parity bits are stripped off to form the well-known 56-bit key. DES is a symmetric cryptosystem that uses a 16-round cipher (an algorithm that is performed a number of times), which was originally designed to be implemented through hardware.

DES is generally considered to be strong enough against weak enemies. However, if you are protecting your data against large corporations or governments, DES is probably not the encryption method you should use. This is due to its vulnerabilities of a brute force attack and the processing power of today's machines, and that it is possible to snoop for patterns within the ciphertext through a "sustained data analysis." It is possible to eliminate sustained data analysis attacks by regularly changing the key, but this may not be feasible.

3DES   *Triple-DES* (3DES) is not a new encryption algorithm based on DES, but a set of algorithms that uses DES multiple times to increase the strength of regular DES. The idea behind reusing this algorithm is to preserve the existing investment in software and equipment.

3DES can be used with two or three keys depending on the implementation. When using two keys, an effective key length of 112 bits exists, whereas three keys provide a combined effective key length of 168 bits. Currently, 3DES can be run on four different modes.

- DES-EEE3
- DES-EDE3
- DES-EEE2
- DES-EDE2

By looking at the four-letter name appended to the DES title, we can discern the implementation of that mode. For example, if we assume the letter E means encrypt, D means decrypt, the number 2 means two keys are used, and 3 means three keys are used, we can see how each of those modes operates in Figure 4-14.

Figure 4-14

3DES's different operating modes

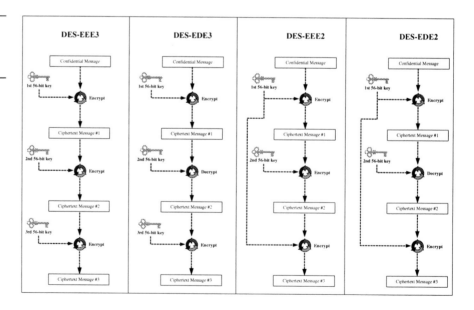

Although each of the encryption operating modes have the same basic intent (to encrypt a message three times using DES), they are variations of a theme. As of the writing of this book, the latest RFC (RFC 2420 - PPP Triple-DES Encryption) uses DES-EDE3-CBC 168-bit key. It also employs the use of a sequence number to ensure the right order of the transmitted packets and detect lost packets.

Currently, no practical cryptanalytical attacks exist on DES. It should also be noted that a brute force key search on 3DES is currently impractical for the machines of today's computational power.

IDEA The *International Data Encryption Algorithm* (IDEA) was developed in the early 1990's to replace the DES standard. It is currently patented in Europe (Austria, France, Germany, Italy, Netherlands, Spain, Sweden, Switzerland, and the United Kingdom), in the United States of America, and in Japan. Many have proposed to replace the aging DES with IDEA. Additionally, IDEA has been included in the *Pretty Good Privacy* (PGP) program after Phil Zimmerman's attempt at a cipher had proven to be weak.

IDEA's algorithm is a block cipher, which works on 64-bit blocks. With a 128-bit key, it uses eight rounds to encrypt the data. Although this may seem weak compared to DES's 16- round cipher, IDEA gets its strength from three incompatible types of arithmetic operations: XOR, modulo addition 16, and a multiplication modulo 216+1.

IDEA is a relative newcomer to the encryption scene and has not been subjected to the intense scrutiny that cryptographic systems like DES have had. However, IDEA is considered to be strong encryption that has withstood many challenges. In addition, it is considered to be immune from differential cryptanalysis. Its weakest point is that a large number of weak keys 2^{51} exist.

RC2 Developed by Ron Rivest for RSA Data Security, RC2 is a symmetric encryption algorithm that uses plain text and ciphertext blocks of 64 bits. It uses a variable key-size block cipher (from 8 to 1,024 bits). The algorithm, originally designed to be implemented on 16-bit microprocessors (which shows proof of its age), is approximately two to three times faster than DES when implemented in software.

An interesting circumstance surrounding the export of RC2 is that in order to qualify for quick export, a product had to limit the key size to 40 bits (56-bits is the maximum allowed for export). However, an extra string between 40 and 88 bits long called a "salt" can be used to prevent attackers from using a brute force to find the key to the ciphertext. This is accomplished by appending the salt to the encryption key during the encryption process for extra security, but instead of keeping the salt a secret, it is sent unencrypted with the message. This loophole allows the cipher to be exported while still abiding by US export laws, but this special status may prove unneeded because as of January 2000, a dramatic reduction has occurred in the restrictions placed on exporting encryption.

RC4   RC4 is a cipher developed by Ron Rivest for RSA Data Security. Unlike RC2, RC4 is a stream cipher that uses a variable key size and is based on the use of a random permutation. It has been designed to run quickly in software and requires from eight to 16 operations per byte to generate ciphertext. It is used in several commercial programs like Lotus Notes and secure Netscape.

The following is an interesting anecdote about RC4. In early 1995, an algorithm claiming to be RC4 was published anonymously in the newsgroups. Tests of this algorithm indicated that it acted identically to the real RC4. To date, RC4 is no longer a trade secret and is no longer proprietary.

RC5   RC5, also developed by Ron Rivest for RSA Data Security, is a block cipher. Using a variable block size, variable key size, and variable number of rounds, it provides flexibility for all levels of security and efficiency. Three different block sizes can be used with RC5: 32 bits for experimentation and evaluation purposes, 64 bits for a drop-in replacement of DES, and 128 bits when it absolutely must be secure. The key can range from zero bits to 2,040 bits in size and the number of rounds can range from zero to 255.

The use of data-dependent rotations in the algorithm along with the mixture of different operations helps defeat any differential and liner cryptanalysis on the algorithm.

Skipjack   Skipjack is a classified algorithm developed by the NSA for use with the "Clipper Chip" and "Capstone Chips," which were pushed by the Clinton Administration. This algorithm is controversial—not based on any technical merit, which was classified until it was released by the U.S. government on June 23, 1998, but because the chips implemented a key escrow system. This key escrow system can be thought of as a backdoor for government agencies. Transmissions would contain an encrypted header containing a session key. Government agencies with access to the header-encryption keys would be able to decrypt the ciphertext. Like that of a wire tap, the idea is that a court order would be required in order for these backdoor keys to be used.

On its technical merits, skipjack is a block cipher using the standard 64-bit block size, an 80-bit key, and has a 32 internal round cipher. Because of the requirement for the escrow mechanism, only hardware implementations of skipjack would be available. This is why the chips "Clipper" and "Capstone" are so closely related to the skipjack cryptographic algorithm. Although an outside review panel concluded that the algorithm was quite strong, its escrow features limited its acceptance into the computing community. The chips are no longer in production; however, various Fortezza products (encrypting modems) used the chips and are still in production today.

Blowfish Developed by Bruce Schneier in 1993, Blowfish is similar to DES in that it is a 64-bit block cipher with variable length keys, which can range in size from 32 to 448 bits in length. By using a Feistel cipher, each round consists of a key-and-data-dependent substitution. It was originally designed specifically for 32-bit machines. Its design makes it significantly faster than DES. Even though Blowfish was found to have certain weak keys, it is still considered to be a secure encryption algorithm.

4.4.1.11 Public/Private Key Algorithms

Public key algorithms, also known as asymmetric key algorithms, provide us with many different ways of providing authentication, data integrity, and confidentiality. Due to the natural paradigm in which they operate, they provide an easy way to scale a security solution. Unfortunately, they are slower and weaker than their shared key counterparts.

Diffie-Hellman The *Diffie-Hellman* (DH) key agreement protocol, developed by Diffie and Hellman in 1976, is a revolutionary protocol that allows two users to exchange a secret key securely over an insecure medium without previously exchanging any secrets. This algorithm is limited only to the unauthenticated exchange of keys.

The limitation to DH is that a person has no way of knowing who is really at the other end of the connection; thus, it is subject to a man-in-the-middle attack. This vulnerability exists because no authentication mechanism is built into the algorithm. In 1992, Diffie, van Oorschot, and

Wiener developed the *Station to Station* (STS) protocol, sometimes known as the Authenticated Diffie-Hellman key-agreement protocol, which defeats the man-in-the-middle attack. This is achieved through the use of digital signatures and public-key certificates.

RSA In 1978, Ron Rivest, Adi Shamir, and Len Adleman at MIT published, in direct response to the pioneering paper by Diffie and Hellman, the RSA cryptosystem. RSA is probably the most common public-key cryptosystem in use today. It can be found in the widely used PGP program.

Note:

So, if PGP uses IDEA encryption, how can it possibly use RSA encryption as well? PGP is a hybrid cryptosystem that provides the best of symmetric and asymmetric encryption. By using a single IDEA key to encrypt the message and the same key to decrypt the message, it utilizes a symmetric encryption scheme. However, once the message is encrypted, the IDEA key is encrypted using RSA public-key encryption and then attached to the message. This allows the recipient to use public-key encryption to decrypt the IDEA key and then decrypt the original message.

RSA is also used in *Secure Sockets Layer* (SSL), found in both Netscape Navigator and Microsoft Explorer as well as by *Secure Electronic Transactions* (SET), utilized by both MasterCard and Visa. It is has also been adopted as the *International Standard Internetworking Operating Service* (ISO) 9796 for widespread use of digital signatures.

Until September 21, 2000, the RSA algorithm was protected by the patent 4,405,829. During its 16-year protection under the federal patent office, the owners of the RSA algorithm and RSA Data Security filed three lawsuits alleging infringement of the RSA patent.

RSA is an asymmetric encryption algorithm that utilizes a variable key-size block cipher that can have key lengths of 768 and 1,024. Future versions are likely to have 2,048 and 4,096 bit keys. Without getting into the mathematical details, RSA's strength comes from the difficulty in factoring large prime numbers.

Note:

To give the reader an understanding of the key size (1,024 bits) in question, we shall make some comparisons ($2^{1,024}$ is roughly equivalent to 10^{300}). Currently, only 10^{77} atoms exist in the universe, which have only existed for 10^{17} seconds. This means we need approximately 10^{200} numbers to describe the relative position in space and time of every atom in the universe for each nanosecond of its existence.

This makes RSA extremely secure, but not because it has been proven secure, but because no mathematical algorithm has been invented yet to factor large prime numbers. Although you may be tempted to think RSA is insecure, it has withstood hundreds, possibly thousands of attempts to crack it.

4.4.1.12 Key Management

We have now looked at the many different types of encryption algorithms in use today. We will now look at approaches to a critical aspect of encryption: key management. Key management deals with the process of generating, distributing, and storing keys.

Multiple methods are available for managing keys. However, the method you choose will be based on the type of encryption you are using (symmetric or asymmetric). The most popular method for exchanging keys is the Diffie-Hellman key exchange algorithm. Diffie-Hellman plays a vital role in symmetric key encryption systems because of the need to establish temporary session keys. This is because each new session requires a new key for good security measure. As previously mentioned, this algorithm has been updated to prevent the man-in-the-middle attacks.

In order for asymmetric encryption to scale, the users must have a method for exchanging public keys. This is where certificate authorities come into play. We can think of certificate authorities (CA) much like a notary republic does for your signature. A CA verifies your identity through the use of digital certificates to other participating routers, as seen in Figure 4-15.

Figure 4-15

Certificate
authority
topology

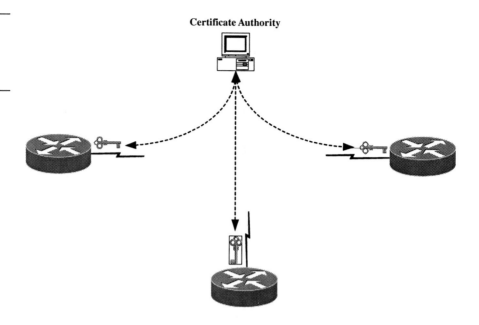

The X.500 series of standards developed by the ITU-T, specifically X.509, addresses the problems associated with registering and retrieving information on a broad range of objects. Often known as *Public Key Infra-structure* (PKI), the X.509 certificate model is based on a hierarchy of trusted authorities. This is quite different from the direction PGP has taken in that authenticity is guaranteed by a set of well-known users signing each other's keys in a face to face meeting. This results in a web of trust in which if you receive a key signed by someone you trust, you can be reasonably certain the user is who they claim to be.

Any PKI should consist of the following:

- A certificate authority that issues and verifies digital certificates

- A registration authority that verifies a certificate authority before issuing a digital certificate to a requestor

- A certificate management system that includes storage of the various certificates

Several efforts are underway to develop a standard PKI. One of the efforts is being driven by the RSA and is known as the *Public Key Cryptography Standard* (PKCS). Another effort underway is through the

Internet Engineering Task Force (IETF). They drive an initiative for PKI called *Public Key Infrastructure Working Group* (PKIX).

Although delving into the various aspects of PKI is a step beyond the direction of this book, it is necessary to understand its importance within a large organization such as a corporation or government.

4.4.2 Authentication

Authentication is typically used prior to being allowed access to a network and the available services provided by the network. Authentication is typically based on something we know (for example, a password), something we have (for example, a token card) or something we are (for example, fingerprints, retinal scans). Environments that require the tightest level of security use all of the above for authentication purposes.

Two different types of protocols are used during authentication of a dial-in user that any network engineer has to deal with. Authentication protocols (at least in this context) deal with the protocols exchanged between a dial-up user and the access server. Security protocols such as *Remote Authentication Dial-In User Services* (RADIUS) and *Terminal Access Controller Access Control System* (TACACS+) deal with centralized authentication, authorization, and accounting. From Figure 4-16, we can get a better sense of where the protocols operate.

In Figure 4-16, it looks like the authentication protocols used are independent of the security protocols. Although this is generally the case, unexpected consequence may exist of selecting two of these protocols to work together. For example, let us say we want to use *Challenge Handshake Authentication Protocol* (CHAP) and RADIUS as our authentication mechanisms for our VPN initiators. In addition, we want the RADIUS

Figure 4-16

Protocols involved with authentication and where they operate

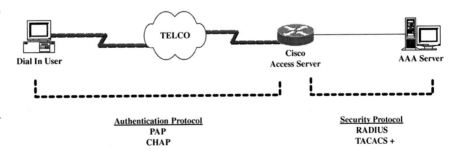

server to use a pre-existing username database, thus minimizing the number of usernames and passwords our end users have to remember. However, several RADIUS servers require the use of a different password in order to authenticate the user with CHAP. Think of this as a second password for the same user. Typically, this stems from the algorithms used to provide the authentication. A good example of this is Novell's BorderManager. Not all implementations of RADIUS are subject to this situation, but it is something to keep in mind when evaluating potential security servers.

Let us now take a look at the various protocols seen in Figure 4-15 and examine how they work and how to implement them.

4.4.2.1 Authentication Protocols

Two commonly used authentication protocols are available: *Password Authentication Protocol* (PAP) and *Challenge Handshake Authentication Protocol* (CHAP).

Password Authentication Protocol (PAP) PAP is the simplest authentication protocol commonly used with *Point-to-Point Protocol* (PPP). When a VPN initiator connects to a Cisco VPN server using PAP authentication, a username/password pair is repeatedly sent to the Cisco VPN server until the authentication is accepted or rejected. Rejection of the authentication is usually in the form of connection termination. When the username/password is sent using PAP, no encryption scheme appears to hide the username or password, as seen in Figure 4-17.

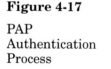

Figure 4-17

PAP
Authentication
Process

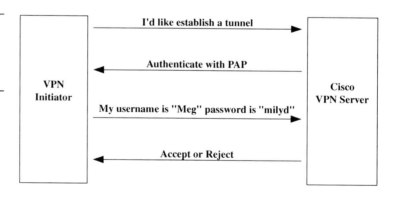

One of the downsides to using PAP is that because the data sent is only the username and password, it is subject to a replay attack. As previously discussed in this chapter, a replay attack is when an attacker "sniffs" the network, intercepts, and records a data stream. In this case, sniffing the network when using PAP during the authentication process would allow an attacker to gain access to the system. Although this is not an easy process, it can be done.

In order to support PAP authentication, you can configure your Cisco VPN Server with the following command:

```
Router (config-if)#ppp authentication pap
```

Remember that in order to configure authentication you must be in interface configuration mode.

Challenge Handshake Authentication Protocol - CHAP   To improve security, we can use a more secure authentication method called CHAP. During a CHAP authentication, the Cisco VPN Server sends a challenge to the VPN Initiator, as seen in Figure 4-18.

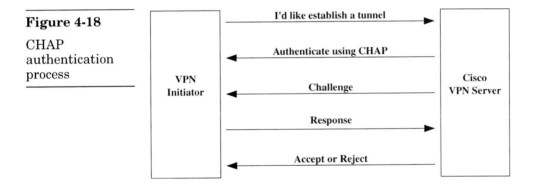

Figure 4-18

CHAP authentication process

The challenge is in the form of a random number. This number, called an "encryption key," is generated by the Cisco VPN Server and must be unique and unpredictable. The host will then encrypt the username and password using a one-way hash function, MD5. This newly encrypted message sent by the host is called the "response." When the Cisco VPN Server receives the response, it calculates a hash using the password it thinks is correct and then compares the two hashes against each other.

The security features in CHAP make it more secure than PAP. Because the random number sent in the challenge is unique and unpredictable, CHAP protects against replay attacks. Because the VPN initiator uses the challenge to form the hash, neither the password nor the username is sent over the wire in clear text form. Lastly, CHAP provides additional protection from session hijacking by repeatedly challenging the host every two minutes. These repeated challenges limit the exposure to any single attack.

Configuration of the Cisco Access Server is almost identical to that of PAP. The format of the command is:

```
Router (config-if)#ppp authentication chap
```

Note:

When a host is trying to authenticate, it is the receiving Cisco VPN Server that determines the authentication method. As an administrator, you specify PAP, CHAP, or both authentication protocols.

4.4.2.2 Security Protocols Related to Authentication

One of the first topics that should be resolved when an organization starts to increase the number of services available to their customer base is authentication. The primary defense against any unauthorized use of a service is authentication and the best way to handle most passwords is through the use of a TACACS+ or RADIUS authentication server. Centralizing authentication minimizes the administrative overhead of keeping multiple authentication systems in sync. In addition, AAA servers

Figure 4-19

An organization
with multiple
dial-in servers

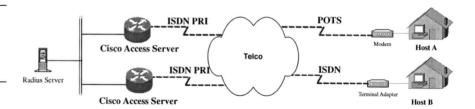

lend flexibility and additional security that is not available through local username databases, as we will see in just a bit.

If we were using a call hunt group, we could roll the phone calls from *Primary Rate Interface* (PRI) #1 to PRI #2 when the first PRI become full, thus giving the appearance of 46 incoming lines (excluding the use of NFAS). Unfortunately, we have now created a problem with authentication. Because each Cisco Access Server maintains its own username/password list and we never know which Cisco Access Server a user may dial into, we need a mechanism that allows both Cisco Access Servers to use the same username/password database. One of the solutions is to manually maintain the usernames and passwords for all users on both machines. This is subject to human error and is really not a viable solution.

By separating the username/password database from the Cisco VPN Server to another device, we can centralize the storage of this information for use by multiple devices on the network. In addition, we can use this information for purposes other than authentication into a Cisco VPN Server. For example, we can use this username/password database to authenticate network administrators who telnet into a Cisco router or switch. This minimizes the number of usernames and passwords that network technicians have to remember (because everything is centralized), and it also allows network administrators to centrally control the username database, instead of having to create a username on every Cisco router so a technician may access the device.

Cisco calls any device that provides external authentication, authorization, or accounting an AAA server. Although we have previously covered authentication, we will now take a quick look at the purpose of authorization and accounting.

Authorization Authorization is the process of determining what services an individual is allowed to access. This is an important aspect of any remote access solution that is running multiple services. For example, a large organization may be running PPP so their sales force can access their NetWare files servers and Web-based applications. They may also run *Apple Remote Access Protocol* (ARAP) for their managers who use Macintosh computers. In addition, they need to control access to their network infrastructure devices (switches and routers). It is easy to see that the need to control who has access to what type of resource is critical in this type of organization. This control can be centralized so that we can take advantage of the centralized username/password database.

Accounting Accounting is the process of determining who is using what resource. Although the accounting aspect of AAA may seem like a minor facet, it actually has three major roles that it can play within any organization:

- Billing
- Audit trail
- Trends

The most obvious use of accounting within a remote access solution is for billing. Whether you are an ISP or a large organization with an internal billing system, many organizations need a method to bill their customers for the services that have been rendered.

In security conscience organizations, it is likely that the use of any resource must have some sort of audit trail. Audit trails allow an organization to go back and find suspicious activities months or even years after an event occurs. Without an audit trail, the information is lost forever, leaving an organization unable to find any misuse of the technology.

As an organization starts to utilize the remote access services put in place, it can be useful to trend the use of a particular service. Depending on the situation, it may be useful to know that in six months your clients can expect to start getting busy signals when they dial in. Obviously, it is not that easy. Many variables go into trending, but looking at the usage statistics can be especially useful in predicting trends.

Overview of Security Protocols (TACACS+/RADIUS) Currently, Cisco routers can use two security protocols; each has its advantages and disadvantages:

- *Terminal Access Controller Access Control System* (TACACS)
- *Remote Authentication Dial-In User Services* (RADIUS)

TACACS has three different variations. The first is just plain TACACS, which the Defense Data Network originally developed. The second variation is *Extended TACACS* (XTACACS), which was introduced in 1990. Both of these versions are defined by RFC 1492. The third version, TACACS+, is a completely new protocol and incompatible with TACACS or XTACACS. TACACS+ is documented as an Internet draft. However, even though it is documented as an Internet draft, it is generally viewed as a Cisco proprietary protocol.

Because of the feature set offered by TACACS+, TACACS, and XTACACS are no longer being deployed in new installations. Therefore, we will only discuss attributes about TACACS+ in this chapter. For more detailed information about the TACACS protocol, see the following URL: `ftp://ftp.isi.edu/in-notes/rfc1492.txt` (An Access Control Protocol, sometimes called TACACS).

RADIUS was originally developed by Livingston Enterprises to control their network access servers. Because RADIUS, defined by RFC 2138, is an Internet standard, many third-party security products support it. It provides a standard mechanism for RADIUS servers and clients to communicate authentication, authorization, and accounting information. For more detailed information about the RADIUS protocol, see the following URLs: `ftp://ftp.isi.edu/in-notes/rfc2138.txt` (Remote Authentication Dial-In User Service (RADIUS) and `ftp://ftp.isi.edu/in-notes/rfc2139.txt` (RADIUS Accounting)

Configuring AAA on a Cisco VPN Server In order to use any of the AAA features on a Cisco VPN Server, you must first activate it. This can be done using the global configuration command:

```
Router (config)#aaa new-model
```

From here, we can now utilize the Cisco VPN Server's AAA security protocols. This means that all lines (con, tty, vty, and aux) are immediately subject to a username and a password for authentication. If you have not thought out your plan, you could inadvertently lock yourself out of the Cisco Access Server. For example, let us say you apply the *aaa new-model* command that activates the advanced security features. If your session times out before you can create a user, at which point you try to enter through the console port, you get the results displayed in Figure 4-20.

Figure 4-20

Accessing the console port with advanced security turned on, but no authentication mechanisms defined

```
% Authorization failed.
```

If you have not saved the results to *Non-Volatile Random Access Memory* (NVRAM), you can power off the router and power it back up. However, if you have saved your configuration, you will need to use the password recovery techniques.

Note:

As with most commands, the "no" form of this command will remove the aaa new-model command as well as all other AAA commands. However, be careful because when you reapply the aaa new-model command, all the other AAA commands that have been installed since bootup are applied immediately.

Configuring Authentication Authentication is typically one of the primary topics of concern for any network administrator. We need to make sure that users are authenticated before they can access a resource. Cisco has provided us with many options based on the type of service that someone is attempting to use.

The general process for authentication when an AAA server appears is illustrated in Figure 4-21.

Figure 4-21

Overview of authentication process

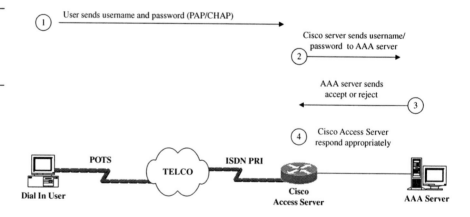

In Step 1 of Figure 4-21, the end user is sending his username and password to the Cisco Access Server using CHAP or PAP for authentication by the Cisco Access Server. The Cisco Access Server in turn forwards the request to the AAA server, where the AAA server determines whether to accept or reject the authentication. The accept/reject notification is sent back to the Cisco Access Server so that it may respond appropriately.

In order to enable AAA authentication, we need to make sure the AAA has been enabled on the Cisco Access Server. Once we have done that, we can use the following command to enable authentication:

```
Router (config)#aaa authentication service method-list security-
protocol
```

service	**arap**	Authenticate incoming ARAP sessions
	ppp	Authenticate incoming PPP sessions
	enable	Authenticate enable sessions on this Cisco router
	login	Authenticate login sessions (telnet)
method-list	**default**	Use the default list
word		Specify a method list
security-protoco	**radius**	Use the RADIUS to authenticate the user
	tacacs+	Use the TACACS+ to authenticate the user
	local	Use the local config file to authenticate user
	local-case	Use the local config file to authenticate user
(case sensitive)		
	none	No authentication required

Figure 4-22

Multiple security protocols being used for authentication

```
!
aaa new-model
aaa authentication login GroupA radius tacacs+
aaa authentication login GroupB tacacs+
                    !
```

The use of method lists allow multiple security protocols to be defined for each authentication service. In Figure 4-22, the method list GroupA uses RADIUS as its first security protocol and then TACACS+. While method list GroupB only uses TACACS+ for authentication purposes. One important note to Figure 4-22 is that with method list GroupA, if the RADIUS server fails to respond to a request, the Cisco Access Server attempts to use the TACACS+ server for authentication purposes. If a RADIUS server returns a "reject" response, the session is terminated and the TACACS+ server is not queried. This is important to keep in mind when designing a remote access solution.

One of the more useful commands to Cisco Access Servers and Cisco routers is the *aaa authentication login* command. This is useful because you can centrally control login access to your Cisco routers. It allows you to centrally maintain the enable password through AAA so that when you have personnel changes, you do not have to login into 50 different routers and manually add or delete user accounts.

In addition to specifying the authentication methods to use, we can also specify some of the cosmetic features when attempting a character-based login, such as what text to display when prompting for a username, password, and after login failure. The command used to modify these cosmetic features is displayed below:

```
Router (config)#aaa authentication message-type message
```

message-type	**banner**	Display this text when attempting to login
	fail-message	Display this text after login failure
	username-prompt	Display this text when prompting for a username
	password-prompt	Display this text when prompting for a password
message	**word**	Specify the phrase to use

Note:

You may need to use a delimiter depending on which message-type you are defining.

Figure 4-23 portrays the use of two commands to customize the output that any incoming telnet sessions will see.

Figure 4-23

Configuring the various login messages on a Cisco router with AAA commands

```
Router(config)#aaa authentication banner z
Enter TEXT message. End with the character 'z'.
Welcome to my Test Router
z
Router(config)#aaa authentication username-prompt WhoAreYou:
Router(config)#end
Router#192.168.103.1
Trying 192.168.103.1 ... Open

Welcome to my Test Router

                          WhoAreYou:
```

We modified the banner on the Cisco router as well as the prompt used to indicate the user's name. The *aaa authentication banner* command can still be used in conjunction with *banner motd* command.

Configuring Authorization   As previously mentioned, AAA authorization allows you to limit the types of services available to a user. When a user authenticates to a Cisco Access Server, the user's profile contains information regarding what services are available to them. These restrictions are in place until the user disconnects and re-authenticates.

A Cisco router can authorize four different types of services through the use of AAA:

* Exec
* Command
* Network
* Reverse access

The exec service deals with the attributes associated with a user's terminal session and whether the user can login to the Cisco router's *Command Line Interface* (CLI). This is useful when you have many routers and you do not want to manually update the telnet password on all of the Cisco routers because of a personnel change.

The command service indicates what commands the user can run after logging into the CLI. Cisco IOS provides for 15 layers of privileges within the CLI. This allows an administrator to give help desk staff commands like "debug," but it can remove commands like "configure terminal," so they do not inadvertently change an attribute.

The network service gives users permission to login with framed services such as PPP, *Serial Line Internet Protocol* (SLIP), and ARAP.

The keyword *reverse access* allows us to limit who can perform reverse telnets on a router. This can be especially important when the router in question is a terminal server connected to many different devices such as other Cisco router console ports and modems. By giving users access to reverse telnet on a terminal server, you have effectively given them access to the physical console port. This should be done with a great amount of care, since password recovery is accomplished through the console port.

The command used to specify the authorization types is listed below.

```
Router (config)#aaa authorization service method-list security-
protocol
```

service	commands <1-15>	Specify the privilege level
	exec	Indicate whether a user can establish a telnet session
	network	Indicate if a user can create a network connection (PPP, SLIP, or ARAP)
	reverse-access	Indicate if a user can reverse telnet
method-list	default	Use the default list
	WORD	Specify a method list
security-protocol	radius	Use the RADIUS for authorization information
	tacacs+	Use the TACACS+ for authorization information
	local	Use the local config file for authorization information
	none	No authentication required

Configuring Accounting   When AAA accounting is enabled, the Cisco Access Server will report the accounting information to the TACACS+ or RADIUS server being used. Like AAA authorization, five types of services can be enabled for accounting.

- Network
- Connection
- Exec
- System
- Command

Network accounting generates accounting information about all framed services such as PPP, SLIP, or ARAP. This includes login name, caller ID information, and start time. The end of session is a separate accounting message, which includes the start and end times of the session, allowing you to see how long someone was using the system.

Connection accounting generates accounting information about all outbound connections made such as Telnet, LAT, TN3270, and PAD.

Exec accounting generates information about terminal sessions on the network access server. This allows you to view when someone accessed the Cisco router, their IP address, date, time, as well as start and stop information.

System accounting generates information regarding all system-level events, such as a system reboot.

Command accounting generates information about the commands being used on a Cisco router. It may be particularly useful in highly secure environments to know what commands have been applied and by whom.

In addition to these five different types of accounting systems, we can indicate what information we want. The keyword *start-stop* indicates that it should record start and stop times, whereas the keyword *stop-only* is used to indicate when a user has stopped using a service. The keyword *wait-start* can be used for additional security. It indicates that the Cisco router should wait until the security server acknowledges the start notice before providing the user access to the requested resources. This keeps attackers from hiding their trail, but also has the potential for not allowing anyone access to the requested resources if the accounting server has gone down.

The command used to specify the accounting types is listed below.

```
Router (config)#aaa authorization service method-list acct-type
security-proto
```

service	commands <1-15>	Track who issued what command on a Cisco router
	exec	Enable accounting information about access to this router
	network	Enable accounting information for PPP, SLIP, or ARAP
	system	Track system event changes (for example, reboot)
	connection	Track who is generating an outbound connection
method-list	default	Use the default list
	WORD	Specify a method list
acct-type	none	No accounting
	start-stop	Record start and stop times

	stop-only	Record stop times only
	wait-start	Same as start-stop, but waits until security server responds before granting request
security-protocol	**radius**	Use the RADIUS for accounting
	tacacs+	Use the TACACS+ for accounting

Applying AAA to an Interface   Now that we have specified all of the attributes necessary for our AAA method lists, we need to apply them to an interface. Because we may have multiple method lists, it might become necessary to be explicit about which lists to use on a particular interface. For example, we may want to configure two different authentication lists for our Cisco Access Server. The first authentication list will be used for PPP connections, whereas the second list will be used to control telnet access to our Cisco Access Server. In addition, we want to use RADIUS for our PPP connections and TACACS+ for our exec sessions. Depending on the interfaces, the commands used to associate an interface to an AAA method list are different.

To associate an AAA method list to an asynchronous interface, we use the following command:

```
Router (config-if)#ppp authentication authentication-type method-list
```

authentication		
-type	**pap**	Use PAP authentication
	chap	Use CHAP authentication
	ms-chap	Use MS CHAP authentication
method-list	**default**	Use default list
	WORD	Use this AAA method list

To associate an AAA method list to a character-based session, like telnet, use the following command:

```
Router (config-line)#login authentication method-list
```

method-list	**default**	Use default list
	WORD	Name of AAA method list

AAA lists multiple authentication sources depending on how the organization is setup. This can be tremendously useful to large organizations that need to control multiple types of access that a Cisco Access Server can provide.

Note:
If you only need to use one method list, then you should use the keyword default. All interfaces will use the default method list unless otherwise specified.

Now that we have covered the three basic components of AAA, authentication, authorization, and accounting, we will take a look at how to configure the Cisco Access Server to specify a specific security server.

Configuring RADIUS To specify the RADIUS server a Cisco Access Server uses requires only two steps. However, other attributes can be configured in order to provide a level of fault-tolerance within any environment. The two components that must be specified in order for RADIUS to be used by any Cisco router are:

- IP address of the server
- Shared key

One of the fundamental components to a radius server is the shared key. This shared key must be known by both ends in order for communication between the client and the server to take place. This is because the shared key is used to encrypt the communication between the two devices.

Even though RADIUS is an Internet standard, many vendors have implemented features that are missing from the RFC. By default, when executing the command to configure a Cisco router to use RADIUS, it uses the Internet standard. However, if your RADIUS server understands the Cisco specific RADIUS attributes and you want to take advantage of them, you can use the keyword *non-standard* when specifying the IP address of the RADIUS server.

To specify the address of the RADIUS server, use the following command:

```
Router (config)#radius-server host radius-ip-address option
```

radius-ip-address	***x.x.x.x***	IP address of the radius server
option	**non-standard**	Use Cisco's extended RADIUS attributes

To specify the shared key used between client and server communication, use the following command:

```
Router (config)#radius-server key shared-key
```

shared-key	*WORD*	The shared key used to encrypt communication

It is possible to use multiple RADIUS servers in order to provide a level of fault tolerance. When using multiple RADIUS servers, you should take care to make sure that each RADIUS server's username database stays in-sync. The easiest way to accomplish this is through the use of network operating systems that share usernames as a natural part of their operation. For example, Novell's NDS and Microsoft's NT Domains have automatic replication schemes for their username database in case one server fails.

Currently, many products can turn a UNIX server, NetWare server, or Windows NT server into a RADIUS server. When evaluating these products, it is important to keep in mind how the RADIUS server stores the user's password. For example, because NetWare stores users' passwords using an encrypted hash function, it is more secure. Unfortunately, this security comes at a price: convenience. Now let us take a look at CHAP authentication. When utilizing CHAP authentication, a challenge is sent from the server to the client. This challenge is used by the client to create a hashed response, which is sent back to the server. Now, because the NetWare RADIUS server also stores hashes of the password, which cannot be reversed, and because they do not use the same hash function, they can not be compared. Thus, it is impossible for a NetWare RADIUS server to use CHAP authentication without the use of a second password, which must be stored in plain text so that the hash value can be calculated during authentication.

Note:

Within the Internet community, some confusion has arisen with the port numbers used for RADIUS. Early deployments of RADIUS used 1645; however, this conflicts with the "datametrics" service. The official port for RADIUS is 1812. Nevertheless, if you are not using the "datametrics" service, you can probably use 1645.

Figure 4-24 shows us an example configuration file that utilizes two RADIUS servers.

It shows that we are utilizing the Cisco specific RADIUS attributes through the use of the keyword *non-standard.*

Figure 4-24

Configuration file with radius server attributes defined

```
!
aaa new-model
aaa authentication ppp Dial-In-AAA radius local
aaa authorization network Dial-In-AAA radius
!
interface async 1
 ppp authentication pap Dial-In-AAA
!
radius-server host 192.168.181.106 non-standard
radius-server host 192.168.181.107 non-standard
radius-server key mysharedkey
                    !
```

Configuring TACACS+ Specifying the use of a TACACS+ server is almost identical to specifying a RADIUS server. The two components that must be specified in order for TACACS+ to be used by any Cisco router are:

- IP address of the server
- Shared key

Like a RADIUS server, both the client and the server need to know the shared key before proper communication can exist between the two devices.

To specify the address of the TACACS+ server, use the following command:

```
Router (config)#tacacs-server host tacacs-ip-address option
```

| ***tacacs-ip-address*** | ***x.x.x.x*** | IP address of the radius server |

To specify the shared key used between client and server communication, use the following command:

```
Router (config)#tacacs-server key shared-key
```

| ***shared-key*** | ***WORD*** | The shared key used to encrypt communication |

Figure 4-25 shows us an example configuration file that could be useful within large organizations trying to control who has access to what resources.

Figure 4-25

Configuration file
with radius
server attributes
defined

```
!
aaa new-model
aaa authentication login IT-Dept tacacs+ local
aaa authorization exec IT-Dept tacacs+ local
!
tacacs-server host 192.168.181.16
tacacs-server host 192.168.181.17
tacacs-server key mysharedkey
!
line vty 0 4
 login authentication IT-Dept
                              !
```

Figure 4-25 shows that we are using two different TACACS+ servers.
They are providing authentication and authorization to the vty sessions
on the Cisco Access Server.

One of the potential problems when setting up a AAA server to control
login access to the router is that if the AAA server is down, the Cisco
router cannot authenticate you, thus locking you out of the Cisco router
until the AAA server comes back online. To prevent getting locked out of
login access, you can use the keyword enable when specifying authentication. This allows you to use the *enable* password to gain access to the Cisco
router. In Figure 4-26, authentication has been set up to try RADIUS first
and then use the enable password.

Figure 4-26

Enabling a
backdoor when
using AAA for
logins and the
AAA server is
down

```
Router(config)#aaa authentication login default local enable
Router(config)#end
Router#telnet 192.168.1.1

User Access Verification

Username: zyx
Password: xyz

Password: abc

              Router>
```

One of the interesting points to notice is that when first attempting to authenticate, the Cisco router responds with a username and password. This is in response to the keyword local in the configuration statement in Figure 5-26. However, if that authentication fails, we are only asked for a password. This is a function of the keyword "enable" in Figure 4-25.

4.5 Chapter Summary

In this chapter, we learned about the various security protocols that are used to secure data from an attacker. Understanding the fundamental nature of each of these protocols will allow you to better choose the appropriate protocol for your VPN.

This is the last chapter in the VPN primer section, the following chapters will focus on particular VPN protocols and their implementation. In the next chapter, we will look at how to take a standard GRE tunnel and turn it into a pseudo VPN using Cisco Encryption Technology.

CHAPTER 5

GRE and CET

Up until now, we have looked at the various technologies that make up a *Virtual Private Network* (VPN), such as encryption, authentication, dialup, and so on. In the next five chapters, we look at how to implement VPNs using Cisco equipment. In this chapter we will also discuss setting up a pseudo-VPN compulsory tunnel using *Generic Routing Encapsulation* (GRE) tunnels and *Cisco Encryption Technology* (CET) encryption. Although these technologies are not generally accepted VPN technologies, they do hold to the definition outlined in the first chapter. One of the other reasons for covering GRE tunnels is that they form the basis of many other VPN protocols.

5.1 Objectives to be Covered in This Chapter

- An overview of GRE tunnels
- Implementing GRE Tunnels
- An overview of CET encryption
- Implementing CET

Unlike many other protocols, VPNs aren't strictly a router-only technology. This is one of the aspects that makes VPNs so flexible. However, in this chapter, the technology we are using is for routers only, and although CET is a Cisco-specific technology, GRE tunnels are not a Cisco proprietary technology.

A quick review of Chapter 1, "Introduction to Implementing Cisco VPNs," shows us that the two key components of a VPN are the virtual aspect and the private aspect (we assume the reader does not need a definition of network). In this chapter, a GRE tunnel provides the virtual component, while CET encryption provides the private component.

5.2 Overview of GRE Tunnels

Tunnels generally refer to the practice of encapsulating a message from one protocol inside another. This enables two protocols to communicate even though the network in between does not support them, as shown in Figure 5-1.

In Figure 5-1, we can see that the protocol being used inside the IP packet is *Internetwork Packet Exchange* (IPX). In this model, a Cisco router at each site encapsulates protocol-specific packets inside an IP header. This paradigm enables the transport of any network layer protocol over an IP network.

Figure 5-1

GRE tunnel encapsulating one protocol inside another

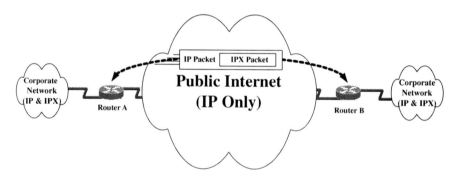

5.2.1 GRE Frame Format

In addition to encapsulating a different network layer protocol, such as AppleTalk, or IPX inside a GRE packet, it is also possible to insert an IP packet inside the GRE packet, as shown in Figure 5-2. This can be useful for connecting discontiguous networks. Additionally, GRE also has the capability to sequence the packets.

Figure 5-2

GRE tunnel encapsulating an IP packet inside an IP packet

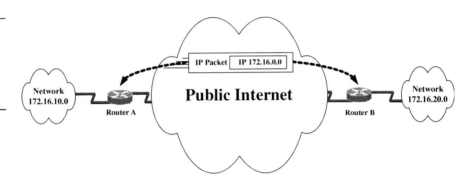

One of the downsides to using GRE packets is performance. It is generally faster to route protocols natively than to use tunnels. This is because of the additional encapsulation headers that must be built before sending the packet to the network. On a router with significant CPU utilization, this may become an issue depending upon the type of router, the speed of the link, and whatever other processes your router might be doing.

When using tunnels, we must be very careful not to introduce the inherent problems of a particular protocol over the network we are using. For example, most large organizations implement an IP-only backbone in an effort to encourage the departments to use applications that use native IP. This is because the native characteristics of protocols such as IPX and AppleTalk do not scale well and can be quite bandwidth-intensive if not implemented with care. If VPNs are set up to transport IPX inside IP packets, it can defeat the purpose of having an IP-only backbone. This is because we still need *Routing Information Protocols* (RIPs) and *Service Access Points* (SAPs) to flow across the backbone every 60 seconds; the only difference is that they are encapsulated by an IP header (which makes them even larger).

A GRE tunnel uses IP port 47 and is composed of three distinct components:

- **Delivery header:** This is the transport used to get the packet from one network to another. Generally, the delivery header is a standard IP header.

- **GRE header:** This component carries information regarding the payload packet, such as whether the packet is sequenced, encrypted, and so on.

- **Payload packet:** This is the passenger protocol for the GRE packet. The passenger protocol can be any protocol such as AppleTalk, DECnet, *Xerox Network Systems* (XNS), Vines, *Connectionless Network Protocol* (CLNP), IPX, Apollo, or even IP.

As shown in Figure 5-3, a GRE header is just a shim between the destination address and the original packet.

The fields that make up a GRE header are as follows:

- **C**—*Checksum Present (bit 0):* If the Checksum Present bit is set to 1, then the Checksum field is present and should be used accordingly.

- **R**—*Routing Present (bit 1):* If the Routing Present bit is set to 1, it indicates that the Offset and Routing fields are present and should be used accordingly.

- **K**—*Key Present (bit 2):* If the Key Present bit is set to 1, it indicates that the Key field is present in the GRE header.

Figure 5-3

GRE packet format

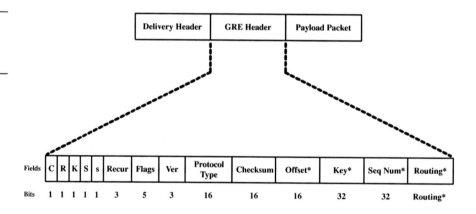

- **S**—*Sequence Number Present (bit 3)*: If the Sequence Number Present bit is set to 1, it indicates that the sequence number field is present and should be used to sequence the packets.

- **s**—*Strict Source Route (bit 4)*: If the Strict Source Route bit is not generally used and is recommended that this bit be set to 1 if all of the routing information consists of strict source routes.

- **Recur**—*Recursion Control (bits 5-7)*: This field contains a three-bit unsigned integer that contains the number of permissible additional encapsulations. This field is reserved for future use and should be set to Flags. *Flags (bits 8-12)* is reserved for future use and should be set to 0.

- **Ver**—*(bits 13-15)*: The Version Number field is used to indicate the version of the GRE packet. Currently, all packets must be set to 0.

- **Protocol Type** *(bits 16-31)*: This mandatory field is used to describe the contents of the payload packet. It is recommended by RFC 1701 that future protocol types be taken from DIX Ethernet encoding. This is to ease the administration of creating appropriate types. However, for historical reasons, a number of other values have been used for some protocols and can be found in Table 5-1.

- **Checksum** *(16 bits)*: This field contains the one's complement checksum of the GRE header and the payload packet. This field is only present if the Routing Present or the Checksum Present bit are set to 1. In addition, it only contains valid data if the Checksum Present bit is set to 1.

- **Offset** *(16 bits)*: This field indicates the octet offset from the start of the Routing field to the first octet of the active source route entry to be examined. This optional field contains valid information only if the Routing Present bit is set to 1.

- **Key** *(32 bits)*: The Key field contains the four-octet number inserted by the encapsulator. If the *Key Present* bit is set to 1, the receiver can authenticate the source of the packet.

- **Sequence** *(32 bits)*: This field is present only if the *Sequence Number Present* bit is set to 1. The receiving device can use this field to reconstruct the data stream in the proper sequence.

- **Routing** *(variable)*: This field contains data that may be used to route a packet, such as source route bridging. It is only present when the Strict Source Route bit is set to 1. It is not generally used.

Note:

You should make note that the Offset, Key, Sequence Number, and Routing fields are all optional and their presence in the GRE header is determined by the first five bits of the GRE header. In addition, most of these optional fields are defined by informational RFC 1701, but not by informational RFC 1702 or proposed standard RFC 2784.

The mandatory Protocol Type field carries in it a value, as shown in Table 5-1, enables us to define the type of packet that is in the payload of the GRE packet. With the capability to describe various protocols within a GRE packet, our tunnel can be multiprotocol-aware.

Table 5-1

List of current protocol types

Protocol Family	PTYPE
Reserved	0000
SNA	0004
OSI network layer	00FE
PUP	0200
XNS	0600
IP	0800
Chaos	0804
Frame Relay ARP	0808
Vines	0BAD
Vines Echo	0BAE
Vines Loopback	0BAF
DECnet (Phase IV)	6003
Transparent Ethernet Bridging	6558
RAW Frame Relay	6559
Apollo Domain	8019
Ethertalk (AppleTalk)	809B
Novell IPX	8137
Reserved	FFFF

For a more complete list of Ether Types values, go to `ftp://ftp.isi.edu/in-notes/iana/assignments/ethernet-numbers`.

5.3 Configuring GRE Tunnels

Now that we have a basic understanding of GRE tunnels and the format, let's examine how to configure them on a Cisco router. Attributes related to a GRE tunnel are similar to those attributes that might be applied to any physical circuit. A few differences can be noticed when setting the tunnel up, but beyond the initial setup, you will find it easier to work with them if you conceptually think of them as a physical interface (once they are working, of course). Four tasks must be completed before a GRE tunnel will operate correctly:

▧ Create tunnel.

▧ Configure GRE encapsulation.

▧ Configure the source and destination IP address of the tunnel.

▧ Configure the network attributes of the tunnel.

We will now take a look at how to configure each of these tasks. Each task is important for the successful operation of a GRE tunnel.

Note:

Because of the discrepancies between configuring a tunnel using IOS 11.3 and IOS 12.0, we will note when the command for each is different.

In order to help the reader categorize specific tasks associated with creating a VPN tunnel, we will categorize these tasks in terms of OSI model-related responsibilities. Realize that our attempt to categorize these tasks is not recognized by any sanctioned group, but they are here to help you understand where to look for problems when they occur and how to use your knowledge of physical circuits to troubleshoot the problems that can appear.

Using the first three layers of the OSI model (physical, data link, and network), we can classify each of these tasks, as shown in Table 5-2.

We will explain these categorizations in each of the subtopics that follow.

	OSI Model	Task
Table 5-2 Tasks for creating a tunnel and their relationship to the IOS model	Physical	Create tunnel
	Data link	Configure encapsulation
	Data link	Configure source and destination IP address of the tunnel
	Network	Configure the network attributes of the tunnel

5.3.1 Create a Tunnel Interface

In order for any communication to occur between two devices, a path must exist between them. Most of the cases that you are familiar with use a physical interface to define that path. However, in VPNs, we use a logical interface between two devices. It is important to understand the characteristics of a tunnel and how they operate so that when you start to have problems you can quickly identify problematic areas.

When configuring a tunnel interface on any router, we need to configure both GRE peers with a tunnel interface. A tunnel interface is required in order to run any kind of tunnel encapsulations (GRE, IPIP, NOS, Cayman) and define network layer addressing. Creating a tunnel interface is almost identical to creating a loopback interface, as shown in this command:

```
Router(config)#interface tunnel tunnel-number
```

tunnel-number 0-2147483647   Unique number to identify the tunnel

Keep in mind that the tunnel number specified in this command is only locally significant. In addition, you should keep in mind that unlike a loopback interface, which goes into an UP/UP state when created, a tunnel interface goes into an UP/DOWN state when created. It won't go into an UP/UP state until after we configure the destination and source of the tunnel, which we will discuss a little later.

Now that we have defined a pseudo-physical interface for our GRE tunnel, we need to look at how to configure the pseudo-data link layer attributes of our GRE tunnel.

5.3.2 Configure GRE Encapsulation for a Tunnel (Tunnel Mode)

When two devices communicate using a physical circuit (T1, Ethernet, or token-ring), both devices must use the same type of encapsulation (packet format). Otherwise, the receiving device will look at an incoming packet differently than the way it was intended, and communication between the two devices will not happen. At first glance, one of the confusing aspects about GRE tunnels on a Cisco router is that the encapsulation on a tunnel interface is referred to as TUNNEL encapsulation. But if you remember that within TUNNEL encapsulation several different modes are available, depending upon your IOS version, it really isn't difficult at all.

Tunnels can be used for many different things, not just for VPNs. Thus, several different modes are available to your TUNNEL encapsulation. Listed here are the tunnel modes available, which are dependent upon your IOS version:

- AURP: AURP TunnelTalk AppleTalk encapsulation
- CAYMAN: Cayman TunnelTalk AppleTalk encapsulation
- DVMRP: *Distance Vector Multicast Routing Protocol* (DVMRP) multicast tunnel
- EON: EON-compatible CLNS tunnel
- GRE: Generic route encapsulation protocol
- IPIP: IP-over-IP encapsulation
- IPTALK: Apple IPTalk encapsulation
- NOS: IP over IP encapsulation (KA9Q/NOS-compatible)

Although multiple types of encapsulation modes can be used over a tunnel, anything other than GRE mode is beyond the scope of this book.

GRE tunnels can be defined in one of two ways: point-to-point or multipoint. Point-to-point GRE tunnels are the simplest form of tunnel to conceptualize, because they only describe a logical circuit between two devices. Multipoint GRE tunnels are a bit more difficult to describe and conceptualize. Looking at Figure 5-4, we can see what appears to be a series of point-to-point tunnels to create a multipoint VPN.

Multipoint GREs operate just like any *Non-Broadcast Multi-Access* (NBMA) network. When using a multipoint GRE tunnel, the links that are connecting our VPN peers use the same address space, just like

Figure 5-4

Multipoint VPN

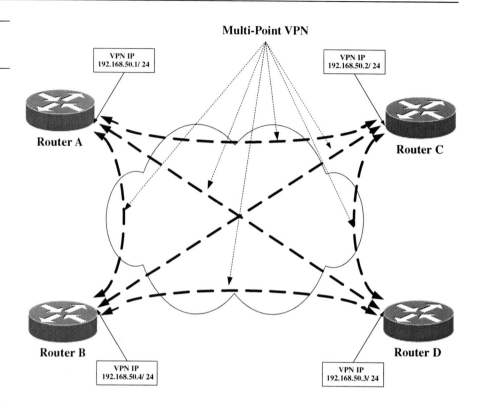

routers on an Ethernet or token-ring network would. For example, in Figure 5-4, we can see that the IP addresses are all within the same logical network. We will see how to configure these a little later in this chapter.

In order to configure the tunnel encapsulation, we must be in tunnel interface configuration mode for the tunnel interface. Although the default encapsulation for a Cisco tunnel is a point-to-point GRE, it is still important to know how to configure it on a tunnel interface in case it has been modified and you need to change it back.

```
Router(config-if)# tunnel mode gre tunnel-mode
```

| *tunnel-mode* | **ip** | Point-to-point tunnel |
| | **multipoint** | Point-to-point tunnel |

We will see a little bit later in this chapter how to verify the mode your tunnel is operating.

5.3.3 Configure the Source and Destination IP Address of the Tunnel

At this point, assuming you have performed the previous two steps, we have configured a tunnel that doesn't start from anywhere or go anywhere. We still need to tell our tunnel where its destination is. Remember that at this point we are only trying to set up a logical tunnel so that our devices can communicate as if a physical circuit existed between them. Once the tunnel has been set up, it does not mean we have secure communication, we still need some sort of encryption. The tunnel only provides the virtual aspect of the VPN.

You should carefully consider the IP address that will be used for the source and the destination of the tunnel. It is recommended that you use the loopback address for the destination of the tunnel. If you have two serial interfaces and you select the IP address of one of the serial interfaces, and if that *wide area network* (WAN) link went down, then your GRE source can't send tunneled packets to the tunnel destination because the IP address is down. However, a loopback address never goes down, unless it is administratively shut down.

Unfortunately, not all networks were designed with loopback addresses. In this case, if a router has more than one serial link, you should select a LAN interface. This is because LAN interfaces are generally more stable than WAN interfaces. WAN circuits frequently take minor hits that force a circuit down, thus; your tunnel becomes unreachable even though a path exists to that router. If, however, you only have a single serial link, then use the IP address of the serial link, because if the WAN circuit goes down, then so does your ability to get to that LAN.

So, you may be asking yourself, does it matter which IP address I use on a router when configuring the source and destination on a point-to-point tunnel? The answer is yes, it does. The source IP address of one tunnel partner must be the destination address of the other tunnel partner. When a Cisco router receives a tunneled packet, it looks at the destination of the packet and then matches it to a tunnel whose source IP address is the same. If the packet's destination does not match any tunnel's current source address, then the packet is discarded. This can be quite confusing when you can see the tunnel interface is receiving the incoming packets, but the other side of the tunnel is discarding them because of an incorrect configuration.

In the previous section, you learned that you could configure your tunnel to operate as a point-to-point link or as a multipoint link. Although this isn't important when defining the source of the tunnel, it is important when defining the destination, as we will see.

5.3.3.1 Configure Source IP Address

At this point in time, our tunnel is still in the UP/DOWN status. In order for our tunnel interface to go into the UP/UP status, we need to configure the source and destination of the tunnel. To configure the source of the tunnel, we can use the following command:

```
Router(config-if)# tunnel source source-ip
```

source-ip	**interface**	Use the IP address on this interface as the source for the tunnel.
	x.x.x.x	Use this IP address as the source for this tunnel.

If you configure the tunnel source as having an address that does not exist on the router, IOS does not complain. It just assumes that you will configure the IP address somewhere on the router at a later date. However, IOS will not let you assign an interface that doesn't exist as the source of the tunnel.

5.3.3.2 Configure Destination IP Address for Point-to-Point Tunnels

We must now configure the destination of our GRE peer. The operating mode of the tunnel, point-to-point versus multipoint, determines how we configure our tunnel interface to communicate with its VPN peers. To configure the destination for a standard point-to-point configuration, use the following command:

```
Router(config-if)# tunnel destination destination-ip
```

destination-ip	**interface**	Use the IP address on this interface as the destination for the tunnel.
	x.x.x.x	Use this IP address as the destination for this tunnel.

As we can see, this command is similar to identifying the source of a GRE tunnel. One of the interesting things about identifying the destination is that as long as it (the destination IP address) is pingable and the tunnel source address has been configured, the tunnel will go into an UP/UP state. At first, you might think that you've successfully configured the tunnel, and as long as the other end is configured, you may have, but do not use this as a tool for verifying the validity of your tunnel because one end of your GRE tunnel may be in an UP/UP status while the other is in an UP/DOWN status.

5.3.3.3 Configure Destination IP Address for Multipoint Tunnels (NHRP)

Similar to Frame Relay, GRE tunnels do not inherently support broadcast traffic. To overcome this limitation for a multipoint tunnel, we need to configure the *Next Hop Resolution Protocol* (NHRP). NHRP is a method used by routers and hosts to dynamically discover the address of other devices connected to a *Non-Broadcast Multi-Access Network* (NBMA). Currently, NHRP works over *Asynchronous Transfer Mode* (ATM), Ethernet, *Switched Multimegabit Data Service* (SMDS), and multipoint tunnel networks.

Note:

Although an overview of NHRP and how to implement it is within the scope of this book, an in-depth discussion of where NHRP came from and how it is used in other technologies is beyond this book's scope.

Using an ARP-like solution, NHRP alleviates the problems created with NBMA networks. Let's look at the purpose of the *Address Resolution Protocol* (ARP). ARP enables us to bridge the gap between layer 2 and layer 3 addresses. For example, a router has just received an IP packet (layer 3) for a device located on an Ethernet segment, but it doesn't know the *Media Access Control* (MAC) address (layer 2). ARP allows any device to learn the MAC address for a layer 3 address. Once ARP has learned this MAC address, it can finish building the frame to send to the device.

NHRP works in a similar fashion, except that instead of returning a layer 2 address, NHRP returns a routable layer 3 address. This enables the router to forward the GRE packet to the correct destination. Just like ARP, NHRP builds a NHRP cache so that it does not have to re-request a routable layer 3 address, as long as our NHRP cache table entry has not expired. Tables 5-3 and 5-4 show us the difference between an NHRP table (refer to Table 5-1) and an ARP table (refer to Table 5-2).

Table 5-3	Local VPN IP Address	NBMA Mapping	Real IP Address
Example of an NHRP table	192.168.10.2	→	20.20.20.1
	192.168.10.3	→	30.30.30.1
	192.168.10.4	→	40.40.40.1

Table 5-4	Local IP Address	ARP Mapping	MAC Address
Example of an ARP table	192.168.10.2	→	0000.0c4a.4a56
	192.168.10.3	→	0000.0c75.f9da
	192.168.10.4	→	00e0.1e3e.8476

The concepts between ARP and NHRP are very similar; just remember that they operate at different levels of the OSI model.

The core of any NHRP solution is the *Next Hop Servers* (NHSs). Every NHRP speaker is a NHS. Within a Multipoint GRE tunnel, all the NHSs cooperatively resolve the GRE next hop addresses. For example, Figure 5-5 shows a multipoint tunnel GRE in which NHRP has been deployed. Each of the IP addresses in the multi-access GRE tunnel are in the 192.168.10.0 range and the NHS servers have been identified in a circular approach, meaning that Router A's NHS is Router B, Router B's NHS is Router C, Router C's NHS is Router D, and Router D's NHS is Router A.

In this configuration, when Router A needs to send a packet to 192.168.10.4 (Router D) and it doesn't know its real IP address, it sends a NHRP request packet to Router B for 192168.10.4 (NHS Query—Hop 1). Router B, not knowing the address, forwards the request packet to its NHS, Router C (NHS query—Hop 2). Router C doesn't know the address either and so it forwards the packet to its NHS, Router D (NHS query—Hop 3). Router D sees the query and responds back to Router C with its real IP address (40.40.40.1) (NHS reply—Hop 1). Router C doesn't just forward the reply back, but it caches the real IP address of 192.168.10.4 in its NHRP cache table before forwarding the packet back to Router B. This keeps Router C from having to do an NHRP request if it needs to send data to that address in the future. Each router in the path does the same the thing until it the packet finally reaches Router A.

Figure 5-5

NHRP
performing an
NBMA resolution

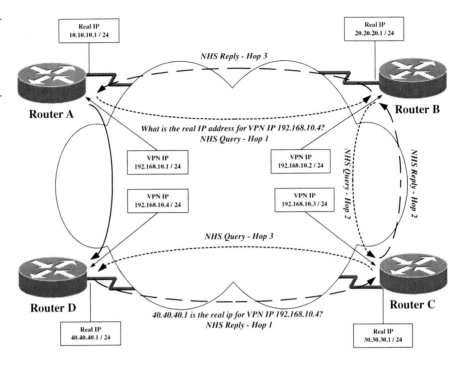

Configuring NHRP in a multipoint tunnel requires the configuration of four different features:

- Configure tunnel for multipoint
- Enable NHRP on an interface
- Configure a NHS
- Configure a single NHS VPN IP to real IP address mapping

Note:
Cisco's implementation of NHRP currently only supports IPv4.

All the preceding tasks are predicated on the fact that you have already configured a network layer address scheme to your tunnel interfaces. The network layer address configured on the tunnel interfaces must logically reside in the same network address space; otherwise, your NHRP will not function correctly. For example, in Figure 5-5, you should notice that all of the VPN addresses in your multipoint tunnel belong to the 192.168.10.0/24 network, while all of the real IP addresses do not belong to the same IP network.

Configure Tunnel for Multipoint Two tasks must be completed in order for a tunnel interface to be ready for multipoint operations. First, we must configure the encapsulation mode of the tunnel interface, as shown with the following command:

```
Router(config-if)# tunnel mode gre multipoint
```

The next step is to identify the tunnel key. Multipoint tunnels require the use of a tunnel key. In point-to-point tunnels, we could easily identify the source and the destination, but with a multipoint tunnel, you don't always know who your GRE partners are. The use of a tunnel key identifies which GRE tunnel the traffic belongs to. The command to identify the tunnel key is as follows:

```
Router(config-if)# tunnel key key-number
```

key-number   0-4294967295   Configure a tunnel identification key.

I recommend that the tunnel key corresponds to the NHRP network identifier, which is covered later.

Enable NHRP on an Interface Enabling NHRP on an interface is a simple process. Only one variable needs to be predetermined before enabling NHRP, the network-id. The network-id should be the same value for all of the routers participating in the multipoint tunnel. Once again, this command must be configured in interface configuration mode within the tunnel interface, as shown here:

```
Router(config-if)# ip nhrp network-id network-number
```

network-number   0-4294967295   Configure a network identifier for the multipoint tunnel.

Remember it is recommended that this value should be the same value as the tunnel key, as previously mentioned.

Statically Configure an NHS   In order for a router to participate in NHRP, it must be configured with at least one NHS server. The idea here is relatively simple; we are looking for a server that can resolve our VPN addresses when we don't know their real value. The command used to do this is as follows:

```
Router(config-if)# ip nhrp nhs VPN-ip-address
```

VPN-ip-address   *x.x.x.x*   This is the VPN IP address of the NHS.

You can have multiple NHS servers configured within a router, but you must have at least one.

Note:

Cisco's documentation references to NBMA addresses are what we are referring to as the VPN IP address. In addition, Cisco's use of the term IP address equates to the term we use, real IP address.

Configure an NHRP Table with Real IP-to-VPN IP Address Mapping

Although a router participating in an NHRP network should dynamically learn the VPN IP address mapping to real IP addresses through the NHS server, we can manually configure an NBMA address mapping using the following command:

```
Router(config-if)# ip nhrp map real-ip-address VPN-ip-address
```

Real-ip-address	*x.x.x.x*	This is the real IP address of the static mapping.
VPN-ip-address	*x.x.x.x*	This is the VPN address that is being statically mapped.

Although this command might not seem significant at first, it is very important. Assuming we have done all of the commands prior to this command, we have enabled NHRP and we even know the VPN IP address of our NHS. However, we can't learn any real IP addresses through our NHS server because we don't know how to get to our NHS server. Thus, every router participating in a NHRP network must have at least one statically configured NHRP mapping of their NHS server.

Note:

When implementing NHRP, it is important that you run the same major Internetworking Operating System (IOS) version on all your VPN peers. This is because as technology moves on, Cisco may implement a different draft of NHRP within their IOS. Cisco IOS releases prior to 12.x implemented NHRP draft version 4, while Cisco IOS Release 12.x and later implemented NHRP draft version 11. Unfortunately, these different NHRP versions are not compatible. Thus, all your VPN peers must all be running 11.0 or 12.0, but not a mix. It is highly recommended that you run the exact same IOS version on all the routers that support NHRP so that you can avoid this pitfall.

5.3.4 Verifying a GRE Tunnel

Several things can be verified within a tunnel to make sure it is configured as you desire. These commands are very important when trying to debug problems that are occurring within your tunnels.

To verify which type of encapsulation is being used on a tunnel interface, we can use the *show interface* command. Figure 5-6 shows an example of what to look for in the show interface output.

Several interesting things need to be pointed out here. First, notice that on line 3 the hardware is *Tunnel* and on line 7 the encapsulation is *TUNNEL*. Also remember that because the status of the tunnel is UP/UP in line 2, this does not mean that it is successfully exchanging packets with the remote tunnel. In line 8, we can also see the source of the tunnel (Ethernet 0) as well as the destination (192.168.30.2).

When troubleshooting a configuration, you need to keep in mind that line 9 displays the mode the tunnel is operating in. In Table 5-5, we can see the various types of modes and their associated output within the show interface command.

Because of the simplicity of point-to-point tunnels, very little can go wrong with them. Multipoint tunnels, on the other hand, have many different things that can go wrong, especially when you start to consider using a routing protocol through your multipoint tunnel. Special care must be taken in order to properly configure a multipoint tunnel. When things start to go wrong, the first place to look for any problems is in the

Figure 5-6

Output from the *show interface tunnel* command

```
1   Router#show interface tunnel1
2   Tunnel1 is up, line protocol is up
3   Hardware is Tunnel
4   Interface is unnumbered.  Using address of Loopback1 (10.10.0.1)
5   MTU 1514 bytes, BW 9 Kbit, DLY 500000 usec,
6      reliability 255/255, txload 1/255, rxload 1/255
7   Encapsulation TUNNEL, loopback not set, keepalive set (10 sec)
8   Tunnel source 192.168.10.1 (Ethernet0), destination 192.168.30.2
9   Tunnel protocol/transport GRE/IP, key disabled, sequencing
    disabled
10  Checksumming of packets disabled,  fast tunneling enabled
11  Last input never, output 00:00:00, output hang never
12  Last clearing of "show interface" counters never
13  Queueing strategy: fifo
14  Output queue 0/0, 7345 drops; input queue 0/75, 0 drops
15    5 minute input rate 0 bits/sec, 0 packets/sec
16    5 minute output rate 0 bits/sec, 0 packets/sec
17    0 packets input, 0 bytes, 0 no buffer
18    Received 0 broadcasts, 0 runts, 0 giants, 0 throttles
19    0 input errors, 0 CRC, 0 frame, 0 overrun, 0 ignored, 0 abort
20    7426 packets output, 6358 bytes, 0 underruns
21    0 output errors, 0 collisions, 0 interface resets
22    0 output buffer failures, 0 output buffers swapped out
```

Table 5-5

Values for the Tunnel protocol/ transport field within the *show interface output* command

Output from show interface command	Tunnel Mode
GRE/IP	Point-to-Point GRE tunnel
multi-GRE/IP	Multipoint GRE tunnel
AURP	AURP TunnelTalk AppleTalk encapsulation
Cayman/UDP	Cayman TunnelTalk AppleTalk encapsulation
EON	EON compatible CLNS tunnel
IP/IP	IP over IP encapsulation
IP/IP (DVMRP)	DVMRP multicast tunnel
IP/IP (NOS)	IP over IP encapsulation (KA9Q/NOS compatible)
IPTalk	Apple IPTalk encapsulation

NHRP mapping table. This can be accomplished using the *show ip nhrp* command, as shown in Figure 5-7.

In this command, we can see the various NHRP mappings and how long ago they were created. In addition, we can see how a mapping was

Figure 5-7

NHRP mapping table

```
Router#show ip nhrp
200.200.0.2/32 , Tunnel100 created 00:03:14 expire 01:56:45
  Type: static Flags: authoritative used
  NBMA address: 192.168.120.1
200.200.0.3/32 , Tunnel100 created 00:00:04 expire 01:59:55
  Type: dynamic Flags: used
  NBMA address: 192.168.130.1
200.200.0.4/32 , Tunnel100 created 00:00:21 expire 01:59:38
  Type: dynamic Flags:
  NBMA address: 192.168.140.1
```

learned through the Type field. A value of *static* means that the address was manually configured using the *ip nhrp map* command, while a value of *dynamic* means that it was learned through the NHRP process. You must have at least one static NHRP address in this table; otherwise, your router can't discover the IP address of any other router.

To verify that NHRP traffic is being sent and received, we can use the command show ip nhrp traffic, as shown in Figure 5-8.

This command enables us to see that we are successfully receiving and sending NHRP traffic. If your values are zero here, check your NHRP mapping table and make sure you have a static mapping.

5.3.5 Troubleshooting a GRE Tunnel

Troubleshooting a GRE tunnel can be a difficult process if you don't know how a tunnel interface will behave. Although currently no strong troubleshooting tools for GRE tunnels are available, the following is a list of steps for making sure they are exchanging data:

- Check the status of both tunnel interfaces.
- Verify the source and destination of each tunnel.
- Verify the encapsulation is set correctly.
- Clear counters and look for matching IN/OUT packet counts.

By using this simple process, in the order as outlined here, you will solve all but the most difficult GRE tunnel problems.

5.3.5.1 Check the Status of Both Tunnel Interfaces

The status of a tunnel interface is dependent upon two things: the source IP address and the destination IP address. If these two items exist, then the tunnel goes into an UP/UP state.

Figure 5-8

Displaying NHRP traffic

```
RouterD#show ip nhrp traffic
Tunnel100
  request packets sent: 7
  request packets received: 5
  reply packets sent: 5
  reply packets received: 7
  register packets sent: 17
  register packets received: 15
  purge packets sent: 0
  purge packets received: 0
  error packets sent: 0
  error packets received: 0
```

A source IP address must be listed in the tunnel interface configuration. The problem here is that any IP address makes our tunnel interface active. This means we could accidentally use an incorrect source IP address and our packets would never be identified correctly at the other end. Thus, the other end would just drop the packets, thinking they were from an unidentified tunnel.

The destination IP address needs to be configured but does not need to be pingable. As long as a route is available in the routing table to that destination, the interface will go active. This means we could be using an incorrect node in our IP address and the tunnel interface will still go into an UP/UP state.

Note:

Remember that a tunnel interface could be misconfigured and still go into an UP/UP state.

5.3.5.2 Verify the Source and Destination of Each Tunnel

In order for two tunnel interfaces to exchange data, a Cisco router must be able to identify which GRE packets belong to which tunnel interface. This is accomplished through the use of the source and destination of the packet. Even if the destination of the IP address exists within the router, unless the destination of the IP address matches the source IP address of a tunnel interface, the packet will get discarded. To understand this better, let's look at the situation in which we have two routers each with a tunnel interface in Figure 5-9.

Figure 5-9

Troubleshooting a
GRE tunnel

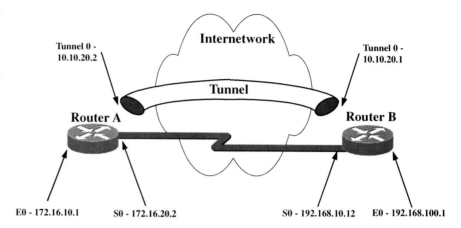

If Router A has a tunnel destination of IP address 192.168.100.1, but
Router B shows a tunnel source IP address of 192.168.10.12, Router B will
dump the packets intended for the tunnel interface. This is because the
destination IP address of the GRE packet does not match the source ip
address of any tunnel interfaces.

Something else to keep in mind is that each tunnel interface operates
independently of the other tunnel interface. Thus, it very easy to create a
situation in which packets sent by Router A are acknowledged by Router
B, but the packets sent by Router B are dropped because Router B has set
the tunnel destination to the Ethernet interface instead of the serial
interface.

5.3.5.3 Verify the Encapsulation Is Set Correctly

This step is relatively straightforward. If either tunnel interface is not
using the same encapsulation, the tunnel will discard the packets, even
though the packets made it to the tunnel interface. Unlike a serial link in
which an incorrect encapsulation brings the serial interface into an
UP/DOWN state, an incorrect matching of encapsulation just causes the
packets to get discarded. This shouldn't present a problem unless you are
attempting to use another type of encapsulation to solve a specific problem.

5.3.5.4 Verify the Tunnel Is Working

If you have verified the three previous steps, you should be able to clear
the counters on a tunnel interface using the *clear counters* command and

see the outgoing packets on one interface match the incoming packets on another interface.

One of the quickest ways to verify that a tunnel is working is to assign IP addresses that aren't in the routing table to each tunnel interface. If your tunnel interface is working correctly, you should be able to ping your psuedo-directly-connected neighbor's interface. For example, in Figure 5-9, if all is working correctly, we should be able to ping 10.10.20.1 from Router A, even if no route exists to that network, because 10.10.20.1 is directly connected to 10.10.20.2 through the tunnel interface, or at least that's the idea.

5.4 Overview of Cisco's CET

CET is a proprietary encryption method introduced in Cisco IOS Release 11.2. CET provides a method of encrypting data that travels across unprotected networks. Although many similarities exist between CET and IPSec, which we will explore in the next chapter, CET is a more mature encryption methodology as compared to IPSec. However, CET can only work with other Cisco devices, while IPSec provides multi-vendor interoperability.

By utilizing a compulsory tunnel paradigm, the burden of encrypting the data is the responsibility of the Cisco router, as shown in Figure 5-10.

Figure 5-10

CET compulsory tunnel

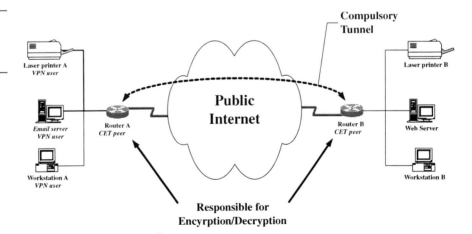

5.4.1 Protocols Used in CET

CET relies on three protocols to successfully encrypt data streams: the *Digital Signature Standard* (DSS), the *Diffie-Hellman* (DH) public key algorithm, and the *Data Encryption Standard* (DES). In the last chapter, we covered the purpose of each of those technologies, but for a quick review we will cover their responsibilities in providing a secure connection:

- DSS is an authentication protocol and is used to authenticate peer routers.
- DH is a public key algorithm used to securely exchange key information over a public medium.
- DES is an algorithm used to encrypt the data.

In order for two routers to communicate securely using CET, an encrypted session must be established. Encrypted sessions can start the negotiation process when a router detects a packet is encrypted and an encrypted session doesn't already exist. In order to establish a session, two CET peers must exchange connection messages. The purpose of the exchange of messages is two-fold: authenticate each other and exchange keys.

Note:

Many similarities exist between CET and IPSec, which we will explore in the next chapter.

5.4.2 Procedure for Establishing Secure Communication Using CET

We will now take a look at how two CET peers create an encrypted tunnel. Configuring any encrypted tunnel is accomplished in four steps:

- Generate DSS public/private keys.
- Exchange DSS public keys.
- Enable the DES encryption algorithm.
- Define crypto maps and assign them to an interface.

These tasks must be performed on both CET peers in order to secure the data stream. Let's now take a closer look at the inner workings of each of these steps.

5.4.2.1 Generate DSS Public/Private Keys

In order to communicate securely, you must use a crypto engine. A crypto engine is a software service provided by a Cisco router. It is responsible for encrypting and decrypting the data stream. Crypto engines must be configured as an encrypting peer, at which point you can configure any interface governed by that crypto engine to perform encryption. Currently, three types of crypto engines are available:

- Cisco IOS crypto engine (software)
- *Versatile Interface Processor* (VIP2) crypto engine (hardware)
- *Encryption Service Adapter* (ESA) crypto engine (hardware)

The purpose of each crypto engine is the same, to encrypt and decrypt the data streams between VPN peers. The difference between the crypto engines is the mechanism used to perform those tasks. Let's take a quick look at each of those different engines:

- **Cisco IOS crypto engine**: The Cisco IOS crypto engine is available on every router whose IOS is capable of performing encryption. For most Cisco routers, the Cisco IOS crypto engine is the only crypto engine available. Its ability to encrypt packets is a direct product of how fast the processor is on the router. This means older 2500 series routers will not be able to encrypt/decrypt packets as fast as a Cisco 3600.

- **VIP2 crypto engine**: A second-generation VIP2 crypto engine governs the adjoining VIP2 port interfaces. The Cisco IOS crypto engine manages the rest of the interfaces on a Cisco router.

- **ESA crypto engine**: This crypto engine is available on Cisco 7000, 7200, and 7500 series routers. On Cisco 7200 routers, the ESA crypto engine governs all the router interfaces, while on a Cisco 7000 and 7500 series router, the ESA plugs directly into a VIP2 board and only governs the interfaces connected directly to the VIP2.

Not all hardware-based encryption crypto engines use VIP2 or ESA for support. A number of routers, such as the Cisco 1700, 2600, and 3600 series routers, support hardware-based encryption using the *Advanced*

Interface Module (AIM). When the AIM is present, it becomes the standard crypto engine for the Cisco router and not the Cisco IOS crypto engine. However, mechanisms are available to turn it off.

Note:

The configuration of these specialized crypto engines is beyond the scope of this book. See your Cisco documentation for more information. Because not every hardware-based crypto engine supports all the various interface/encapsulation combinations for encryption, it is important to review your Cisco documentation to make sure the interface/encapsulation combination you are planning on using supports encryption. In particular, x.25 and SMDS encapsulation is not always supported by the various hardware-based crypto engines.

5.4.2.2 Exchanging DSS Public Keys

Exchanging keys with a CET peer is a multi-step process that requires someone at each end of the router to configure each router. Looking at Figure 5-11, we can see the basic flow of events and the order in which they must occur.

The following is the generic process used to exchange DSS public keys with VPN peers. This process will be used later in this chapter when we explain the commands used to perform this process:

1. Router B enters passive mode.
2. Router A enters active mode and sends its public key to Router B.
3. The network engineer(s) must now verify that the serial number and fingerprint are the same on both routers.
4. If step 4 is successful, Router B accepts Router A's DSS key.
5. Router B sends its public key to Router A.
6. The network engineer must now verify that the serial number and fingerprint are the same on both routers.
7. If step 7 is successful, Router A accepts Router B's DSS key.

This is a fairly straightforward process. It is, however, critical to understand the importance of verifying that the serial number and fingerprint

Figure 5-11

Process of exchanging DSS keys between two Cisco routers

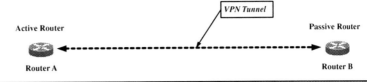

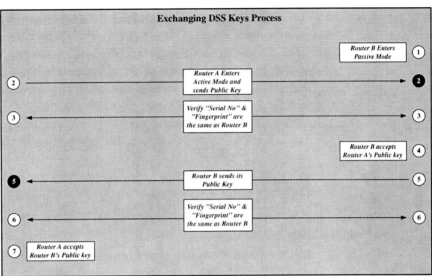

are the same on both routers. This helps to defeat the man-in-the-middle scenarios.

5.4.2.3 Enabling Encryption

As mentioned in Chapter 4, in order for two routers to communicate securely over a public medium, they must agree on the encryption method used to secure the data. Cisco routers have four different types of DES encryption algorithms available to encrypt the data:

- 40-bit DES with an eight-bit *cipher feedback* (CFB)
- 40-bit DES with an 64-bit CFB
- 56-bit DES with an eight-bit CFB
- 56-bit DES with an 64-bit CFB

In order for a Cisco router to use one of these encryption algorithms, it must be enabled globally. The encryption algorithm you choose should be based on several factors: CPU speed, speed of the WAN link, and hardware support for encryption (AIM, VPN module, and so on), and, last but not least, export laws. You should pay particular attention to the various export laws as it is a federal crime to export certain IOS images out of the country due to the laws that govern the encryption algorithms.

As discussed in Chapter 4, CFB is a cipher feedback. This is used to give the data an appearance of randomness to the data stream; otherwise, it might be possible to logically guess the data inside the stream by using techniques that enable you to examine the consistency of characters within the data stream compared to their frequency in the language used. The larger the cipher feedback, the more random the data appears when encrypted. So what is the cost of a more random encrypted data stream? Latency. The router must perform more calculations when using a 64-bit cipher feedback as opposed to an eight-bit cipher feedback.

Note:

When we refer to secure communications, we are talking about a two-way path, while a secure data stream only denotes an encrypted data stream in one direction.

5.4.2.4 Defining Crypto Maps and Assigning Them to an Interface

Crypto maps bring all the previous steps together and apply them to an interface, thus enabling secure communications. In order for secure communication to take place, we must configure a crypto map on each CET peer. This is accomplished through several different steps that must be performed on both routers:

- Create a crypto map.
- Specify the remote peer router.
- Define access-lists and assign them to a crypto map.
- Define encryption used within a crypto map.
- Apply the crypto map to the interface.

Creating a crypto map is a simple task and is analogous to a holding container that we will apply to a physical interface. The primary function of a crypto map is threefold: Identify the remote peer that you will be exchanging encrypted data with, identify the data stream that needs to be encrypted between the two peers, and select the type of encryption that will be used.

An additional function of a crypto map is to specify the encryption algorithms that will be used. Remember that in the previous step, enabling encryption, we only activated the encryption globally. In order to apply an encryption algorithm to a particular data stream, we specify the encryption algorithm, previously enabled globally, which will be used by the crypto map. Figure 5-12 shows us that encryption of a data stream is defined by the use of an access-list.

Figure 5-12

Using crypto maps to encrypt a data stream

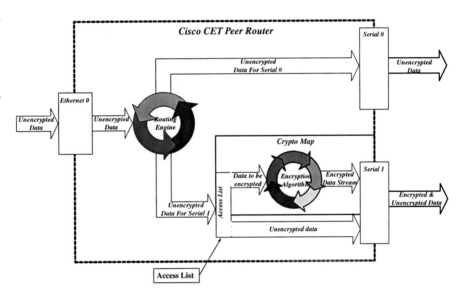

By using access-lists, a crypto map can tell your router which data streams to encrypt and which not to encrypt. In order to decrypt your data, the inverse of this access-list must be used by your VPN peer. By using extended access-lists, Cisco provides a high degree of granularity for encrypting the exact data stream you desire.

When starting to learn crypto maps, many people seem to be misled by the statement that only a single crypto map can be applied to a physical interface. Although this seems fairly straightforward, it isn't. If you don't understand this concept, you will not understand the power of a crypto map.

A crypto map is defined by the name of the crypto map. However, when creating a crypto map globally we specify a sequence number. By creating crypto maps using multiple unique sequence numbers, we are still configuring a single crypto map that will eventually get applied to a physical interface. These crypto maps with subdefinitions are useful when we have multiple data streams that we want to secure, as seen in Figure 5-13.

Figure 5-13

Crypto maps defining traffic to a different destination

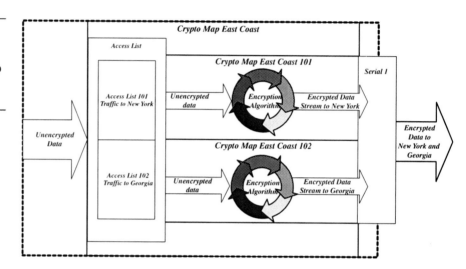

So, now you may be asking yourself, if an access-list can be used to define which traffic to encrypt and which data not to encrypt, what is the point of learning GRE tunnels? Learning about GRE tunnels is good for three reasons. First, many of the other VPN protocols that we will cover utilize a GRE tunnel in their infrastructure. Second, instead of applying an extended access-list to a crypto map and having to be careful about which data you encrypt and which you don't, you can select to encrypt all the data that traverses a GRE tunnel. This eases the configuration aspects of your VPN, especially if you aren't very good at calculating subnet masks. Third, a GRE tunnel has support for multiple protocols enabling you to pass IPX, DECnet, and AppleTalk traffic over an IP backbone. Couple this capability with encryption and you have support for more than just an IP VPN, but for a Multiprotocol VPN.

5.5 Configuring CET

In order to have secure communications between two routers, encryption must be configured at both ends. In this section, we will be describing the tasks necessary to configure encryption. One of the problems associated with writing a book on this topic is the dynamic nature of VPN technology.

Cisco's latest and greatest IOS 12.x, has been released relatively recently. However, it is recognized that 11.x code will be around for a very long time, and as the old adage goes, "if it ain't broke, don't fix it." Although some of the commands are the same between IOS versions 11.x and 12.x, enough variation exists to make it difficult to cover both commands within the same section. Therefore, in order to help the reader locate the information he or she is looking for, each IOS version has been broken into its own topic within this chapter. Although we will be covering the steps for both IOSs, we would not be surprised to find that a reader does not read both sections, as there will be a lot of overlap between the two different sections because not all of the commands have changed and the tasks that are being performed are identical. However, we will make sure to point out the differences in behavior and screen output between IOS 12.x and 11.x.

Note:

The IOS images that have been used in this chapter are specifically the Enterprise version of IOS 11.3(11a) and the Enterprise version of IOS 12.0(3). There may be slight variations of the commands within your IOS; however, they should for the most part, be very similar.

5.5.1 Configuring CET Using IOS 11.3

In this section, we will be covering the commands required to configure CET using IOS 11.3. The steps to perform these tasks have already been outlined from a previous section; therefore, we are going to focus on implementation-specific information within IOS 11.3.

Note:

This does not apply to IOS 11.3T. For IOS 11.3T, use the commands found in IOS 12.0.

5.5.1.1 Generate and Verify DSS Public/Private Keys

In order to encrypt the data, you must have a pair of public/private keys. The crypto engine that will be performing the encryption/decryption creates these keys. Therefore, when creating the public/private keys, you must specify the source of the crypto engine. To create a public/private key, we can use the following command:

```
Router(config)#crypto gen-signature-keys crypto-engine-name slot
```

crypto-engine-name	*WORD*	**required**	Name to identify the key crypto engine.
slot	*WORD*	**optional**	Slot to identify hardware encryption device.

When generating the public/private key pairs, the *slot* option is used to identify where in the Cisco router the hardware-based encryption crypto engine resides. This option is only available for the Cisco 7200, RSP7000, and 7500 series routers.

Note:

What about the Cisco 1700 series router? Cisco currently does not make a version of 11.3 IOS that supports the 1700 series router. If you are using a 1700 series router, you will need to go to the next section on configuring encryption for Cisco's 1700 series routers.

Figure 5-14 shows us an example of creating the public/private keys using IOS 11.3. One of the common misconceptions is that we generate a unique public/private key pair on a per-destination basis.

Figure 5-14

Generating DSS
public/private key
with IOS 11.3

```
RouterA(config)#crypto gen-signature-keys RouterA_IOS_crypto_engine
Generating DSS keys ....
  [OK]
```

When generating a public/private key pair, we need to generate a unique pair for each of the different crypto engines.

You should note that if you attempt to recreate the DSS public/private key pair after already having created them, you will have to re-exchange the keys; otherwise, your CET peer will not have the correct public key. Thus, you will receive the output seen in Figure 5-15 if you attempt to regenerate the keys.

Figure 5-15

Regenerating
DSS
public/private key
with IOS 11.3

```
Router_A(config)#crypto gen-signature-keys
RouterA_IOS_crypto_engine
% Generating new DSS keys will require re-exchanging
    public keys with peers who already have the public key
    named RouterB!
Generate new DSS keys? [yes/no]: y
Generating DSS keys ....
  [OK]
```

Once the public/private key pair has been created, we may, from time to time, verify the public key that we created. We can do this using the following command:

`Router(config)#show crypto mypubkey`

A little bit later in this chapter, you will see how to verify that a router's CET peer has the same public/private key pair. In Figure 5-16, we can see the use of this command to view the public key.

Figure 5-16

Displaying your
public key with
IOS 11.3

```
Router_A#show crypto mypubkey
crypto public-key RouterA_IOS_crypto_engine 02368817
  88BE7197 C0C55FB8 8E4A225E 17D941E8 2F5121FB 57507EAC C8E54F02
976B5938
  DB9DA5A4 14C1BE3E 9DE90D0F CEDD1495 F6895F5A 9532FA4B C2B202A3
DFEBD087
quit
```

Although the previous command shows us how to view the public key, how do we view the private key? There really is no way to view the private key. As a matter of fact, when saving your configuration using IOS 11.3 on a router that has created a public/private key pair, the private key is stored in a non-viewable area of NVRAM, as seen in Figure 5-17, A router's public key is viewable using the command found in Figure 5-16.

Figure 5-17

Saving memory DSS public/private key with IOS 11.3

```
Router_A#write memory
Building configuration...

Building private configuration...
[OK]
```

This is good from a security point of view. However, let's take the situation in which we've successfully built our public/private key pair. We then back up our configuration to our TFTP server. The only component that gets included in the viewable configuration file is your CET peer's public key, and neither your public nor private key are included. This is okay as long as we only restore the configuration file to the original router. If we try to copy the configuration file to a new router because of a router upgrade, the new router will not have a copy of its public or private key because it isn't stored in the viewable configuration file that was backed up, but on the non-viewable portion of the NVRAM. This means that we need to recreate our public/private key, which in turn means that we need to re-exchange keys with our VPN peer.

We've seen how to create a public/private key; we now need to see how to exchange public keys between VPN peers.

5.5.1.2 Exchanging DSS Public Keys

As previously discussed, seven steps are used to exchange DSS public/private key pairs. As we walk through configuring a Cisco router running IOS 11.3 to use CET, we will refer back to Figure 5-11, because unlike most configurations, only one command is entered on each router. A whole procedure must be followed in order to successfully exchange keys.

The first is to determine which router will be in active mode and which will go into passive mode. It makes no difference which router will be active and which router will be passive; it only defines the starting point for the exchange of public keys. In our example that follows, Router A will be the active router and Router B will be the passive router.

Step 1—Configure Router B (CET Peer) for Passive Mode To configure a router for passive mode, we can use the following command:

```
Router(config)#crypto key-exchange passive
```

Once we've entered this command, we will be asked to confirm that we want to wait for the connection. After we've confirmed that we do want to wait for a connection, the router starts waiting for a connection from the active router, as seen in Figure 5-18. If we've made a mistake, we can exit this mode by hitting the esc key.

Figure 5-18

Entering passive mode during the exchange of public keys

```
Router_B(config)#crypto key-exchange passive
Enter escape character to abort if connection does not complete.
Wait for connection from peer[confirm]
Waiting ....
```

Step 2—Configure Router A (CET Peer) for Active Mode and Send Public Key To configure a router for active mode (Step 2) we use the following command:

```
Router(config)#crypto key-exchange VPN-peer-ip-address crypto-engine
```

VPN-peer-ip-address	*x.x.x.x*	IP address of the VPN peer in passive mode.
Crypto-engine	*WORD*	Name of the crypto engine used to generate public key.

It is important to configure the router that will go into passive mode first, because when configuring the second CET peer for active mode, we specify the IP address of the CET peer. At that point, it contacts the passive CET peer to exchange keys.

Note:

The rest of the steps that follow are events that have been triggered by the commands from Step 1 and Step 2.

Step 3a—Router B and Router A both Verify Serial Number and Fingerprint If we have correctly configured the VPN peer to be in passive mode, then both VPN peers will display a *serial number* and *fingerprint* simultaneously. The network engineer(s) must validate that the serial number and fingerprint information displayed on both Router A and Router B is identical. The fingerprint is a hash of the identity and public key so that you can tell if the public key has been altered while in transit. The serial number identifies the certificate of the transaction.

Once the serial number and fingerprint have been verified, the active mode CET peer (Router A in our case) must then wait for its CET peer (Router B) to send its public key, which is accomplished by selecting the default answer *confirm,* as shown in Figure 5-19.

Figure 5-19

Router A sending public key to Router B and then going into passive mode waiting for Router B's public key

```
Router_A(config)#crypto key-exchange 192.168.40.1
RouterA_IOS_crypto_engine
Public key for RouterA_IOS_crypto_engine:
    Serial Number 02368817
    Fingerprint   D862 598B C63A 4EAA 7714

Wait for peer to send a key[confirm]
Waiting ....
```

Step 3a—Router B (Passive CET Peer) Accepts Router A's Public Key At this point, the passive mode CET peer will then enter active mode. The network engineer is prompted to save the public key information in the config file stored in running memory (not NVRAM), as seen in Figure 5-20. Remember that only a router's CET peers public key will be stored in the configuration file and not in its own public or private key. They are stored in a special section of NVRAM that is not viewable.

Figure 5-20

Router B adding Router A's public key to configuration

```
Waiting ....
Public key for RouterA_IOS_crypto_engine:
    Serial Number 02368817
    Fingerprint   D862 598B C63A 4EAA 7714

Add this public key to the configuration? [yes/no]: y
```

Note:

Step 3a and Step 3b can happen in either order; however, it is important that Router A be waiting to receive the public key before moving onto Step 4.

Step 4—Router B Sends Its Public Key Back to Router A   Once Router B has added Router A's public key to its configuration, Router B will prompt the network engineer if you want to send a public key back to the CET peer router, in this case Router A. If you have multiple crypto engines, you will have the opportunity to select them. If you only have a single crypto engine (Cisco IOS crypto engine), you will only have one choice, as seen in Figure 5-21.

Figure 5-21

Router B sending its public key back to Router A

```
Send peer a key in return[confirm]
Which one?

RouterB_IOS_crypto_engine? [yes]:
Public key for RouterB_IOS_crypto_engine:
    Serial Number 02368515
    Fingerprint   7A8C 83DB 7D8C B86A C738
```

Step 5—Router A Accepts Router B's Public Key   This step is almost identical to Step 3a, except that Router A is accepting Router B's public key instead of the other way around (see Figure 5-22).

Once this step has been completed, both routers have successfully exchanged public keys.

Figure 5-22

Router A adding Router A's public key to configuration

```
Public key for RouterB_IOS_crypto_engine:
    Serial Number 02368515
    Fingerprint   7A8C 83DB 7D8C B86A C738

Add this public key to the configuration? [yes/no]:yes
```

5.5.1.3 Enabling Encryption

Enabling encryption on a Cisco router for use with CET is a fairly easy task to do because the only thing to do is enable encryption globally. Two different types of DES encryption can be used with CET: 40-bit encryption and 56-bit encryption. To enable 40-bit encryption, use the following command:

```
Router(config)# crypto algorithm 40-bit-des cfb-type
```

cfb-type   **cfb-64**   Use 64 bits of feedback for ciphertext.

            cfb-8   Use eight bits of feedback for ciphertext.

To enable 56-bit encryption, use the following command:

```
Router(config)# crypto algorithm des cfb-type
```

cfb-type   **cfb-64**   Use 64 bits of feedback for ciphertext.

            cfb-8   Use eight bits of feedback for ciphertext.

By default, a 56-bit DES with a 64-bit CFB is enabled on most IOSs equipped to handle CET. To view the encryption algorithms that are currently enabled on your router, you can use the following command:

```
Router(config)# show crypto algorithms
```

In Figure 5-23, we can see that all four algorithms are available on Router A. Although we wouldn't normally want to enable all of the encryption algorithms available, it is useful for troubleshooting our crypto connections.

Figure 5-23

Output from show crypto algorithms that displays what encryption algorithms are active

```
Router_A#show crypto algorithms
  des cfb-64
  des cfb-8
  40-bit-des cfb-64
  40-bit-des cfb-8
```

5.5.1.4 Defining Crypto Maps and Assigning Them to an Interface

At this point, we've seen how to enable crypto engines, create public and private key pairs, how to exchange keys with your CET peers, and enable encryption. We shall now look at the final piece of the puzzle that brings it all together: *crypto maps.*

As discussed earlier this chapter, crypto maps enable us to define which data streams to encrypt and which not to encrypt. Selection of the data streams to encrypt is handled by access-lists. By using extended access-lists, we are afforded a tremendous amount of granularity.

When setting up a crypto map, five tasks must be completed:

- Create a crypto map
- Specify the remote peer router
- Define access-lists and assign them to a crypto map
- Define the encryption used within a crypto map
- Apply a crypto map to an interface

Create a Crypto Map   A crypto map is a vessel used to carry all of the configuration-specific information about our VPN tunnel. When creating a crypto map, two different aspects are used to configure: the name for the crypto map and the sequence number. The crypto map is a name that is only significant to the network administrator, while the sequence number, used when defining a crypto map, is used to identify a different destination within the crypto map. When creating a crypto map, we must use the following global configuration command:

```
Router(config)#crypto map crypto-map-name sequence-number
```

crypto-map-name	**WORD**	Name for the VPN peer.
sequence-number	**0-65535**	Unique number identifying destination-specific—information for the remote VPN peer.

The sequence number enables us to identify multiple destinations within the same crypto map. When the crypto map is applied, it is applied without a sequence number because the Cisco IOS lumps them together and places them on the physical interface. Thus, when configuring a crypto map globally, we can think of it as a destination-specific device.

Specify the Remote Peer Router   Specifying the remote peer router is performed within a crypto map and tells the crypto map which public key to use to encrypt the data stream. This is accomplished in the crypto map configuration mode using the command displayed in the following:

```
Router(config-crypto-map)#set peer crypto-engine-name
```

Crypto-engine-name   ***WORD***   Name of the crypto engine used to generate the public key by the VPN peer.

This name identifies the public key of the remote CET peer. This key name is received by the router during the exchange of DSS keys and is placed in the configuration file. If you don't know what keys are currently available, you can use the command *show pubkey* to display a list of keys that are available. In Figure 5-24, we can see that Router A used the public keys that were generated by Router B.

Figure 5-24

Router A identifying the peer router to set up a secure data stream

```
RouterA(config-crypto-map)#set peer RouterB_IOS_crypto_engine
```

Define Access-Lists and Assigning Them to a Crypto Map   Crypto maps require the use of an extended access-list to define traffic that should be encrypted by the CET peer. Extended access-lists offer a high degree of control by filtering a data stream based on the session-layer protocol, source address, destination address, and application port number.

Note:

Standard access-lists differ from extended access-lists in that they have limited capability to define a data flow. Every IP packet consists of a source address, destination address, and application port number. Standard access lists can only address a single address (source or destination depending on how it is configured), while extended access-lists can easily deal with the source address, destination address, and application port. Thus, it is no wonder that extended access-lists are used to define data flows for a VPN!

As you probably already know, extended access-lists can be identified as any access-list between 100 and 199. Although most of you already understand access-lists and how to use them, we will briefly cover how to configure an access-list for use with a crypto map.

```
Router (config)#access-list list-number permission protocol source
source-wildcard {protocol-specific-option} destination destination-
wildcard {protocol-specific-option}
```

list-number	**100-199**	Specify the extended access-list.
permission	**deny**	Deny specified protocol (simple form).
	permit	Permit specified protocol (simple form).
protocol	**ip**	Identifies IP traffic within this stream.
	tcp	Identifies TCP traffic within this stream.
	udp	Identifies UDP traffic within this stream.
	gre	Identifies GRE traffic within this stream.
source & destination	*x.x.x.x*	Identifies the IP addresses.
source-wildcard & destination-wildcard	*x.x.x.x*	Wildcard mask to used to identify the size of the address space being addressed.

Extended access-lists are a very powerful tool that can identify very granular data streams. For example, let's look and see how to keep users on the 192.168.8.0 / 22 network from communicating with Web servers in the 10.10.10.16 / 28. The three tasks to identify are the source, the destination, and the port. The user's would be the source of starting any transaction, the Web servers are the destination (of the initial session), and the port used is port 80 (HTTP). Using these guidelines, we could create an access-list that would enable all other data flows, but eliminate this particular data stream, as seen in Figure 5-25.

Figure 5-25

Using an extended IP access-list to identify a data stream

```
Router_A(config)# access-list 101 deny tcp 192.168.8.0 0.0.1.255
10.10.10.0 0.0.0.15 eq www
```

A crypto map subdefinition can only have a single access-list applied to it. All of these subdefinitions get grouped together when applied to a physical interface. To apply an access-list to a crypto map, we can use the command as displayed in the following:

```
Router(config-crypto-map)#match address access-list
```

`access-list`	**100-199**	Extended access list to use for crypto map.

Define Encryption Used Within Crypto Map   When defining the encryption to be used within a crypto map, we need to make sure that both CET peers will be using the same encryption algorithm. This is where we determine the encryption algorithm to be used within the crypto map. This command must be configured within the crypto map configuration mode.

Depending upon the IOS feature set you have, different options will be available. Two types of encryption are generally used with CET, 40-bit DES, and 56-bit DES. They are configured using the following commands:

```
Router(config-crypto-map)#set algorithm encrypt-algorithm cfb-type
```

`encrypt-algorithm`	**40-bit-des**	Use 40-bit DES.
	des	Use 56-bit DES.
`cfb-type`	**cfb-64**	Use 64 bits of feedback for ciphertext.
	cfb-8	Use eight bits of feedback for ciphertext.

Apply Crypto Map to an Interface   As previously mentioned, only a single crypto map can be applied to a physical interface. However, this is not as limiting as it might sound. This is because a crypto map can have multiple subdefinitions. Applying a crypto map to an interface is done through interface configuration mode using the following command:

```
Router(config-if)#crypto map crypto-map-name
```

`crypto-map-name`	***WORD***	Name of the crypto map.

When using this command, the crypto map must already exist. You cannot apply a crypto map to an interface before you configure the crypto map; otherwise, you end up with the error seen in Figure 5-26.

Figure 5-26

Assigning a
crypto map to a
physical
interface, in
which the crypto
map does not
exist

```
RouterA(config-if)#crypto map Alaska
ERROR: Crypto Map with tag "Alaska" does not exist.
```

In Figure 5-27, we can see that a crypto map has been supplied with two subdefinitions, at which point they were both applied to the physical interface.

Figure 5-27 demonstrates how we can apply only a single crypto map "NorthCarolina" to a single physical interface, but still be able to have multiple destinations within that single physical interface.

Figure 5-27

Creating two
subdefinitions
within a single
crypto map and
applying to a
physical interface

```
RouterA(config)#crypto map NorthCarolina 10
RouterA(config-crypto-map)#set peer NewYork
RouterA(config-crypto-map)#set algorithm 40-bit-des cfb-8
RouterA(config-crypto-map)#match address 101
RouterA(config-crypto-map)#exit
RouterA(config)#crypto map NorthCarolina 20
RouterA(config-crypto-map)#set peer Florida
RouterA(config-crypto-map)#set algorithm des cfb-64
RouterA(config-crypto-map)#match address 102
RouterA(config-crypto-map)#exit
RouterA(config)#interface serial 0
RouterA(config-if)#crypto map NorthCarolina
```

5.5.1.5 Fine-Tuning CET

Although the default settings defined by CET are okay for most network engineers, there will be a handful of times in which the default values just don't fit the bill. Two areas in particular can be modified to help network engineers adjust the configuration to fit their particular solution:

▨ Adjusting the expiration timer on encrypted sessions

▨ Pre-generate DH numbers

Changing the Expiration Timer on Encrypted Sessions   By default, all encrypted sessions last only 30 minutes. Once this default time has expired, the encryption session must be renegotiated. Adjusting these values is a simple global configuration command:

```
Router(config)#crypto key-timeout timeout
```

timeout	1-1440	Number of minutes to wait before timing out encrypted session.

This command is important if your router will be hosting lots of VPN sessions; no need to keep an encrypted session open if the connection is not being used.

Pre-generate DH numbers   When setting up an encrypted session, DH numbers are generated. Setting up these keys can be CPU-intensive and depending upon any other activity your router is doing, it can cause your sessions to time out before they can even begin. Therefore, Cisco has given us a way to generate those numbers before starting a session, enabling us to decrease the time required to set up an encrypted session. Using the following command, you can pre-generate up to 10 pairs of DH keys:

```
Router(config)#crypto pregen-dh-pairs number-of-pairs
```

number-of-pairs	1-10	Number of pairs of DH numbers to pregenerate.

On slower CPUs, this pre-generation of DH numbers can decrease the amount of time required to set up an encrypted session.

5.5.1.6 Verifying CET

When trying to debug CET, a handful of commands really help you understand how your router is configured. One of the more important commands for verifying your configuration is the command *show crypto map* (see Figure 5-28). This will give you an accurate assessment of your crypto map and verify that it is correct.

Figure 5-28

Output from the show crypto map command

```
Router#show crypto map
Crypto Map "NorthCarolina" 10
  Connection Id = 3          (3 established,     0 failed)
   Algorithm = des cfb-64
   Peer = NewYork
   PE = 192.168.110.0
   UPE = 192.168.120.0
   Extended IP access list 102
    access-list 102 permit tcp 192.168.110.0 0.0.0.255 192.168.120.0
   0.0.0.255
```

The values in Table 5-6 show how to interpret the output from Figure 5-28.

The *show crypto connections* command, as seen in Figure 5-29 enables us to see all of the currently active encrypted sessions. Once again, using Table 5-6, we can interpret most of the output from the command found in Figure 5-29. The one field displayed in Figure 5-29 that is not found in Table 5-6 is the field Time. The Time field indicates when the connection was established.

Table 5-6

Descriptions of the fields within the *show crypto map* Command

Field	Description
Connection ID	Identifies the connection. Values of 1-299 indicate an active encrypted session, whereas a value of UNSET indicates no connection currently exists.
Established	Number of successful encrypted connections using that crypto map.
Failed	Number of failed encrypted connections using that crypto map.
Algorithm	Indicates the type of algorithm used by the crypto map.
Peer	Name of the peer router used in the crypto map.
Protected Entity (PE)	Displays a representative source IP address as specified by the access-list.
Unprotected Entity (UPE)	Displays a representative destination IP address as specified by the access-list.
Extended IP access-list	Indicates the access-list being used by the crypto map.

Figure 5-29

Output from the *show crypto connections* command

```
Router#show crypto connections
Connection Table
PE              UPE           Conn_id New_id Algorithm    Time
192.168.120.0  192.168.110.0  8      0        DES_56_CFB64 Oct 25 2000
11:29:22
```

Two last commands that can be used to determine the status of an encrypted session are the *show crypto engine connections active* and *show crypto engine connections dropped-packet* (see Figure 5-30). These two commands can tell us a lot about the performance of the encrypted sessions. For example, if the drop count is high, we might consider raising the timeout of encrypted sessions or pre-generating DH numbers.

Figure 5-30

Output from show crypto engine connections

```
Router#show crypto engine connections active
ID    Interface   IP-Address   State  Algorithm       Encrypt  Decrypt
 8     Serial0     192.168.20.2 set     DES_56_CFB64      25       22

Router#show crypto engine connections dropped-packet
Interface           IP-Address     Drop Count

Serial0             192.168.20.2   15
```

5.5.2 Configuring CET Using IOS 11.3T and 12.x

Passing secure data streams between two routers requires encryption to be configured at both ends. In this section, we will be describing the tasks necessary to configure encryption for IOS 11.3T and IOS 12.0. Using the steps outlined earlier in the chapter, we will focus on implementation-specific information for Cisco's IOS version 12.0 as well as the differences between 11.3 and 12.0.

Note:

Note that the T train within Cisco's IOS is developed with the latest and greatest features. Thus, IOS 11.3T uses the same commands as IOS 12.x to implement CET.

5.5.2.1 Generate and Verify DSS Public/Private Keys

Like all encryption algorithms, there must be a key to lock and unlock the data. Because CET utilizes asymmetric encryption, we must generate a pair of public/private keys. When creating the public/private keys, the crypto engine that will be performing the encryption and decryption must create these keys. Therefore, when creating the public/private keys, you must specify the source of the crypto engine. To create a public/private key, we can use the following command:

```
Router(config)# crypto key generate dss crypto-engine-name slot
```

crypto-engine-name	*WORD*	required	Name to identify the key crypto engine.
slot	*WORD*	optional	Slot to identify the hardware encryption device.

When generating the public/private key pairs, the *slot* option is used to identify where in the Cisco router the hardware-based encryption crypto engine resides. This option is only available for the Cisco 7200, RSP7000, and 7500 series routers. If you are using Cisco 1700 series routers with a VPN module, the VPN modules become the default crypto engine and do not need to be specified. By using the following command, you can disable hardware encryption and use Cisco's IOS crypto engine.

```
Router(config)#crypto engine accelerator
```

In this section, we see an example of creating the public/private keys using IOS 12.0. One of the great aspects of asymmetric (public/private) key encryption is that we only need to generate a single pair of keys for use with all other encryption peers, unlike symmetric key encryption that requires a unique key for each encryption peer relationship.

You should note that if you attempt to recreate the DSS public/private key pair after already having created them, you will have to re-exchange the keys; otherwise, your peer VPN router will not have the correct public key for you. Thus, you will receive the output seen in Figure 5-31 if you attempt to regenerate the keys.

Once the public/private key pair has been created, we may, from time to time, verify the public key that we created. We can do this using the following command:

```
Router(config)# show crypto key mypubkey dss
```

Figure 5-31

Regenerating DSS public/private key with IOS 12.0

```
RouterC(config)#crypto key generate dss RouterC
% Generating new DSS keys will require re-exchanging
   public keys with peers who already have the public key
   named RouterC!
Generate new DSS keys? [yes/no]: y
Generating DSS keys ....
   [OK]
```

In Figure 5-32, we can see the use of this command to view the public key. Notice that we can easily identify the serial number of the key as well as its name. These fields were difficult to find in version 11.3, but in IOS 12.0, they are much easier to find.

Figure 5-32

Displaying your public key with IOS 12.0

```
RouterC#show crypto key mypubkey dss
Key name: RouterC
 Serial number: 06107486
 Usage: Signature Key
 Key Data:
  49FA1E6E 25A1E2E9 2E587C90 DACC23E0 256207AF 4D17DCB4 DD059AD9
  CDEEBA60
  9EF59648 BA72EAFC 7AAC5967 EE8F98D8 48D1E1EB E81001AA F7ADF1F6
  83939F6D
```

In Cisco IOS 11.3, when saving your configuration, the router would tell you that it was building a private area of NVRAM to save your public/private keys. However, in IOS 12.0 you do not get this indicator. However, it is important to remember that the keys are still saved in NVRAM in a private, non-viewable area and that if you attempt to copy your config file to another router without regenerating your public/private keys and then exchanging them again, your VPN tunnel will not work.

5.5.2.2 Exchanging DSS Public Keys

As discussed earlier in this chapter, seven steps are used to exchange DSS public/private key pairs. Although configuring a router to exchange keys is started by a single command on each router, the whole procedure must be followed in order; otherwise, we won't successfully exchange keys. Using Figure 5-11 as a guideline, we have outlined the following steps.

In order to exchange keys between routers we must have one router in passive mode and the other in active mode. There is no difference in the final outcome, only who will start the process. In our example that follows, Router C will be the active router and Router D will be the passive router.

Step 1—Configure Router D (CET Peer) for Passive Mode To configure a router for passive mode, we can use the following command:

```
Router(config)# crypto key exchange dss passive
```

Once we've entered this command, we must confirm that we want to wait for a connection from an active CET peer. Until our CET peer activates a session, we can't do anything on our local router, as seen in Figure 5-33.

Figure 5-33

Entering passive mode during the exchange of public keys

```
RouterD(config)#crypto key exchange dss passive
Enter escape character to abort if connection does not complete.
Wait for connection from peer[confirm]
Waiting ....
```

Step 2— Configure Router C (CET Peer) for Active Mode and Send Public Key
To configure a router for active mode, we use the following command:

```
Router(config)# crypto key exchange dss VPN-peer-ip-address crypto-
engine
```

VPN-peer-ip-address	*x.x.x.x*	IP address of the VPN peer in passive mode.
Crypto-engine	***WORD***	Name of the crypto engine used to generate public key.

If you skip Step 1 when performing this configuration, then Step 2 will time out, because it is expecting to connect with a device that is ready to exchange keys.

Note:
The rest of the steps that follow are events that have been triggered by the commands from Step 1 and Step 2.

Step 3a—Router D and Router C Both Verify Serial Number and Fingerprint
Assuming Steps 1 and 2 have been successfully completed, the network engineer(s) must validate the serial number and fingerprint information displayed on their corresponding routers. The fingerprint is a hash of the identity and public key so that you can tell if the public key

has been altered while in transit, while the serial number identifies the certificate of the transaction.

Once the serial number and fingerprint have been verified, the active mode VPN peer (Router C in our case) must then wait confirm to send its public key back to its VPN peer (Router D), as seen in Figure 5-34.

Figure 5-34

Router C sending public key to Router D and then going into passive mode waiting for Router D's public key

```
RouterC(config)#crypto key exchange dss 192.168.140.1 RouterC
Public key for RouterC:
    Serial Number 06107486
    Fingerprint   F1D5 15C1 32DD E87B D69E

Wait for peer to send a key[confirm]
Waiting ....
```

Step 3b—Router D (Passive CET peer) Accepts Router C's Public Key   Once Step 3a has been completed, Router D will receive key information for Router C at which point Router C can add the public key to its configuration. Once the key has been saved, the network engineer is prompted to save the public key, as seen in Figure 5-35. Remember that only a router's CET peers public key will be stored in the configuration file and not its own public or private key. They are stored in a special section of NVRAM that is not viewable.

Figure 5-35

Router D adding Router C's public key to configuration

```
Waiting ....
Public key for RouterA_IOS_crypto_engine:
    Serial Number 02368817
    Fingerprint   D862 598B C63A 4EAA 7714

Add this public key to the configuration? [yes/no]: y
```

Note:

Step 3a and Step 3b can happen in either order; however, it is important that Router A be waiting to receive the public key before moving onto Step 4.

Step 4—Router D Sends Its Public Key Back to Router C After Router D has saved Router C's public key, Router D will prompt the network engineer to send a public key back to the VPN peer router. If you have multiple crypto engines, you will have the opportunity to select them. If you only have a single crypto engine (Cisco IOS crypto engine), you will only have one choice, as seen in Figure 5-36.

Figure 5-36

Router B sending its public key back to Router A

```
Send peer a key in return[confirm]
Which one?

RouterD? [yes]:
Public key for RouterD:
    Serial Number 01771306
    Fingerprint   49F9 66DA 5692 5490 BEAF
```

Step 5—Router A Accepts Router B's Public Key This step is almost identical to Step 3a, except that Router A is accepting Router B's public key instead of the other way around (see Figure 5-37).

Once this step has been completed, both routers have successfully exchanged public keys. Although these steps are not terribly difficult, it is important to do them in the appropriate order.

Figure 5-37

Router A adding Router A's public key to the configuration

```
Public key for RouterD:
    Serial Number 01771306
    Fingerprint   49F9 66DA 5692 5490 BEAF

Add this public key to the configuration? [yes/no]: y
```

5.5.2.3 Enabling Encryption

Enabling encryption on a Cisco router is a fairly easy task to do because the only thing we need to do is enable encryption globally. Two different types of DES encryption can be used with CET, 40-bit encryption, and 56-bit encryption. To enable 40-bit encryption, use the following command:

```
Router(config)# crypto cisco algorithm 40-bit-des cfb-type
```

| *cfb-type* | **cfb-64** | Use 64 bits of feedback for ciphertext |
| | **cfb-8** | Use eight bits of feedback for ciphertext |

To enable 56-bit encryption, use the following command:

```
Router(config)# crypto cisco algorithm cfb-type
```

cfb-type   **cfb-64**   Use 64 bits of feedback for ciphertext

cfb-8   Use eight bits of feedback for ciphertext

By default, a 56-bit DES with a 64-bit CFB is enabled on most IOSs equipped to handle CET.

To view the encryption algorithms that are currently enabled on your router, you can use the following command:

```
Router# show crypto algorithms
```

In Figure 5-38, we can see that all four algorithms are available on Router C. Although we wouldn't normally want to enable all of the encryption algorithms available, it is useful for troubleshooting our crypto connections.

Figure 5-38

Output from the *show crypto cisco algorithms* command

```
RouterC#show crypto cisco algorithms
    des cfb-64
    des cfb-8
    40-bit-des cfb-64
    40-bit-des cfb-8
```

5.5.2.4 Defining Crypto Maps and Assigning Them to an Interface

Crypto maps bring together all of the work we have done so far in a single package. Using this package (crypto map) we can create a VPN by applying it to an interface.

By using access-lists to define the data streams that get encrypted, we can create our secure communications. Because we need to have great flexibility when defining our secure data streams, we use extended access lists, as seen later in this chapter.

When setting up a crypto map, five tasks must be completed:

- Create a crypto map
- Specify the remote peer router
- Define access-lists and assigning them to a crypto map

- Define the encryption used within the crypto map
- Apply the crypto map to an interface

Note:

Crypto maps have changed very little from IOS 11.3 to IOS 12.0.

Create a Crypto Map   A crypto map is simply a container that holds all of the encryption configuration information about our VPN tunnel. Crypto maps have two different variables that need to be defined: name and sequence number. The name is used to identify the crypto map, while the sequence number is used to define a subdefinition of the crypto map. When creating a crypto map, we must use the following global configuration command:

```
Router(config)#crypto map crypto-map-name sequence-number
```

crypto-map-name	**WORD**	Name for the VPN peer.
sequence-number	**0-65535**	Unique number identifying destination-specific information for the remote VPN peer.

All crypto maps are created using the same crypto map name, but different crypto sequence numbers get combined into a single crypto map that is applied to the physical interface.

Specify the Remote Peer Router   Identifying your CET peer enables Cisco's IOS to associate a specific CET peer's public key and crypto engine with a crypto map. Although we aren't specifically indicating the crypto engine to use on our Cisco router, the fact that our CET peer will be using the key we exchanged with him dictates the crypto engine to be used by the router. Specifying a crypto map is done in crypto map configuration mode using the following command:

```
Router(config-crypto-map)#set peer crypto-engine-name
```

Crypto-engine-name	**WORD**	Name of the crypto engine used to generate the public key by the VPN peer.

In order to specify a peer CET partner, you must have already exchanged keys with the CET peer. Failure to exchange keys with the CET peer prior to indicating its name will generate an error.

Define Access-Lists and Assign Them to a Crypto Map   Identifying a data stream to be encrypted by a crypto map requires the use of an extended access-list. Extended access provides a very high degree of granularity for defining our encrypted data stream. We can filter based upon a number of attributes, such as the source address, destination address, and application port number.

As you probably already know, extended access-lists can be identified as any access-list between 100 and 199. Implementing an extended access-list not only requires an understanding of the format of the command, but it also requires an understanding of how TCP/IP addressing works. The command used to configure an extended access list is displayed in the following:

```
Router (config)#access-list list-number permission protocol source
source-wildcard {protocol-specific-option} destination destination-
wildcard {protocol-specific-option}
```

list-number	**100-199**	Specify the extended access-list.
permission	**deny**	Deny specified protocol (simple form).
	permit	Permit specified protocol (simple form).
protocol	**ip**	Identifies IP traffic within this stream.
	tcp	Identifies TCP traffic within this stream.
	udp	Identifies UDP traffic within this stream.
	gre	Identifies GRE traffic within this stream.
source & destination	*x.x.x.x*	Identifies the IP addresses.
source-wildcard & destination-wildcard	*x.x.x.x*	Wildcard mask to used to identify the size of the address space being addressed.

Extended access-lists can identify very specific types of data streams. For example, let's look and see how to keep users on the 192.168.108.0 / 28 network from communicating via telnet with Unix servers in the 172.16.31.0 / 27 network. The three tasks to identify are the source, the destination, and the port. The users would be the source of starting any transaction, the Web servers are the destination (of the initial session), and the port used is port 80 (HTTP). Using these guidelines, we could create an access-list that would allow all other data flows but eliminate this particular data stream, as seen in Figure 5-39.

Figure 5-39

Using an
extended IP
access list to
identify a data
stream

```
Router_A(config)# access-list 101 deny tcp 192.168.108.0 0.0.0.31
172.16.31.0 0.0.0.63 eq www
```

To apply an access-list to a crypto map, we can use the command as displayed in the following:

```
Router(config-crypto-map)#match address access-list
```

access-list	100-199	Extended access list to use for crypto map.

Define the Encryption Used Within the Crypto Map Depending upon the IOS feature set you have, different options will be available. Two types of encryption are generally used with CET: 40-bit DES and 56-bit DES. In order to have secure communications between two entities, the same algorithm must be used on both VPN peers. Thus, the following command must be performed on both routers.

They are configured using the following commands:

```
Router(config-crypto-map)#set algorithm encrypt-algorithm cfb-type
```

encrypt-algorithm	40-bit-des	Use 40-bit DES.
	des	Use 56-bit DES.
cfb-type	cfb-64	Use 64 bits of feedback for ciphertext.
	cfb-8	Use eight bits of feedback for ciphertext.

Apply a Crypto Map to an Interface Applying a crypto map to an interface is as easy as applying an access-list to an interface. It is important not to forget that crypto maps can have multiple destinations. Applying a crypto map to an interface is done through interface configuration mode using the following command:

```
Router(config-if)#crypto map crypto-map-name
```

crypto-map-name	WORD	Name of the crypto map.

When using this command, the crypto map must already exist. You cannot apply a crypto map to an interface before you configure the crypto map; otherwise, you end up with the error seen in Figure 5-40.

Figure 5-40

Assigning a crypto map to a physical interface, in which the crypto map does not exist

```
RouterC(config-if)#crypto map Ithaca
ERROR: Crypto Map with tag "Ithaca" does not exist.
```

5.5.2.5 Fine-Tuning CET

As with any technology, there will be times when the default settings will not do. Particular attention must be paid to the establishment of the encrypted tunnels. These CET encrypted sessions can be considered more like Dial-On-Demand routing; connections expire after a certain period of time. During a session's establishment, low-end routers may have difficulty establishing a tunnel before the initial packet that initiated the session expires. Thus, two areas can be modified to help reduce a session's establishment:

▪ Adjusting expiration timer on encrypted sessions

▪ Pre-generate DH numbers

Changing Expiration Timer on Encrypted Sessions   By default, all encrypted sessions last only 30 minutes. Once this default time has expired, the encryption session must be renegotiated. Adjusting these values is a simple global configuration command:

```
Router(config)#crypto cisco key-timeout timeout
```

timeout   **1-1440**   Number of minutes to wait before timing out encrypted session.

This command is important if your router will be hosting lots of VPN sessions. Keeping an encrypted session open is not necessary if the connection is not being used.

Pre-generate DH Numbers   In order to establish an encrypted session, DH numbers must be used during the DH exchange. The generation of these keys can be very CPU-intensive. In order to minimize the amount of time required to set up a tunnel, Cisco enables us to pre-generate up to 10 pairs of DH keys. Using the following command, you can pre-generate up to 10 pairs of DH keys:

```
Router(config)#crypto pregen-dh-pairs number-of-pairs
```

number-of-pairs   1-10   Number of pairs of DH numbers to pre-generate.

5.5.2.6 Verifying CET

When attempting to verify the configuration of CET, we still use the same commands from IOS 11.3 that we do in 12.0. Whereas the output has been reformatted from IOS 11.3 to 12.0, the contents of the output are almost the same. One of the first commands used to verify your configuration is the command *show crypto map*. This will give you an accurate assessment of your crypto map and verify that it is correct (see Figure 5-41).

Figure 5-41

Output from the *show crypto map* command from IOS 12.0

```
RouterD#show crypto map
Crypto Map "RouterD" 20 cisco
    Peer = RouterC
    PE = 192.168.140.0
    UPE = 192.168.130.0
    Extended IP access list 101
        access-list 101 permit ip 192.168.140.0 0.0.0.255
192.168.130.0 0.0.0.25
    Algorithm = 40-bit-des cfb-8
    Connection Id = 1          (1 established,     0 failed)
```

The values in Table 5-7 show how to interpret the output from Figure 5-41. Note that in IOS 11.3, the encryption algorithm statement is missing from the output of the show crypto map.

The final two commands that can be used to determine the status of an encrypted session (which are also the same from IOS 11.3) are *show crypto engine connections active* and *show crypto engine connections dropped-packet*. These two commands can tell us a lot about the performance of the encrypted sessions. For example, if the drop count is high, we might consider either raising the timeout of encrypted sessions, or pre-generating DH numbers (see Figure 5-42).

Table 5-7

Descriptions of the fields within the *show crypto map* command

Field	Description
Connection ID	Identifies the connection. Values of 1-299 indicate an active encrypted session, whereas a value of UNSET indicates no connection currently exists.
Established	Number of successful encrypted connections using that crypto map.
Failed	Number of failed encrypted connections using that crypto map.
Algorithm	Indicates the type of algorithm used by the crypto map.
Peer	Name of the peer router used in the crypto map.
Protected Entity (PE)	Displays a representative source IP address as specified by the access-list.
Unprotected Entity (UPE)	Displays a representative destination IP address as specified by the access-list.
Extended IP Access-List	Indicates the access-list being used by the crypto map.

Figure 5-42

Output from *show crypto engine* connections

```
RouterD#show crypto engine connections active

 ID Interface   IP-Address    State  Algorithm          Encrypt  Decrypt
  1 Serial0     192.168.40.2   set   DES_40_CFB8            5        5

Crypto adjacency count : Lock: 0, Unlock: 0
RouterD#show crypto engine connections dropped-packet

Interface           IP-Address           Drop Count
Serial0             192.168.40.2                  4
```

5.5.3 Troubleshooting CET

Troubleshooting CET can be a difficult process because not many debug tools are provided by Cisco to help in these situations. Luckily, most of the problems that can occur are with key exchanges. Because key exchanges are a manual process, you will immediately be aware that you are having a problem. In this section, some of the more common problems that occur when exchanging DSS keys will be addressed.

5.5.3.1 Common Key Configuration Problems

As Murphy's law has proven time and time again, if something can go wrong, it will. This section is here to help you solidify your understanding of VPNs, as well as the tasks and events that must happen in order to create a VPN.

Connection refused by remote host when exchanging keys
Problem: When I attempt to exchange keys with my VPN peer, the connection is refused.

```
RouterA(config)#crypto key-exchange 192.168.40.1 RouterB
Error! TCP open failed: Connection refused by remote host
```

Resolution: This problem occurs because your VPN peer is not ready to accept a connection. Make sure that the remote router is ready to accept a connection as shown below.

```
RouterB(config)#crypto key-exchange passive
Enter escape character to abort if connection does not complete.
Wait for connection from peer[confirm]
Waiting ....
```

No Key Present for Peer Router When Creating Crypto Map
Problem: When I attempt to set a peer within a crypto map, I get the message

```
Router_A(config-crypto-map)#set peer RouterB
WARNING: No key present for peer "RouterB".
```

Resolution #1: You have not exchanged keys with your VPN peer.
Resolution #2: You are using the incorrect name for your crypto map. Use the show crypto pubkey command to see the list of VPN peers in which you have exchanged keys.

What Public Keys do I currently have?
Problem: I don't know if I have my VPN peer's public key. How can I tell?
Resolution: Use the show crypto pubkey to display all the current public keys available.

```
Router_A#show crypto pubkey
crypto public-key RouterB_IOS_crypto_engine 02368515
 57F18438 2D5DA56B 14F592E6 8701D27F 62DB7F19 B5A10624 9A7FE7F3
92932E66
 61827342 5B270957 E5FF4C6D 57A09156 AA9B904E 7741045B 1D127BB7
4E1B5E4C
quit
crypto public-key Router_C_VIP2_crypto_engine 06107486
 BDB01B40 8EC12286 F1CB9515 4DFE448E E5FF4590 C3E6A103 5DB8FD42
58430E69
 51D0139C AB64B4FD F04AB771 543674D4 26BEF7F0 41ACD48E 9146C725
6E13530D
quit
```

Assuming that you have successfully exchanged keys with your VPN peer, other problems may still arise. By following the steps, you should be able to resolve any problems that occur.

- Verify the encryption algorithm being used.
- Verify that the access-lists are the inverse of each other.
- Verify that the key has been identified within the crypto map.

5.5.3.2 Verify the Encryption Algorithm Being Used

In order for encryption to work correctly, both CET peers must be using the same encryption algorithms. To verify that the encryption algorithms are the same, use the *show crypto map* command on both routers if you are using IOS 12.x. If you are using IOS 11.3 and IOS 11.3T, you will need to use the *show crypto cisco algorithms* to view the currently active encryption algorithms.

5.5.3.3 Verify that the Access-Lists Are the Inverse of Each Other

This is a fairly easy task unless you are not familiar with how access-lists work. If you are not familiar with how they work, check out the case analysis in Case study #2 of this chapter.

5.5.3.4 Verify That the Key Has Been Identified Within the Crypto Map

When keys are exchanged, the local router names the key so it can apply it to a crypto map. By using the show crypto map command, we can see what key is being used. Don't be confused by the fact that the name of the field is Peer, as shown in Figure 5-41, because it still identifies the name of the key that is stored in NVRAM.

5.6 GRE with CET Encryption VPN Case Studies

This chapter section is one of the most important parts of any hands-on book. We have shown you how to configure a router to participate in a VPN, but how do we take a take a technical problem and solve it with a VPN? In each of the three case studies that follow, we will explain the five following things before moving on to configuration specific information.

- VPN type
- Tunnel type
- When to deploy
- Verifying our VPN
- VPN configurations

Note:

Most of our case studies consist of three Cisco 2500 series routers (except for Case Study #3). The middle router between the two devices will be an IP only router.

5.6.1 Case Study #1—Tunnel IPX over IP Backbone Using CET (IOS 113)

VPN type: Intranet VPN
Tunnel type: Compulsory Tunnel
When to deploy: This type of tunnel is useful within an enterprise network when the core network is only routing IP and you need to run IPX between the various sites. Many large enterprises choose to only run IP at the core of the network in order to provide a stable backbone. However, it can cut off those departments that rely on IPX for their business functions.
Verifying VPN has been enabled: Verify that you are not running IPX on the Internet router, but can still see remote IPX networks. Use the *show ipx route* command (see Figure 5-47).

Figure 5-43

Case Study #1

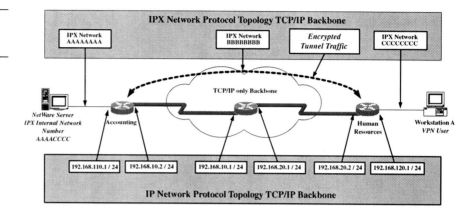

5.6.1.1 Human Resources Config File

Figure 5-44

Human resources
config file

```
1   version 11.3
2   service timestamps debug uptime
3   service timestamps log uptime
4   no service password-encryption
5   !
6   hostname Accounting
7   !
8   enable secret 5 $1$SCEM$ChedgD8pbI9c7/GuqMBfl/
9   !
10  ipx routing 0000.0c4a.4a56
11  !
12  crypto public-key HR 02368515
13  1778C95D DBA18D04 09A806F0 989077A6 620573EC 2AEC8B5D E9803239
    CDFC391A
14  210A6438 998A848F F868E80E BBB39F35 C3250A7C 0907F4C2 4CC90125
    0610BE42
15  quit
16  !
17  crypto map Accounting.HR 20
18    set algorithm des
19    set peer HR
20    match address 101
21  !
22  interface Tunnel1
23    no ip address
24    ipx network BBBBBBBB
25    tunnel source Serial0
26    tunnel destination 192.168.20.2
27    crypto map Accounting.HR
28  !
29  interface Ethernet0
30    ip address 192.168.110.1 255.255.255.0
31    ipx network AAAAAAAA encapsulation SAP
32  !
```

Figure 5-44

Human resources
config file (cont.)

```
33  interface Serial0
34   ip address 192.168.10.2 255.255.255.0
35   crypto map Accounting.HR
36  !
37  router eigrp 10
38   network 192.168.10.0
39   network 192.168.110.0
40  !
41  ip classless
42  !
43  access-list 101 permit gre host 192.168.10.2 host 192.168.20.2
44  !
45  line con 0
46   exec-timeout 0 0
47  line aux 0
48  line vty 0 4
49   exec-timeout 0 0
50   password cisco
51   login
52  !
```

5.6.1.2 Accounting Config File

Figure 5-45

Accounts
config file

```
53   version 11.3
54   service timestamps debug uptime
55   service timestamps log uptime
56   no service password-encryption
57   !
58   hostname HR
59   !
60   enable secret 5 $1$ZAZ5$Lv5KyXumwVac0Pk3bDX6T0
61   !
62   ipx routing 0000.0c75.f9da
63   !
64   crypto public-key Accounting 02368817
65   480275E4 9EC46FCB 3E939A22 A8387E2D 639BE1CB 8CAA4FB4 0CA906A5
     5D331D91
66   2E669952 0B4DFB8E 56F1EF7E C318C127 0F177726 86E4E515 B2A82005
     D42B636B
67    quit
68   !
69   crypto map HR.Accounting 10
70    set algorithm des
71    set peer Accounting
72    match address 101
73   !
74   interface Tunnel1
75    no ip address
76    ipx network BBBBBBBB
77    tunnel source Serial0
78    tunnel destination 192.168.10.2
79    crypto map HR.Accounting
80   !
81   interface Ethernet0
```

Figure 5-45

Accounts config file (cont.)

```
82   ip address 192.168.120.1 255.255.255.0
83   ipx network CCCCCCCC encapsulation SAP
84  !
85  interface Serial0
86   description Going to Backbone Router
87   ip address 192.168.20.2 255.255.255.0
88   crypto map HR.Accounting
89
90  !
91  router eigrp 10
92   network 192.168.20.0
93   network 192.168.120.0
94  !
95  ip classless
96  !
97  access-list 101 permit gre host 192.168.20.2 host 192.168.10.2
98  !
100 line con 0
101  exec-timeout 0 0
102 line aux 0
103 line vty 0 4
104  exec-timeout 0 0
105  password cisco
106  login
```

5.6.1.3 Backbone Router Configuration File

Figure 5-46

Backbone router config

```
107 version 11.0
108 service udp-small-servers
109 service tcp-small-servers
110 !
111 hostname Campus_Backbone
112 !
113 enable secret 5 $1$1fuK$c7nwnmcRolYgWpRKDliEk.
114 !
115 interface Serial0
116  description Human Resources
117  ip address 192.168.20.1 255.255.255.0
118  no fair-queue
119  clockrate 2000000
120 !
121 interface Serial1
122  description Accounting
123  ip address 192.168.10.1 255.255.255.0
124  clockrate 2000000
125 !
126 router eigrp 10
127  network 192.168.10.0
128  network 192.168.20.0
129 !
130 !
131 line con 0
```

Figure 5-46

Backbone router config (cont.)

```
132  exec-timeout 0 0
133 line aux 0
134  transport input all
135 line vty 0 4
136  exec-timeout 0 0
137  password cisco
138  login
139 !
140 end
```

5.6.1.4 Verifying VPN

Figure 5-47

Verifying IPX over VPN

```
141 HR#show ipx route
142 Codes: C - Connected primary network, c - Connected secondary
    network
143 S - Static, F - Floating static, L - Local (internal), W -
IPXWAN
144      R - RIP, E - EIGRP, N - NLSP, X - External, A - Aggregate
145       s - seconds, u - uses, U - Per-user static
146
147 4 Total IPX routes. Up to 1 parallel paths and 16 hops allowed.
148
149 No default route known.
150
151 C    BBBBBBBB (TUNNEL),        Tu1
152 C    CCCCCCCC (SAP),           Et0
153 R    AAAAAAAA [151/01] via BBBBBBBB.0000.0c4a.4a56,   37s, Tu1
154 R    AAAACCCC [152/02] via BBBBBBBB.0000.0c4a.4a56,   38s, Tu1
155 HR#show crypto connections
156 Connection Table
157 PE           UPE        Conn_id New_id Algorithm    Time
158 192.168.20.2 192.168.10.2  1     0        DES_56_CFB64 Mar 01
    1993 00:32:22
159
156                    flags:TIME_KEYS ACL: 101
```

5.6.1.5 Case Study Analysis

In this case study, all of our VPN peer routers are running IOS 11.3 and not IOS 11.3T. The most interesting aspect of this case study is that we show how a GRE tunnel has multiprotocol support. Notice that in lines 24 and 76, we used the same IPX network number. This is how IPX defines the network portion of an address. Because IPX RIP is enabled by default, we did not have to do anything special other than configure IPX on our Ethernet interfaces to get IPX working. We can verify that IPX is working because in lines 153 and 154, we can see that we have learned about two networks, AAAACCCC and AAAAAAAA from IPX RIP, whereas IPX networks BBBBBBBB and CCCCCCCC are directly connected to our router (lines 151 and 152). One last point about this setup is that our backbone router (lines 107 through 140) show no indication that IPX is being routed through it. As far as the backbone router is concerned, it is only transporting IP packets from one router to another. It has no idea that IPX is embedded inside of the GRE packet.

The encryption algorithm used in this case study was DES (lines 18 and 70). By using CET, two options are DES with a standard 56-bit key, or DES with a 40-bit key. In instances in which hardware replacement is not an option and security is not critical, you may consider using 40-bit encryption. Using 56-bit encryption will dramatically increase CPU performance. On a Cisco 2500 with 16MB of RAM, we can see a decrease in performance by as much as 10 percent to 15 percent by using 40-bit DES over 56-bit DES.

In our two VPN routers, notice that we only needed to encrypt the data stream between the two GRE points (line 97 and 43). Because all IPX data flowing between these two networks is going through our tunnel interface which is sourced from the serial interface, our access-list only needed to include those two host IP addresses and not an entire network. In other case studies, we will see instances where we have to be less specific, as well as defining the encrypted data stream between two networks instead of two hosts.

In this particular case study, pay close attention to the fact that the IP address designated in line 25 matches the IP address designated in line 78. While line 25 does not exactly identify the IP address, line 34 shows that serial 0's IP address is 192.168.10.2, which does match line 78. This also goes the other way; line 77 and line 26 must match IP addresses. Remember that we can have a situation in which one of the tunnel interfaces is configured incorrectly and discards all of the GRE packets that are sent to it, whereas the other tunnel interface successfully receives the GRE packets. This unidirectional communication can show itself in bizarre ways. For instance, we could see the SAPS from a NetWare server, but not be able to log in to it. GRE tunnel problems can appear to be quite strange if you do not understand how they work. Most GRE tunnel problems can be resolved by validating the information as presented in the troubleshooting GRE section of this chapter.

5.6.2 Case Study #2—Using CET Encryption (IOS 12.0)

VPN type: Extranet VPN

Tunnel type: Compulsory Tunnel

When to deploy: This type of tunnel is useful when setting up a business relationship between two businesses. Using the Internet as the backbone, we want the staff computer at Router to communicate securely with the Web server.

Verifying VPN has been enabled: Verify you can connect to the Web server from a staff machine (see Figure 5-48).

Figure 5-48

Case Study #2

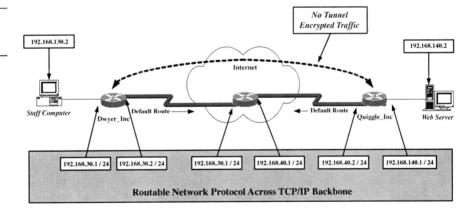

5.6.2.1 Quiggle Router Configuration File

Figure 5-49

Quiggle router config

```
1   version 12.0
2   service timestamps debug uptime
3   service timestamps log uptime
4   no service password-encryption
5   !
6   hostname Quiggle_Inc
7   !
8   ip subnet-zero
9   !
10  crypto cisco algorithm des
11  crypto cisco algorithm des cfb-8
12  !
13  crypto key pubkey-chain dss
14   named-key Dwyer signature
15    serial-number 06107486
16    key-string
17     ED1ECA34 0519D5BE 5B37B22F 49218269 DADE011D E138385C
       3EF5DC12 505894F3
18     DBC6523F EB965EA9 41A6FCAA 563C7B8D 00CF969D A7D03A74
       9293E9DE
       C50EF532
19    quit
20   !
21   crypto map Quiggle.Dwyer 11
22    set peer Dwyer
23    set algorithm des cfb-8
24    match address 130
25   !
26  interface Serial0
27   ip address 192.168.40.2 255.255.255.0
28   no ip directed-broadcast
29   crypto map Quiggle.Dwyer
30  !
31  interface TokenRing0
32   ip address 192.168.140.1 255.255.255.0
33   no ip directed-broadcast
34   ring-speed 16
35  !
36  ip classless
37  ip route 0.0.0.0 0.0.0.0 192.168.40.1
38  !
39  access-list 130 permit ip host 192.168.140.2
       192.168.130.0.0.0.0.255
40  !
41  !
42  line con 0
43   exec-timeout 0 0
44   transport input none
45  line aux 0
46  line vty 0 4
```

5.6.2.2 Dwyer Router Configuration File

Figure 5-50

Dwyer router config

```
47 version 12.0
48 service timestamps debug uptime
49 service timestamps log uptime
50 no service password-encryption
51 !
52 hostname Dwyer_Inc
53 !
54 !
55 ip subnet-zero
56 !
57 crypto cisco algorithm des cfb-8
58 !
59 crypto key pubkey-chain dss
60  named-key Quiggle signature
61    serial-number 01771306
62    key-string
63      2344C06F D2A99E0E 3D722969 E512EA64 44FCA7B0 21B594CC
        0771D1C4 2D05F350
64      3CDCD484 0FF6BA03 687DF9AE 53FEA022 F44CE737 5B081800
        B9CFC8A6
        9DE3187E
65    quit
66  !
67  crypto map Dwyer.Quiggle 14
68  set peer Quiggle
69  set algorithm des cfb-8
70  match address 140
71 !
72 interface Ethernet0
73  ip address 192.168.130.1 255.255.255.0
74  no ip directed-broadcast
75 !
76 interface Serial0
77  ip address 192.168.30.2 255.255.255.0
78  no ip directed-broadcast
79  crypto map Dwyer.Quiggle
80 !
81 ip classless
82 ip route 0.0.0.0 0.0.0.0 192.168.30.1
83 !
84 access-list 140 permit ip 192.168.130.0 0.0.0.255 host
   192.168.140.2
85 !
86 !
87 line con 0
88  exec-timeout 0 0
89  transport input none
90 line aux 0
91 line vty 0 4
```

5.6.2.3 Pseudo Internet Router (No Routing Information Being Exchanged)

Figure 5-51

Backbone router config

```
92   version 11.0
93   service udp-small-servers
94   service tcp-small-servers
95   !
96   hostname Internet
97   !
98   enable secret 5 $1$1fuK$c7nwnmcRolYgWpRKDliEk.
99   !
100  no ip domain-lookup
101  !
102  interface Ethernet0
103   no ip address
104   shutdown
105  !
106  interface Serial1
107   description To Dwyer Router
108   ip address 192.168.30.1 255.255.255.0
109   clockrate 2000000
110  !
111  interface Serial2
112   description To Quiggle Router
113   ip address 192.168.40.1 255.255.255.0
114   clockrate 2000000
115  !
116  ip route 192.168.130.0 255.255.255.0 192.168.30.2
117  ip route 192.168.140.0 255.255.255.0 192.168.40.2
118  !
119  !
120  line con 0
121   exec-timeout 0 0
122  line aux 0
123   transport input all
124  line vty 0 4
125   exec-timeout 0 0
126   password cisco
127   login
128  !
129  end
```

5.6.2.4 Case Analysis

When looking at this case study, the first thing to notice is that we are not running any routing protocol. The static default routes on router Quiggle_Inc (line 37) and Dwyer_Inc (line 82) were done on purpose. In most instances, you will be connecting to another router in which you do not share routing information. The default route to the ISP is the only thing that either router will know. In this situation, both routers have their default route point to the same router; however, that is insignificant. It is significant however, that neither router knows a route, other than the default route, to its VPN peer.

So how does the crypto map on Quiggle_Inc know what key to use to encrypt the data? It knows what key to use because the key indicated on line 22. The key used in line 22 must match one of the keys found under the crypto key pubkey-chain (line 13). In this case, it can be found on line 14.

When setting up crypto maps, it is important that our access-lists be mirror images of each other as shown in lines 39 and 84. Each access-list denotes the traffic to encrypt from its perspective. When setting up that access-list, you need to remember that the source address indicates where data will be sent from, whereas the destination indicates where the encrypted data is being sent to. It is easy to get these turned around. For this reason, extra care must be given to make sure they work as designed.

5.6.3 Case Study #3—Multipoint GRE VPN (NHRP)

VPN type: Intranet VPN

Tunnel type: Compulsory Tunnel

When to deploy: This type of tunnel is useful when you have multiple locations that need to correspond with each other and want to provide a pseudo firewall between the Internet and the organization.

Verifying VPN has been enabled: Any LAN device should be able to get to any other LAN device, whereas the Internet cannot reach any of these devices (see Figure 5-52).

Note:

In an effort to minimize the complications involved using NHRP, we have specifically left CET out of this case study.

Figure 5-52

Case Study #3

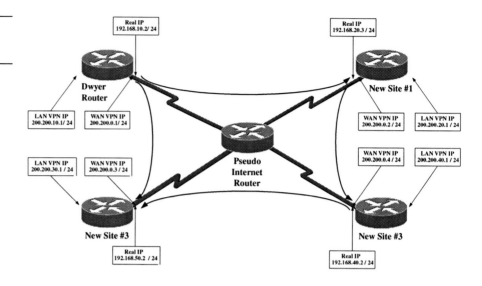

5.6.3.1 Dwyer Router Configuration File

Figure 5-53

Dwyer router
config

```
1    version 11.3
2    service timestamps debug uptime
3    service timestamps log uptime
4    no service password-encryption
5    !
6    hostname Dwyer_Inc
7    !
8    interface Loopback100
9     ip address 1.1.1.1 255.255.255.0
10   !
11   interface Tunnel100
12    ip address 200.200.0.1 255.255.255.0
13    no ip redirects
14    ip nhrp map 200.200.0.2 192.168.20.2
15    ip nhrp network-id 200
16    ip nhrp nhs 200.200.0.2
17    ip ospf network non-broadcast
18    tunnel source Serial0
19    tunnel mode gre multipoint
20    tunnel key 200
21   !
22   interface Ethernet0
23    ip address 200.200.110.1 255.255.255.0
24   !
25   interface Serial0
26    ip address 192.168.10.2 255.255.255.0
27   !
28   interface Serial1
29    no ip address
30    shutdown
```

Figure 5-53

Dwyer router
config (cont.)

```
31 !
32 router eigrp 10
33   network 192.168.10.0
34 !
35 router ospf 25
36   network 200.200.0.0 0.0.255.255 area 0
37   neighbor 200.200.0.2 priority 1
38   neighbor 200.200.0.3 priority 1
39   neighbor 200.200.0.4 priority 1
40 !
41 ip classless
42 !
43 !
44 !
45 line con 0
46   exec-timeout 0 0
47 line aux 0
48 line vty 0 4
49   exec-timeout 0 0
50   login
51 !
52 end
```

5.6.3.2 Dwyer Router Routing Table

Figure 5-54

Dwyer routing
table

```
53 RouterA#show ip route
54 Codes: C - connected, S - static, I - IGRP, R - RIP, M - mobile,
   B - BGP
55 D - EIGRP, EX - EIGRP external, O - OSPF, IA - OSPF inter area
56 N1 - OSPF NSSA external type 1, N2 - OSPF NSSA external type 2
57 E1 - OSPF external type 1, E2 - OSPF external type 2, E - EGP
58 i - IS-IS, L1 - IS-IS level-1, L2 - IS-IS level-2, * - candidate
   efault
59 U - per-user static route, o - ODR
60
61 Gateway of last resort is not set
62
63 O 200.200.140.0/24 [110/11117] via 200.200.0.4, 00:15:20,
   Tunnel100
64 1.0.0.0/24 is subnetted, 1 subnets
65 C 1.1.1.0 is directly connected, Loopback100
66 D 192.168.30.0/24 [90/46738176] via 192.168.10.1, 00:26:48,
   Serial0
67 C 200.200.0.0/24 is directly connected, Tunnel100
68 C 192.168.10.0/24 is directly connected, Serial0
69 D 192.168.40.0/24 [90/46738176] via 192.168.10.1, 00:26:48,
   Serial0
70 D 192.168.20.0/24 [90/46738176] via 192.168.10.1, 00:26:48,
   Serial0
71 O 200.200.120.0/24 [110/11121] via 200.200.0.2, 00:15:21,
   Tunnel100
72 C 200.200.110.0/24 is directly connected, Ethernet0
73 O 200.200.130.0/24 [110/11121] via 200.200.0.3, 00:15:21,
   Tunnel100
```

5.6.3.3 New Site #1 Configuration File

Figure 5-55

New site #1
configuration file

```
74   version 11.3
75   service timestamps debug uptime
76   service timestamps log uptime
77   no service password-encryption
78   !
79   hostname RouterB
80   !
81   interface Loopback100
82    ip address 200.200.120.1 255.255.255.0
83   !
84   interface Tunnel100
85    ip address 200.200.0.2 255.255.255.0
86    no ip redirects
87    ip nhrp map 200.200.0.3 192.168.130.1
88    ip nhrp network-id 200
89    ip nhrp nhs 200.200.0.3
90    ip ospf network non-broadcast
91    tunnel source Ethernet0
92    tunnel mode gre multipoint
93    tunnel key 200
94   !
95   interface Ethernet0
96    ip address 192.168.120.1 255.255.255.0
97   !
98   interface Serial0
99    ip address 192.168.20.2 255.255.255.0
100  !
101  interface Serial1
102   no ip address
103   shutdown
104  !
105  router eigrp 10
106   network 192.168.20.0
107   network 192.168.120.0
108  !
109  router ospf 25
110   network 200.200.0.0 0.0.255.255 area 0
111   neighbor 200.200.0.4 priority 1
112   neighbor 200.200.0.3 priority 1
113   neighbor 200.200.0.1 priority 1
114  !
115  line con 0
116   exec-timeout 0 0
117  line aux 0
118  line vty 0 4
119   exec-timeout 0 0
120   login
```

5.6.3.4 New Site #2 Configuration File

Figure 5-56

New site #2
configuration file

```
121 version 11.3
122 service timestamps debug uptime
123 service timestamps log uptime
124 no service password-encryption
125 !
126 hostname RouterC
127 !
128 interface Loopback100
129   ip address 3.3.3.3 255.255.255.255
130   no ip directed-broadcast
131 !
132 interface Tunnel100
133   ip address 200.200.0.3 255.255.255.0
134   no ip redirects
135   ip nhrp map 200.200.0.4 192.168.40.2
136   ip nhrp network-id 200
137   ip nhrp nhs 200.200.0.4
138   ip ospf network non-broadcast
139   tunnel source Serial0
140   tunnel mode gre multipoint
141   tunnel key 200
142 !
143 interface Ethernet0
144   ip address 200.200.130.1 255.255.255.0
145   no ip directed-broadcast
146 !
147 interface Serial0
148   ip address 192.168.30.2 255.255.255.0
149   no ip directed-broadcast
150 !
151 router eigrp 10
152   network 192.168.30.0
153 !
154 router ospf 25
155   network 200.200.0.0 0.0.255.255 area 0
156   neighbor 200.200.0.1 priority 1
157   neighbor 200.200.0.2 priority 1
158   neighbor 200.200.0.4 priority 1
159 !
160 line con 0
161   exec-timeout 0 0
162   transport input none
163 line aux 0
164 line vty 0 4
165   exec-timeout 0 0
166   login
167 !
168 end
```

5.6.3.5 New Site #3 Configuration File

Figure 5-57

New site #3
configuration file

```
169 version 11.3
170 service timestamps debug uptime
171 service timestamps log uptime
172 no service password-encryption
173 !
174 hostname RouterB
175 !
176 interface Loopback100
178  ip address 2.2.2.2 255.255.255.255
179 !
180 interface Tunnel100
181  ip address 200.200.0.2 255.255.255.0
182  no ip redirects
183  ip nhrp map 200.200.0.3 192.168.30.2
184  ip nhrp network-id 200
185  ip nhrp nhs 200.200.0.3
186  ip ospf network non-broadcast
187  tunnel source Serial0
188  tunnel mode gre multipoint
189  tunnel key 200
190 !
191 interface Ethernet0
192  ip address 200.200.120.1 255.255.255.0
193 !
194 interface Serial0
195  ip address 192.168.20.2 255.255.255.0
196 !
197 router eigrp 10
198  network 192.168.20.0
199 !
200 router ospf 25
201  network 200.200.0.0 0.0.255.255 area 0
202  neighbor 200.200.0.1 priority 1
203  neighbor 200.200.0.3 priority 1
204  neighbor 200.200.0.4 priority 1
205 !
206 line con 0
207  exec-timeout 0 0
208 line aux 0
209 line vty 0 4
210  exec-timeout 0 0
211 login
```

5.6.3.6 Pseudo Internet Router

Figure 5-58

Pseudo
internet router
configuration file

```
212 version 11.0
213 service udp-small-servers
214 service tcp-small-servers
215 !
216 hostname INTERNET
217 !
218 enable secret 5 $1$1fuK$c7nwnmcRolYgWpRKDliEk.
219 !
230 no ip domain-lookup
231 !
232 interface Serial0
233   description RouterB
234   ip address 192.168.20.1 255.255.255.0
235   no fair-queue
236   clockrate 2000000
237 !
238 interface Serial1
239   description RouterA
240   ip address 192.168.10.1 255.255.255.0
241   clockrate 2000000
242 !
243 interface Serial2
244   description RouterC
245   ip address 192.168.30.1 255.255.255.0
246   clockrate 2000000
247 !
248 interface Serial3
249   description RouterD
250   ip address 192.168.40.1 255.255.255.0
251   clockrate 2000000
252 !
253 router eigrp 10
254   network 192.168.10.0
255   network 192.168.20.0
256   network 192.168.30.0
257   network 192.168.40.0
258 !
259 !
260 line con 0
261   exec-timeout 0 0
262 line aux 0
263   transport input all
264 line vty 0 4
265   exec-timeout 0 0
266   password cisco
267   login
268 !
269 end
```

5.6.3.7 Pseudo Internet Router Routing Table

Figure 5-59

Output from
show crypto
engine
connections

```
270 INTERNET#show ip route
271 Codes: C-connected, S-static, I-IGRP, R-RIP, M-mobile, B-BGP
272 D-EIGRP, EX-EIGRP external, O-OSPF, IA-OSPF inter area
273 E1-OSPF external type 1, E2-OSPF external type 2, E-EGP
274 i-IS-IS, L1-IS-IS level-1, L2-IS-IS level-2, *-candidate
    default
275
276 Gateway of last resort is not set
277
288 C    192.168.40.0 is directly connected, Serial3
289 C    192.168.10.0 is directly connected, Serial1
290 C    192.168.30.0 is directly connected, Serial2
291 C    192.168.20.0 is directly connected, Serial0
```

5.6.3.8 Case Analysis

This particular case study is very interesting. In it, we use EIGRP to
establish connectivity between all of the serial interfaces on the routers
and OSPF to connect all the LAN segments to each other. Whereas this is
not a recommended solution, it does provide an interesting view of NHRP
and NBMA networks. In this case study, EIGRP can be configured in a
normal manner. However, OSPF must treat the multipoint GRE tunnel as
an NBMA network, which leads to the configurations found in lines 17,
37, 38, and 39 for Router A. This OSPF configuration is repeated between
all four routers.

Lines 53-73 shows us the routing table from Router A. You can see that
it knows how to get to both the OSPF network and the EIGRP network.
Whereas the Pseudo Internet Router (lines 270-291) only knows about the
EIGRP network, which in this case it happens to be directly connected to
all of those routers. Notice that the Pseudo Internet Router cannot get to
any of the LAN IP addresses. This keeps our LAN users from even knowing about the Internet even though they use it for a transport! Whereas
the data that is being sent is not encrypted, we could simply apply a
crypto map to each of the serial interfaces to take care of that problem.

Making NHRP work requires that we have at least one statically
mapped NHRP address. Notice that we have configured each router to
point to the next router in a circular fashion so the NHRP can resolve
NHRP requests. Lines 14, 87, 135, and 183 show us how the map statements are used to create this circular approach to resolve the real IP
address for the VPN IP address.

Once you get over the fact that the GRE multipoint tunnel appears to be a single network (even though there are multiple networks that are being used to support this pseudo network), this case study becomes trivial to understand. The key is isolating the configuration of NHRP and how the different networks interoperate.

5.7 Summary of GRE and CET for VPN

Multiprotocol Support	Yes, IPX, AppleTalk, DECNet
IP Protocol Number	Decimal: 47 (Hex:2F)
Port Number	1701
What ports need to be opened in order to use through a firewall?	
	permit tcp host X.X.X.X eq 1723 any
	permit 47 host X.X.X.X any
TCP Dependent	No
UDP Dependent	No
Encryption Strength	Weak
IOS Support for GRE Tunnels	IOS 10.0 and later
IOS Support for CET	IOS 11.2 and later

RFC's related to GRE Tunnels

RFC	Status	Title
1701	Informational	*Generic Routing Encapsulation* (GRE)
1702	Informational	GRE Over IPv4 Networks
2784	Proposed Standard	GRE
2890	Proposed Standard	Key and Sequence Number Extensions to GRE

RFC's Related to CET Encryption	None, CET is a Cisco proprietary solution

5.8 Command Summary

5.8.1 IOS 11.3 and 12.0 Tunnel Interface Commands

Command	Config Mode	Function
interface tunnel	Global Config	Creates a tunnel interface or changes to a previously created tunnel
tunnel mode gre ip	Tunnel Interface	Specifies the tunnel to operate in point to point mode
tunnel mode gre multipoint	Tunnel Interface	Specifies the tunnel to operate in multipoint mode
tunnel source	Tunnel Interface	Specifies the source IP address to use for the tunnel
tunnel destination	Tunnel Interface	Specifies the destination IP address to use for the tunnel
ip nhrp network-id	Tunnel Interface	Specifies the network ID of the NHRP network.
ip nhrp nhs	Tunnel Interface	Specifies the Next Hop Server the NHRP device should use
ip nhrp map	Tunnel Interface	Manually maps an NHRP address to a NBMA address
show interface tunnel	User/Enable	Shows the status of the current tunnel
show ip nhrp	User/Enable	Shows current NHRP mappings
show ip nhrp traffic	User/Enable	Shows traffic over the NHRP network

5.8.2 CET IOS 11.3 Enterprise Commands

Command	Config Mode	Function
crypto gen-signature-keys	Global Config	Generate public/private key pair
crypto engine accelerator	Global Config	Enables VPN module for crypto engine on Cisco 1700 series router
show crypto mypubkey	User/Enable	Displays your public key
crypto key-exchange passive	Global Config	Specifies a router go into passive mode during a key exchange

continued

crypto key-exchange x.x.x.x	Global Config	Specifies a router contact a VPN peer at the IP address to exchange keys
crypto algorithm	Global Config	Enables a cryptography algorithm globally
show crypto algorithms	User/Enable	Shows all the current enabled algorithms
crypto *crypto-map-name sequence-number*	Global Config	Creates a crypto map, or enters a previously created crypto map
set peer	Crypto Map Config Mode	Defines the peer you will exchange encrypted data with in this crypto map
match address	Crypto Map Config Mode	Defines the data stream that should be encrypted
set algorithm	Crypto Map Config Mode	Defines the encryption algorithm to be used by the crypto map
crypto map	Interface Config Mode	Applies the crypto map to an interface
crypto key-timeout	Crypto Map Config Mode	Specifies the length of time to use before expiring an encrypted connection
crypto pregen-dh-pairs	Crypto Map Config Mode	Specify the number of DH numbers that can be pre-generated
show crypto connections	User/Enable	Show the active encryption sessions
show crypto engine connections	User/Enable	Show active and disabled encryption sessions

5.8.3 CET IOS 11.3T and 12.0 Enterprise Commands

Command	*Config Mode*	*Function*
crypto key generate dss	Global	Generates public/private key pair
crypto engine accelerator	Global	Enables VPN module for crypto engine on Cisco 1700 series router
show crypto key mypubkey dss	User/Enable	Displays your public key
crypto key exchange dss passive	Global Config	Specifies a router to go into passive mode during a key exchange

continued

crypto key exchange dss x.x.x.x	Global Config	Specifies a router contact a VPN peer at the IP address to exchange keys
crypto cisco algorithm	Global Config	Enables a cryptography algorithm globally
show crypto algorithms	User/Enable	Show all the current enabled algorithms
crypto *crypto-map-name sequence-number*	Crypto Map Config Mode	Creates a crypto map, or enters a previously created crypto map
set peer *crypto-engine-name*	Crypto Map Config Mode	Defines the peer you will exchange encrypted data with in this crypto map
match address		Defines the data stream that should be encrypted
set algorithm	Crypto Map Config Mode	Defines the encryption algorithm to be used by the crypto map
crypto map	Crypto Map Config Mode	Applies the crypto map to an interface
crypto cisco key-timeout	Crypto Map Config Mode	Specifies the length of time to use before expiring an encrypted connection
crypto pregen-dh-pairs	Crypto Map Config Mode	Specify the number of DH numbers that can be pre-generated
show crypto map	User/Enable	Shows the active encryption sessions
show crypto engine connections	User/Enable	Show active and disabled encryption sessions

6

IPSec

In the last chapter we looked at a method of creating a pseudo VPN using standard features found on most Cisco routers, specifically *Cisco Encryption Technology* (CET) and *Generic Routing Encapsulation* (GRE). Cisco's proprietary CET received a large part of its foundation in the *Internet Security Protocol* (IPSec) before IPSec became a standard, so it is no surprise that many similarities exist between configuring IPSec and CET on a Cisco router.

Although IPSec services outlined in this chapter are similar to the previous chapter on CET, CET cannot provide some functions that IPSec can. For example, both CET and IPSec can encrypt a data stream, however, only IPSec can authenticate the source of the data stream, and provide protection against replay attacks. It also has many other features, which we will examine later in this chapter.

6.1 Objectives to be Covered in This Chapter

■ Overview of IPSec
■ Describe IPSec authentication methods

- Describe IPSec encryption methods
- Describe IPSec key management
- Describe tunnel mode versus transport mode
- Configure IPSec on a Cisco router
- Review design considerations for IPSec
- Troubleshoot IPSec

We will first discuss the architecture of IPSec in detail, including the various components: authentication, encryption, key management, and how these components interoperate with each other. As you read this chapter, it is more important to understand how the various components interoperate with each other rather than what commands to use. If you understand the protocol and how it operates, finding the appropriate commands becomes easy.

6.2 Overview of IPSec Architecture

IPSec is a generic framework developed and maintained by the *Internet Engineering Task Force* (IETF). The design goals for IPSec is to provide a modular component-oriented structure that would enable the replacement of the protocols, causing minimal impact to a network. It has been designed from the ground up to be a security protocol for both IPv4 and IPv6. In addition, it has been designed so that it can operate as a compulsory tunnel or a voluntary tunnel. Like any technologies that enable two devices to communicate, the protocol(s) used must be agreed upon prior to the actual use of the technology. IPSec is no exception to this rule.

Request for Comment (RFC) 2411 outlines the interrelationship of all the IPSec documents. In Figure 6-1, we can see that in an effort to maintain a modular approach to IPSec, the IETF has divided all of the IPSec protocols into seven different groups.

Each of these different groups has a specific purpose in the IPSec paradigm. By breaking down IPSec into seven different areas, it becomes easier to understand which group of documents is responsible for each objective, and it minimizes the possibility of overlap in such a complex suite of protocols.

- **IPSec architecture** - These documents describe the general concepts, security requirements, definitions, and mechanisms used in IPSec technology.

Figure 6-1

Interrelationship
of IPSec
documents/
protocols

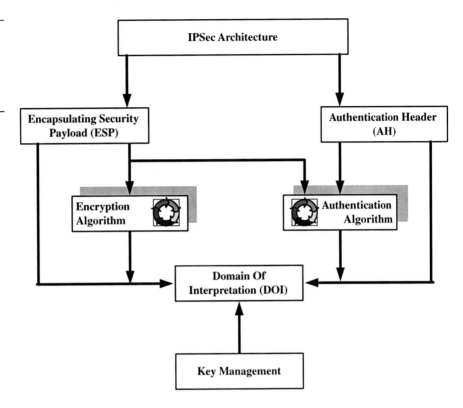

- ***Encapsulating Security Protocol* (ESP)** - These documents
  describe packet format, default values (when appropriate), padding
  contents, mandatory algorithms, and general issues associated with
  encryption.
- ***Authentication Header* (AH)** - These documents describe packet
  format, default values (when appropriate), padding contents,
  mandatory algorithms, and general issues associated with
  authentication.
- **Encryption algorithm** - This set of documents illustrates the
  various encryption algorithms used for ESP. These documents should
  avoid overlap with the ESP protocol and authentication algorithm
  documents. For example, documents related to the *Data Encryption
  Standard* (DES) would fall under this category. When certain values
  are not provided by a document, it is left to the *Domain of
  Interpretation* (DOI) to indicate values.

- **Authentication algorithm** - This describes the set of documents used for authentication for both ESP and AH. These documents should avoid overlap with the AH protocol documents and the encryption algorithm documents. Examples of authentication algorithm documents are HMAC-MD5 and HMAC-SHA-1 documents. When these algorithms are used for ESP and AH, the domain of interpretation has to indicate certain values.

- **Key management** - This set of documents describes the IETF standards-track key management schemes. When appropriate, they provide default values for the domain of interpretation documents. Examples of key management documents include ISAKMP and OAKLEY.

- **Domain of Interpretation** (DOI) - The set of documents that fall into the domain of interpretation contain values that enable each of the other documents to relate to each other. Assigned values and constants of negotiable items go in DOI documents. The purpose of these values is to enable the establishment of *Security Associations* (SAs).

Note:

If you are unfamiliar with some of the above acronyms, specifically ISAKMP, OAKLEY, and SA, do not worry, it is because we have not covered them yet. Once we have discussed these protocols and you have become familiar with their purpose, the above definitions may make more sense to you. You may want to review this section after you read the rest of this section. Note that this information is not critical when trying to configure IPSec. It is important if you need to find some definitive source describing the nitty-gritty aspects of a particular protocol's operational characteristics.

6.2.1 Security Associations

Now that we understand how the various documents that describe IPSec have been grouped to provide a modular solution to our security problem, we will look at the various IPSec components that make IPSec work. SAs are a fundamental aspect to IPSec. In order for two parties to encrypt/

decrypt a data stream, they must agree on many different attributes used to encrypt their data stream, such as, whether they will authenticate a data stream, which cryptographic algorithms to use for either authentication or encryption, as well as many other components. Because of the many components that must be agreed upon between two IPSec peers, IPSec can be confusing. However, these components give IPSec its flexibility. In addition, the components must agree on a key management paradigm that will be used and if needed, how to exchange keys, how often to exchange keys, and the process of actually exchanging keys.

Note:

To more quickly understand security associations, think of encryption and authentication as different processes. These different processes do not need to use the same key or algorithm. They are a separate and distinct process from each other and neither one relies on the other. This enables us to authenticate a data stream, encrypt a data stream, and authenticate-encrypt a data stream.

An SA is a one-way relationship between the sender and receiver that groups all the components required in order to communicate securely with another entity. If a peer relationship is required (which it is for a VPN), then two SAs are required. An IPSec SA between two IPSec peers defines the following:

- **Sequence number counter** - This 32-bit parameter is used to generate the sequence number field in AH or ESP headers.
- **Anti-replay window** - This parameter is used to determine whether an inbound AH or ESP packet has been replayed. If a packet has already been received or fails authentication, the packet is discarded and an auditable event is generated.
- **AH information** - These parameters describe the algorithm, keys, key lifetimes, and related parameters used with the AH.
- **ESP information** - These parameters describe the algorithm, keys, key lifetimes, and related parameters used with the AH.
- **Life of security association** - This parameter describes a time interval or byte count that cannot be exceeded. If either factor (time or byte count) is exceeded, a new SA must be established.

In order to minimize the amount of risk that any group of encrypted messages has due to brute force attacks, security associations are generally associated with a time limit. This forces the IPSec peers to renegotiate all of the SA components. Some SAs not only have time limits, but message limits as well. For example, a typical SA might be defined so that after 60 minutes or after 20Mb of data has been exchanged, the SA is renegotiated.

Although an SA can be either an authentication SA or an encryption SA, it cannot be both. An IPSec peer uses the following three parameters to identify an SA.

- *Security Parameters Index (SPI)* - This locally significant field is carried in the AH and/or ESP headers. This enables the receiving device to select the SA under which a packet should be processed.

- **IP destination address** - This is the destination address of the IPSec peer. The destination address can either be an end user or a network device, such as a router or firewall. Currently, only unicast addresses are supported.

- **Security protocol identifier** - This is used to indicate whether an association is an AH or ESP SA.

One of the key benefits derived from compliance with the IPSec suite of protocols is that any product or service can interoperate with any other IPSec product. Thus, you do not have to be locked into any single vendor's product for security; you can mix and match as your business demands. We will now take a look at the building blocks of each of the different protocols that utilize SAs.

6.2.2 Authentication Header (AH)

The authentication header provides a crucial aspect of a VPN. Although authentication protocols like *Password Authentication Protocol* (PAP) and *Challenge Handshake Authentication Protocol* (CHAP) deal with Layer 2 authentication, IPSec is a Layer 3 technology and uses a completely different paradigm for authenticating. IPSec authentication header enables a connectionless method of providing data origin authentication, message integrity, and protection against a replay attack. This is accomplished using a shared key-hashing algorithm, such as HMAC-MD5 and HMAC-SHA-1.

Note:

SHA-1 HMAC is considered the stronger hash function by using a 160-bit authenticator, compared to HMAC-MD5's 128-bit authenticator.

The authentication header is inserted between the IP header and the rest of the packet's contents, including the *Transmission Control Protocol (TCP)/User Datagram Protocol* (UDP) header and packet's payload, as seen in Figure 6-2.

Figure 6-2

AH header format

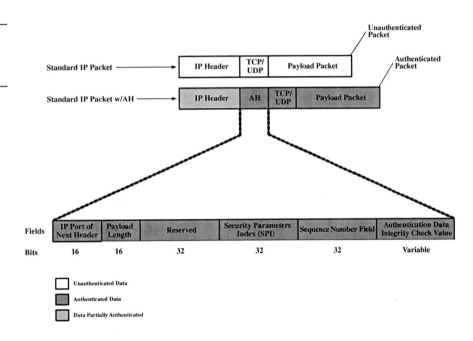

AH attempts to protect as much of the IP header as possible, but some IP header fields may change in transit; therefore, the sender does not protect the value of these fields. As can be seen in Figure 6-2, AH authenticates everything in the entire IP packet except for those fields that are changeable, which we will discuss soon.

The various fields that make up the AH header are as follows:.

- **IP Port of Next Header** - *(bits zero-seven)* - This field describes the type of payload after the authentication header. The value of this field comes from the IP protocol numbers defined by the *Internet Assigned Number Authority* (IANA) in STD-2.

- **Payload Length** - *(bits eight-15)* - This field specifies the length of the AH in 32-bit words.

- **Reserved** - *(bits 16-31)* - This field is reserved for future use and must be set to zero. It is included when calculating the *Integrity Check Value* (ICV), but is otherwise ignored.

- ***Security Parameters Index (SPI)*** - *(bits 32-63)* - This field, in combination with the destination IP address and security protocol, uniquely identifies the security association for this datagram. The values one-255 are reserved for future use by the IANA. Generally this value is selected by the destination system when the SA is established.

- **Sequence number** - *(bits 64-95)* - This field contains an increasing counter value. Its presence is mandatory, although the receiver is not required to act upon it. If anti-replay is disabled, the sender and receiver's counters are initialized to zero when an SA is established. If anti-replay is enabled, which is the default, the transmitted sequence number is never reset.

- **Authentication data integrity check value (variable)** - This variable length field contains the *Integrity Check Value* (ICV) for this packet. Its size will be a multiple of 32 bits.

For fields that are not protected by AH, the system uses a value of zero for the ICV calculation. As a general rule of thumb, if a value in the IP header is predictable, the value is included within the ICV. If a value in the IP header is not predictable, a zero is used by the ICV calculation as opposed to omitting the field. This preserves the alignment of the ICV calculation. Examples of fields that are zeroed during ICV calculation are

- Type of service
- DF flag
- TTL field
- Fragment offset
- Header checksum

Note:

In addition to using a value of zero when calculating the ICV, the authentication data integrity check value field is set to zero for the purpose of the calculation.

Currently, two RFCs are related to AH: RFC 1828, *IP Authentication using Keyed MD5,* and RFC 2402, *IP Authentication Header.* RFC 1828 does not provide protection against replay attacks, whereas the updated AH protocol does. Cisco has implemented the updated authentication algorithms MC5 and SHA (HMAC variants).

6.2.3 Encapsulating Security Protocol (ESP)

The primary reason for implementing a VPN of any sort is for security. IPSec's ESP is responsible for encrypting and decrypting a packet. In addition, ESP can be used for connectionless data origin authentication, data integrity, and protection against a replay attack.

Note:

Remember that connectionless data origin authentication does not require the exchange of a username and password in a manner with which we are familiar. Instead, using techniques from Chapter 4, we can encrypt data in such a way that we know who it comes from (assuming that our keys have not been compromised).

Like the AH header, the ESP header is inserted between the IP header and any subsequent packet content, as seen in Figure 6-3.

ESP attempts to protect as much of the IP header as possible, but some IP header fields may change in transit; therefore, the sender does not protect the value of these fields. In Figure 6-2, AH authenticates everything in the entire IP packet except for those fields that are changeable, which we will discuss soon.

▓ **Security parameters index** - *(bits zero-31)* - This field, in combination with the destination IP address and security protocol, uniquely identifies the security association for this datagram. The

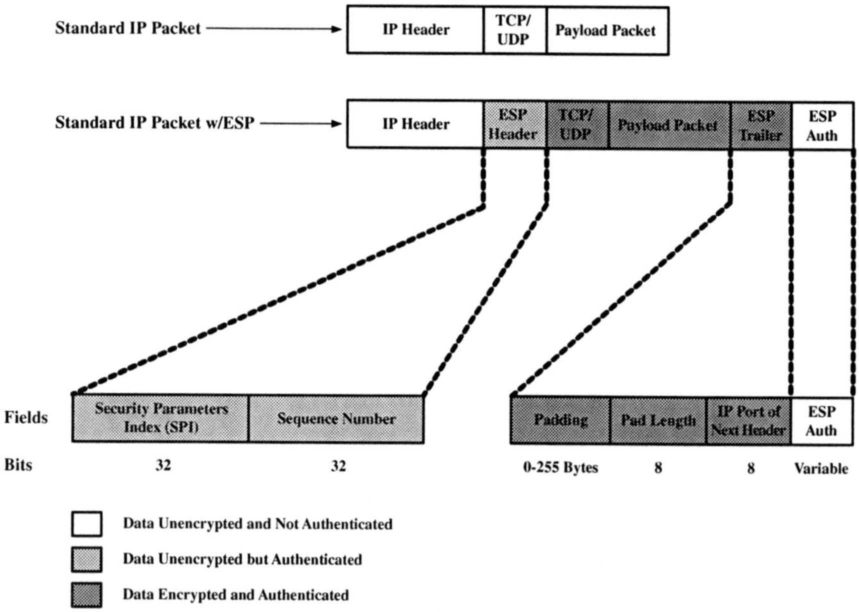

Figure 6-3

ESP header format

Standard IP Packet ⟶ | IP Header | TCP/UDP | Payload Packet

Standard IP Packet w/ESP ⟶ | IP Header | ESP Header | TCP/UDP | Payload Packet | ESP Trailer | ESP Auth

Fields | Security Parameters Index (SPI) | Sequence Number | Padding | Pad Length | IP Port of Next Header | ESP Auth

Bits | 32 | 32 | 0-255 Bytes | 8 | 8 | Variable

☐ Data Unencrypted and Not Authenticated

▨ Data Unencrypted but Authenticated

▩ Data Encrypted and Authenticated

values of one-255 are reserved for future use by the IANA. Generally this value is selected by the destination system when the SA is established.

- **Sequence number** - *(bits 32-63)* - This field contains an increasing counter value. Its presence is mandatory, although the receiver is not required to act upon it. If anti-replay is disabled, the sender and receiver's counters are initialized to zero when an SA is established. If anti-replay is enabled, which is the default, the transmitted sequence number is never reset.

- **Padding** - *(zero-255 bytes)* - If an encryption algorithm requires the plain text block to be a multiple of some number of bytes for use with a block cipher, the padding field is used to fill the plain text to the size required by the algorithm.

- **Pad length** - *(eight bits)* - This field indicates the number of bytes used in the padding field. The pad length field is mandatory. A value of zero should be used to indicate that no padding bytes are present.

- **IP port of next header** - *(eight bits)* - This mandatory field describes the type of payload contained in the payload data field. The value of this field comes from the IP protocol numbers defined by the *Internet Assigned Number Authority* (IANA) in STD-2.

■ **ESP authentication** - *(variable length)* - This variable length field contains the *Integrity Check Value* (ICV) for this packet. Its size will be a multiple of 32 bits.

Notice that the ESP header can provide authentication services as well as encryption services. This might be confusing because you would think that only AH provides authentication services. ESP can provide limited authentication for our data streams, which we will address in the "Tunnel Mode versus Transport Mode" section of this chapter.

Although ESP provides data-origin authentication, it cannot authenticate all of the data within the packet like AH can. As seen in Figure 6-3, ESP's scope for providing authentication is quite extensive; however, it does not provide any authentication to the IP header. Thus, if your business requirement is for absolute security, you may need to deploy both ESP and AH. Remember that there is a performance penalty for each protocol that is used.

When choosing to use ESP to provide authentication as well as encryption, encryption is always performed first. Because the authentication field is not encrypted, it enables the receiver of the packet to rapidly detect and reject replayed or bogus packets. This is an attempt by the designers to reduce the impact of *denial of service* (DoS) attacks.

According to RFC 2406, if authentication is being used within ESP and the receiver calculates a mismatched ICV, the event should be logged. The following data should be included within the event:

■ SPI value

■ Date/time received

■ Source address

■ Destination address

■ Sequence number

■ Clear text flow ID (IPv6 only)

Currently, several RFCs are related to ESP. It is important to keep in mind that RFC 1829, *The ESP DES-CBC Transform,* does not provide protection against replay attacks, whereas the updated ESP protocol RFC 2405, *The ESP DES-CBC Cipher Algorithm With Explicit IV,* does. Cisco has implemented the updated ESP protocol found in RFC 2405.

6.2.4 Key Management

With all of the encryption algorithms and authentication algorithms used within IPSec, it should be obvious that key management is a fundamental issue for any IPSec solution. Two possible solutions exist to key management in any IPSec solution:

- Manual
- Automatic

As mandated by IPSec, every implementation must be able to support both manual and automatic key management. For quite a while in fact, manual keying was the only way for vendors to perform interoperability testing.

When the number of peers that you must communicate with is minimal, you should consider using the manual method. Manual key configurations are practical in small static environments, but are still prone to errors when entering the IPSec SA keys. In addition, when rolling out large VPN infrastructures, a manual key infrastructure does not scale, as it requires too much administrative overhead to be a viable solution.

Several different key management protocols are available: for example, KDC-based systems such as Kerberos, and public-key systems such as SKIP. However, IPSec's default key management protocol is *Internet Key Management Protocol* (IKMP), frequently referred to as *Internet Key Exchange* (IKE).

6.2.4.1 Internet Key Exchange (IKE)

IKE, defined by RFC 2409, is a hybrid protocol that is used to negotiate authentication and provide authentication material for SAs in a secure manner. IKE has been designed for four primary functions:

- To provide a means for two IPSec peers to agree on which protocols, algorithms, and keys to use for a key exchange
- To ensure that you are talking to the right person from the beginning of the conversation
- To manage the keys after they have been agreed upon
- To guarantee that the keys are kept secret

These functions are implemented from the following two protocols:

- *ISAKMP* - is designed as a framework for authentication and key exchanges, but does not define them. It defines procedures and packet formats to establish, negotiate, modify, and delete security associations.

- *Oakley* - describes multiple modes of key exchanges and provides details for perfect forward secrecy for keys, identity protection, and authentication services. It is based on the Diffie-Hellman algorithm.

Note:

IKE is a relatively new name for ISAKMP/Oakley. Many IPSec documents refer to the key-exchange protocols as ISAKMP/Oakley. You will see us use ISAKMP and IKE interchangeably.

ISAKMP's primary function is to establish SAs for IPSec. In order to negotiate an IPSec SA relationship with another VPN peer, IKE must negotiate its own SA first. Think of it as securing a channel so that you can then negotiate the parameters of the IPSec SA. This enables the negotiation of the IPSec parameters to be confidential, as seen in Figure 6-4.

Four steps are required to establish an IPSec SA. Using Figure 6-4, the following process occurs:

1. Router A and Router B negotiate an ISAKMP SA.
2. Router A has an ISAKMP SA for its VPN peer (Router B). Router B has an ISAKMP SA for its VPN peer (Router A).
3. Router A and Router B to negotiate an IPSec SA, using the encrypted tunnel established by ISAKMP.
4. Router A has an IPSec SA for its VPN peer (Router B). Router B has an IPSec SA for its VPN peer (Router B).

Note:

Although the RFC defines IPSec peers as "devices," we are using the term "router" to help clarify any confusion that could be caused by using the generic term "device." This is especially true because in the end we are trying to show how to configure routers as IPSec peers.

In order to accomplish this task, each protocol (ISAKMP and Oakley) has their own set of stages they utilize to establish an SA. ISAKMP operates in two different phases, whereas Oakley operates in three different modes.

Figure 6-4

ISAKMP
negotiating an
IPSec SA

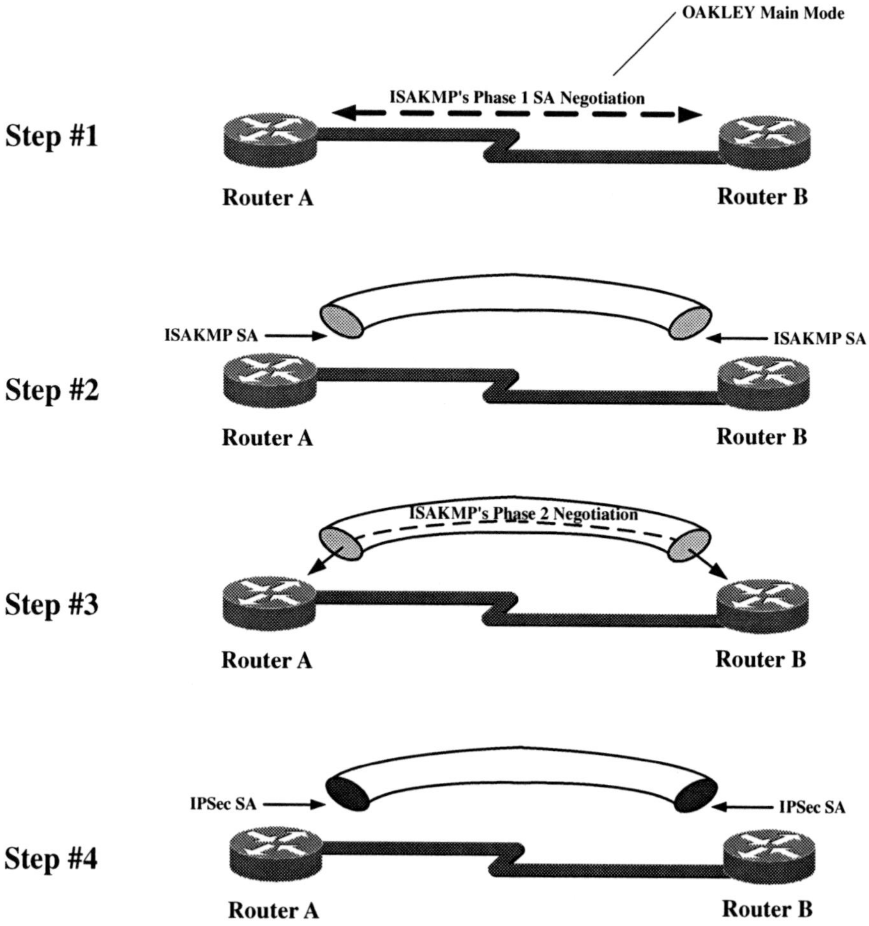

Step #1

OAKLEY Main Mode

ISAKMP's Phase 1 SA Negotiation

Router A

Router B

Step #2

ISAKMP SA

ISAKMP SA

Router A

Router B

Step #3

ISAKMP's Phase 2 Negotiation

Router A

Router B

Step #4

IPSec SA

IPSec SA

Router A

Router B

ISAKMP's first phase is used to establish a secure channel for performing ISAKMP operations (Step #1 in Figure 6-4). ISAKMP's second phase is used to negotiate general-purpose SAs (AH or ESP) through the ISAKMP SA (Step #3 in Figure 6-4). This prevents outside parties from knowing what type of encryption we are going to use, which makes an attacker's job much more difficult.

In support of creating the SAs, the Oakley protocol operates in three different modes:

- Main mode
- Aggressive mode
- Quick mode

Main mode provides a mechanism for establishing ISAKMP's first phase. Oakley main mode operation uses three, two-way exchanges between the SA initiator and the recipient. During the first exchange, they agree on the basic algorithms and hashes to use. In the second exchange, the SA initiator and the recipient exchange public keys using DH and pass each other a random number that they must each sign and return to prove their identity. In the third exchange, (the last exchange), they both verify each other's identity, completing the exchange and establishment of the SA.

Quick mode uses encrypted packets to negotiate general-purpose IPSec services after a secure tunnel has already been established. Quick mode, which utilizes a hash payload with the agreed-upon psuedo-random function, employs a three-packet exchange like the aggressive mode. After ISAKMP's first phase has been completed (ISAKMP SA established), ISAKMP's second phase will use quick mode to establish the remaining SAs. Do not forget that up to four SAs may need to be established because each IPSec protocol (ESP or AH) will require an SA at each end.

6.2.4.1 Public Key Infrastructure (PKI)

One of the greatest challenges facing implementers of large IPSec installations is the distribution and management of public keys. By utilizing digital certificates, a large organization can provide an easy way for devices to authenticate each other. PKIs are not just a VPN authentication mechanism, they also support electronic mail, Web access, and variety of other applications that require security. PKI gives you the ability to issue, revoke, and distribute public keys in a secure manner.

Even though it is easier to distribute public keys than secret keys, we still need a method in which we can deliver public keys in a trusted manner. Otherwise, we could be subject to a man-in-the-middle attack in which an attacker could fool a couple of public key users to request a public key from an attacker instead of the PKI *Certificate Authority* (CA). The attacker could then send a public key in which he or she knew the private key, thus corrupting our public key. Requiring a CA to use a digital signature allows you to avoid this man-in-the-middle type of attack.

Generally, public keys are delivered to a requestor through a digital certificate. In Figure 6-5, Router A is requesting the public key for Router B. The CA server sends Router B's public key to Router A, but it is encrypted with the CA's private key. Router A then uses the CA's public key to decrypt the message, allowing Router A to verify that the digital certificate really came from our CA.

Figure 6-5

Example of PKI
in action

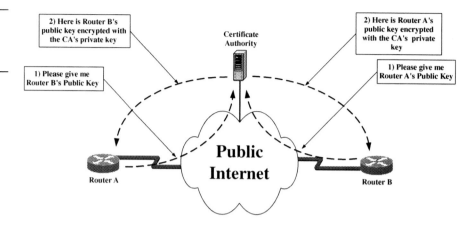

So then, where do CAs get their authority? Two generally accepted distributions systems are available: a hierarchical system, and a web of trust. Although the intricacies of how these things work is beyond the scope of this book, we can tell you that a hierarchical system relies on a top-level agency to provide a CA. The easiest way to describe a web of trust is with the phrase "any friend of yours is a friend of mine." The idea is that you only trust those peers who are trusted by someone you trust. Unfortunately, this paradigm does not scale to meet the needs of an enterprise.

In most cases, a large organization that is interested in deploying large scale IPSec VPNs will deploy their own CA server without bothering to link to any national or international hierarchy. However, if you plan on creating an extranet, you will probably have to depend on some third party CA to validate certificates.

6.2.5 Tunnel Mode versus Transport Mode

IPSec can operate in one of two modes: transport mode and tunnel mode. Both the ESP and AH protocols have been designed to work in either transport mode or tunnel mode. In transport mode, only the transport layer field and higher layers of the datagram are processed by AH or ESP. Tunnel mode enables AH or ESP to process the network layer protocol. In Figure 6-6, we can examine the differences between tunnel mode and transport mode when using the AH protocol.

Notice that the AH header comes directly after the first IP header. In tunnel mode, this enables AH to treat the original IP header as data, and

Figure 6-6

Differences
between
transport mode
and tunnel mode
on AH

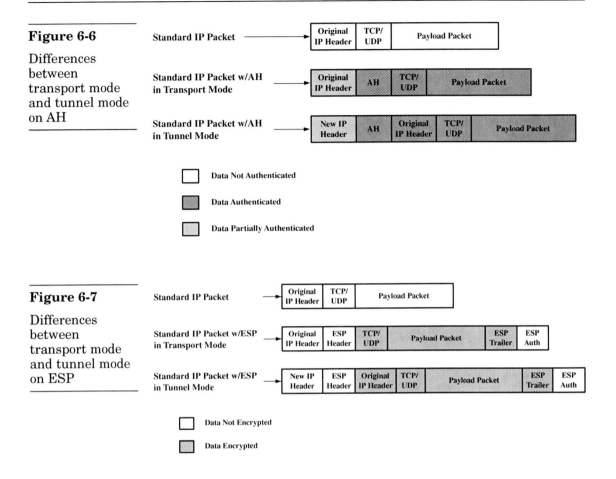

Figure 6-7

Differences
between
transport mode
and tunnel mode
on ESP

it can fully authenticate everything because none of the changeable fields
will be modified as it crosses the internetwork to the IPSec peer.

Figure 6-7 illustrates the differences between tunnel mode and transport mode when using the ESP protocol.

When using IPSec in tunnel mode, like the AH protocol, the ESP
header is inserted immediately after the new IP header, encrypting the
original IP header. This is useful for protecting the inside of a network
because the original source IP address and destination IP address are
encrypted. The rest of the world can only see the source and destination of
the two IPSec peers, but not those of the two communicating devices.

After reviewing the differences between these two modes, it should be
clear that you should use transport mode for voluntary tunnels, and use

the tunnel mode for compulsory tunnels. Although you can use the tunnel mode on voluntary tunnels, and the transport mode on compulsory tunnels, it will not fit the mold in which they were designed. Let us look at why you should use transport mode on voluntary tunnels.

The main advantage of tunnel mode is that you can fully encrypt and authenticate the IP header. In addition, you can use the IP address of the VPN initiator to hide the VPN client's IP address.

However, in the case of a voluntary tunnel, in which the end user initiates the VPN with an IPSec terminating device, the IP address of the VPN client would be the same as the VPN initiator. Therefore, you would be exposing the IP address of the VPN client to the public anyway. In addition, we take a performance hit because we have to build a second IP header for our encrypted packet.

Deciding to use transport mode on a compulsory tunnel should be determined by the business requirements and the level of security required. In a case where you are providing LAN-to-LAN connectivity, it is probably essential that you hide the IP addresses of the VPN clients from the rest of the world; the tunnel mode can accomplish this with no problem. However, if you have routers that are short on *Central Processing Unit* (CPU) processing power, you might make a trade-off between performance (building the second header) and security. However, it is recommended that you use the tunnel mode for compulsory tunnels whenever possible because of the security factor.

6.3 Cisco IOS Support for IPSec

Because IPSec was not available when 11.2 was released, Cisco introduced their proprietary security solution: CET. However, IPSec provides more security and is standards-based, making it a preferred security solution.

IPSec was first available starting with IOS 11.3T. It was introduced into the mainline IOS, starting with IOS 12.0. However, support for Triple DES first appeared in IOS 12.0(1)XA. If you need Triple DES support, you will have to apply for a license through Cisco's Web site.

Verifying support for IPSec within an IOS is a relatively simple task. This is because any IOS that supports IPSec will have a *56i* designation with the IOS name.

6.4 Configuring IPSec (IOS 11.3T, 12.0, and 12.1)

As with the communication between any devices, an agreement as to the format of the communication must exist between those devices. In this section, we will describe the tasks required to configure IPSec between two devices. As in Chapter 5, "GRE with CET," we will outline the necessary steps for configuring your router for IPSec. Unlike Chapter 5, however, the commands used for both IOS 11.3T and IOS 12.0 are very similar. For this reason, we will not have separate sections for each IOS, but we will show you when differences appear among IOS 11.3T, IOS 12.0, and IOS 12.1.

In order to configure IPSec in a bare minimum configuration, we must perform the following tasks:

- Configure transform set.

  - Specify encapsulating security protocol.
  - Specify authentication header protocol.
  - Specify tunnel mode versus transport mode.

- Create and configure crypto maps.

  - Specify IPSec peer.
  - Specify which data stream to encrypt.
  - Specify transform set.

- Configure key management.
- Apply crypto map to interface.

Key management is a crucial and potentially complex component to configure. Because of this, several different types of crypto maps can be configured, each with its own task list. Keep in mind that although we will discuss these different types of crypto maps, only a single type of crypto map should be used between two IPSec peers.

6.4.1 Configure Transform Set (AH, ESP, and Mode)

In a nutshell, transform sets are used to define IPSec policies (do not confuse these with ISAKMP policies). A transform set represents a grouping of the various AH protocols, ESP protocols, and modes used to enact a security policy. When configuring a transform set, three components can be configured.

▓ Encapsulating security protocol (up to two per transform set)

▓ Authentication header protocol (single encryption per transform set)

▓ Mode (transport or tunnel)

6.4.1.1 Configuring AH and ESP Protocols

When configuring a transform set to be used for IPSec encryption and authentication, no negotiation of the protocols occurs. Either the two IPSec peers agree on encryption and authentication protocols, or they do not. When configuring the AH and ESP protocols to be used by a transform set, each of the protocols are listed on the same configuration line as the name of the transform set. The format of the command for all three IOSs (11.3T, 12.0, and 12.1) is:

```
Router(config)#crypto ipsec transform-set transform-name protocol1
protocol 2 protocol3
```

transform-name	*WORD*	Name of the transform set
protocol	**ah-md5-hmac**	Use AH-HMAC-MD5 for auth
	ah-rfc1828	Use AH-MD5 transform (RFC1828) for auth
	ah-sha-hmac	Use AH-HMAC-SHA transform for auth
	esp-des	Use ESP transform using DES cipher (56 bits)
	esp-md5-hmac	Use ESP transform using HMAC-MD5 auth
	esp-null	Use ESP transform w/o cipher
	esp-rfc1829	Use ESP-DES-CBC transform (RFC1829)
	esp-sha-hmac	Use ESP transform using HMAC-SHA auth

Table 6-1	Transform Type	Protocol
Categorization of ESP and AH protocols	AH	ah-md5-hmac
		ah-sha-hmac
	ESP (encryption)	esp-3des
		esp-null
	ESP (authentication)	esp-md5-hmac
		Esp-sha-hmac

When specifying which encryption/authentication protocols to use, you can choose only one AH protocol, one ESP encryption protocol, and one ESP authentication protocol. Table 6-1 shows us which category each of the various transform types fall into.

Note:

IOS 12.1 has another transform available: comp-lzs. *Comp-lzs is a transform that provides compression. This protocol is important to those who are more concerned about bandwidth than CPU performance. Although applying compression to an interface can be effective for unencrypted data streams, it is not effective for data streams that are encrypted. This is because compression works by finding repetitive patterns within the data stream, removing them, and telling the remote end about these repetitive patterns. However, good encryption algorithms employ a mechanism that eliminates any repetitive pattern, preventing attackers from seeing patterns within the ciphertext that could enable them to determine the contents. Unfortunately, this makes it impossible for compression to operate because all of the repetitive patterns have disappeared. However, by first compressing the data and then encrypting it, we can reduce the size of the data stream while enjoying the benefits of encryption.*

In Figure 6-8, we have specified multiple ESP protocols, but specified only a single AH protocol. This is because only a single authentication protocol can be specified within a transform set.

Figure 6-8

Router A
specifying the
encryption
protocols to use
for IPSec

```
Router(config)#crypto ipsec transform-set VPN2CentralOffice ah-md5-
hmac esp-des esp-md5-hmac
```

6.4.1.2 Configuring Mode of Transform Set

The last item to configure within a transform set is the mode in which
IPSec will operate. Earlier in this chapter we discussed the two different
modes that IPSec can operate: tunnel mode and transport mode. The
mode you select will be based on the purpose of the VPN. Although you
can configure your VPN to operate either way, most of the time you will
configure compulsory tunnels in tunnel mode and voluntary tunnels in
the transport mode. The command to change the mode of your transport
set for IOS 11.3T, 12.0, and 12.1 is:

```
Router(cfg-crypto-trans)#mode mode-of-operation
```

mode-of-operation	**tunnel**	transform set will operate in tunnel mode
	transport	transform set will operate in transport mode

By default, a transform set is configured to operate in tunnel mode.

Once we have configured the transform set, we still need to apply it to
the crypto map, which we will see later in this chapter.

6.4.2 Configuring Crypto Maps

Crypto maps in IPSec are similar to crypto maps in CET. A crypto map is
a device that defines the configuration-specific information about how to
apply encryption. Within the generic crypto map, you can have multiple
crypto map entries, as seen in Figure 6-9.

Figure 6-9

Crypto map
versus crypto
map entry

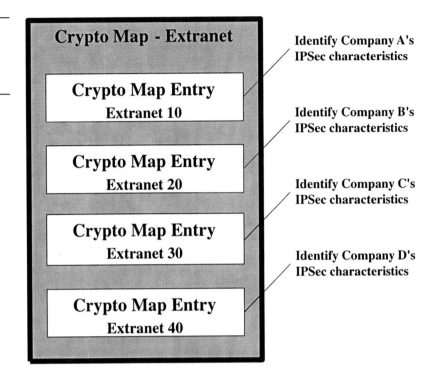

Notice that each crypto map entry that specifies a crypto map entry actually falls under the umbrella of the generic crypto map, even though we never created a crypto map umbrella for it to fall under. This will make more sense a little later when you see that in order to create a crypto map, you must specify a sequence number. With the ability to create multiple crypto map entries, we can define parameters for different VPN peers.

Because IPSec is such a flexible and extensible protocol, a crypto map can be configured in multiple ways. Figure 6-10 illustrates the various types of crypto maps that can be configured.

Each leaf (end node) represents a unique type of crypto map representing unique attributes that must be configured regarding that crypto map. The first type of crypto map we will concentrate on is a crypto map in which the encryption and authentication keys are manually configured. When IPSec was first introduced and ISAKMP was still in its infancy, many engineers used manually configured crypto maps. It was the only way to guarantee interoperability between vendors.

Figure 6-10

Different types of
crypto maps

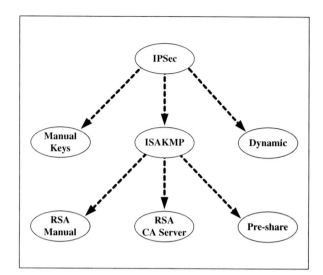

As time went on, ISAKMP became more mature. Now the bulk of IPSec configurations use ISAKMP pre-share. The main reason ISAKMP pre-share installations greatly outnumber ISAKMP RSA installations is the cost of the infrastructure. PKI infrastructures are expensive, time consuming, and cumbersome to build, whereas ISAKMP pre-shares can be set up in a matter of hours.

Three different types of crypto map entries can be used with IPSec. The type you select will depend on the VPN, you are deploying (compulsory or voluntary), and how you approach key management for your VPN. The three different types are

▨ Crypto maps that have manually configured keys for security associations

▨ Crypto maps that utilize ISAKMP for security associations

▨ Dynamic crypto maps

We will look at each of these different types of crypto maps and how to configure each one. As in Figure 6-10, when setting up IPSec between two peers, we should only complete the tasks associated with a single crypto map leaf. Because you can configure IPSec in many different ways, it is easy to become confused as to what tasks need to be completed.

6.4.2.1 Crypto Maps—Manual SAs versus ISAKMP SAs

The type of key management we have chosen will dictate the parameters used to specify the transform set. We can either manually configure the encryption keys that will be used for the security association, or we can use ISAKMP to negotiate the encryption keys. The advantage of using ISAKMP over manually configuring the encryption is that you can negotiate which type of encryption and authentication algorithms to use to set up your ISAKMP SAs.

6.4.2.2 Dynamic Crypto Maps versus Standard Crypto Maps

Unlike their CET cousin, IPSec crypto maps come in one of two flavors. Because IPSec can operate in a compulsory VPN and voluntary VPN, we need to distinguish between the two types of crypto maps. This is because with a compulsory VPN we already know who our VPN peer will be. We can then configure many of the options statically. Voluntary VPNs, which can only be configured to use ISAKMP, are essentially a crypto map without all of the parameters configured. We can think of it more as a template where all the missing information is determined dynamically (as a result of SA negotiations). Figure 6-11 shows us the difference between when to use a standard crypto map (for compulsory tunnels) and a dynamic crypto map (for voluntary tunnels).

In order to create a working crypto map, we must perform the following six tasks:

- Create a crypto map entry.
- Specify which data stream to encrypt.
- Specify the peer router.
- Specify which transform set to use (which encryption and authentication algorithms to use).
- Specify key management.
- Apply crypto map to an interface.

We will now look at the steps involved with creating crypto maps for the three types of crypto maps by utilizing the six steps outlined above. Although all of the steps listed above need to be performed on all crypto maps, the commands and protocols used to accomplish this task are not the same; therefore, only a single crypto map section should be used from the three different types; manual, ISAKMP and dynamic.

Figure 6-11

Dynamic crypto map versus standard crypto map

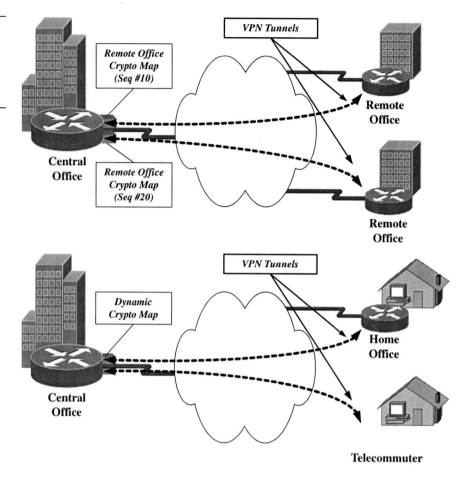

6.4.3 Crypto Maps that Use Manually Configured IPSec SA Keys

Crypto maps in which SAs are manually configured are probably the easiest crypto maps to configure. This is not because they use the fewest number of commands to implement, but because no negotiation occurs, and you always know how your crypto map is configured (except for IOS 12.0, see Author Note later in this section). In order to support manual crypto maps, you must reach an agreement with your VPN peer prior to configuring your crypto maps as to which type of encryption and authentication algorithms will be used.

Note:

When getting started with static crypto maps, it is possible to become confused about the command no crypto ipsec isakmp. *A Cisco router can operate with crypto maps that use manual key configuration and crypto maps that use ISAKMP simultaneously. However, this command is not required when configuring crypto maps in which the keys are manually configured. However, it can be useful if you need to disable ISAKMP activities while trying to troubleshoot manual crypto maps.*

To configure a crypto map in which the IPSec SA keys are manually configured, we must perform the following tasks:

- Create a crypto map.
- Specify which the data stream to encrypt.
- Specify the peer router.
- Specify the transform set.
- Specify keys.
- Apply crypto map to an interface.

Each of these tasks are described in detail in the sections to follow. Many of the tasks for creating a crypto map in which the IPSec SA keys are manually configured are the same for creating crypto maps that utilize ISAKMP. However, subtle differences may appear, so make sure you follow the steps outlined in this section.

6.4.3.1 Create a Crypto Map Entry

When creating a standard IPSec crypto map, three components must be identified (as opposed to only two for CET): the name of the crypto map, the sequence number, and the type of key management that will be used with the tunnel. The global configuration command used, which is the same for IOS 11.3T, 12.0, and 12.1, is:

```
Router(config)#crypto map name-of-map sequence-number ipsec-manual
```

name-of-map	*WORD*	Name for the crypto map
sequence-number	**0-65535**	Unique number identifying destination specific information for the remote VPN peer

Because an interface can only have a single crypto map applied to it, we need a method to identify different VPN peers. This is accomplished by using a sequence number to identify a crypto map entry. Once you have created the crypto map, which is created the first time you use the command, you should not specify its key management (for example, ipsec-manual or ipsec-isakmp) when modifying parameters of a crypto map entry after it has already been created.

All crypto maps are case sensitive. Although this is not a big deal when creating the crypto maps, it becomes important when you need to change parameters of any existing crypto map or when you attempt to apply the crypto map to an interface. When setting up a crypto map, it might be useful to use all capital letters when defining a crypto map. This enables the network engineer to pick out any crypto map references in your configuration more easily.

6.4.3.2 Specify which Data Stream to Encrypt

When configuring a crypto map, we must use an extended access-list to define traffic that should be encrypted by the VPN peer. Extended access-lists offer a high degree of flexibility by filtering a data stream based on the source address, destination address, and application port number. Extended access-lists are identified in Cisco's IOS as those access-lists whose number is between 100 and 199. Once the access-list has been created, we can associate it with a crypto map using the following global configuration mode command (for IOS 11.3T, 12.0, and 12.1):

```
Router(config-crypto-map)#match address access-list
```

access-list	**100-199**	Extended access-list used to identify data stream to encrypt

6.4.3.3 Specify the Peer Router

A crypto map must be associated with a unique VPN peer. You cannot have two VPN peers using the crypto map entry; only one VPN peer is allowed per crypto map entry, although you can have multiple crypto map entries within a single crypto map (see Figure 6-9). To specify the VPN peer, use the following command, which is available in IOS 11.3T, 12.0, and 12.1:

```
Router(config-crypto-map)#set peer VPN-ip-address
```

VPN-ip-address	*x.x.x.x*	IP address of the VPN peer

When specifying the VPN peer IP address, it must be the IP address of the interface that has the crypto map applied on the remote end. If you choose a different IP address on the remote IPSec peer, your IPSec SA negotiations will fail.

6.4.3.4 Specify the Transform Set

Remember that the transform set identifies the encryption/authentication protocols that will be used within a crypto map entry. Thus, it is at this point when we will determine which algorithms are used for encryption and authentication. Because we can only specify a single transform set within a crypto map entry, no room is available for negotiations of the IPSec encryption and authentication protocols. IOS 11.3T, 12.0, and 12.1 use the same command to specify which transform set a crypto map should use. The command is

```
Router(config-crypto-map)#set transform-set transform-set-name
```

transform-set-name　　　　*WORD*　　　Name of existing transform set

Only a single transform set can be used within a crypto map entry, which is denoted by the sequence number. However, you can specify multiple crypto map entries within a crypto map.

6.4.3.5 Specify Keys

Because we will be using a manual crypto map, we will configure the keys that are used by the ESP and AH protocols by hand. Four different components must be specified when manually configuring the keys between two VPN peers. They are:

- Are we configuring an ESP encryption key, an ESP authentication key, or an AH key?
- Is the key for inbound traffic or outbound traffic?
- What is the *security parameters index* (SPI)?
- What is the key?

Because we can have multiple encryption entries within our crypto map, we must make sure that we have defined this type of encryption/authentication within our transform set. We must also ensure that our IPSec peer is using the same key with the same encryption/authentication within the transform set. It is also important to remember that the outbound key for one IPSec peer is the inbound key for the other IPSec peer.

To protect ourselves from replay attacks, we can use the SPI to identify the starting sequence number associated with our data streams. Once again, the starting value of the inbound key on one IPSec peer is the starting value of the outbound key on the other IPSec peer.

The commands used to configure keys are different depending on whether you are using IOS 11.3T or 12.0/12.1. To configure your encryption keys manually using IOS 11.3T, use the following command:

```
Router(config-crypto-map)#set security-association direction esp SPI
protocol key
```

direction	**inbound**	Decrypt packets using this key
	outbound	Encrypt packets using this key
SPI	**256-4294967295**	Starting sequence number to use for SPI
protocol	**cipher**	This key is for encryption
	authenticator	This key is for authentication
key	**WORD**	The key in hexadecimal format (without leading 0x)

To configure your encryption keys manually using IOS 12.0 and 12.1, use the following command:

```
Router(config-crypto-map)#set session-key direction esp SPI protocol
key
```

direction	**inbound**	Decrypt packets using this key
	outbound	Encrypt packets using this key
SPI	**256-4294967295**	Starting sequence number to use for SPI
protocol	**cipher**	This key is for encryption
	authenticator	This key is for authentication
key	**WORD**	The key in hexadecimal format (without leading 0x)

To configure your authentication keys manually using IOS 11.3T, use the following command:

```
Router(config-crypto-map)#set security-association direction ah SPI
key
```

direction	**inbound**	Decrypt packets using this key
	outbound	Encrypt packets using this key*SPI*
	256-4294967295	Starting sequence number to use for SPI
key	**WORD**	The key in hexadecimal format (without leading 0x)

To configure your authentication keys manually using IOS 12.0 and 12.1, use the following command:

```
Router(config-crypto-map)#set session-key direction ah SPI key
```

direction	**inbound**	Decrypt packets using this key
	outbound	Encrypt packets using this key
SPI	**256-4294967295**	Starting sequence number to use for SPI
key	***WORD***	The key in hexadecimal format (without leading 0x)

One of the most commonly overlooked subjects is key length. Each encryption algorithm has its own minimum key length for each encrypting/decrypting of a data stream. Unfortunately, if you use the wrong key length, IOS will not inform you of your mistake (it will let you know that the key must be an even number of digits). If you use a key that does not meet the minimum key length requirement, your encryption algorithms will not work correctly. The encryption algorithms will attempt to encrypt, but fail, and it will appear to you (at least on the surface) as if your keys do not match. The minimum key lengths for each algorithm are displayed in Table 6-2. You will probably use longer key lengths when actually deploying it, but if you are testing your configuration, you can easily fall into this trap.

Note:

IOS 11.3T and 12.1 will both display the actual keys in the configuration file. For whatever reason, IOS 12.0 does not display the key in the configuration file, which can make troubleshooting difficult if you rely on the show config *command to see the key. You would think that if they removed the keys from the configuration file in IOS 12.0 for security reasons, they would not have put them back in IOS 12.1. It seems that Cisco may have had a change of position on this particular subject.*

Table 6-2	Algorithm	Minimum Length (in bits)
Minimum key lengths for each encryption algorithm	DES	16 hexadecimal digits
	MD5	32 hexadecimal digits
	SHA	40 hexadecimal digits

6.4.3.6 Apply Crypto Map to an Interface

Now that we have created our crypto map and specified all of the parameters associated with the crypto map, we will examine how to apply a crypto map to an interface. The command used is the same for IOS 11.3T, 12.0, and 12.1:

```
Router(config-if)#crypto map name-of-map
```

name-of-map **WORD**   Name for the previously created crypto map

If the crypto map has not already been created, this command will give you an error, as illustrated in Figure 6-12. When applying your crypto map, you should remember that crypto maps are case sensitive.

Figure 6-12

Example of trying to specify a crypto map which does not exist on a serial interface

```
RouterA(config-if)#crypto map DoesNotExist
ERROR: Crypto Map with tag "DoesNotExist" does not exist.
```

6.4.3.7 Example - Two IPSec Peers with Manually Configured Keys

Let us now take a look at everything we have learned, and see what the relevant combination of commands look like from two VPN peers. In Figure 6-13 and 6-14, you can see the necessary commands to configure two IPSec peers to communicate when manually configuring the keys. Pay close attention to the keys being used and their direction in Figure 6-13 and 6-14 examples. For examples of manual key configuration other than IOS 11.3T, see the case studies later in this chapter.

6.4.4 Configuring Crypto Maps Using ISAKMP for IPSec SAs

Now that we have seen how to configure a crypto map without ISAKMP (manual configuration), let us look at how to configure a crypto map that utilizes ISAKMP for key exchanges. Crypto maps that utilize ISAKMP have more steps that must be completed to create a working IPSec VPN.

Figure 6-13

Example of a
manual mode
IPSec VPN
Router A running
IOS 11.3T

```
Hostname RouterA
!
crypto ipsec transform-set Project esp-des
!
 !
 crypto map ManualExtranet 30 ipsec-manual
 set peer 192.168.20.2
 set security-association inbound esp 256 cipher abcdabcdabcdabcd
 set security-association outbound esp 1257 cipher 1010101010101010
 set transform-set Project
 match address 103
 !
interface Ethernet0
 ip address 192.168.1.1 255.255.255.0
 !
interface Serial0
 ip address 192.168.10.2 255.255.255.0
 crypto map ManualExtranet
 !
access-list 103 permit ip 192.168.1.0 0.0.0.255 192.168.120.0
0.0.0.255
```

Figure 6-14

Example of a
manual mode
IPSec VPN
Router B running
IOS 11.3T

```
Hostname RouterB
!
crypto ipsec transform-set TempTransform esp-des
!
 !
 crypto map ManualModeExtranet 20 ipsec-manual
 set peer 192.168.10.2
 set security-association inbound esp 1257 cipher 1010101010101010
 set security-association outbound esp 256 cipher abcdabcdabcdabcd
 set transform-set TempTransform
 match address 104
 !
interface Ethernet0
 ip address 192.168.120.1 255.255.255.0
 !
interface Serial0
 ip address 192.168.20.2 255.255.255.0
 crypto map ManualModeExtranet
 !
access-list 104 permit ip 192.168.120.0 0.0.0.255 192.168.1.0
0.0.0.255
```

However, ISAKMP can help eliminate the possibility of entering an incorrect key. In addition, it provides for a more flexible environment because IPSec peers can negotiate the settings that they will use for the new security associations. The steps for creating a crypto map that use ISAKMP are similar to the commands in which we manually specified the keys; however, more steps are involved because we still must configure ISAKMP, which will create exchange keys for us.

During ISAKMP security association negotiations, both peers search for a transform that each of them can support, as seen in Figure 6-15.

If the two IPSec peers fail to find a common set of protocols, the ISAKMP security association negotiation will fail. Subsequently, the IPSec SA negotiations will fail. Just because two ISAKMP peers have a policy that has common attributes, it does not necessarily mean that the ISAKMP SA will be created. The creation of the ISAKMP SA still depends on successful authentication.

To configure a crypto map using ISAKMP in which the IPSec SA keys are negotiated, we must perform the following tasks:

- Create a crypto map.

- Specify which data stream to encrypt.

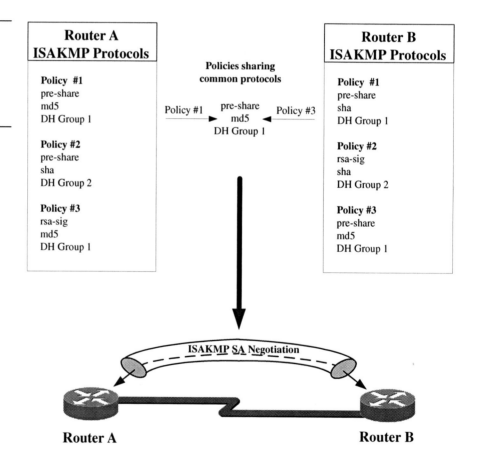

Figure 6-15

Negotiation of ISAKMP protocols to create ISAKMP SAs

- Specify the peer router.
- Specify the transform set.
- Configure ISAKMP.
- Apply crypto map to an interface.

Each of these tasks are described in detail in the sections to follow. Many of the tasks for creating a crypto map in which the IPSec SA keys are manually configured are the same for creating crypto maps that utilize ISAKMP. However, subtle differences may appear, so make sure you follow the steps outlined in this section.

6.4.4.1 Create a Crypto Map Entry

When creating a standard IPSec crypto map, three components must be identified (as opposed to only two for CET): the name of the crypto map, the sequence number, and the type of key management that will be used with the tunnel. The global configuration command used, which is the same for IOS 11.3T, 12.0, and 12.1, is

```
Router(config)#crypto map name-of-map sequence-number ipsec-isakmp
```

name-of-map	**WORD**	Name for the crypto map
sequence-number	**0-65535**	Unique number identifying destination specific information for the remote VPN peer

Because an interface can only have a single crypto map applied to it, we need a method to identify different VPN peers. This is accomplished by using a sequence number to identify a crypto map entry. Once you have created the crypto map, which is created the first time you use the command, you should not specify its key management (for example, ipsec-manual or ipsec-isakmp) when modifying parameters of a crypto map entry after it has been created.

All crypto maps are case sensitive. Although this is not a big deal when creating crypto maps, it becomes important when you need to change parameters of any existing crypto map or when you attempt to apply the crypto map to an interface. When setting up a crypto map, it might be useful to use all capital letters when defining a crypto map. This enables the network engineer to pick out any crypto map references in your configuration more easily.

6.4.4.2 Specify which Data Stream to Encrypt

When configuring a crypto map, we must use an extended access-list to define traffic that should be encrypted by the VPN peer. Extended access-lists offer a high degree of flexibility by filtering a data stream based on the source address, destination address, and application port number. Extended access-lists are identified in Cisco's IOS as those access-lists whose number is between 100 and 199. Once the access-list has been created, we can associate it with a crypto map using the following global configuration mode command (for IOS 11.3T, 12.0, and 12.1):

```
Router(config-crypto-map)#match address access-list
```

access-list	**100-199**	Extended access-list used to identify data stream to encrypt

6.4.4.3 Specify the Peer Router

A crypto map must be associated with a unique VPN peer. You cannot have two VPN peers using the same crypto map entry; only one VPN peer is allowed per crypto map entry, although you can have multiple crypto map entries within a single crypto map (refer to Figure 6-9). To specify the VPN peer, use the following command, which is available in IOS 11.3T, 12.0, and 12.1:

```
Router(config-crypto-map)#set peer VPN-ip-address
```

VPN-ip-address	**x.x.x.x**	IP address of the VPN peer

When specifying the VPN peer IP address, it must be the IP address of the interface that has the crypto map applied on the remote end. If you choose a different IP address on the remote IPSec peer, your IPSec SA negotiations will fail.

6.4.4.4 Specify the Transform Set

Remember that the transform set identifies the encryption/authentication protocols that will be used within a crypto map entry. Thus, it is at this point when we will determine which algorithms are used for encryption and authentication. Because we can only specify a single transform set within a crypto map entry, no room is available for negotiations of the IPSec encryption and authentication protocols. IOS 11.3T, 12.0, and 12.1

use the same command to specify the transform set that a crypto map should use. The command is

```
Router(config-crypto-map)#set transform-set transform-set-name
```

transform-set-name   ***WORD***   Name of existing transform set

Only a single transform set can be used within a crypto map entry (denoted by the sequence number). However, you can specify multiple crypto map entries within a crypto map.

6.4.4.5 Configure ISAKMP

Before we configure our crypto maps, let us examine the various components that need to be configured when using ISAKMP. In Figure 6-4, we saw how ISAKMP negotiated encryption parameters before negotiating the parameters to be used during an IPSec session. This enables two IPSec peers to determine what keys they will be using in an encrypted session, instead of communicating in the clear what type of encryption/authentication algorithms will be used. Think of this as an extra level of protection.

Like IPSec's encryption algorithms, ISAKMP also needs to have a key in order to create a SA so that IPSec can securely negotiate the parameters of an IPSec SA. This means that we need another key. We can use either a pre-existing key to setup the ISAKMP SA, or we can have a CA server provide us with a key. In any event, the following items need to be configured in order for ISAKMP to work:

- Enable ISAKMP.
- Create ISAKMP policy.
- Configure ISAKMP policy to use keys (RSA or pre-share).

Enable ISAKMP   By default, ISAKMP is enabled on Cisco's 11.3T, 12.0, and 12.1. However, if it has been previously disabled and you need to enable it, use the following global configuration command:

```
Router(config)#crypto isakmp enable
```

Create ISAKMP Policy   AN ISAKMP policy defines the security parameters that will be defined during the ISAKMP SA negotiation. An ISAKMP policy is the same to ISAKMP as a crypto map is to IPSec except that we can have multiple policies. Because an ISAKMP peer can have multiple policies, they must first exchange all of their policies so that each ISAKMP peer can determine what policies they have in common.

By default, a 56-bit DES-CBC will be used during the negotiation of ISAKMP. However, two other options must be configured within an ISAKMP policy as well as two optional attributes.

When two peers begin the ISAKMP process, they must first exchange all of their ISAKMP policies. The peers, starting with their own highest value policy, start working their way down the list of their remote peer's policy, looking for a match. If the local peer cannot find a policy that matches its highest priority policy, the local peer will look to its own second highest value policy, continuing the search until it has exhausted its own list of ISAKMP policies. If the peers cannot find a mutually agreeable policy, the peers refuse negotiation and an IPSec SA will not be estab-

Table 6-3	Security Mechanism	Required/Optional	Option
Options to be configured in an ISAKMP policy	HASH	Required	sha
			md5
	Authentication	Required	rsa-sig
			Rsa-encr
			pre-share
	Diffie-Hellman Group	Optional	1 (768 bit)
			2 (1024 bit)
	Lifetime	Optional	Seconds

lished. To define an ISAKMP policy in IOS 11.3T, 12.0, and 12.1, we can use the global configuration command:

```
Router(config)#crypto isakmp policy policy-number
```

policy-number **1-10000**   Priority of policy number

To define the hash within an ISAKMP policy, use the following command for IOS 11.3T, 12.0, and 12.1:

```
Router(config-isakmp)#hash hash-protocol
```

| *hash-protocol* | **md5** | Use Message Digest 5 for the hash algorithm |
| | **sha** | Use Secure Hash Standard for the hash algorithm |

When setting up encryption within an ISAKMP policy, three different protocols can be used to encrypt the ISAKMP SA, which will be used for IPSec negotiations. It is important to understand their distinctions when implementing IPSec with ISAKMP because non-trivial ramifications can exist when using each one. The three different protocols that can be used are

- **Pre-share**—Like any symmetric encryption, both parties must know the key. This is useful for small environments where the number of peers is small because we do not need to use a CA server.
- **RSA encryption**—In order to utilize this protocol, you must already have a CA server in which you can exchange keys. By utilizing a CA server, you can considerably improve the scalability of an IPSec network. Because it is only encryption, it does not provide nonrepudiation. However, it is useful if you want to prevent a third party from knowing your activity.
- **RSA signature**—n order to utilize this protocol, you must already have a CA server in which you can exchange public keys. By utilizing a CA server, you can considerably improve the scalability of an IPSec network. Unlike RSA encryption, RSA signature provides nonrepudiation.

To define the authentication protocol that will be used during ISAKMP negotiations, we can use the following command for all three IOSs:

```
Router(config-isakmp)#authentication auth-protocol
```

auth-protocol	**pre-share**	Use a pre-shared key
	rsa-encr	Use RSA encryption
	rsa-sig	Use RSA signature

Depending on the type of authentication you have selected, you must enable a policy to handle that type of authentication. Pre-share authentication uses a symmetric encryption algorithm, whereas both RSA algorithms utilize an asymmetric encryption algorithm. If you are using RSA keys, we must configure our ISAKMP policy to handle RSA keys. Two different methods can be used for handling RSA public/private keys. We can either use a PKI Infrastructure (CA Server), or we can manually exchange public keys with our ISAKMP peer.

To summarize, three different methods can be used to handle ISAKMP authentication:

▪ Configure pre-share keys for an ISAKMP policy.

▪ Configure RSA keys manually for an ISAKMP policy.

▪ Configure RSA keys using a CA server for an ISAKMP policy.

Remember that we can only configure a policy to handle a specific type of ISAKMP policy. This means that we should only configure one of the above ISAKMP policies. Let us now take a look at how to configure each of these ISAKMP policies.

Configure Pre-Share Keys for an ISAKMP Policy Two possible types of keys can be used when configuring ISAKMP: RSA keys and pre-share keys. RSA keys can be configured to use a CA server, or you can manually configure RSA keys, whereas a pre-share key enables the use of an agreed upon key for encryption. You cannot use a pre-share key in combination with an RSA key for an ISAKMP encryption. However, you can use a pre-share key for one ISAKMP policy, and an RSA key encryption for another policy. If you choose a pre-shared key for authentication, you must use the following global configuration command (available in all three IOSs) on both ISAKMP peers:

```
Router(config)#crypto isakmp key key address ISAKMP-peer-ip-address
```

key	***WORD***	Key to be used for encryption
ISAKMP-peer-ip-address	*x.x.x.x*	IP address of the ISAKMP peer

or

```
Router(config)#crypto isakmp key key hostname ISAKMP-peer-name
```

key	***WORD***	Key to be used for encryption
ISAKMP-peer-name	***WORD***	Name of the ISAKMP peer (requires name resolution)

How your ISAKMP identifies itself in the ISAKMP process determines which command to use. By default, Cisco IOS uses the IP address. Unless someone has changed how the router identifies itself during ISAKMP negotiations, you should use the IP address.

For each ISAKMP peer, you must configure an independent pre-share identifying which key the router will use (you do not need to use a different key, you only need to identify other ISAKMP peers). In a large environment where security is of extreme importance, it is easy to see that using a pre-shared key is not a recommended solution due to the number of pre-shared keys that would have to be established.

Configure RSA Keys Manually for an ISAKMP Policy   When using RSA keys, you can configure them manually or you can use a CA server. Manually configuring RSA keys can be cumbersome, and if this is done incorrectly, it can pose a security risk. In environments where security is important, you may want to utilize RSA keys with a CA server. Although configuring a CA server and building a PKI infrastructure is beyond the scope of this book, they are serious topics for discussion and should not be taken lightly. PKI infrastructures can be expensive and time consuming to build, so you may want to look to a third party vendor to provide a PKI infrastructure. Keep in mind that if you do not trust your CA, or their practices and procedures, all of your hard work could be for nothing.

In order to configure an ISAKMP policy to use RSA keys, we must make sure that the ISAKMP policy has been configured to use RSA (rsa-sig or rsa-encr). Once this is completed, we must perform the following three tasks:

- Generate RSA keys.
- Define our ISAKMP identity.
- Specify the RSA public keys of our ISAKM peers.

Note:

Before deploying RSA manually, you should consider its effects on Non- Volatile Random Access Memory *(NVRAM). Because each key is of considerable size and NVRAM is generally fairly small, you must be careful that your RSA key requirements do not exceed your available NVRAM.*

Generating RSA Keys When generating your RSA key, you can specify the size of the modulus ranging from 360 to 2048 bits. The default value is 512 bits. Before you can generate your RSA keys, you must specify the hostname of the router and the IP domain name of the router. Although these features are probably already deployed on your existing routers, it is not something that you would normally do in a test environment. Failure to do this will cause your router to generate an error when attempting to generate the keys. To generate the RSA keys for a router, use the following global configuration command, which is available in IOS 11.3T, 12.0, and 12.1:

```
Router(config)#crypto key generate rsa option
```

option	**usage-keys**	Generate different RSA keys for signing and encrypting

Figure 6-16 illustrates the process of generating an RSA key. Notice that the name of the key is RouterA.quiggle.com. By specifying a hostname and the IP domain name, we have hopefully created a unique name.

Define Our ISAKMP Identity When using RSA keys in a PKI environment, you need to specify your identity so you can be identified. You can be identified two different ways: IP address or name. The default within IOS 11.3T, 12.0, and 12.1 is to use your IP address. It is recommended that whatever you choose as an identifier, (IP address or hostname), you use it throughout your VPN infrastructure to minimize confusion.

To set a router's ISAKMP identity for use with RSA keys, use the following global configuration command (available in IOS 11.3T, 12.0, and 12.1).

```
Router(config)#crypto isakmp identity isakmp-identity
```

isakmp-identity	**address**	Use the IP address as the ISAKMP's identity
	hostname	Use the hostname as the ISAKMP's identity

Specify the RSA Public Keys of Our ISAKMP Peers At this point we have configured everything that a router needs to know about itself. Now we must focus on configuring the details of our ISAKMP peer. Unlike CET, which had a mechanism for exchanging keys, no method is available

Figure 6-16

Generating
RSA keys

```
RouterA(config)#crypto key generate rsa
The name for the keys will be: RouterA.quiggle.com
Choose the size of the key modulus in the range of 360 to 2048 for
your
  General Purpose Keys. Choosing a key modulus greater than 512 may
take
  a few minutes.
How many bits in the modulus [512]:
Generating RSA keys ...
[OK]
```

when using IPsec so we must enter them by hand if we do not have a CA server. Therefore, we must be careful about how we exchange keys with any ISAKMP identity otherwise we could compromise our key. This is where it is important to understand the fundamentals of public/private key encryption so that you understand those risks.

To enter our public key chain in which we can specify a remote ISAKMP's identity and key, use the following command:

```
Router(config)#crypto key pubkey-chain rsa
```

Once in this configuration mode, we can specify the remote peer's ISAKMP identity by using the following command:

```
Router(config-pubkey-chain)#named-key isakmp-identity option
```

isakmp-identity	**address**	Identity the ISAKMP peer will use
option	**encryption**	Use for encryption only (use only with the usage-key option)
	signature	Use for signature only (use only with the usage-key option)

Now comes the difficult part: entering your ISAKMP peer's key into your configuration without compromising it. Most of the time this should be entered by hand; however, if you are in the position of having the routers physically close to each other, you can use a hyperterminal to copy and paste the keys into each other. If you display the key when telnetted to the router, the key will traverse the network unencrypted. This may be fine if it is your internal network, but if it is the public Internet, the world just had a quick look at your key. The process used to identify the RSA key for a manually configured ISAKMP peer has three steps:

Step #1 - **Router(config-pubkey-key)#key-string**

Step #2 - **Router(config-pubkey)#***key*

Step #3 - **Router(config-pubkey)#quit**

The exchange looks something like Figure 6-17, but with a much larger key. Remember that this key is not one of your choosing, but it is half of a mathematically generated public/private key combination.

You can see from this example that it could become a cumbersome process without a CA server.

Configure RSA Keys Using a CA Server for an ISAKMP Policy When using RSA keys, you can configure them manually or you can use a CA server. Manually configuring RSA keys can be cumbersome and if this is done incorrectly, it can pose a security risk. By utilizing a CA server, you can minimize this administrative burden and make your IPSec solution scalable.

| **Figure 6-17**<br><br>Configuring a remote peer's public key | ```
RouterE(config-pubkey-key)#key-string
Enter a public key as a hexidecimal number ....
RouterE(config-pubkey)# 305C300D 06092A86 4886F70D 01010105
00034B00 30480241 00C15333 7B874CD6 A58F4A27 45405DEE 5159C1E8
C74B9C84 89EA32F9 E5AA02D3 C13459CC 4A42A4BF 2C5BBA46 94425BD4
1896D8C6 288E0779 65F757D9 45F562A3 61020301 0001
RouterE(config-pubkey)#quit
``` |

In order to configure an ISAKMP policy to utilize a CA server for use with RSA keys, we must make sure that the ISAKMP policy has been configured to use RSA (rsa-sig or rsa-encr). Once this is completed, we must perform the following four tasks:

▓ Generate RSA keys.

▓ Declare a Certificate Authority.

▓ Authenticate the Certificate Authority.

▓ Request a certificate.
```

Note:

Before deploying RSA manually, you should consider its effects on NVRAM. Because each key is of considerable size and NVRAM is generally fairly small, you must be careful that your RSA key requirements do not exceed your available NVRAM.

Generating RSA Keys   When generating your RSA key, you can specify the size of the modulus ranging from 360 to 2048 bits. The default value is 512 bits. Before you can generate your RSA keys, you must specify the hostname of the router and the IP domain name of the router. Although these features are probably already deployed on your existing routers, it is not something that you would normally do in a test environment. Failure to do this will cause your router to generate an error when attempting to generate the keys. To generate the RSA keys for a router, use the following global configuration command, which is available in IOS 11.3T, 12.0, and 12.1:

```
Router(config)#crypto key generate rsa option
```

option	**usage-keys**	Generate different RSA keys for signing and encrypting

Figure 6-18 illustrates the process of generating an RSA key. Notice that the name of the key is RouterA.quiggle.com. By specifying a hostname and the IP domain name, we have (hopefully) created a unique name.

Figure 6-18

Generating RSA keys

```
RouterA(config)#crypto key generate rsa
The name for the keys will be: RouterA.quiggle.com
Choose the size of the key modulus in the range of 360 to 2048 for
your
    General Purpose Keys. Choosing a key modulus greater than 512 may
take
    a few minutes.
How many bits in the modulus [512]:
Generating RSA keys ...
    [OK]
```

Declare a Certificate Authority Declaring a CA is a four-step process. You should only declare a single CA for any router. The following four steps are available in all three IOSs (11.3T, 12.0, and 12.1):

Step #1 - declaring a CA is to declare the domain name of the CA.

```
Router(config)#crypto ca identity name
```

name   **WORD**   Name of the CA's domain

Step #2 - declaring a CA is to specify the URL of the CA, including any cgi-bin script locations within the URL.

```
Router(ca-identity)#enrollment url url
```

url   **WORD**   Specifies the URL of the CA

Note:

Cisco has provided a way to use an http proxy server for registrations with the enrollment url http-proxy command.

Step #3 - declaring a CA is to specify RA mode if your CA provides a registration authority.

```
Router(ca-identity)#enrollement mode ra
```

Step #4 - declaring a CA is to specify the location of the *Lightweight Directory Access Protocol* (LDAP) server.

```
Router(ca-identity)#query url url
```

url   **WORD**   Specifies the URL of the LDAP server

Although these commands are the commands that are required to declare a CA authority, they are not all the commands available when configuring a router to use a CA. For example, if we need to change the retry period during which to receive a certificate, we can use the following command:

```
Router(ca-identity)#enrollment retry period minutes
```

minutes   **WORD**   Number of minutes to wait before timing out

Authenticate the Certificate Authority   At this point, we will need to receive the CA's public key so that we can decrypt any future digital certificates that the CA sends to our router. This command is accomplished by using the command

```
Router(config)#crypto ca authenticate name
```

name   ***WORD***   Name of the CA (same name as when declaring the CA)

Request a Certificate   The last step in configuring ISAKMP to support a CA server is to request a certificate for all of the RSA key pairs. You will receive one certificate for every RSA key pair that you generate. If you used the usage-key option when generating your RSA key pairs, you will receive two certificates. To request all of your certificates, use the following command.

```
Router(config)#crypto ca enroll name
```

name   ***WORD***   Name of the CA (same name as when declaring the CA)

The certificates that you receive will not be viewable in your config file and are saved in a private part of NVRAM for security reasons. In addition, they will not be copied out when saving your configuration to a *tftp* server. Therefore, if you have to replace a router that is using IPSec and utilizing a CA server for ISAKMP, you will have to rebuild the certificates.

6.4.4.6 Apply Crypto Map to an Interface

Now that we have created our crypto map and specified all of the parameters associated with the crypto map, let us look at how to apply a crypto map to an interface. The command used is the same for IOS 11.3T, 12.0, and 12.1:

```
Router(config-if)#crypto map name-of-map
```

name-of-map   ***WORD***   Name for the previously created crypto map

If the crypto map has not already been created, this command will send you an error, as seen in Figure 6-19. When applying your crypto map, you should remember that crypto maps are case sensitive.

Figure 6-19

Appyling a non-existent crypto map to an interface

```
RouterA(config-if)#crypto map DoesNotExist
ERROR: Crypto Map with tag "DoesNotExist" does not exist.
```

6.4.4.7 Example—Two IPSec Peers Using ISAKMP Pre-Share

Figure 6-20 and 6-21 illustrate the necessary configurations to make IPSec work by utilizing ISAKMP for key management. As we can see from these two working configuration files, the amount of additional work required to make our configurations work using ISAKMP is minimal compared to manually configuring the SAs.

Figure 6-20

Example of VPN Router A running IOS 11.3T that utilizes ISAKMP

```
hostname RouterA
!
crypto isakmp policy 100
 hash md5
 authentication pre-share
crypto isakmp key yabadabadoo address 192.168.20.2
!
!
crypto ipsec transform-set Project esp-des
!
 !
 crypto map ISAKMPExtranet 30 ipsec-isakmp
 set peer 192.168.20.2
 set transform-set Project
 match address 103
!
interface Ethernet0
 ip address 192.168.1.1 255.255.255.0
!
interface Serial0
 ip address 192.168.10.2 255.255.255.0
 crypto map ISAKMPExtranet
!
access-list 103 permit ip 192.168.1.0 0.0.0.255 192.168.120.0
0.0.0.255
```

Figure 6-21

Example of VPN
Router B running
IOS 11.3T that
utilizes ISAKMP

```
hostname RouterB
!
crypto isakmp policy 200
 hash md5
 authentication pre-share
crypto isakmp key yabadabadoo address 192.168.10.2
!
crypto ipsec transform-set TempTransform esp-des
!
 !
 crypto map ISAKMPModeExtranet 20 ipsec-isakmp
 set peer 192.168.10.2
 set transform-set TempTransform
 match address 104
!
interface Ethernet0
 ip address 192.168.120.1 255.255.255.0
!
interface Serial0
 ip address 192.168.20.2 255.255.255.0
 crypto map ISAKMPModeExtranet
!
access-list 104 permit ip 192.168.120.0 0.0.0.255 192.168.1.0
0.0.0.255
```

In addition, we get the benefit of the routers not employing encryption
until after the SAs have been negotiated. If we were not using ISAKMP to
negotiate the SA parameters, the data stream we are trying to protect
immediately is encrypted once the crypto map is applied to the interface.
If the other side is not set up, we have cut off communication between the
two entities until our IPSec VPN peer configures its SA parameters.

6.4.5 Dynamic Crypto Maps

Dynamic crypto maps are used when you do not know the IP address of
the IPSec peer; such is the case with mobile users or telecommuters.
Dynamic crypto maps are almost identical to standard crypto maps except
that they are missing key parameters within the configuration. The
remote peer fills in these missing parameters at a later date.

Note:

Dynamic crypto maps are used only to host incoming IPSec sessions. They are never used to establish an SA with a remote peer.

So, what kind of information is missing within a dynamic crypto map? Let us take a look at the paradigm of a telecommuter or mobile user. Generally, this user connects to a public infrastructure of some sort (usually an outsourced ISP), and they rarely know their IP address in advance. However, standard crypto maps require the IP address of the IPSec peer in advance. This situation creates a catch 22.

To overcome these limitations, we can use dynamic crypto maps, which enable us to specify the VPN peer during IPSec negotiations. Using dynamic crypto maps requires the use of ISAKMP for key negotiation.

When creating a dynamic crypto map, the priority value of the crypto map entry should be as high as possible (higher value means a lower priority). Because crypto map entries are evaluated on a priority basis, the higher priority entries are evaluated for a match before the lower priority crypto entries. By setting the dynamic crypto map entries with a low priority, you make it the last priority to be evaluated, enabling your standard crypto maps to be selected first over your dynamic crypto map.

Unlike the previous crypto maps, dynamic crypto maps only require that a crypto map is created and a transform set is identified. This makes dynamic crypto maps simple to configure. Other commands are used in dynamic crypto maps, such as match address and set peers, which were also used in standard crypto maps. It is highly recommended that you do not use these commands when using dynamic crypto maps because they hold little advantage. In order to use these commands, you must have a high degree of certainty to be able to predict the user's IP address. If you can predict the user's IP address, you should not use a dynamic crypto map.

6.4.5.1 Create a Crypto Map Entry

When creating a dynamic IPSec crypto map, two components must be identified: the name of the crypto map and the sequence number. The global configuration command used, which is the same for IOS 11.3T, 12.0, and 12.1, is

```
Router(config)#crypto dynamic-map name-of-map sequence-number
```

name-of-map	**WORD**	Name for the crypto map
sequence-number	**0-65535**	Unique number identifying destination specific information for the remote VPN peer

All crypto maps are case sensitive. Although this is not a big deal when creating them, it becomes important when you need to change parameters of any existing crypto map or when you attempt to apply the crypto map to an interface. It might be useful to use all capital letters when defining a crypto map. This enables the network engineer to pick out any crypto map references in your configuration more easily.

6.4.5.2 Specify the Transform Set

Remember that the transform set identifies the encryption/authentication protocols that will be used. Thus, it is at this point when we will determine which algorithms are used for encryption and authentication. IOS 11.3T, 12.0, and 12.1 use the same command to specify the transform set that a crypto map should use. The command is

```
Router(config-crypto-map)#set transform-set transform-set-name
```

transform-set-name	**WORD**	Name of existing transform set

Only a single transform set can be used within a crypto map entry (denoted by the sequence number). However, you can specify multiple crypto map entries within a crypto map.

6.4.5.3 Apply Crypto Map to an Interface

Now that we have created our crypto map and specified all of the parameters associated with the crypto map, we will examine how to apply a crypto map to an interface. The command used is the same for IOS 11.3T, 12.0, and 12.1:

```
Router(config-if)#crypto map name-of-map
```

name-of-map	**WORD**	Name for the previously created crypto map

If the crypto map has not already been created, this command will send you an error, as seen in Figure 6-22. When applying your crypto map, you should remember that crypto maps are case sensitive.

Figure 6-22

Applying a crypto map to a non-existent interface

```
RouterA(config-if)#crypto map DoesNotExist
ERROR: Crypto Map with tag "DoesNotExist" does not exist.
```

6.4.6 Optional Crypto Map Attributes

In each of the previous segments of this section on "Configuring IPSec," we have identified the necessary commands that make IPSec operational. However, some commands can be used to fine-tune your IPSec configurations. In all of these cases, the commands enable us to adjust the standard security policies that Cisco has defined, and insert our own policies.

6.4.6.1 Security-Association Lifetimes

When IPSec security associations are negotiated, the security-association lifetime parameter is one of the parameters that is negotiated. This variable indicates how much time or data must pass before a new security association is negotiated. By default, Cisco only allows an ISAKMP SA to age to 86,400 seconds (one day) with no limit on the amount of traffic that can pass through the ISAKMP SA. An IPSec SA, by default, will only last for 3,600 seconds or transport 4500 Mb before expiring an IPSec SA.

Although these limits may be reasonable for standard IPSec installations, some installations will always require a different policy. To configure the security association lifetime on an IPSec SA, use the following command (available in IOS 11.3T, 12.0, and 12.1):

```
Router(config-crypto-map)#set security-association lifetime seconds
num-of-seconds
```

num-of-seconds	**120-86400**	Security association duration in seconds

```
Router(config-crypto-map)#set security-association lifetime kilobytes
num-of-seconds
```

num-of-seconds	**2560-536870912**	Security association duration in seconds

6.4.6.2 Perfect Forward Secrecy (PFS)

Perfect Forward Secrecy (PFS) is a method of providing an extra level of protection. PFS ensures that your IPSec SA key is not derived from any previous secret. If an attacker were to break one of the keys used during encryption and you were not using PFS, it is hypothetically possible to compromise additional keys. However, PFS makes certain that an attacker would have to break each IPSec SA individually. The cost of this advantage is time because during an ISAKMP SA negotiation, an extra DH exchange must take place.

```
Router(config-crypto-map)#set pfs group
```

| *group* | **group1** | Use 768-bit key for DH when utilizing PFS |
| | **group2** | Use 1,024-bit key for DH when utilizing PFS |

6.5 Design Considerations

6.5.1 Crypto Map Sequence Numbers

You should note that the sequence number indicates a priority. The lower the sequence number, the higher the priority within a crypto map. Crypto maps with multiple crypto map entries evaluate a data stream for encryption starting with the lowest sequence number and working their way to the higher numbers.

6.5.2 Identifying Data Streams

When creating your access-list, you should be cautious when defining the data stream you want to encrypt. In certain situations, you can potentially compromise your VPN's security due to an inadequate analysis of the network. For example, in Figure 6-23 and 6-24, we can see the configuration of Router A and Router B, (IPSec peers) respectively, in Figure 6-25. Router C is not a participant in the VPN, it is just a normal router.

Figure 6-23

Example of a
misconfigured
ACL for Router A
in Figure 6-23

```
1  hostname RouterA
2  !
3  crypto isakmp policy 100
4   hash md5
5   authentication pre-share
6  crypto isakmp key yabadabadoo address 192.168.20.2
7  !
8  crypto ipsec transform-set Project esp-des
9  !
10  !
11  crypto map ISAKMPExtranet 30 ipsec-isakmp
12   set peer 192.168.20.2
13   set transform-set Project
14   match address 103
15  !
16  interface Ethernet0
17   ip address 192.168.130.1 255.255.255.0
18  !
19  interface Serial0
20   ip address 192.168.30.2 255.255.255.0
21   crypto map ISAKMPExtranet
22  !
23  access-list 103 permit ip 192.168.130.0 0.0.0.255 192.168.110.0
    0.0.0.255
```

Figure 6-24

Example of a
misconfigured
ACL for Router B
in Figure 6-23

```
24  hostname RouterB
25  !
26  crypto isakmp policy 200
27   hash md5
28   authentication pre-share
29  crypto isakmp key yabadabadoo address 192.168.30.2
30  !
31  crypto ipsec transform-set TempTransform esp-des
32  !
33   !
34   crypto map ISAKMPModeExtranet 20 ipsec-isakmp
35   set peer 192.168.30.2
36   set transform-set TempTransform
37   match address 104
38  !
39  interface Ethernet0
40   ip address 192.168.110.65 255.255.255.192
41  !
42  interface Serial0
43   ip address 192.168.20.2 255.255.255.0
44   crypto map ISAKMPModeExtranet
45  !
46  access-list 104 permit ip 192.168.110.0 0.0.0.255 192.168.130.0
    0.0.0.255
```

Figure 6-25

Example of a
misconfigured
ACL

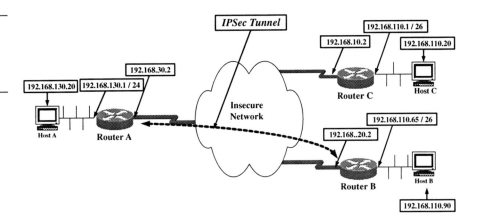

In line 23 of Figure 6-23, the destination network is a /24 network, whereas in Figure 6-25, we can see that Router B and Router C are each configured with a /26 network, which falls within access-list 103 in Figure 6-23 and 6-24.

So, what would happen within this configuration? Assuming that all of the other protocols were configured correctly anytime Host A (192.168.130.20) needed to communicate with Host B (192.168.110.90), everything would be encrypted as expected and communication would be fine.

However, let us take a look at what would happen if network Host A needed to communicate with Host C (192.168.110.20). Once Router A received the packet from Host A, it would queue the packet for its only serial interface (routing table decision). Next, the crypto map would encrypt the packet because of access-list 103 and send the packet to Router B in tunnel mode (meaning the packet has a destination IP for Router B and not the true destination). Router B would receive and decrypt the packet because access-list 104 said it was a packet to decrypt (line 46 in Figure 6-24). Router B then determines from its routing table that the packet must be forwarded to Router C. Router B forwards the unencrypted packet through its serial interface. Remember that the source and destination of access-list 104 no longer match through the insecure network. Router C receives the unencrypted packet and forwards it to Host C (192.168.110.25). Host C responds to Host A and sends the packet back to Router C, at which point Router C knows nothing of the IPSec tunnel and sends the packet back to Router A's serial interface. Router A views the incoming packet and matches it against access-list 103 (line 27), but recognizes that the packet is not encrypted and sends and alert to the console, as seen in Figure 6-26.

This situation is problematic for two reasons. First and most obvious is that our hosts cannot communicate. Secondly, our data is passing unencrypted over an insecure network. From this example, it is easy to see where a misconfigured access-list can potentially cause not only communication problems, but security problems as well.

Figure 6-26

Example of an IPSec router expecting a packet to be encrypted, but receiving it is unencrypted

```
00:17:11: %CRYPTO-4-RECVD_PKT_NOT_IPSEC: Rec'd packet not an IPSEC
packet.
(ip) dest_addr= 192.168.130.20, src_addr= 192.168.110.20, prot= 1
```

6.5.3 Migration from Pre-Shared Keys to a PKI

Sometimes the need to have a task done quickly can be the overriding factor in certain circumstances. This often leaves the network engineer in a precarious position as they try to correct a poor design. For example, the executives at Company A want to secure a data stream to their business partner as soon as possible. However, the executives have also made it clear that they will have hundreds, even thousands more business partners in the near future as they take advantage of VPNs.

Most network engineers would come to the conclusion that they need to utilize a CA server to minimize the overhead required to exchange all of the keys with the new business partners. Unfortunately, the executives at Company A do not give the network engineers a chance to deploy such an infrastructure because they need it completed immediately. In haste, the network engineer deploys pre-shared keys using ISAKMP to complete the job. Now that the job is done, how do you convert from ISAKMP to a PKI infrastructure?

This situation can be solved easily with minimal impact to the encrypted data streams. When defining a crypto map entry, you also specify a sequence number that indicates the priority of the crypto map entry.

When configuring the original pre-shared ISAKMP infrastructure, make sure you select a number high enough so you can insert a lower value (higher priority) crypto map sequence number. Remember that once the IPSec SAs are in place, they are not renegotiated until the lifetimes are about to expire. Thus, by creating a higher priority crypto map entry on both VPN peers, both peers will utilize the new crypto map that makes use of a CA server during the next IPSec SA negotiation. If you are in a hurry, you can clear the SAs using the *clear crypt sa* command and enable the routers to renegotiate their IPSec SAs.

Note:

If you let the SA expire naturally, you can take advantage of the fact that 30 seconds or 256Kb before an SA expires, ISAKMP will renegotiate the SAs and you will not experience any downtime to your IPSec VPN.

6.5.4 Redundant Interfaces Using IPSec

When it comes to *wide area network* (WAN) links, a trouble-free circuit is virtually non-exisitent. A good designer will take this into account when designing a VPN that requires high availability. In the case of IPSec, how can we minimize disruptions to a VPN service?

In Figure 6-27, Router A has two WAN links: Serial 0 and Serial 1. If the WAN link connected to Serial 1 were to go down, what could we as VPN designers do to minimize the impact?

Figure 6-27

Redundant links for an IPSec VPN

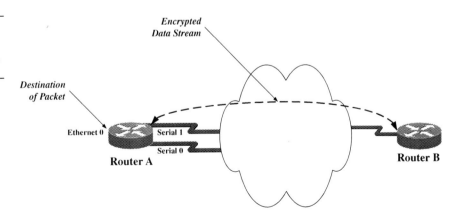

Unfortunately, crypto maps are specific about the VPN peer with which they communicate. One might think that we could start by using a loop-back address to terminate a VPN peer. Unfortunately, this does not work because the outgoing packets are not encrypted because they do not go through the loopback interface. Even if the packets did go through the loopback interface, they would end up in the bit bucket anyway. What can we do?

Cisco has given us the ability to specify a primary link within our crypto map entry. Thus, we can apply the crypto map to any interface without having the fear that encrypted streams are not being carried because of a down WAN link. Using the following command, we can specify which IP address an interface should use for encryption, regardless of its local IP address.

```
Router(config-crypto-map)# Crypto map name-of-map local-ip-address
interface
```

name-of-map	***WORD***	Name for the crypto map
local-ip-address	*x.x.x.x*	IP address of the VPN peer.
interface	**serialx**	The interface whose IP address is specified in the previous parameter

Figure 6-28 depicts this command.

Figure 6-28

Example of configuring a redundant link for IPSec

```
Router(config-crypto-map)#Crypto map RedundantCrypto primary crypto
map 192.168.2.1 serial0
```

6.6 Verify and Troubleshoot IPSec

Cisco has provided quite a few commands that enable us to view the specific attributes of an IPSec VPN. Using a handful of commands, you can have almost every aspect that you need to perform a simple analysis and troubleshooting of an IPSec solution.

6.6.1 Verify IPSec

One of the most useful commands that will provide a brief synopsis of your crypto maps is the *show crypto map* command. In Figure 6-29, all of the most important details about this crypto map entry are at our finger tips.

Figure 6-29

Output from the *show crypto map* command

```
1 RouterA#show crypto map
2 Crypto Map "ISAKMPExtranet" 30 ipsec-isakmp
3       Peer = 192.168.20.2
4       Extended IP access list 103
5               access-list 103 permit ip 192.168.1.0 0.0.0.255
6 192.168.120.0 0.0.0.255
7       Current peer: 192.168.20.2
8       Security association lifetime: 4608000 kilobytes/600 seconds
9           PFS (Y/N): N
10          Transform sets={ Project, }
```

In line two of Figure 6-29, we can see the name of our crypto map and that it utilizes ISAKMP. Line four shows us the access list used to define the data stream for encryption. In addition, line 9 shows us whether or not Perfect Forward Secrecy is enabled.

If we want to view the details about our current IPSec SA associations we can use the *show crypto ipsec sa* command. In Figure 6-30, we can see that a lot of detail in any single IPSec SA.

In Figure 6-30, we see everything we need to know about IPSec SAs. Table 6-4 shows us how to read the information provided in the show crypto ipsec sa command.

We have examined how to tell what parameters are being used for an IPSec SA. Now let us look at the ISAKMP policies. Figure 6-31 illustrates three different policies: two we have configured and one in default.

The *show crypto isakmp policy* command is useful for troubleshooting an ISAKMP problem.

6.6.2 Troubleshoot IPSec

At times, viewing the configurations of an IPSec configuration alone does not provide enough detail to tell you what is wrong with a configuration. Because so many variables exist in IPSec, it is impossible for anyone to describe all the possible problems that you could encounter when imple-

Figure 6-30

Output from the
*show crypto ipsec
sa* command

```
1   RouterB#show crypto ipsec sa
2
3   interface: Serial0
4     Crypto map tag: ISAKMPModeExtranet, local addr. 192.168.20.2
5
6     local  ident (addr/mask/prot/port):
      (192.168.120.0/255.255.255.0/0/0)
7     remote ident (addr/mask/prot/port):
      (192.168.1.0/255.255.255.0/0/0)
8     current_peer: 192.168.10.2
9      PERMIT, flags={origin_is_acl,}
10    #pkts encaps: 19204, #pkts encrypt: 19204, #pkts digest 0
11    #pkts decaps: 15446, #pkts decrypt: 15446, #pkts verify 0
12    #send errors 0, #recv errors 0
13
14    local crypto endpt.: 192.168.20.2, remote crypto endpt.:
      192.168.10.2
15    path mtu 1500, media mtu 1500
16    current outbound spi: BA515E3
17
18    inbound esp sas:
19     spi: 0x109D2107(278733063)
20       transform: esp-des ,
21       in use settings ={Tunnel, }
22       slot: 0, conn id: 46, crypto map: ISAKMPModeExtranet
23       sa timing: remaining key lifetime (k/sec): (4607900/133)
24       IV size: 8 bytes
25        replay detection support: N
26
27
28    inbound ah sas:
29
30
31    outbound esp sas:
32     spi: 0xBA515E3(195368419)
33       transform: esp-des ,
34       in use settings ={Tunnel, }
35       slot: 0, conn id: 47, crypto map: ISAKMPModeExtranet
36       sa timing: remaining key lifetime (k/sec): (4606529/132)
37       IV size: 8 bytes
38       replay detection support: N
39
40
41    outbound ah sas:
```

Table 6-4

Defining the
Output from
Figure 6-30

Line	Field	Description
4	Crypto map tag	Name of the crypto map applied to the interface
6	local ident	Source address for access list
7	Remote ident	Destination address for access list
8	Current_peer	IPSec peer identified in crypto map
10	pkts encaps	Number of packets encrypted
11	pkts decaps	Number of packets decrypted
20	Transform	Encryption and Authentication algorithms specified in crypto map
21	in use settings	Tunnel mode or Transport Mode
23 & 36	Remaining key lifetime	Volume of traffic/time left before a new SA is negotiated.
25 & 38	Replay detection support	Does current IPSec session protect against replay attacks

Figure 6-31

Output from the
*show isakmp
policy* command

```
1   Router#show crypto isakmp policy
2   Protection suite of priority 20
3           encryption algorithm:      DES - Data Encryption Standard (56
                                       bit keys).
4           hash algorithm:            Secure Hash Standard
5           authentication method:     Pre-Shared Key
6           Diffie-Hellman group:      #1 (768 bit)
7           lifetime:                  86400 seconds, no volume limit
8   Protection suite of priority 200
9           encryption algorithm:      DES - Data Encryption Standard (56
                                       bit keys).
10          hash algorithm:            Message Digest 5
11          authentication method:     Pre-Shared Key
12          Diffie-Hellman group:      #1 (768 bit)
13          lifetime:                  86400 seconds, no volume limit
14  Default protection suite
15          encryption algorithm:      DES - Data Encryption Standard (56
                                       bit keys).
16          hash algorithm:            Secure Hash Standard
17          authentication method:     Rivest-Shamir-Adleman Signature
18          Diffie-Hellman group:      #1 (768 bit)
19          lifetime:                  86400 seconds, no volume limit
```

menting IPSec. However, you can use the debugs that Cisco provides along with your understanding of how the technology works to find and resolve problems.

Note:

Before you start troubleshooting your IPSec configurations or even after you have tried everything under the sun to get your configurations working, try removing your crypto maps from the interface and make sure that your IP infrastructure works without IPSec. Many times IPSec installations fail because the basic routing infrastructure is not operational.

When experiencing problems with an IPSec session, it may be difficult to know where to begin. However, you can break down these problems into three areas:

- Troubleshooting ISAKMP SAs
- Troubleshooting IPSec SAs
- Identifying which data stream to encrypt

By breaking down where problems can occur, we can focus on where the problems are and not based on the symptoms that we are seeing. We will not address troubleshooting problems that stem from identifying the data stream incorrectly because this is a simple access-list problem. The other two can be more difficult to determine.

6.6.2.1 Troubleshooting ISAKMP SAs

In any IPSec session utilizing ISAKMP, two negotiations must take place. ISAKMP is the first negotiation that takes place. Then, IPSec will negotiate a connection within the secure ISAKMP SA. Therefore, if you do not have any idea of where to start looking, start with the ISAKMP negotiation. If this is unsuccessful, your VPN peers will not move onto IPSec SA negotiations.

In Figure 6-32, we can see the output from *debug crypto isakmp* during an ISAKMP SA negotiation.

In Figure 6-32, the ISAKMP VPN peer is sending its ISAKMP policies in main mode to its ISAKMP peer (192.168.20.2) in lines 1 and 2. In lines 3 through 9, the router is checking its ISAKMP peer's policies against its own crypto ISAKMP policy 50 (lines 6 through 9 are the remote ISAKMPs policies). In line 10, it rejects the policy and moves on to its next policy. In lines

Figure 6-32

Output from the *debug crypto isakmp* during ISAKMP negotiations

```
 1 22:18:19: ISAKMP(63): beginning Main Mode exchange
 2 22:18:19: ISAKMP(63): sending packet to 192.168.20.2 (I)
                         MM_NO_STATE
 3 22:18:20: ISAKMP(63): received packet from 192.168.20.2 (I)
                         MM_NO_STATE
 4 22:18:20: ISAKMP(63): processing SA payload. message ID = 0
 5 22:18:20: ISAKMP(63): Checking ISAKMP transform 1 against
                         priority 50 policy
 6 22:18:20: ISAKMP:     encryption DES-CBC
 7 22:18:20: ISAKMP:     hash MD5
 8 22:18:20: ISAKMP:     default group 1
 9 22:18:20: ISAKMP:     auth pre-share
10 22:18:20: ISAKMP(63): atts are not acceptable. Next payload is 0
11 22:18:20: ISAKMP(63): Checking ISAKMP transform 1 against
                         priority 100 policy
12 22:18:20: ISAKMP:     encryption DES-CBC
13 22:18:20: ISAKMP:     hash MD5
14 22:18:20: ISAKMP:     default group 1
15 22:18:20: ISAKMP:     auth pre-share
16 22:18:20: ISAKMP(63): atts are acceptable. Next payload is 0
17 22:18:22: ISAKMP(63): SA is doing pre-shared key authentication
18 22:18:22: ISAKMP(63): sending packet to 192.168.20.2 (I)
                         MM_SA_SETUP
19 22:18:22: ISAKMP(0):  received packet from 192.168.20.2 (N) NEW
                         SA
20 22:18:24: ISAKMP(63): received packet from 192.168.20.2 (I)
                         MM_SA_SETUP
21 22:18:24: ISAKMP(63): processing KE payload. message ID = 0
22 22:18:26: ISAKMP(63): processing NONCE payload. message ID = 0
23 22:18:26: ISAKMP(63): SKEYID state generated
24 22:18:26: ISAKMP(63): processing vendor id payload
25 22:18:26: ISAKMP(63): speaking to another IOS box!
26 22:18:26: ISAKMP(63): sending packet to 192.168.20.2 (I)
                         MM_KEY_EXCH
27 22:18:26: ISAKMP(63): received packet from 192.168.20.2 (I)
                         MM_KEY_EXCH
28 22:18:26: ISAKMP(63): processing ID payload. message ID = 0
29 22:18:26: ISAKMP(63): processing HASH payload. message ID = 0
30 22:18:26: ISAKMP(63): SA has been authenticated
31 22:18:26: ISAKMP(63): beginning Quick Mode exchange, M-ID of
                         1915447014
32 22:18:26: ISAKMP(63): sending packet to 192.168.20.2 (I) QM_IDLE
33 22:18:27: ISAKMP(63): received packet from 192.168.20.2 (I)
                         QM_IDLE
34 22:18:27: ISAKMP(63): processing SA payload. message ID =
                         1915447014
35 22:18:27: ISAKMP(63): Checking IPSec proposal 1
36 22:18:27: ISAKMP:     transform 1, ESP_DES
37 22:18:27: ISAKMP:     attributes in transform:
38 22:18:27: ISAKMP:     encaps is 1
39 22:18:27: ISAKMP:     SA life type in seconds
40 22:18:27: ISAKMP:     SA life duration (basic) of 600
41 22:18:27: ISAKMP:     SA life type in kilobytes
42 22:18:27: ISAKMP:     SA life duration (VPI) of  0x0 0x46 0x50
                         0x0
43 22:18:27: ISAKMP(63): atts are acceptable.
44 22:18:27: ISAKMP(63): processing NONCE payload. message ID =
                         1915447014
45 22:18:27: ISAKMP(63): processing ID payload. message ID =
                         1915447014
```

Figure 6-32

Output from the
*debug crypto
isakmp* during
ISAKMP
negotiations
(cont.)

```
46 22:18:27: ISAKMP(63): processing ID payload. message ID =
                         1915447014
47 22:18:27: ISAKMP(63): Creating IPSec SAs
48 22:18:27:        inbound SA from 192.168.20.2    to 192.168.10.2
                    (proxy 192.168.120.0   to 192.168.1.0    )
49 22:18:27:        has spi 290393453 and conn_id 64 and flags 4
50 22:18:27:        lifetime of 600 seconds
51 22:18:27:        lifetime of 4608000 kilobytes
52 22:18:27:        outbound SA from 192.168.10.2      to
192.168.20.2
                    (proxy 192.168.1.0     to 192.168.120.0  )
53 22:18:27:        has spi 305012560 and conn_id 65 and flags 4
54 22:18:27:        lifetime of 600 seconds
55 22:18:27:        lifetime of 4608000 kilobytes
56 22:18:27: ISAKMP(63): sending packet to 192.168.20.2 (I) QM_IDLE
```

11 through 15, the router is checking the remote ISAKMP's policies against its own internal crypto policy number 100, which according to line 16 are acceptable. Lines 17 through 34 show us the steps involved with creating an ISAKMP SA. On line 25, notice that the router has figured out that its ISAKMP peer is another IOS box! Lines 35 through 47 show us ISAKMP checking the proposal of IPSec for encryption, and line 43 shows us that they are agreeable and that the router proceeds to create the SAs for IPSec.

If we determine that our ISAKMP negotiations are failing, we can always use the *show crypto isakmp policy*, on both ISAKMP peers to make sure matching policies are present.

6.6.2.2 Troubleshooting IPSec SAs

Once you have determined that your ISAKMP SAs are negotiated, you can start troubleshooting IPSec SAs. If you are having difficulties establishing an IPSec SA, one of the most informational commands you can use is the *debug crypto ipsec* command. This debug does not provide any useful information until the router attempts to establish an IPSec SA. Figure 6-33 illustrates the output generated from a debug command during an IPSec negotiation.

In line 1, the local IPSec device makes a request to its IPSec peer. In the request, it specifies the following items:

Lines 15 through 17 display an incoming request from its VPN peer. After seeing that they agree upon a session, lines 18 and 19 show the router creating two connections (incoming and outgoing). Line 21 through 34 depict an initialization of the two connections (notice the values in lines 27 and 34 compared to the value of the lines in 7 and 17, respectively). Finally, in lines 35 and 39, two SAs are created and assigned to the two newly created connections.

Figure 6-33

Output from the *debug crypto ipsec* command during an IPSec SA negotiation

```
 1  21:29:30: IPSEC(sa_request): ,
 2    (key eng. msg.) src= 192.168.10.2, dest= 192.168.20.2,
 3      src_proxy= 192.168.1.0/255.255.255.0/0/0 (type=4),
 4      dest_proxy= 192.168.120.0/255.255.255.0/0/0 (type=4),
 5      protocol= ESP, transform= esp-des ,
 6      lifedur= 600s and 4608000kb,
 7      spi= 0x0(0), conn_id= 0, keysize= 0, flags= 0x4004
 8  21:29:31: IPSEC(key_engine): got a queue event...
 9  21:29:31: IPSEC(spi_response): getting spi 304286340 for SA
10          from 192.168.20.2    to 192.168.10.2    for prot 3
11  21:29:31: IPSEC(validate_proposal_request): proposal part #1,
12    (key eng. msg.) dest= 192.168.20.2, src= 192.168.10.2,
13      dest_proxy= 192.168.120.0/255.255.255.0/0/0 (type=4),
14      src_proxy= 192.168.1.0/255.255.255.0/0/0 (type=4),
15      protocol= ESP, transform= esp-des ,
16      lifedur= 0s and 0kb,
17  spi= 0x0(0), conn_id= 0, keysize= 0, flags= 0x4
18  21:29:31: CRYPTO: Allocated conn_id 48 slot 0, swidb 0x0,
19  21:29:32: CRYPTO: Allocated conn_id 49 slot 0, swidb 0x0,
20  21:29:32: IPSEC(key_engine): got a queue event...
21  21:29:32: IPSEC(initialize_sas): ,
22  (key eng. msg.) dest= 192.168.10.2, src= 192.168.20.2,
23  dest_proxy= 192.168.1.0/255.255.255.0/0/0 (type=4),
24  src_proxy= 192.168.120.0/255.255.255.0/0/0 (type=4),
25  protocol= ESP, transform= esp-des ,
26  lifedur= 600s and 4608000kb,
27  spi= 0x12230A84(304286340), conn_id= 48, keysize= 0, flags= 0x4
28  21:29:32: IPSEC(initialize_sas): ,
29  (key eng. msg.) src= 192.168.10.2, dest= 192.168.20.2,
30  src_proxy= 192.168.1.0/255.255.255.0/0/0 (type=4),
31  dest_proxy= 192.168.120.0/255.255.255.0/0/0 (type=4),
32  protocol= ESP, transform= esp-des ,
33  lifedur= 600s and 4608000kb,
34  spi= 0x16ED183C(384636988), conn_id= 49, keysize= 0, flags= 0x4
35  21:29:32: IPSEC(create_sa): sa created,
36    (sa) sa_dest= 192.168.10.2, sa_prot= 50,
37      sa_spi= 0x12230A84(304286340),
38      sa_trans= esp-des , sa_conn_id= 48
39  21:29:32: IPSEC(create_sa): sa created,
40    (sa) sa_dest= 192.168.20.2, sa_prot= 50,
41      sa_spi= 0x16ED183C(384636988),
42      sa_trans= esp-des , sa_conn_id= 49
```

Table 6-5

Description of the various parameters in the *debug crypto ipsec* command

Line	Description
1	Source and Destination of the IPSec session (from the local router's perspective)
2	source network to encrypt
3	Destination network to encyrpt
4	Requested encryption protocol
5	SA lifetimes (seconds and kb)

In the output from Figure 6-34, there is a problem. Can you identify it? In lines 15 and 17, not enough bits are available in the cipher to successfully encrypt a data stream. If the key fails, so does the IPSec SA.

Figure 6-34

Output from a *debug crypto ipsec* command during a failed IPSec SA negotiation

```
1   00:27:12: IPSEC(sa_request): ,
2      (key eng. msg.) src= 192.168.50.1, dest= 192.168.60.1,
3        src_proxy= 192.168.1.0/255.255.255.0/0/0 (type=4),
4        dest_proxy= 192.168.120.0/255.255.255.0/0/0 (type=4),
5        protocol= ESP, transform= esp-des ,
6        lifedur= 3600s and 4608000kb,
7        spi= 0x0(0), conn_id= 0, keysize= 0, flags= 0x4004
8   00:27:13: IPSEC(sa_request): ,
9      (key eng. msg.) src= 192.168.50.1, dest= 192.168.60.1,
10       src_proxy= 192.168.1.0/255.255.255.0/0/0 (type=4),
11       dest_proxy= 192.168.120.0/255.255.255.0/0/0 (type=4),
12       protocol= ESP, transform= esp-des ,
13       lifedur= 3600s and 4608000kb,
14       spi= 0x0(0), conn_id= 0, keysize= 0, flags= 0x4004
15  00:27:13: IPSEC(manual_key_stuffing): not enough cipher keymat,
                 8 bytes
16  needed for addr 192.168.60.1/prot 50/spi 256
17  00:27:13: IPSEC(manual_key_stuffing): not enough cipher keymat,
                 8 bytes
18  needed for addr 192.168.60.1/prot 50/spi 256
19  00:27:14: IPSEC(sa_request): ,
20     (key eng. msg.) src= 192.168.50.1, dest= 192.168.60.1,
21       src_proxy= 192.168.1.0/255.255.255.0/0/0 (type=4),
22       dest_proxy= 192.168.120.0/255.255.255.0/0/0 (type=4),
23       protocol= ESP, transform= esp-des ,
24       lifedur= 3600s and 4608000kb,
25       spi= 0x0(0), conn_id= 0, keysize= 0, flags= 0x4004
```

6.7 IPSec Case Studies

6.7.1 Case Study #1 - Using IPSec with a GRE Tunnel

VPN Type: Intranet VPN
Tunnel Type: Compulsory tunnel
When to deploy: This type of tunnel is useful within an enterprise network when the core network is only routing IP and you need to run IPX between the various sites. Using the Internet as your backbone, you can tunnel IPX securely across the Internet.
Verifying that VPN has been enabled: A remote workstation can login to NetWare server.

Note:

All links are considered to have a subnet mask of 255.255.255.0 unless otherwise specified.

Figure 6-35

Case Study #1—
Routing IPX/SPX
across a TCP/IP
backbone
encrypted with
IPSec

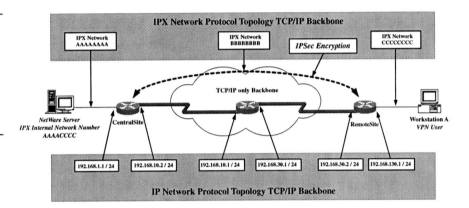

Case Study Note:

It is assumed that the reader can configure the backbone router for simple IP address assignments and OSPF routing. If you need help, use the "Backbone Router Configuration File" from Chapter 5's Case Study #1 for guidance.

6.7.1.1 CentralSite Router Configuration File

Figure 6-36

CentralSite
configuration file
for Chapter 6
Case Study #1

```
1   version 11.3
2   service timestamps debug uptime
3   service timestamps log uptime
4   no service password-encryption
5   !
6   hostname CentralSite
7   !
8   ipx routing 0000.0c4a.4a56
9   !
10  no crypto isakmp enable
11  !
12  crypto ipsec transform-set Encryption2RemoteOffice ah-md5-hmac esp-
    des
13  !
14  !
15  crypto map ManualModeIntranet local-address Serial0
16  crypto map ManualModeIntranet 20 ipsec-manual
17  set peer 192.168.30.2
18  set security-association inbound esp 300 cipher 1234567890abcdef
19  set security-association outbound esp 300 cipher fedcba0987654321
20  set security-association inbound ah 300
    1234567890abcdef1234567890abcdef
21  set security-association outbound ah 300
    fedcba0987654321fedcba0987654321
22  set transform-set Encryption2RemoteOffice
23  match address 101
24  !
25  interface Loopback0
26  ip address 1.1.1.1 255.255.255.255
27  !
28  interface Tunnel1
29  no ip address
30  ipx network BBBBBBBB
31  tunnel source Serial0
32  tunnel destination 192.168.30.2
33  crypto map ManualModeIntranet
34  !
35  interface Ethernet0
36  ip address 192.168.1.1 255.255.255.0
37  no ip route-cache
38  ipx network AAAAAAAA encapsulation SAP
39  !
40  interface Serial0
41  ip address 192.168.10.2 255.255.255.0
42  no ip route-cache
43  crypto map ManualModeIntranet
44  !
45  interface Serial1
46  shutdown
47  no fair-queue
48  !
49  router ospf 10
50  network 1.1.1.1 0.0.0.0 area 0
51  network 192.168.1.0 0.0.0.255 area 0
52  network 192.168.10.0 0.0.0.255 area 0
53  !
54  access-list 101 permit gre host 192.168.10.2 host 192.168.30.2
55  !
56  !
57  line con 0
58  exec-timeout 0 0
59  line aux 0
60  line vty 0 4
61  password cisco
62  login
63  !
64  end
```

6.7.1.2 RemoteSite Router Configuration File

Figure 6-37

RemoteSite
configuration file
for Chapter 6
Case Study #1

```
65   version 12.0
66   service timestamps debug uptime
67   service timestamps log uptime
68   no service password-encryption
69   !
70   hostname RemoteSite
71   !
72   ipx routing 00e0.1e3e.8476
73   !
74   no crypto isakmp enable
75   !
76   crypto ipsec transform-set Encryption2CentralOffice ah-md5-hmac esp-
     des
77   !
77a  crypto map ManualModeIntranet local-address Serial0
78   crypto map ManualModeIntranet 20 ipsec-manual
79    set peer 192.168.10.2
79a   set session-key inbound esp 300 cipher fedcba0987654321
79b   set session-key outbound esp 300 cipher 1234567890abcdef
79c   set session-key inbound ah 300 fedcba0987654321fedcba0987654321
79d   set session-key outbound ah 300 1234567890abcdef1234567890abcdef
80    set transform-set Encryption2CentralOffice
81    match address 101
82   !
83   interface Loopback0
84    ip address 3.3.3.3 255.255.255.255
85    no ip directed-broadcast
86   !
87   interface Tunnel1
88    no ip address
89    ipx network BBBBBBBB
90    tunnel source Serial0
91    tunnel destination 192.168.10.2
92    crypto map ManualModeIntranet
93   !
94   interface Ethernet0
95    ip address 192.168.130.1 255.255.255.0
96    no ip directed-broadcast
97    no ip route-cache
98    ipx network CCCCCCCC encapsulation SAP
99   !
100  interface Serial0
101   ip address 192.168.30.2 255.255.255.0
102   no ip directed-broadcast
103   no ip route-cache
104   crypto map ManualModeIntranet
105  !
106  interface Serial1
107   no ip address
108   no ip directed-broadcast
109   shutdown
110  !
111  router ospf 10
112   log-adjacency-changes
113   network 3.3.3.3 0.0.0.0 area 0
114   network 192.168.30.0 0.0.0.255 area 0
115   network 192.168.130.0 0.0.0.255 area 0
116  !
117  ip classless
118  !
119  access-list 101 permit gre host 192.168.30.2 host 192.168.10.2
120  !
121  line con 0
122   exec-timeout 0 0
123   transport input none
124  line aux 0
125  line vty 0 4
126   exec-timeout 0 0
127   password cisco
128   login
129  !
130  end
```

6.7.1.3 Case Study Analysis

In this case study, one router is running IOS 11.3 (CentralSite), and the other is running IOS 12.0 (RemoteSite). We have done this to highlight the difference between these IOS configuration files.

The first section that must be highlighted is found in Figure 6-37, between lines 79 and 80 (79a, 79b, 79c, and 79d). These commands are used to configure the encryption and keys used for the IPSec SAs. However, unlike IOS 11.3T and IOS 12.1, when entered into a router using IOS 12.0, they disappear. You cannot view any of the keys used for the IPSec key. If you forget what the key is, you cannot view it and must therefore change it at both ends. In addition, this makes the configuration file non-portable because the keys are not copied with the configuration file. Thus, if you have to replace a router with the IPSec SA keys manually configured, you must re-enter the keys. To help with the discussion, we have identified the missing lines as 79a through 79d. Remember that we are running IOS 12.0 and these commands would be missing from the configuration file.

In this case study, we are using MD5 for IPSec authentication and DES for encryption (lines 12 and 76). When manually configuring the keys for an IPSec SA, you must use the correct key size. Failure to do so will cause the tunnel to be non-operational. Configuring the keys in this paradigm can become confusing because you have a key for each protocol in each direction. In order for it to work, the key that was used to encrypt a data stream must also decrypt it. Therefore, the key must be the same between the following lines in our configuration files: 18 and 79b, 19 and 79a, 20 and 79c, and 21 and 79d. Not only must the keys be the same for these encryption/decryption pairs, but the *Security Parameters Index* (SPI) must also be the same between the pair.

When applying the crypto map to this configuration, two interesting actions had to take place to make this configuration work. First, we had to specify the crypto map, not only on the physical interface (serial zero, and lines 53 and 104), but on the logical interface as well (tunnel one, and lines 33 and 92). If the crypto map is missing from either interface, the configuration does not work. Secondly, because we are technically using two interfaces, we had to use the local-address option within a crypto map (although not visible in IOS 12.0, but added for clarity within our configuration file, line 77a), which specifies the source address of our local VPN.

The last action to note about this configuration and the other IPSec configurations is that we must disable the fast switching if we are going to use IPSec. Unfortunately, the requirements for using fast switching seem random. For example, while writing the configuration files for these case studies, I had two Cisco 2503's both running Cisco IOS 11.3(11a)T1, with 5.2(8a) BOOT ROM's. During my analysis, I came to the conclusion that I could enable fast switching on the CentralOffice router and not the RemoteSite router. As soon as fast switching was turned on the Remote-site router, the VPN did not work.

The advantage of this configuration (manually configuring your IPSec SA keys) is that you can get it working quickly. However, it should become obvious that trying to scale a solution like this to meet the needs of a large VPN solution could be unmanageable, especially because certain IOSs will not even let you see the encryption key, whereas others will!

6.7.2 Case Study #2 - IPSec with Pre-Shared Keys with IOS 12.0 and IOS 11.3

VPN Type: Extranet VPN

Tunnel Type: Compulsory tunnel

When to deploy: This type of tunnel is useful when you are a small company that needs to conduct secure communication with a couple of business partners. Using multiple ISAKMP policies, crypto maps, and transform sets, we will demonstrate the use of different encryption and authentication algorithms between the partners.

Verifying that VPN has been enabled: hosts at each site can ping each other.

Note:

All links are considered to have a subnet mask of 255.255.255.0 unless otherwise specified.

Figure 6-38

Multiple IPSec peers using ISAKMP with pre-shared keys

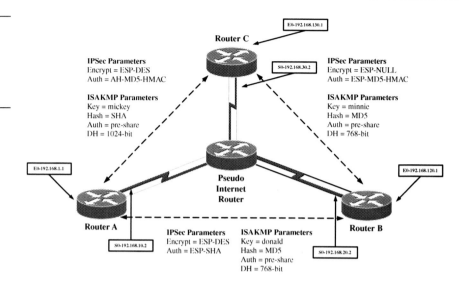

6.7.2.1 Router A Configuration File

Figure 6-39

Router A configuration file for Chapter 6 Case Study #2

```
1  !
2  version 11.3
3  service timestamps debug uptime
4  service timestamps log uptime
5  no service password-encryption
6  !
7  hostname RouterA
8  !
9  crypto isakmp policy 100
10  hash md5
11  authentication pre-share
12  !
13 crypto isakmp policy 200
14  authentication pre-share
15  group 2
16 crypto isakmp key donald address 192.168.20.2
17 crypto isakmp key mickey address 192.168.30.2
18 !
19 !
20 crypto ipsec transform-set IPSecToRouterC esp-des esp-md5-hmac
21 crypto ipsec transform-set IPSecToRouterB esp-des esp-sha-hmac
22 !
23  !
24  crypto map ISAKMPExtranet 20 ipsec-isakmp
25  set peer 192.168.20.2
26  set transform-set IPSecToRouterB
27  match address 102
```

Figure 6-39

Router A
configuration file
for Chapter 6
Case Study #2
(cont.)

```
28 crypto map ISAKMPExtranet 30 ipsec-isakmp
29  set peer 192.168.30.2
30  set transform-set IPSecToRouterC
31  match address 103
32 !
33 interface Loopback0
34  ip address 1.1.1.1 255.255.255.255
35 !
36 interface Ethernet0
37  ip address 192.168.1.1 255.255.255.0
38  no ip route-cache
39 !
40 interface Serial0
41  ip address 192.168.10.2 255.255.255.0
42  no ip route-cache
43  crypto map ISAKMPExtranet
44 !
45 interface Serial1
46  shutdown
47 !
48 router ospf 10
49  network 1.1.1.1 0.0.0.0 area 0
50  network 192.168.1.0 0.0.0.255 area 0
51  network 192.168.10.0 0.0.0.255 area 0
52 !
53 access-list 102 permit ip 192.168.1.0 0.0.0.255 192.168.120.0
   0.0.0.255
54 access-list 103 permit ip 192.168.1.0 0.0.0.255 192.168.130.0
   0.0.0.255
55 !
56 !
57 line con 0
58  exec-timeout 0 0
59 line aux 0
60 line vty 0 4
61  password cisco
62  login
63 !
64 end
```

6.7.2.2 Router B Configuration File

Figure 6-40

Router B
configuration file
for Chapter 6
Case Study #2

```
65 !
66 version 11.3
67 service timestamps debug uptime
68 service timestamps log uptime
69 no service password-encryption
70 !
71 hostname RouterB
72 !
73 !
74 crypto isakmp policy 100
75  hash md5
76  authentication pre-share
```

Figure 6-40

Router B
configuration file
for Chapter 6
Case Study #2
(cont.)

```
77   !
78   crypto isakmp policy 200
79    hash md5
80    authentication pre-share
81   crypto isakmp key minnie address 192.168.30.2
82   crypto isakmp key donald address 192.168.10.2
83   !
84    !
85   crypto ipsec transform-set IPSecToRouterC esp-null esp-md5-hmac
86   crypto ipsec transform-set IPSecToRouterA esp-des esp-sha-hmac
87   !
88    !
89    crypto map ISAKMPModeExtranet 20 ipsec-isakmp
90    set peer 192.168.30.2
91    set transform-set IPSecToRouterC
92    match address 103
93   crypto map ISAKMPModeExtranet 30 ipsec-isakmp
94    set peer 192.168.10.2
95    set transform-set IPSecToRouterA
96    match address 101
97   !
98   interface Loopback0
99    ip address 2.2.2.2 255.255.255.255
100  !
101  interface Ethernet0
102   ip address 192.168.120.1 255.255.255.0
103   no ip route-cache
104   no ip mroute-cache
105  !
106  interface Serial0
107   ip address 192.168.20.2 255.255.255.0
108   no ip route-cache
109   crypto map ISAKMPModeExtranet
110  !
111  interface Serial1
112   shutdown
113  !
114  router ospf 10
115   network 2.2.2.2 0.0.0.0 area 0
116   network 192.168.20.0 0.0.0.255 area 0
117   network 192.168.120.0 0.0.0.255 area 0
118  !
119  access-list 101 permit ip 192.168.120.0 0.0.0.255 192.168.1.0
       0.0.0.255
120  access-list 103 permit ip 192.168.120.0 0.0.0.255 192.168.130.0
       0.0.0.255
121  !
122  !
123  line con 0
124   exec-timeout 0 0
125  line aux 0
126  line vty 0 4
127   login
128  !
129  end
```

6.7.2.3 Router C Configuration File

Figure 6-41

Router C
configuration file
for Chapter 6
Case Study #2

```
130 !
131 version 12.0
132 service timestamps debug uptime
133 service timestamps log uptime
134 no service password-encryption
135 !
136 hostname RouterC
137 !
138 crypto isakmp policy 100
139  authentication pre-share
140  group 2
141 !
142 crypto isakmp policy 200
143  hash md5
144  authentication pre-share
145 crypto isakmp key minnie address 192.168.20.2
146 crypto isakmp key mickey address 192.168.10.2
147 !
148 crypto ipsec transform-set IPSecToRouterA esp-des esp-md5-hmac
149 crypto ipsec transform-set IPSecToRouterB esp-null esp-md5-hmac
150 !
151 crypto map ISAKMPExtranet 10 ipsec-isakmp
152  set peer 192.168.10.2
153  set transform-set IPSecToRouterA
154  match address 101
155 crypto map ISAKMPExtranet 20 ipsec-isakmp
156  set peer 192.168.20.2
157  set transform-set IPSecToRouterB
158  match address 102
159 !
160 interface Loopback0
161  ip address 3.3.3.3 255.255.255.255
162 !
163 interface Ethernet0
164  ip address 192.168.130.1 255.255.255.0
165  no ip route-cache
166 !
167 interface Serial0
168  ip address 192.168.30.2 255.255.255.0
169  no ip route-cache
170  crypto map ISAKMPExtranet
171 !
172 interface Serial1
173  shutdown
174
175 router ospf 10
176  network 3.3.3.3 0.0.0.0 area 0
177  network 192.168.30.0 0.0.0.255 area 0
178  network 192.168.130.0 0.0.0.255 area 0
179 !
180 access-list 101 permit ip 192.168.130.0 0.0.0.255 192.168.1.0
     0.0.0.255
181 access-list 102 permit ip 192.168.130.0 0.0.0.255 192.168.120.0
     0.0.0.255
182 !
```

Figure 6-41

Router C
configuration file
for Chapter 6
Case Study #2
(cont.)

```
183 !
184 line con 0
185   exec-timeout 0 0
186   transport input none
187 line aux 0
188 line vty 0 4
189   login
190 !
191 end
```

6.7.2.4 Case Study Analysis

In this case study, two routers are running IOS 11.3 (Router A and Router B) and one router is running IOS 12.0 (Router C). In this particular configuration, the commands appear to be no different from one router to the next. This is good to know for you *Cisco Certified Internetworking Experts* (CCIE) candidates because you do not know what IOS will be running in your CCIE Lab. With no change in the commands, you do not need to remember variations of the commands.

Each of these configuration files is a pretty simple ISAKMP pre-share IPSec configuration. What can really make this particular lab a challenge is that you have multiple negotiations occuring simultaneously to different peers. At times, isolating the errors to one negotiation can be difficult. I find that by shutting down the third router link and focusing on a single link at a time, you can conquer each of these configurations. In addition, when you do have multiple VPN peers, it is important to make sure you choose names that mean something in your configuration files. Otherwise you will spend a lot of time trying to remember which policy, transform set, or crypto map goes to which VPN peer. For example, you should try to pair up a local policy of 100 to a remote policy of 200. This means that you always know which two pairs of policies you have to analyze.

Notice that in the case study, we indicated that we wanted to use the SHA hash algorithm in our ISAKMP policy between Router A and Router B. In both configuration files, this configuration parameter is missing. This is because it is the default hash for an ISAKMP policy.

One of the interesting things to point out about the encryption algorithms that can be used is on lines 20 and 148. In this configuration pair, we have chosen not to use an AH protocol for authentication, but an ESP protocol. Remember earlier in the chapter when we mentioned that the ESP protocol had the ability to authenticate? You should remember that although ESP can protect most of the packet, it cannot protect the entire packet like an AH protocol. Another interesting point in this case study is that we used ESP to authenticate only between Router C and Router B (lines 85 and 148). In order to use ESP as an authentication tool, we still need to use an encryption protocol of some sort. Cisco has given us the null option so that we can take advantage of the authentication abilities of ESP.

This case study is straightforward to implement as long as you can keep the different policies, transform sets, and crypto maps straight. This particular configuration can scale better than the previous case study in which we manually configured the encryption algorithms by the SAs, but it is still limited in its growth potential.

6.7.3 Case Study #3 - Redundant IPSec Configuration

VPN Type: Intranet VPN
Tunnel Type: Compulsory tunnel
When to deploy: This type of IPSec configuration is useful when you need to build an IPSec solution with redundant links.
Verifying that VPN has been enabled: Any LAN device should be able to reach to any other LAN device, even after shutting down either link.

Figure 6-42

Redundant IPSec configuration

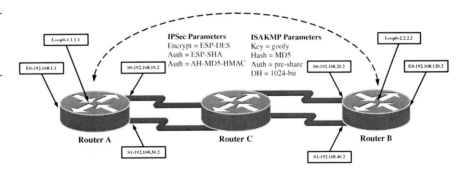

6.7.3.1 Router A Configuration File

Figure 6-43

CentralSite
configuration file
for Chapter 6
Case Study #3

```
1   version 11.3
2   service timestamps debug uptime
3   service timestamps log uptime
4   no service password-encryption
5   !
6   hostname RouterA
7   !
8   crypto isakmp policy 200
9    hash md5
10   authentication pre-share
11   group 2
12  crypto isakmp key goofy address 2.2.2.2
13  !
14  crypto ipsec transform-set RedundantLink ah-md5-hmac esp-des
    esp-sha-hmac
15  !
16   !
17   crypto map RedundantIntranet local-address Loopback0
18   crypto map RedundantIntranet 10 ipsec-isakmp
19   set peer 2.2.2.2
20   set transform-set RedundantLink
21   match address 102
22  !
23  interface Loopback0
24   ip address 1.1.1.1 255.255.255.255
25  !
26  interface Ethernet0
27   ip address 192.168.1.1 255.255.255.0
28   no ip route-cache
29  !
30  interface Serial0
31   ip address 192.168.10.2 255.255.255.0
32   no ip route-cache
33   crypto map RedundantIntranet
34  !
35  interface Serial1
36   ip address 192.168.30.2 255.255.255.0
37   no ip route-cache
38   crypto map RedundantIntranet
39  !
40  interface BRI0
41   no ip address
42   shutdown
43  !
44  router ospf 10
45   network 1.1.1.1 0.0.0.0 area 0
46   network 192.168.0.0 0.0.255.255 area 0
47  !
48  access-list 102 permit ip 192.168.1.0 0.0.0.255 192.168.120.0
    0.0.0.255
49  !
50  line con 0
51   exec-timeout 0 0
52  line aux 0
53  line vty 0 4
54   password cisco
55   login
56  !
57  end
```

6.7.3.2 Router B Configuration File

Figure 6-44

CentralSite
configuration file
for Chapter 6
Case Study #3

```
58   version 11.3
59   service timestamps debug uptime
60   service timestamps log uptime
61   no service password-encryption
62   !
63   hostname RouterB
64   !
65   crypto isakmp policy 740
66    hash md5
67    authentication pre-share
68    group 2
69   crypto isakmp key goofy address 1.1.1.1
70   !
71   crypto ipsec transform-set IntranetIPSec ah-md5-hmac esp-des
     esp-sha-hmac
72   !
73    crypto map RedundantIPSecLink local-address Loopback0
74    crypto map RedundantIPSecLink 10 ipsec-isakmp
75    set peer 1.1.1.1
76    set transform-set IntranetIPSec
77    match address 101
78   !
79   interface Loopback0
80    ip address 2.2.2.2 255.255.255.255
81   !
82   interface Ethernet0
83    ip address 192.168.120.1 255.255.255.0
84    no ip route-cache
85   !
86   interface Serial0
87    ip address 192.168.20.2 255.255.255.0
88    no ip route-cache
89    crypto map RedundantIPSecLink
90   !
91   interface Serial1
92    ip address 192.168.40.2 255.255.255.0
93    no fair-queue
94    crypto map RedundantIPSecLink
95   !
96   router ospf 10
97    network 2.2.2.2 0.0.0.0 area 0
98    network 192.168.0.0 0.0.255.255 area 0
99   !
100  access-list 101 permit ip 192.168.120.0 0.0.0.255 192.168.1.0
     0.0.0.255
101  !
102  line con 0
103   exec-timeout 0 0
104  line vty 0 4
105   login
106  !
107  end
```

6.7.4 Case Study Analysis

In this case study, we have a configuration that seems straightforward, but it really is not. It is the second link that really causes a problem for our configuration. As we saw in Case Study #1, having two interfaces that use the same crypto can be problematic when they both need to support the same VPN peer. One way to solve this problem would be to set up a second IPSec session, but we only double the confusion by having two IPSec sessions to the same router. The easiest way to solve this problem is to source everything from an interface that does not go down, that is, use a loopback interface. By using a loopback interface, we can source all of our negotiations from that address; it does not matter which interface actually routes the packet. However, in order to do this we must use the local address option in the crypto map as can be seen in lines 73 and 17.

Why could we not just source everything from the Ethernet interface? By sourcing, we mean the IP address, not the application of the crypto map to an interface. We could do this, but we would not want to for a couple of reasons. First, let us look at a scenario in which a second Ethernet network is present whose data streams were being encrypted in addition to the first Ethernet interface. If the first Ethernet interface is disconnected from the network, the second Ethernet network would lose its VPN connection even though none of the WAN circuits is down. Secondly, one of the reasons we use IPSec in tunnel mode is so that we can hide the IP addresses of our protected users. By default, an IPSec session is in tunnel mode. This means that the real IP address becomes hidden behind the IPSec source IP address. By using the Ethernet network as the source, you have just allowed an attacker to see the IP address of your protected network.

One interesting trick that you can use in this particular case study is to increase the *Open Shortest Path First* (OSPF) cost of one of the links and then remove the crypto map from that interface. By forcing the traffic over one of the links, we can remove the crypto map because the router will not route any traffic across that link. We can think of this trick as the "look ma, only one hand!" trick. It is important to keep in mind that underlying all of the crypto maps, transform sets, and access-lists is just basic IP routing.

At times when using encryption, we will need to balance CPU/WAN performance with the security of our solution. In this case study, we used ah-md5-hmac, esp-des, and esp-sha-hmac protocols (lines 14 and 71). One action to increase performance is to remove a protocol in our IPSec session. We can then put more packets through the encryption process (especially on slower older routers). While copying files through your IPSec VPN, remove the esp-sha-hmac algorithm from the transform set (do not worry, this will not disrupt your VPN session). If you remove the transform set and reapply a new one, make sure that you configure your new transform on both sides before they decide to renegotiate their SAs! If the IPSec peers attempt to renegotiate their SAs while the transform set is removed, or the IPSec peers transform sets do not match, you will lose your VPN until you configure it correctly.

6.8 Summary of IPSec

Table 6-6	**Authentication**	**Machine only, no user authentication**
Summary of IPSec features	Multiprotocol Support	No (Use a GRE tunnel for Multiprotocol support)
	IP protocol Number	50 - ESP, 51 - AH
	UDP Port Number	500 - IKE
	Data Confidentiality	Yes
	Data Integrity	Yes
	Data Origin Authentication	Yes
	Anti-Replay	Yes
	Encryption Strength	Strong
	IOS support for IPSec	IOS 11.3T and later
	What IOS naming convention value supports IPSec	56i
	What IOS naming convention value supports Triple DES	k2

Current RFCs Related to IPSec

Table 6-7	RFC	Title
Current RFCs related to IPSec	2401	Security Architecture for the Internet Protocol
	2402	IP Authentication Header
	2403	The Use of HMAC-MD5-96 within ESP and AH
	2404	The Use of HMAC-SHA-1-96 within ESP and AH
	2405	The ESP DES-CBC Cipher Algorithm with Explicit IV
	2406	IP Encapsulating Security Payload
	2407	The Internet IP Security Domain of Interpretation fo ISAKMP
	2408	Internet Security Association and Key Management Protocol (ISAKMP)
	2409	The Internet Key Exchange
	2410	The NULL Encryption Algorithm and Its Use with IPSec
	2411	IP Security Document Roadmap
	2412	The OAKLEY Key Determination
	2207	RSVP Extensions for IPSec Data Flows
	2410	The NULL Encryption Algorithm and Its Use With IPSec
	2709	Security Model with Tunnel-mode IPSec for NAT Domains
	1828	IP Authentication using Keyed MD5
	2857	The Use of HMAC-RIPEMD-160-96 within ESP and AH
	1829	The ESP DES-CBC Transform
	1851	The ESP Triple DES Transform
	2451	The ESP CBC-Mode Cipher Algorithms
	2587	The Use of HMAC-RIPEMD-160-96 within ESP and AH
	2631	Diffie-Hellman Key Agreement Method

CHAPTER 7

PPTP

7.1 Chapter Introduction

In the last two chapters, we have looked at strictly compulsory *virtual private network* (VPN) tunneling technologies. In this chapter and the next chapter, we will look at VPN technologies that support voluntary tunnels. Although compulsory VPNs are easy to set up and maintain, voluntary VPNs are extremely flexible in their capability to be deployed. One of the distinct advantages that the *Point-to-Point Tunneling Protocol* (PPTP) has over competing voluntary VPN technologies is its widespread distribution of the client on Windows 95, Windows 98, Windows ME, Windows NT, and Windows 2000. This fact alone makes it a significant contender for market share.

Note:

In instances in which a compulsory tunnel will be used, two VPN PPTP servers will need to be configured, which in most circumstances will be the same type of device, NT servers. If the two VPN peers are Cisco devices, then a network designer will most likely implement IP Security *(IPSec),* Layer Two Tunneling Protocol *(L2TP), or* Generic Routing Encapsulation *(GRE) with CET and not PPTP. This is because network engineers will use those protocols that are very mature protocols (from a Cisco support perspective). Thus, in this chapter, we will only discuss voluntary tunnels in which a Cisco Router is the VPN terminating device. We will not be discussing using a Cisco router as a PPTP initiator.*

In this chapter and the next chapter, we will be focusing on technologies that are known as *Virtual Private Dial-up Networks* (VPDNs). This naming convention is twofold. First, in voluntary tunnels the method used to establish a connection with a VPN terminator is very similar to dialing into a PPP dial-up router. Second, some VPDN technologies, when implemented as a compulsory tunnel allows, a VPN terminator to authenticate a user even when using a third-party ISP to terminate the user's physical layer and data-link layer PPP connection.

The objectives to be covered in this chapter are:

- Overview of PPTP
- Describe PPTP authentication methods
- Describe PPTP encryption methods
- Configure PPTP on a Cisco router
- Configure PPTP on Windows 98, NT, and 2000
- Review design considerations for PPTP
- Troubleshoot PPTP

The basic premise of PPTP is to enable a remote user to dial into any ISP and then tunnel their way to the corporate network as seen in Figure 7-1. This is why you will frequently hear PPTP referred to by Cisco as a VPDN technology. We are going to embrace this term within this chapter and the next chapter because the term VPDN is embedded within many of the Cisco commands that enable PPTP.

Although we will use the term VPN to refer to a VPDN technology, not all VPN technologies are VPDN technologies. PPTP, L2TP, and L2TP's

Figure 7-1

PPTP paradigm

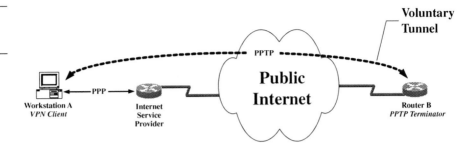

cousin *Layer Two Forwarding* (L2F) are considered VPDN technologies, while IPSec is still referred to as just VPN.

When establishing a PPTP connection, the same data-link layer and network layer characteristics that are negotiated during a PPP connection are negotiated during a PPTP connection such as authentication, encryption, compression, IP address, IPX network address, and so on. The same protocols (LCP and NCP) that are used during PPP negotiations are used during PPTP negotiations. For example, the *Password Authentication Protocol* (PAP) and the *Challenge Handshake Authentication Protocol* (CHAP) are used for authenticating a PPTP tunnel.

Note:

For those of you who already have a firm understanding of how PPP connections are negotiated, this should be a simple concept to understand. For more information about PPP negotiations, review Chapter 3, "Implementing Dialup over Cisco routers."

7.2 Overview of PPTP Architecture

PPTP, developed by a consortium of vendors (Microsoft, Ascend, 3Com, ECI Telematics, and Copper Mountain Networks), is currently defined by RFC 2637. Its purpose is to specify a protocol that encapsulates PPP packets inside an IP packet. PPTP can be broken down into two different components: the transport, which makes the virtual connection, and the encryption, which makes it private.

PPTP uses an extended version of GRE to transport PPP packets, allowing for low-level congestion and flow control. PPTP gets its multiprotocol support from PPP and not GRE. It is easy to see where you can get confused on this issue, because the GRE protocol has multiprotocol support. However, GRE is only the transport used by PPTP to tunnel the packets to the VPN terminator.

Security for PPTP is provided by the use of *Microsoft Point-to-Point Encryption* (MPPE). MPPE can use either 40-bit or 128-bit encryption, depending upon whether you intend to use encryption domestically or internationally (export laws currently prohibit the exportation of strong encryption, thus 128-bit encryption is not available for international use). In addition, the payload of a PPTP packet can be compressed.

As with any voluntary VPN, only two components exist: the VPN user, which is also the VPN initiator, and the VPN server. Depending upon the group discussing PPTP several other names are used for these two devices as seen in Table 7-1.

Table 7-1	Vendor/Group	VPN Client Terminology	VPN Server Terminology
Different names used for the PPTP device terminology	Microsoft	VPN Client	Front-End Processor
	IETF	*PPTP Access Concentrator* (PAC)	*PPTP Network Server* (PNS)

7.2.1 PPTP Control Messages and Data Tunneling

In order for a computer to use PPTP, the computer must already have access to an IP-based internetwork. The connection can be either LAN-based through an Ethernet connection or through a modem dialed up to an ISP.

PPTP utilizes two different types of messages, one for PPTP control connections and the other for PPTP data tunneling. Each of these messages has a different frame format and utilizes a different identifier, which must be taken into account when defining security at the edge of your network through access-lists or firewalls.

PPTP control connection uses a TCP port 1723 for messages relating to the creation, maintenance, and termination of a tunnel. In Figure 7-2, we can see the format of a PPTP control connection packet.

Figure 7-2

PPTP control connection packet format

Data-Link Layer Header	IP Header	TCP Header	PPTP Control Message	Data-Link Layer Trailer

A number of different messages are used in support of a PPTP tunnel. They are as follows:

▨ *Start-Control-Connection-Request* **(SCCRQ)**—This type of message is sent by the PPTP client to establish a control connection. Each PPTP tunnel must have a control connection established before any other control messages are sent.

▨ *Start-Control-Connection-Reply* **(SCCRP)**—This is a reply to the SCCRQ.

▨ *Outgoing-Call-Request* **(OCRQ)**—This is sent by the PPTP client to create a PPTP tunnel. In this message, a Call ID is specified that is used in the GRE header to identify the tunnel traffic.

▨ *Outgoing-Call-Reply* **(OCRP)**—This message is sent by the PPTP server in response to an OCRQ.

▨ **Echo-Request**—This PING-like message is a keep-alive mechanism used to make sure the other end (PPTP client or PPTP server) is still there.

▨ **Echo-Reply**—This message is sent in response to an echo-request. Neither the echo-request nor echo-reply is related to ICMP echo messages; however, it is that behavior which is being emulated.

▨ **WAN-Error-Notify**—This message is sent from the PPTP server to indicate errors on the PPP interface of the PPTP server.

▨ **Set-Link-Info**—This message is sent by the PPTP client or server to start PPP-related negotiated options.

▨ **Call-Clear-Request**—This message is sent by the PPTP client and it indicates that the tunnel should be terminated.

- **Call-Disconnect-Notify**—This message is in direct response to the call-clear-request.

- **Stop-Control-Connection-Request**—This message is sent by either the PPTP client or server to inform the other device that the control connection is being terminated.

- **Stop-Control-Connection-Reply**—This message is sent in response to the Stop-Control-Connection-Request.

Note:

Because ISPs sometimes forward routing information using GRE tunnels, an ISP may filter GREs from being forwarded to Internet backbone routers. As a result, you could set up a PPTP tunnel using PPTP control messages, but PPTP tunneled data never makes it through. If you suspect that is your problem, contact your ISP and see if they can open GRE tunnels.

Now take a look at the PPTP data tunneling packet format as seen in Figure 7-3.

Figure 7-3

PPTP packet being assembled

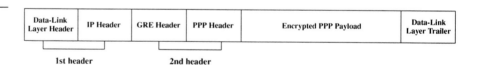

In Figure 7-3, we can see that two different headers are used. The first IP header is used for transporting the packet to the VPN server. The GRE header, which utilizes IP port 47, is used to encapsulate the PPP packet inside of it. The VPN server strips the IP and GRE header off so that the second header can be revealed and acted upon. The second header may contain an IP packet or an IPX packet. Packets that are sent back to the PPTP client are encapsulated by the PPTP server, which must add the first header back to the packet so that it can get routed back to the VPN client.

PPTP utilizes two standard security features to secure the data stream: authentication and encryption. We will now take a closer look at how each of these security features operates.

7.2.2 PPTP Authentication

PPTP authentication can take two different forms: user authentication and data authentication. User authentication requires the exchange of a password (PAP) or hash (CHAP or MS-CHAP). Data authentication is achieved through the use of a cryptographic checksum based on an encryption key known only by the sender and receiver, which will be discussed in the next section.

Because PPTP is so closely related to PPP, PPTP authentication uses the same authentication protocols as PPP. In Chapters 2, "Windows Support for Dialup," and 3, "Dialup over Cisco Routers," we discussed the various dial-up protocols and their authentication mechanisms, specifically PAP and CHAP. Microsoft products also have an additional authentication protocol, *Microsoft Challenge Handshake Authentication Protocol* (MS-CHAP), available for authenticating PPP/PPTP sessions.

PAP authentication is rarely used in the creation of PPTP tunnels because PAP uses clear text to send usernames and passwords. Thus, why bother encrypting your data if you are just going to send your password in clear text across the network anyway?

When authenticating a PPTP session, the PC client acts more like a router performing CHAP authentication than a PC client using CHAP during PPP negotiations. This is because a VPN client, in a PPTP session, can do mutual authentication, providing protection against masquerading VPN servers.

7.2.3 Microsoft Point-to-Point Encryption (MPPE)

PPTP incorporates authentication and encryption into MPPE. Authentication utilizes an encrypted checksum to verify the data-origin of the packet. In order to achieve this, a PPTP peer will calculate a checksum against the PPP payload and then generate a hash of the checksum using the user's password. Authentication occurs when the remote PPTP peer performs the same operation and compares the newly calculated checksum with the checksum sent with the packet. If the checksums match, then the packet is authenticated.

MPPE incorporates data encryption (up to 128-bit encryption) on the PPP payload through the use of RSA's RC4 stream cipher using the user's password as the "shared secret." Because encryption occurs only at the PPP payload and not the entire PPTP packet, it is similar to IPSec's transport mode. Remember that you can't encrypt the header information; otherwise, the packet would not be able to get to its destination.

Note:

Despite the controversy surrounding PPTP's security flaws, it is adequate for preventing casual observers from viewing the data. However, if security is a factor and real monetary consequences will occur if a third party should reveal your information, then you should look to IPSec for encryption.

7.2.3.1 Establishing a PPTP Session

Now that we've seen how the two different types of data streams (control messages and data tunneling packets) work together to provide the requisite information for a PPTP session, let's look at the process used to establish that connection, as seen in Figure 7-4.

1. Workstation A initiates a standard PPP connection to the ISP through a standard analog telephone or an *Integrated Services Digital Network* (ISDN). The ISP accepts the connection and a network layer connection is established.

2. Workstation A then contacts Router B to establish a PPTP tunnel using a SCCRQ message.

3. The PPTP server establishes a new PPTP tunnel and replies with an SCCRP message.

4. The PPTP client then initiates the session by sending an OCRQ message.

5. The PPTP server then creates a virtual interface and replies with an OCRP message.

Figure 7-4

Process used to
establish a
voluntary PPTP
tunnel

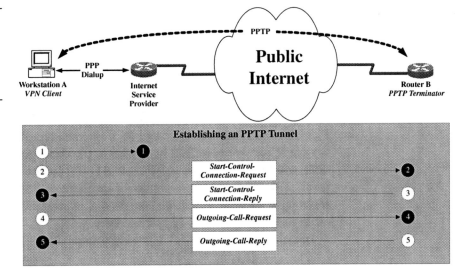

7.2.4 Cisco Support for PPTP

PPTP clients have traditionally been Windows 95, Windows NT, and Windows 2000 hosts, while the server typically requires a Windows NT or Windows 2000 device to terminate the PPTP sessions. However, Cisco has added PPTP functionality to a handful of Cisco devices. The following Cisco hardware can host a PPTP connection:

- Cisco 1700 series router
- Cisco 7100/7200 series router
- Cisco PIX firewall
- Cisco 3000 VPN concentrator

As most of us are aware, just having the right Cisco hardware does not necessarily mean we have support for PPTP. Your IOS must support PPTP as well, and only recently has Cisco made PPTP available in its IOS for the 1700 series router and 7100/7200 series routers. PPTP was first made available in release 12.0(5)XE5.

Even though the Cisco 3000 VPN concentrator supports PPTP, it is not within the scope of this book because they do not run standard Cisco IOS.

7.3 Configuring PPTP

The task list when configuring PPTP is much simpler with PPTP than it is with IPSec or even CET. In addition, the concepts used are completely different. When configuring PPTP, and L2TP for that matter, it is easier to think of the incoming connection as similar to a dial-up connection. Concepts such as authentication and interface configuration become easy if we equateVPDN to dial-up technologies.

In order to configure PPTP, we need to perform the following tasks:

- Enable VPDN
- Configure usernames and passwords for VPN clients
- Configure virtual interfaces
- Configure network attributes of virtual interface (optional)
- Configure a PPTP server to accept incoming connections

Using the steps outlined here, we will show you the steps required to configure PPTP on a Cisco 1700, 7100, and a 7200 series router. Although the commands used might be different between the various Cisco hardware devices, the concepts used are the same.

7.3.1 PPTP Server on a Cisco Series Router (1700, 7100, and 7200)

Configuring PPTP on a Cisco router is a fairly easy task because there aren't a lot of options. Because PPTP and L2TP operate in fairly similar paradigms, it is important to recognize that the commands used to configure PPTP and L2TP are similar. Using the steps outlined, we will show you the steps required to configure a PPTP on Cisco 1700, 7100, and 7200 series routers.

7.3.1.1 Enable VPDN

In order to configure any VPDN technology, we must first enable it. Enabling VPDN is a simple task that is carried out using the following command:

```
Router (config)#vpdn enable
```

This command is not used just for PPTP; it applies to all VPDN technologies including L2F and L2TP.

7.3.1.2 Configure Usernames and Passwords for VPN clients

When using PPP, we need to have a username and password in which a user is authenticated. PPTP is no different than PPP in this regard. We can authenticate PPTP users in one of two ways, either through a locally configured username and password or through a AAA server, such as the *Remote Access Dial-In User Serivce* (RADIUS) or the *Terminal Access Controller Access Control System* (TACACS). In order to use a AAA server, you must also configure the various parameters that are used for those devices to communicate, which is discussed extensively in Chapters 3, "Dialup over Cisco Routers" and 4, "VPN Security Primer." As a matter of convenience, the command to configure a username and password locally is included here:

```
Router (config)#username username password password
```

username	*WORD*	Name used by the VPDN client to authenticate
password	*WORD*	Password used by the VPDN client to authenticate

---

Note:
Usernames and passwords are case-sensitive.

7.3.1.3 Configure Virtual Interfaces

After the generic VPDN configuration has been set up, we can concentrate on defining the attributes necessary for a VPDN server to operate. A

VPDN server needs an interface to terminate a PPTP connection. Because these connections are dynamic, we do not configure the attributes directly on a physical interface. The whole point of a VPN is that the interface that the physical "outside" world sees does not support the logical attributes that we need to define, (such as IPX, bridging, or discontiguous IP addresses). So, if we don't configure the attributes of our tunnel on the physical interface, where are the attributes located for our VPN tunnel? Virtual access interfaces are the logical elements that terminate our PPTP tunnel (and other types of tunnels as we will see in the next chapter). These dynamic interfaces are created when the router detects an incoming connection. As long as the connection lasts, so does the virtual access interface.

So, where do these dynamic interfaces get their configuration if we cannot configure them directly? The virtual template interface is a template that is used to create virtual access interfaces when an incoming connection is detected. This template contains all the configuration settings required to configure the virtual access interface, as seen in Figure 7-5.

Figure 7-5

Virtual template interface versus virtual access interface

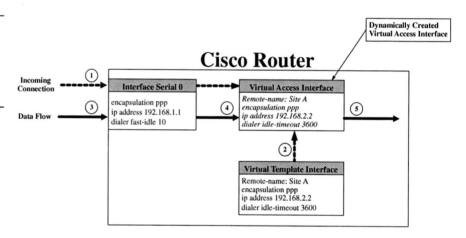

Once this virtual access interface is created, it is used during the entire length of the VPDN session. You will notice that no way to modify the virtual access interface exists. The only way to modify your connection is to modify the virtual template interface and then reestablish your connection. When the PPTP client disconnects, the VPDN server destroys the virtual access interface created by that session.

To create a virtual template, use the following command:

```
Router (config)#interface virtual-template virtual-template-number
```

virtual-template-number **1-25**   Number of the virtual template.

Note:

The default encapsulation method for a virtual template interface is PPP, so there is no need to manually configure it.

Once we have created the interface, we still need to configure it with the various attributes that enable a VPDN client and a VPDN server to establish a connection. You will notice that the attributes configured on a virtual template interface are very much like an interface that needs to support PPP. This is because PPTP uses PPP for its payload and thus must adhere to the same type of rules bound to PPP (such as authentication, compression, network layer attributes, and so on). In Chapter 3, which covered PPP dialup, remember that four different characteristics need to be agreed upon in order for a connection to be established. When using PPTP, only two attributes are needed to be agreed upon: authentication and compression.

Note:

Although callback is negotiated during the establishment of a PPTP tunnel, its use in PPTP does not make sense. PPP callback is generally used for two reasons: to transfer the costs of the incoming telephone call to the central site and for security (determine that a user is a pre-defined location). The logic of using PPP callback on a VPDN connection makes no sense because the cost associated with a PPTP server is identical no matter who establishes the connection (remember PPTP only establishes a connection to an IP address not to a phone number). In addition, trying to use PPP callback for security is absurd because an IP address does not define a physical location like phone numbers can (within reason).

When establishing a PPTP connection, the two VPDN peers must agree on which authentication protocol to use. To specify the authentication protocol to use during the initialization of a VPDN connection, use the following command:

```
Router (config-if)#ppp authentication authentication-protocol
```

authentication-protocol		
	PAP	Use PAP as the authentication protocol
	CHAP	Use CHAP as the authentication protocol
	MS-CHAP	Use MS-CHAP as the authentication protocol

Note:

Even though MS-CHAP is supported as an authentication protocol, you should make sure that your PPTP clients do not use MS-CHAP v2. Although the two devices will negotiate the type of authentication to use for a connection, if a PPTP client only uses MS-CHAP2, the connection will fail because Cisco routers currently do not support MS-CHAP v2 authentication.

Some network engineers will only be interested in using PPTP as a multiprotocol transport over an IP backbone. However, if you need to secure the data streams between these two devices, make sure that you specify the encryption by using the following command:

```
Router (config-if)#ppp encrypt mppe num-encryption--bits use-of-
enncryption-option
```

num-encryption—bits	**40**	Use 40-bit encryption (uses 40-bit DES)
	128	Use 128-bit encryption (requires 3DES)
use-of-encryption-option	**passive**	Will allow an encrypted session, but will not require an encrypted session
	required	Connection must use encryption, otherwise disconnect

Note:

Two different encryption types can be selected within MPPE: stateful and stateless. Stateful encryption provides better performance but can be affected by networks that experience a high number of lost packets. Stateless encryption is slower than stateful encryption but provides for a higher level of reliability with your PPTP tunnel. This is due to the fact the RC4 reinitializes its tables and the fact that two packets may be encrypted using the same key.

7.3.1.4 Configure Network Attributes of VPN Connection

When two devices communicate, they must use a common network protocol to communicate. Because we are using PPTP, which is just an extension, the commands used to configure the virtual interface for IP, IPX, and NetBEUI are identical to that of a PPP. Thus, we can use the following commands to configure our network layer attributes.

Network Layer Configuration of TCP/IP   When configuring TCP/IP for our VPN, three basic steps need to be completed:

▨ Configure dynamically assigned IP addresses.

▨ Configure IP related services (DNS, WINS, and so on).

▨ Use IP unnumbered for routing purposes.

Assuming our VPDN client does not have a statically configured IP address to use inside the VPN, we need to assign it an IP address. The first step to accomplishing this task is to define the range of IP addresses to be assigned. Use the following command to assign a block of IP addresses to hand out when clients tunnel in.

```
Router (config)#ip local pool address-pool-name first-ip-address last-
ip-address
```

`address-pool-name`	**default**	Make this IP address pool the default
	WORD	The name for this IP address pool block
`first-ip-address`	***a.b.c.d***	The first ip address in the block of IP addresses
`last-ip-address`	***a.b.c.d***	The last ip address in the block of IP addresses

Having just a TCP/IP address and no other attributes makes using TCP/IP difficult at best. Therefore, we also need to give our PPTP client TCP/IP information. Using the command listed below, we can hand out a variety of information:

```
Router (config)#async-bootp ip-attribute a.b.c.d
```

ip-attribute	dns-server	a.b.c.d	Sets DNS server for PPTP client to use
	lpr-server	a.b.c.d	Sets LPR server for PPTP client to use
	nbns-server	a.b.c.d	Sets WINS server for PPTP client to use
	time-server	a.b.c.d	Sets time server for PPTP client to use

To set the local IP address on a VPN infrastructure, we will use the IP unnumbered command just like we did in Chapter 3 to specify the VPN server's IP address. By using IP unnumbered, we do not have to assign a point-to-point network between each of our VPN clients. This command is used on the virtual template interface and is as follows:

```
Router (config-if)#ip unnumbered interface
```

interface	Ethernet slot/port	Use this Ethernet interface for IP unnumbered
	Async slot/port	Use this Async interface for IP unnumbered
	Loopback slot/port	Use this Ethernet interface for IP unnumbered
	Serial slot/port	Use this Ethernet interface for IP unnumbered

The next step is to tell the virtual template interface the IP address it can assign to the remote client. The ports you can use are directly related to the type of hardware found in your router. It is recommended that you create a loopback adapter and assign that loopback adapter an IP address that is not used on your network (preferably from the private IP range).

```
Router (config-if)#peer default ip address pool ip-pool-name
```

| ip-pool-name | WORD | IP pool to use for incoming connections |

Because this interface configuration command allows you to select from multiple pools of IP addresses, you can define your security models at an IP layer. We can use one pool of addresses for those who need tight security and one pool of address for those who have a higher security clearance. In order for this to be achieved, we need a way to authenticate different users, which can be accomplished using Cisco's AAA.

Network Layer Configuration of IPX/SPX Configuring a VPN server for use with IPX/SPX requires the use of a loopback interface to specify the IPX network address. Four steps are needed to configure IPX/SPX on your VPN server:

1. Enable IPX routing.
2. Create a loopback interface.
3. Configure the loopback interface with the IPX network number.
4. Associate the loopback interface with the asynchronous interface.

Unlike TCP/IP, the default for a Cisco router is not to route IPX; we must manually turn IPX routing on. If you are using IPX, most likely this has already been done for a router's other IPX interfaces. Using the following command, we can enable IPX routing:

```
Router (config)#ipx routing mac-address
```

mac-address	*xxxx.xxxx.xxx*	(Optional) use a non-duplicate MAC address

Now that the loopback adapter has been created, we can configure the IPX network number that our PPP remote clients will use. This command must be executed within the loopback interface configuration mode. We will then associate this loopback interface to our virtual template.

```
Router (config-if)#ipx network ipx-network-number
```

ipx-network-number	*xxxxxxxx*	any hexadecimal number between 00000001 and FFFFFFFE

Once the loopback interface is configured, we need to associate the loopback interface with our asynchronous interface. Typically, we will associate the group-async interface.

```
Router (config-if)#ipx ppp-client loopback loopback-number
```

loopback-number	*x*	This is the loopback number used to define our IPX address

Figure 7-6 shows the association of an asynchronous interface to the loopback interface for use with IPX over PPP.

For more information about the configuration of IPX on PPP networks, see Chapter 3.

Figure 7-6

Association of a
loopback interface
with a virtual
template
interface to
provide IPX over
PPTP

```
Router(config)#interface virtual-template 1
Router(config-if)#ipx ppp-client loopback 0
```

7.3.1.5 Configure PPTP Server to Accept Incoming Connections

We have seen all the commands that enable two devices to communicate within a VPN tunnel. However, we haven't seen the commands that tell a Cisco router that it can host a PPTP session.

Starting with IOS 12.0(5)T, Cisco modified the paradigm in which PPP UPDN connections would be configured. Fortunately, PPTP wasn't available until after this change was made, so we only need to learn the new paradigm to configure PPTP.

Configuring a router to accept an incoming PPTP connection involves four steps performed in the following order:

1. Create a VPDN group.

2. Allow incoming connections for the VPDN group.

3. Specify the VPDN protocol to use for the VPDN group.

4. Specify the virtual template to clone during incoming connections.

A VPDN group allows us to associate a VPDN protocol (PPTP, L2F, L2TP) with a virtual template (an interface configuration that is cloned when a VPDN connection is attempted). In order to create a VPDN group, we can use the following command:

```
Router (config)#vpdn-group vpdn-group-name
```

vpdn-group-name **WORD** *Name of the VPDN group*

To enable a VPDN group to accept incoming connections, we use the following command:

```
Router (config-vpdn)#accept-dialin
```

Until we've established whether a VPDN group is responsible for incoming or outgoing connections, we cannot configure any of the protocols (PPTP, L2F, L2TP) that can be associated with a VPDN group. That is why it is important to follow the steps that are being outlined here. One additional note about VPDN groups: once we've specified a group is a dial-in VPDN group, it cannot be configured for dialout. You must create another VPDN group to handle dialout connections.

Once we've configured a VPDN group that is responsible for dialin, we must now specify what type of incoming connections this particular VPND group will support. You can use the following command to specify PPTP as the supported protocol.

```
Router (config-vpdn-acc-in)#protocol pptp
```

The last step to enabling a VPDN group to accept an incoming connection is to specify the virtual template interface to clone when an incoming connection is detected. Use the following command to specify the virtual template interface to use:

```
Router (config-vpdn-acc-in)#virtual-template virtual-template-
interface
```

virtual-template-interface   **1-25**   The number of the virtual template interface that should be cloned in support of this VPDN protocol

In Figure 7-7, we can see an example of a PPTP configuration. From this example, we can note that the amount of work required to configure a Cisco router to accept PPTP connections is minimal.

Figure 7-7

Example of PPTP configuration

```
vpdn enable
!
vpdn-group PPTP Group
! Default PPTP VPDN group
 accept-dialin
  protocol pptp
  virtual-template 10
!
interface Virtual-Template10
 ip unnumbered Ethernet 0
 peer default ip address pool default
 ppp encrypt mppe 40 required
 ppp authentication ms-chap
!
ip local pool default 192.168.1.115 192.168.1.125
```

Now that we've seen how to configure a PPTP server on a Cisco router, we will now look at how to configure PPTP on the three different Windows platforms: Windows 95/98, Windows NT, and Windows 2000.

7.3.2 PPTP Client on Windows 98

Configuring PPTP on Windows 98 is very similar to configuring PPP. The main difference between setting up a PPP connection and a PPTP connection is that a PPP connection will establish a connection by dialing a number, while a PPTP connection will establish a connection using an IP address.

Setting up a PPTP connection between a PPTP client and a PPTP server requires the following steps to be performed:

- Install Virtual Private Networking software
- Create a connection
- Define authentication and encryption parameters
- Define the username and password for connection script

Even though Windows 95 supports PPTP connections, it is not in the normal installation. You must download a patch, *Msdun13.exe,* from Microsoft's Web site. This update will give you the PPTP functionality that is found in Windows 98. In addition, a patch for PPTP and Windows 98, *vpnupd.exe,* should be applied to PPTP clients before trying to connect to a PPTP server.

7.3.2.1 Install Virtual Private Networking Software

To install new Windows 98 software, make sure that you have installed the VPN software. The installation is simple and can be accomplished using the following five steps:

1. Open Control Panels under My Computer.
2. Open Add/Remove Programs.
3. Select **Windows Setup** tab as shown in Figure 7-8.
4. Select the **Communications** option and click on **Details.**
5. Select **Virtual Private Networking,** as seen in Figure 7-9 (if they are already selected, skip this step).

Figure 7-8

Windows Setup
tab

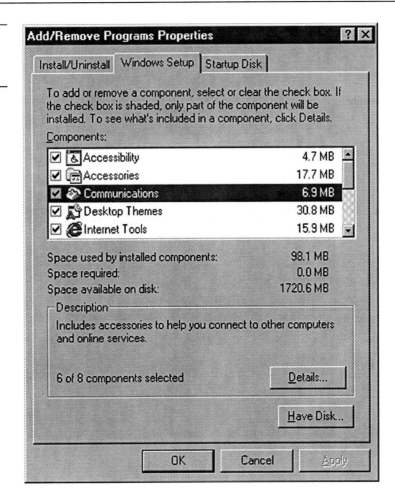

7.3.2.2 Create a Connection Script

Dialup scripts specify all the attributes necessary to connect to an ISP.
Each script specifies the connection requirements for a particular ISP. To
create a PPTP connection script in Windows 98, use the following process
that utilizes the Make New Connection Wizard:

1. Open Dial-Up Networking under My Computer.
2. Open Make New Connection.
3. Enter the name of the connection script and select **Microsoft VPN
   Adapter**, as shown in Figure 7-10, and select **Next**.

Figure 7-9

Windows 98
Communications
window

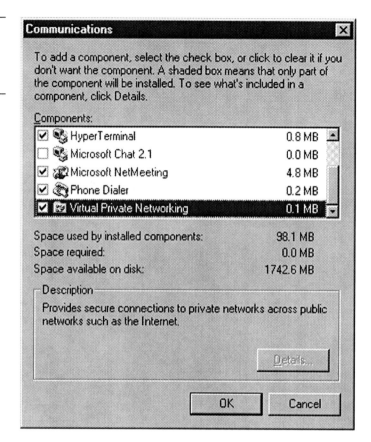

4. Enter the IP address of the PPTP server, as seen in Figure 7-11, and select **Next**.

5. Select **Finish** to complete the creation of the PPTP connection script.

This script is not quite ready to connect to our PPTP server. We still need to establish our identity and configure any authentication and encryption protocols that will be used (assuming the default is not acceptable).

Figure 7-10

Make New
Connection
window

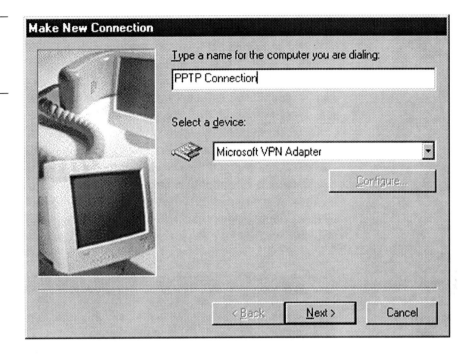

Figure 7-11

Defining the
destination of the
PPTP tunnel

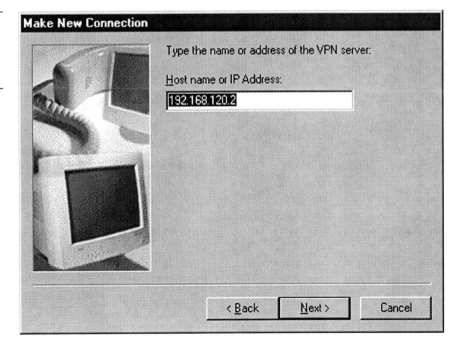

7.3.2.3 Define Authentication and Encryption Parameters

The two protocols that can be configured for a PPTP connection are the authentication protocols and encryption protocols. It is possible to establish a PPTP connection but not use any encryption. This is useful if security is not a real concern for us and we only need to use PPTP as a transport for non-IP packets.

Only three authentication protocols exist that a Cisco router, acting as a PPTP server, can use. Unfortunately, Windows 98 does not elaborate on those choices. Instead they've chosen to use a more user-friendly approach to selecting authentication and encryption algorithms. By right-clicking on the newly created PPTP connection script, we can view the properties of this script. Under the Server Types tab, as seen in Figure 7-12, really only two choices for authentication and encryption exist.

Figure 7-12

Advanced options for a PPTP connection

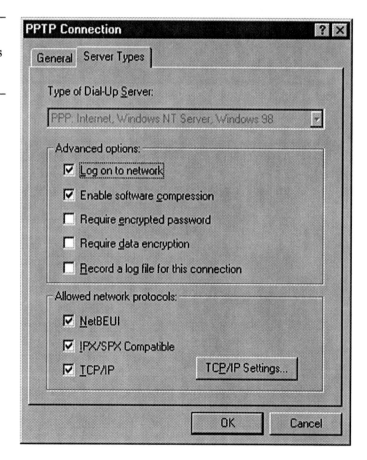

Either one of these processes can be encrypted or not. If we do not select encrypted authentication or data encryption, then by default, we will let the PPTP server determine whether or not we will be encrypting the data.

By selecting "Require encrypted password," our Windows 98 computer will only use CHAP or MS-CHAP. It will not use PAP authentication. This is because PAP sends passwords as clear text, thus allowing anyone to see it. This is especially critical with PPTP connections, because the data is passing through many networks in which people could easily get the user's login name and password simply by sniffing the network. In addition, if a client machine is enabled for using PAP, a Windows 98 machine will attempt to use a PAP first.

If we want to use MPPE with our VPN, we should select "Require data encryption." If we don't select this option, it does not necessarily mean our VPN isn't going to use MPPE, only that we will let the PPTP server decide if we are going to use encryption for our VPN. Earlier in this chapter, we showed you how to configure a Cisco router, acting as a PPTP server to require encrypted data streams using the ppp encrypt mppe 40 required command.

7.3.2.4 Define the Username and Password for a Connection Script

We've now defined all the attributes required for our PPTP connection, except the username and password our PPTP script will use. By opening up the script and entering our username and password in the corresponding fields as seen in Figure 7-13, we have completed the task of creating a PPTP script on a Windows 98 script.

Note:

The "Save password" check box only saves the password after a successful logon connection.

Figure 7-13

Entering the
username and
password to be
used for a PPTP
connection

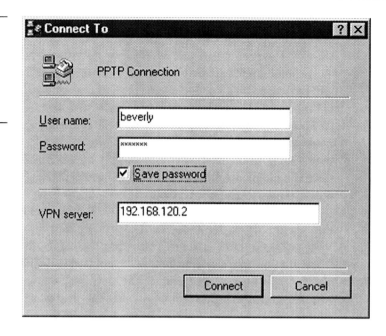

7.3.3 PPTP Client on Windows NT

Like Windows 98, configuring PPTP on a Windows NT is very similar to
configuring PPP. One of the main distinctions between Windows 98 PPTP
and Windows NT PPTP is that it is very easy to make Windows NT a
PPTP server, not just a PPTP client, even a Windows NT workstation.

Setting up a PPTP connection between a Windows NT PPTP client and
a PPTP server requires the following five tasks to be performed:

1. Install PPTP.

2. Install *Remote Access Service* (RAS).

3. Create a connection.

4. Define authentication and encryption parameters.

5. Define the username and password for the connection script.

Microsoft has developed an add-on to Microsoft's NT RAS called "Routing and Remote Access." This add-on enables an NT server to turn into a
full-fledged router that can utilize *Routing Information Protocol* (RIP) and
Open Shortest Path First (OSPF) routing protocols. This add-on is not
required for the successful operation of Windows NT acting as a PPTP
client, but it is in order for Windows NT to be a PPTP server.

7.3.3.1 Install PPTP

Installing the PPTP is a crucial aspect to this process and must be done first, before we can do any of the additional steps that are outlined. The following six steps outline the process of adding the PPTP protocol to a Windows NT server or Windows NT workstation:

1. Open Control Panels under My Computer.
2. Open the **Network** control panel.
3. Select **Protocol** tab, as shown in Figure 7-14.

Figure 7-14

Services tab in Network Control Panel

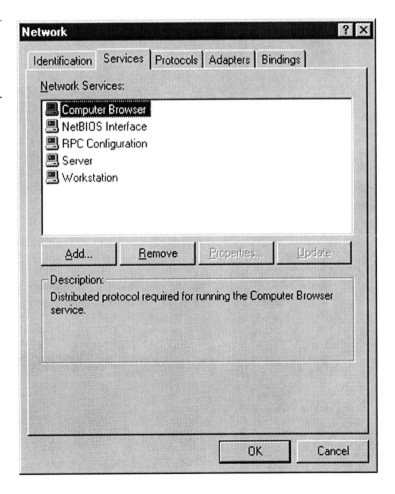

4. Click **Add** to add a new protocol.

5. Select Microsoft's PPTP, as seen in Figure 7-15.

Figure 7-15

Adding PPTP

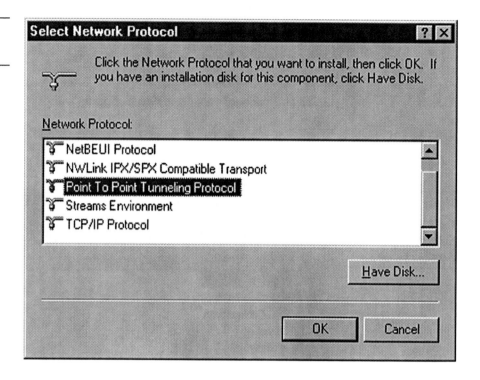

You may be prompted to find the installation directory (such as C:\I386).

6. Select the number of simultaneous VPN connections you want to support and then click **OK**. In most instances you will only want a single connection, as seen in Figure 7-16.

Figure 7-16

Selecting the number of simultaneous VPN connections for Windows NT to support

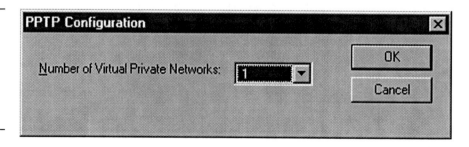

7.3.3.2 Install RAS

Installation of RAS can be performed in nine steps:

1. Open Control Panels under My Computer.
2. Open the **Network** control panel.
3. Select **Services** tab as shown in Figure 7-17.

Figure 7-17

Services tab in
Network Control
panel

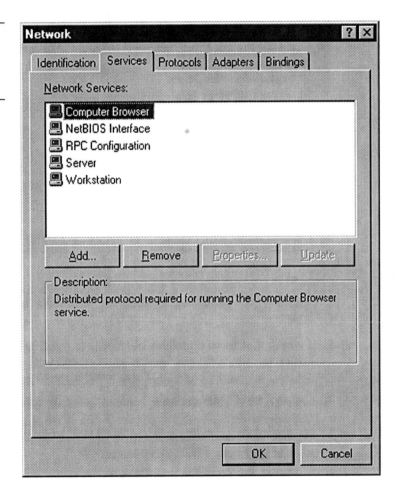

4. Click Add to add a new service.

5. Select **Remote Access Service**, as seen in Figure 7-18.

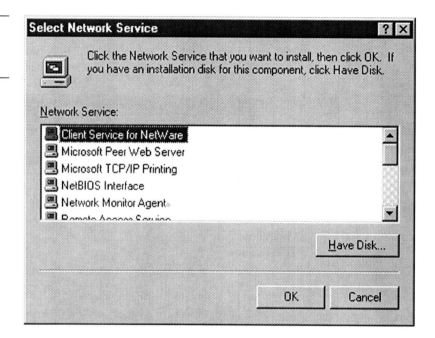

You may be prompted to find the installation directory (such as C:\I386).

6. If you do not have a modem installed, you will be asked to install a modem so that RAS can bind to the interface. In this particular instance, we will be installing the VPN RAS device.

7. Adding a VPN RAS device is accomplished by selecting Add to the RAS Access Setup tool (see Figure 7-19). If we specified two simultaneous connections when configuring the PPTP protocol, we can add up to two VPN RAS devices.

8. Configure the direction of calls to be placed by selecting the **Configure** button as shown in Figure 7-20 (you must select an option that allows for dial-out calls).

9. Select **Continue** to finish the configuration of RAS.

Figure 7-19

RAS properties

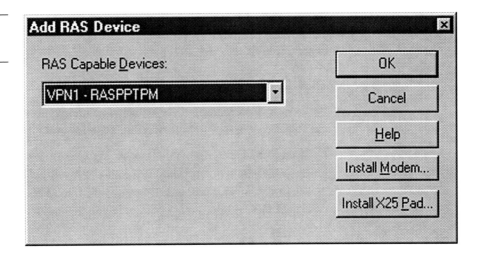

Figure 7-20

RAS window

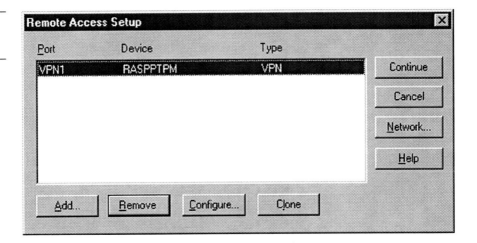

Note:
If, during installation, you needed to access the installation media, you will need to reapply the service packs.

At this point you will probably have to reboot your computer; however, you can now consider PPTP installed in Windows NT. We now have to create scripts that can use this newly installed service.

7.3.3.3 Create a Connection

The process for creating a PPTP connection script, which is almost identical to setting up a PPP connection, is as follows:

1. Open Dial-Up Networking under My Computer.

2a. If no scripts are available, Windows NT will inform you that no scripts exist and will ask if you would like to create a new script. Select **OK**.

Or

2b. If scripts are available, Windows NT will bring you to the phonebook. Select new to start the dial-up script creation wizard.

3. Name the dial-up script and click **next**.

4. Select "I am calling the Internet" and click **next.**

5. Enter the IP address of the PPTP server.

6. Click Finished to end the dial-up script creation wizard.

A screen will now appear that looks like Figure 7-21.

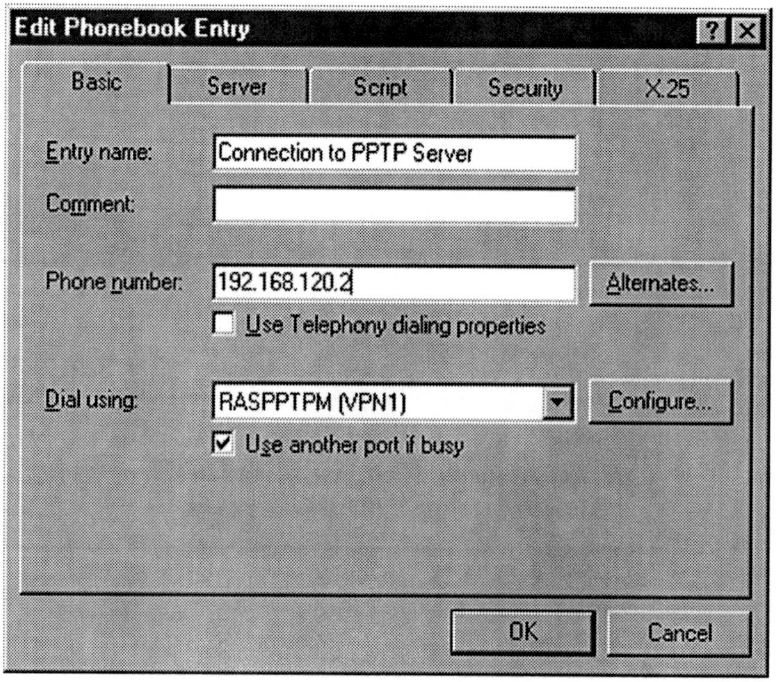

Figure 7-21

Editing a dial-up script

7.3.3.4 Define Authentication and Encryption Parameters

When defining authentication and encryption for network administrators, it is generally customary to use the name of the authentication protocol or encryption protocol, because we are used to dealing with specifics. When it comes to Windows 95/98 and Windows NT, Microsoft made the options more easily readable for a user than for a network engineer. If both devices don't use the same protocol, they will fail. So, we always want to know which protocol, not just the encryption, that will be required.

When configuring authentication and encryption for Windows NT, we will need to select the Security tab as seen in Figure 7-22.

Figure 7-22

Edit security settings

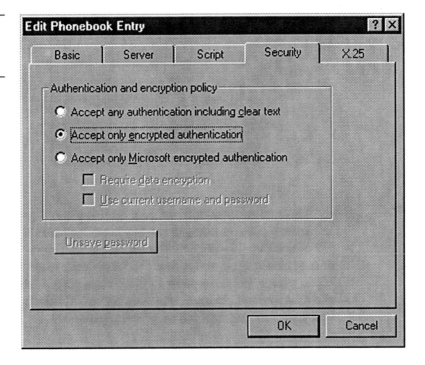

Our first option, Accept any authentication including clear text, is the easiest to use as an administrator and will enable the PPTP client to use any type of authentication (PAP, CHAP, and MS-CHAP). The second option is a bit more restrictive in that it requires we use some type of encrypted authentication (CHAP or MS-CHAP). The third option is the most restrictive and requires that we only use MS-CHAP authentication.

7.3.3.5 Define the Username and Password for the Connection Script

When using this newly created dialup script for the first time, you will be required to enter a username and password, as shown in Figure 7-23.

Figure 7-23

Example of dialup connection script

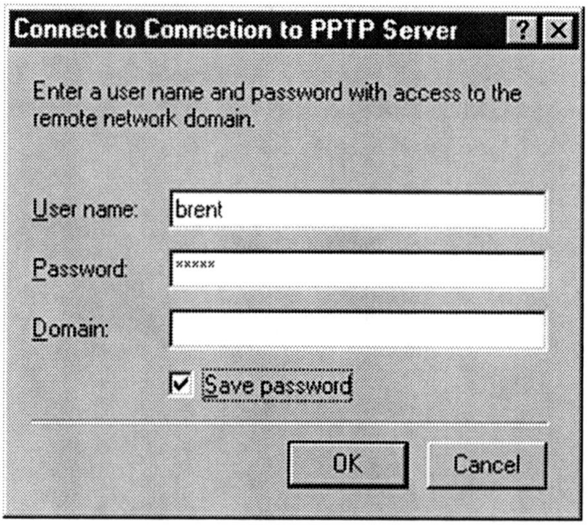

This is where you will put your username and password. However, do not enter a domain name in the box provided (even if you are primarily an NT shop). This is only for Windows NT dialin remote access service. You should also keep in mind that the "Save password" check box only works if you successfully complete a PPTP connection. If the connection fails on the first connect attempt, Windows NT will think that the password used was incorrect and will fail to save the password.

7.3.4 PPTP Client on Windows 2000

Unlike Windows 98 and Windows NT, Windows 2000 has PPTP built into the operating system. It isn't an optional attribute that needs to be installed; it is there right from the beginning of the installation. Setting up a PPTP connection on a Windows 2000 machine is the easiest of all the previous Microsoft Operating Systems. Using the Make New Connection wizard, as seen in Figure 7-24, found in the Network and Dial-up Con-

Figure 7-24

Windows 2000
Network and
Dial-Up
Connections

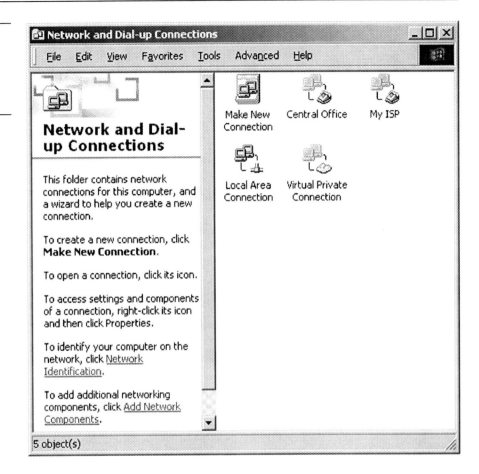

nections folder, we can create a VPN connection very easily because the
only thing to do is create a PPTP script.

7.3.4.1 Creating PPTP Connection Scripts

To create a PPTP connection script, use the following procedure:

1. Open **Network and Dial-Up Connections** in the control panel
   window.
2. Select Make New Connection.
3. Select Connect to a private network through the Internet, as seen in
   Figure 7-25.

Figure 7-25

Network
Connection
Wizard

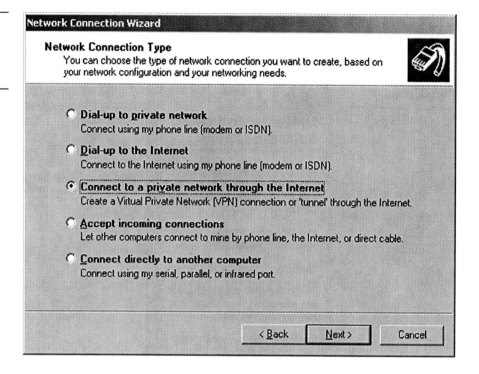

4. Select whether you want to establish the initial connection or not.

5. Enter the IP address of the PPTP server.

6. Select whether this connection is for **all users** or **only for myself**.

7. Name the PPTP Connection script and click **finish**.

Just like Windows 95 and Windows NT, we have the opportunity to modify the connection attributes. By opening the dialup script we get a window shown in Figure 7-26.

Windows 2000 supports multiple authentication types, which can be configured under the properties of the login script. Those authentication protocols are:

Figure 7-26

PPTP connection
script

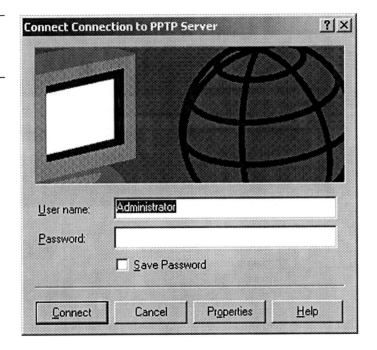

- PAP
- *Shiva Password Authentication Protocol* (SPAP)
- CHAP
- MS-CHAP
- MS-CHAPv2

Keep in mind that a Cisco router will only support PAP, CHAP, and MS-CHAP for authentication protocols.

Because Windows 2000 also supports L2TP, we may find it necessary to make sure we only use PPTP. Therefore, Microsoft has given us the opportunity to specify the type of VPN protocol to use for a connection script as seen in Figure 7-27.

For those of you who are aware that L2TP is the next chapter, this is a glimpse into how easy it is to configure L2TP on a Windows 2000 machine.

Figure 7-27

Specifying the
VPN protocol to
use for a
connection script

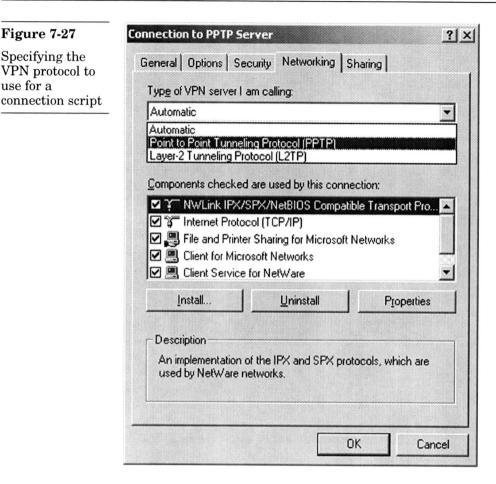

7.4 Design Considerations

7.4.1 Mobile User Versus Telecommuter

As we've pointed out several times throughout this chapter, PPTP is very
similar to PPP. The main difference is that that PPP establishes a layer
two connection, while PPTP requires an already existing layer two section. This means we must already have an IP connection before we can
attempt to establish a PPTP connection.

Even though PPTP requires an IP connection, it does not require that we use a PPP connection to establish that layer tunnel. We could be connected to an Ethernet, Fast Ethernet, or Token-Ring *local area network* (LAN). As long as we have IP connectivity to our PPTP server, our connection should work.

Given these circumstances, you can see that a telecommuter with a cable modem or DSL connection does not need to use PPP to establish a secure tunnel to the office. This is great for telecommuters because they can work at home securely using a connection that is much faster than any dial-up connection can provide. However, you will still find that mobile users will continue to use a PPP connection to establish a layer two connection to their local ISP and then tunnel to the corporate network. However, as the Internet becomes more ubiquitous, major hotels are installing Ethernet connections into hotel rooms so that their guests can have high-speed access to the Internet. Unfortunately, you can't guarantee that all hotel rooms will have this type of connection and you will probably still have to outfit your mobile users with PPP connections for a very long time.

7.4.2 IP Addressing and a PPTP Connection

Because PPTP is quite flexible, it is possible to enable a client to specify the IP address he wants to use within the PPTP tunnel. Although there may be times that this is a rational explanation to this approach, generally it is a bad idea. If the address space for the VPN has to change, it could be very cumbersome to have to modify hundreds of computers.

In addition, an important note that is often forgotten, if the actual destination of the connection is not on the same network as the PPTP server and the packet must get routed through the corporate network, there must be a route back to the client's VPN IP address and that path must lead back to the PPTP server. This enables the PPTP server to capture the packet and put a GRE header on it, encrypt if necessary, and send it back through the VPN to the VPN client.

7.5 Verify PPTP

Many times it may become necessary to see how many users are connected to your PPTP server. Although these types of devices are generally the type that are set up and forgotten about until an issue arises, it does become helpful to know how many connections are active. Using the command *show vpdn*, as seen in Figure 7-28, we can see not only PPTP sessions, but L2F and L2TP sessions (which we will cover in the next chapter).

Figure 7-28

Output from
Show vpdn
command

```
 1  Cisco1720# show vpdn
 2
 3  % No active L2TP tunnels
 4
 5  % No active L2F tunnels
 6
 7  PPTP Tunnel and Session Information (Total tunnels=1 sessions=1)
 8
 9  LocID RemID Remote Name    State   Remote Address   Port  Sessions
10  23    23    192.168.130.3  estabd  192.168.120.2    1136  1
11
12  LocID RemID TunID Intf    Username        State    Last Chg
13  23    0     23    Vi1                      estabd   000030
```

In lines 3 and 5, we can see no active L2TP or L2F tunnels, but in line 7, we can see 1 tunnel. Lines 9 through 12 show us the details of that single connection.

7.6 Troubleshooting PPTP

In this chapter, we've looked at using a Cisco router as a PPTP server instead of a NT server. When troubleshooting PPTP, four areas should be scrutinized in order to resolve difficulties with a PPTP connection:

- User account
- Authentication protocol
- Encryption
- Network layer attributes

We will now focus on troubleshooting these elements. However, all of these tips are predicated on the fact that our PPTP client can ping the PPTP server (or at least have IP visibility, and we haven't blocked ports TCP port 1723 and IP port 47).

7.6.1 User Account

In most instances, it should become obvious that a user account and password do not match when attempting to authenticate a PPTP connection, because the PPTP client, in most instances, will tell you that your username and password is incorrect. However, if you are not at the PPTP client, your user may not be able to recognize the symptoms. In those events, we can use the *debug ppp authentication* command to see whether authentication is the problem. In Figure 7-29, we can see the output from the command during a successful PPTP connection.

Figure 7-29

Output from
debug ppp
authentication

```
1   %LINK-3-UPDOWN: Interface Virtual-Access1, changed state to up
2   Vi1 PPP: Treating connection as a dedicated line
3   %LINEPROTO-5-UPDOWN: Line protocol on Interface Virtual-Access1,
    changed
4   state to up
5   Vi1 MS-CHAP: O CHALLENGE id 3 len 21 from "1720      "
6   Vi1 MS-CHAP: I RESPONSE id 3 len 61 from "meg"
7   Vi1 MS-CHAP: O SUCCESS id 3 len 4
```

In lines 1 through 4, we can see the incoming PPTP connection. Line 5 shows us the MS-CHAP challenge sent from the local PPTP router named 1720 to the remote device. Lines 6 and 7 show us that the response from "meg" was successful.

7.6.2 Authentication Protocol

In some instances, we may have mismatched authentication protocols. This is a bit harder to detect from the PPTP client's machine. Using *debug ppp negotiations* command, we can see these mismatched connections as seen in Figure 7-30.

Looking at lines 4-6 in Figure 7-30, we can see that the Cisco router sent out a CONFREQ (configuration request) to use MS-CHAP authentication. However, on lines 7 and 8, the remote PPTP peer wants to use CHAP authentication. This request and rejection happens several times until finally on line 58, the remote PPTP peer rejected MS-CHAP and on line 59, the local PPTP server disconnected the session because it could negotiate an authentication with the remote VPN device.

Figure 7-30

Output from
debug ppp
negotiations with
mismatched
authentication
protocols

```
 1  %LINK-3-UPDOWN: Interface Virtual-Access1, changed state to up
 2  Vi1 PPP: Treating connection as a dedicated line
 3  Vi1 PPP: Phase is ESTABLISHING, Active Open [0 sess, 1 load]
 4  Vi1 LCP: O CONFREQ [Closed] id 30 len 15
 5  Vi1 LCP:    AuthProto MS-CHAP (0x0305C22380)
 6  Vi1 LCP:    MagicNumber 0x55102EFC (0x050655102EFC)
 7  Vi1 LCP: I CONFNAK [REQsent] id 30 len 9
 8  Vi1 LCP:    AuthProto CHAP/129 (0x0305C22381)
 9  Vi1 LCP: O CONFREQ [REQsent] id 31 len 15
10  Vi1 LCP:    AuthProto MS-CHAP (0x0305C22380)
11  Vi1 LCP:    MagicNumber 0x55102EFC (0x050655102EFC)
12  Vi1 LCP: I CONFNAK [REQsent] id 31 len 9
13  Vi1 LCP:    AuthProto CHAP/129 (0x0305C22381)
14  Vi1 LCP: O CONFREQ [REQsent] id 32 len 15
15  Vi1 LCP:    AuthProto MS-CHAP (0x0305C22380)
16  Vi1 LCP:    MagicNumber 0x55102EFC (0x050655102EFC)
17  Vi1 LCP: I CONFNAK [REQsent] id 32 len 9
18  Vi1 LCP:    AuthProto CHAP/129 (0x0305C22381)
19  Vi1 LCP: O CONFREQ [REQsent] id 33 len 15
20  Vi1 LCP:    AuthProto MS-CHAP (0x0305C22380)
21  Vi1 LCP:    MagicNumber 0x55102EFC (0x050655102EFC)
22  Vi1 LCP: I CONFNAK [REQsent] id 33 len 9
23  Vi1 LCP:    AuthProto CHAP/129 (0x0305C22381)
24  Vi1 LCP: O CONFREQ [REQsent] id 34 len 15
25  Vi1 LCP:    AuthProto MS-CHAP (0x0305C22380)
26  Vi1 LCP:    MagicNumber 0x55102EFC (0x050655102EFC)
27  Vi1 LCP: I CONFNAK [REQsent] id 34 len 9
28  Vi1 LCP:    AuthProto CHAP/129 (0x0305C22381)
29  Vi1 LCP: O CONFREQ [REQsent] id 35 len 15
30  Vi1 LCP:    AuthProto MS-CHAP (0x0305C22380)
31  Vi1 LCP:    MagicNumber 0x55102EFC (0x050655102EFC)
32  Vi1 LCP: I CONFNAK [REQsent] id 35 len 9
33  Vi1 LCP:    AuthProto CHAP/129 (0x0305C22381)
34  Vi1 LCP: O CONFREQ [REQsent] id 36 len 15
35  Vi1 LCP:    AuthProto MS-CHAP (0x0305C22380)
36  Vi1 LCP:    MagicNumber 0x55102EFC (0x050655102EFC)
37  Vi1 LCP: I CONFNAK [REQsent] id 36 len 9
38  Vi1 LCP:    AuthProto CHAP/129 (0x0305C22381)
39  Vi1 LCP: O CONFREQ [REQsent] id 37 len 15
40  Vi1 LCP:    AuthProto MS-CHAP (0x0305C22380)
41  Vi1 LCP:    MagicNumber 0x55102EFC (0x050655102EFC)
42  Vi1 LCP: I CONFNAK [REQsent] id 37 len 9
43  Vi1 LCP:    AuthProto CHAP/129 (0x0305C22381)
44  Vi1 LCP: O CONFREQ [REQsent] id 38 len 15
45  Vi1 LCP:    AuthProto MS-CHAP (0x0305C22380)
46  Vi1 LCP:    MagicNumber 0x55102EFC (0x050655102EFC)
47  Vi1 LCP: I CONFNAK [REQsent] id 38 len 9
48  Vi1 LCP:    AuthProto CHAP/129 (0x0305C22381)
49  Vi1 LCP: O CONFREQ [REQsent] id 39 len 15
50  Vi1 LCP:    AuthProto MS-CHAP (0x0305C22380)
51  Vi1 LCP:    MagicNumber 0x55102EFC (0x050655102EFC)
52  Vi1 LCP: I CONFNAK [REQsent] id 39 len 9
53  Vi1 LCP:    AuthProto CHAP/129 (0x0305C22381)
54  Vi1 LCP: O CONFREQ [REQsent] id 40 len 15
55  Vi1 LCP:    AuthProto MS-CHAP (0x0305C22380)
56  Vi1 LCP:    MagicNumber 0x55102EFC (0x050655102EFC)
57  Vi1 LCP: I CONFREJ [REQsent] id 40 len 9
58  Vi1 LCP:    AuthProto MS-CHAP (0x0305C22380)
59  Vi1 LCP: Failed to negotiate with peer
60  Vi1 LCP: State is Closed
61  Vi1 PPP: Phase is DOWN [0 sess, 1 load]
```

Note:

For a more complete description of LCP negotiations, see Chapter 3.

7.6.3 Encryption

Within the PPTP protocol, it is not a requirement to do encryption. However, either side can choose to require encryption, at which point the VPN peer must comply or the connection is disconnected. In most instances, we can easily determine if that is causing a problem by enabling the PPTP server to operate in passive mode for encryption instead of requiring it. Figure 7-31 shows us an example of the configuration necessary to allow the PPTP client to decide whether or not to choose encryption.

Figure 7-31

Example of configuration allowing client to choose whether to encrypt or not

```
vpdn enable
!
vpdn-group LetClientChooseEncryption Group
! Default PPTP VPDN group
 accept-dialin
   protocol pptp
   virtual-template 15
!
interface Virtual-Template15
 ip unnumbered Ethernet 0
 ppp encrypt mppe 40 passive
 ppp authentication ms-chap
!
```

7.7 Cisco Router to Cisco Router Case Studies

This section in the chapter is one of the most important part of any hands-on book. We have shown you how to configure a router to participate in a VPN, but how do we take a take a technical problem and solve it with a VPN? In the following case study, we will explain the five following things before moving to configuration-specific information:

- VPN type
- Tunnel type

▩ When to deploy

▩ Verifying our VPN

▩ VPN configurations

7.7.1 Case Study #1—Using PPTP Without Access to the Corporate Network

VPN type: Intranet VPN

Tunnel type: Voluntary tunnel

When to deploy: This type of tunnel is useful within an enterprise network when the core network is only routing IP and you need to run IPX between the various sites. In many situations, a department within an enterprise may find it unable to access the corporate network routers, which can be very limiting.

Verifying VPN has been enabled: Remote workstation can log in to NetWare server.

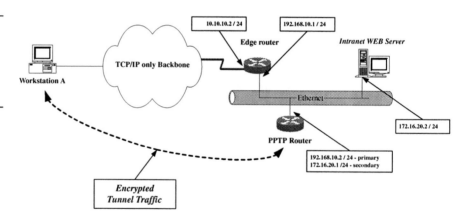

Figure 7-32

Case Study #1—
Access a
departmental
Intranet

Note:

All links are considered to have a subnet mask of 255.255.255.0 unless otherwise specified.

7.7.1.1 Edge Router Configuration File

Figure 7-33

Edge router configuration file

```
1  !
2  version 12.0
3  service timestamps debug uptime
4  service timestamps log uptime
5  service password-encryption
6  !
7  hostname Edgerouter
8  !
9  interface Ethernet0
10  description Connection to Research & Development LAN
11  ip address 192.168.10.1 255.255.255.0
12  no ip directed-broadcast
13  !
14  interface Serial0
15  description Connection to Corporate backbone
16  ip address 10.10.10.1 255.255.255.0
17  no ip directed-broadcast
18  no ip mroute-cache
19  !
20  router eigrp 100
21  network 192.168.0.0
22  network 10.0.0.0
23  no auto-summary
24  !
25  ip classless
26  no ip http server
27  !
28  line con 0
29  transport input none
30  line aux 0
31  line vty 0 4
32  login
33  !
34  end
```

7.7.1.2 PPTP Server Configuration File

```
35 version 12.1
36 no service single-slot-reload-enable
37 service timestamps debug uptime
38 service timestamps log uptime
39 no service password-encryption
40 !
41 hostname PPTPRouter
42 !
43 enable secret 5 $1$r4fV$I9xIQwLMshIboXc8bW67a0
44 !
45 vpdn enable
46 !
47 vpdn-group Intranet
48 ! Default PPTP VPDN group
49  accept-dialin
50   protocol pptp
51   virtual-template 1
52 !
53 interface FastEthernet0
54  ip address 192.168.10.2 255.255.255.0 secondary
55  ip address 172.16.20.1 255.255.255.0
56  speed auto
57  half-duplex
58 !
59 interface Serial0
60  no ip address
61  shutdown
62 !
63 interface Serial1
64  no ip address
65  shutdown
66 !
67 interface Virtual-Template1
68  ip unnumbered FastEthernet 0
69  peer default ip address pool Pool4PPTP
70  ppp encrypt mppe 40 required
71  ppp authentication ms-chap
72 !
73 ip local pool Pool4PPTP 172.16.20.5 172.16.20.25
74 !
75 ip route 0.0.0.0 0.0.0.0 192.168.10.1
76 no ip http server
77 !
78 !
79 line con 0
80  exec-timeout 0 0
81  transport input none
82 line aux 0
83 line vty 0 4
84  password cisco
85  login
86 !
87 end
```

7.7.2 Case Study Analysis

In this case study, the edge router is part of the corporate network, while the PPTP router is a router that does not belong to the central IT department, but to a department that wants a secure method of communicating within their network.

In this case, the address space 172.16.20.0/24 is their private network. No one from outside their network can access it, except those that can tunnel into the PPTP server. This is all made possible by the use of a secondary address on the PPTP router's FastEthernet interface (line 54 and 55). If the devices on the 192.168.10.x network use a default gateway of 192.168.10.1, then they cannot communicate with the private address space of 172.16.20.x. However, if hosts use 192.168.10.2 as the default gateway, then they can communicate with both the 172.16.20.x network as well as the rest of the corporate network.

For example, we can take a look at a host JoeUser whose address is 192.168.10.5 and who uses 192.168.10.1 (edge router) as his default gateway. Host JoeUser cannot communicate with the 172.16.20.x network because the edge router knows nothing about the 172.16.20.x network. However, if host JoeUser were to use 192.168.10.2 (PPTP router) as his default gateway, he can communicate with the 172.16.20.x network. But what about communication with the outside world? The PPTP router has a default route pointing to the edge router so that any packet it can't deliver directly will get forwarded to the edge router and thus be forwarded the outside world. The return trip of that packet will completely bypass the PPTP router and will be delivered directly to JoeUser from the edge router.

Lines 69 and 73 show us that the IP addresses used are on the same IP server network as the intranet Web. To the PPTP clients, it appears to only be a single hop through the PPTP Router to communicate with the intranet Web server. In this particular situation, it is important to be careful that broadcast traffic doesn't flood our VPN tunnel, rendering it useless. However, using the situation as described above, there isn't any reason we couldn't introduce a second IP network that the PPTP router knows about, thus isolating each other from broadcasts.

7.8 Summary of PPTP

Table 7-2	**Authentication**	**User Authentication**
Summary of PPTP Features	Multiprotocol Support	Yes
	PPTP Control Messages	TCP - 1723
	PPTP Data Messages	IP port 47
	Data Confidentiality	Yes
	Data Integrity	Yes
	Data Origin Authentication	Yes
	Anti-Replay	Yes
	IOS Support for PPTP	IOS 12.0(5)XE and later
	What IOS Naming Convention Value Supports PPTP	s

7.9 RFCS Related to PPTP

Table 7-3	**RFC**	**Title**
Current RFC's related to PPTP	2637	*Point-to-Point Tunneling Protocol* (PPTP)
	2784	*Generic Routing Encapsulation* (GRE)

CHAPTER 8

L2TP

In the last chapter, we looked at using *Point-to-Point Tunneling Protocol* (PPTP) to carry *Point-to-Point Protocol* (PPP) traffic through voluntary tunnels via an internetwork. This chapter will focus on L2TP, a successor to Cisco's *Layer Two Forwarding* (L2F) technology and Microsoft's PPTP. Just like PPTP, L2TP is a VPN technology that supports voluntary tunnels. However, L2TP also supports compulsory tunnels.

Because L2TP can support both voluntary and compulsory tunnels, it can provide a lot of flexibility. L2TP has the ability to break apart the physical attributes (flowcontrol, stopbits, and modem speed) associated with a dialup PPP connection and the logical attributes (IP address, IPX address, authentication, and so on). By breaking apart the responsibilities of each of these attributes, we can completely change the paradigm in which PPP dialup connections are deployed by large organizations.

8.1 Objectives to be Covered in This chapter

- Overview of L2TP
- Describe L2TP Authentication Methods

- Configure L2TP on a Cisco Router
- Configure L2TP on Windows 2000
- Review Design Considerations for L2TP
- Troubleshoot L2TP

L2TP is commonly referred to as a *Virtual Private Dialup Networking* (VPDN) technology by Cisco. For this reason, we will embrace this term within this chapter because the term VPDN is entrenched within the nomenclature used to describe L2TP.

Although we use the term VPN to refer to a VPDN technology, not all VPN technologies are VPDN technologies. PPTP, L2TP and L2TP's cousin L2F are considered VPDN technologies, whereas IPSec is still referred to as just VPN.

8.2 Overview of L2TP Architecture

Historically, organizations that needed their workforce to access their network remotely had to either set up their own dialup service, or outsource their dialup needs to an *Internet Service Provider* (ISP). By building their own dialup service, an organization had to invest in dialup technology and personnel to maintain that technology as well as pay the long distance bills generated by their mobile workforce.

Through traditional dialup outsourcing methods, an organization could eliminate many of the "difficult to manage characteristics" associated with dialup (specialized hardware, specialized personnel, dialup circuits). In addition, this paradigm could enable an organization to immediately take advantage of an ISP's geographically dispersed environment, greatly reducing, even eliminating, long distance phone calls (long distance phone calls related to a mobile workforce can be exceedingly high). Unfortunately, in this paradigm an organization typically loses the ability to create accounts, restrict users, and so on, in a timely fashion.

L2TP changes this paradigm by enabling ISPs to focus on their core competencies, build and maintain dialup infrastructures, and enable an organization to control access to their resources without involving the ISP.

L2TP was designed to enable a user to dial into an ISP and, unbeknownst to the dialin user, tunnel their connection into the corporate network as seen in Figure 8-1. This enables the corporate network to provide

Figure 8-1

L2TP paradigm

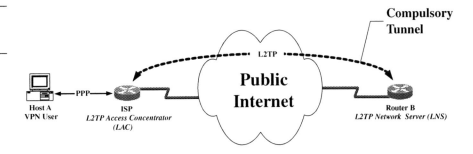

all the logical attributes to the dialin connection, such as authentication and network layer attributes. It also enables the ISP to maintain its focus on the physical attributes.

As seen in Figure 8-1, two VPN peers make up the L2TP tunnel: the *L2TP Access Concentrator* (LAC) and the *L2TP Network Server* (LNS). The user will dial into the LAC, at which point the LAC will initiate the L2TP connection to the LNS. The LNS can sit on the edge of a corporate network or behind a firewall within the corporate network.

L2TP can also operate in the same manner as PPTP, enabling users who already have IP connectivity, to connect to the corporate network. Although this type of voluntary tunnel appears to use the same methodology as PPTP, the way in which L2TP works is fundamentally different.

When establishing an L2TP connection, the same data-link layer and network layer characteristics that are negotiated during a PPP connection are negotiated during an L2TP connection such as: authentication, encryption, compression, IP address, IPX network address, and so on. This is one of the reasons why it is important to have a good understanding of how PPP operates before attempting to understand how L2TP operates.

Note:

For more information about PPP negotiations, review Chapter 3, "Dialup over Cisco Routers."

Just like PPTP, L2TP provides multiprotocol support through the use of PPP for the data transport. However, unlike PPTP, L2TP has no built-in encryption. The only mechanisms built into L2TP are the use of a random number during the generation of tunnel ID and call id to protect against blind attacks aimed at L2TP. For those who need to encrypt the L2TP data stream, they can utilize an even stronger encryption mechanism: IPSec.

8.2.1 L2TP Control Messages and Data Tunneling

Many of the paradigms that are used in PPTP can be found in L2TP, such as the use of two different types of messages to make L2TP operate. L2TP uses two types of messages in an L2TP tunnel: control messages and data tunneling messages. L2TP messages are responsible for the creation, maintenance, and termination of an L2TP tunnel. A L2TP data tunnel packet is responsible for the actual transmission of the user's PPP data. However, unlike PPTP, L2TP uses the same frame format for both sending control messages and data messages. There is only a single field within the frame that indicates whether the frame is a data message or a control message. The L2TP frame header can be seen in Figure 8-2.

Figure 8-2

L2TP control message format

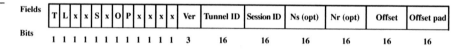

The fields that make up an L2TP header are found in the following list:

▪ **T**—*Type bit (bit 0)*: This field is used to specify whether a message is a control message or a data message. Value of one indicates a control message. A value of zero is used for data messages.

▪ **L**—*Length Bit* (bit 1): This bit indicates whether the length field is present in the message. For all control messages, this bit must be set to one.

- **x**—*Key Present (bits 2,3,5,8,9,10,11)*: These bits are reserved for future extensions. All reserved bits must be set to zero on outgoing messages, and ignored on incoming messages.

- **S**—*Sequence Bit (bit 4)*: This bit is used to indicate whether the Ns and Nr fields are present. For all control messages, this bit must be set to one.

- **O**—*Offset Bit (bit 5)*: This bit is used to indicate whether the Offset field is present. For all control messages, this bit must be set to zero.

- **P**—*Priority Bit (bit 6):* This field is used to indicate whether this data message should receive preferential treatment as well as queuing and transmission.

- **Ver**—*Version (bits 12-14)*: This field indicates the version of the L2TP data message header. According to RFC 2661, this field must be set to 2, because the value of 1 is reserved for L2F packets. Packets with an unknown Version field must be discarded.

- **Tunnel ID**—*(bits 13-15)*: This field is used to indicate the identifier for the control connection and is only locally significant. When a L2TP tunnel is established with a L2TP peer, Tunnel IDs are exchanged. Thus, a packet sent to a L2TP peer will use the Tunnel ID of the recipient and not the sender.

- **Session ID**—*(bits 16-31)*: This field is used to identify a session within a L2TP tunnel. The Session ID is only locally significant, thus a packet sent to a PPP peer will use the Session ID of the recipient and not the sender.

- **Ns**—*Next sent (16 bits)*: This field contains a value that identifies the sequence number of a message. The control messages and the data messages each have their own sequence number state. The presence of this field is dependent on the S bit being set to one.

- **Nr**—*Next Received (16 bits)*: This field contains the next expected value that the sender is expecting to see in the N's field.

- **Offset**—*(32 bits)*: This field is only available if the O bit is set to zero. It indicates the number of octets past the L2TP header that the payload data is expected to start. Data within the offset padding is undefined and meaningless. The L2TP header ends after the last octet of the offset padding.

- **Offset Pad**—*(32 bits)*: The field is present only if the *Offset Bit* is set to zero. Its size is indicated by the *Offset* field. Its contents are ignored; it is recommended that the contents be initialized to zero by the sender.

When control messages are sent, a non-zero *Attribute Value Pair* (AVP) follows the L2TP packet header. Instead of using static fields to define control messages, the L2TP protocol uses AVPs. This extensible format makes future extensions to the L2TP protocol very easy. In addition, mechanisms exist within the AVP field that enable *AVP Hiding*, a method that allows a control message to be encrypted.

As previously mentioned, management of an L2TP tunnel is handled through the control messages. The different control messages are displayed here:

- **Start-Control-Connection-Request (SCCRQ):** This type of control message is used to initialize a tunnel between two L2TP peers. It can either be sent by the LAC or the LNS. It should include the Protocol version, hostname, framing capabilities, and the locally assigned tunnel ID.

- **Start-Control-Connection-Reply (SCCRP):** This control message is used in direct response to an SCCRQ message. It indicates the SCCRQ was accepted and that tunnel establishment should continue. The message should include the protocol version, hostname, and the locally assigned tunnel ID.

- **Start-Control-Connection-Connected (SCCCN):** This control message is sent in direct response to an SCCRP message completing the tunnel establishment process. The two L2TP peers can now start negotiating L2TP characteristics.

- **Stop-Control-Connection-Notification (StopCCN):** This control message indicates that the tunnel is being shut down. It can be sent by either the LAC or the LNS. Only an acknowledgement of this message needs to be sent, because there is no reply message. The message must include the locally assigned tunnel id.

- **Hello (HELLO):** This is a "keepalive" used by the tunnel to verify the operation of the tunnel. An L2TP peer receiving this message must respond with either a ZLB ACK, or another unrelated message piggybacking the necessary acknowledgement. Interestingly enough, according to RFC 2661, an L2TP peer must not expect to see HELLO messages. This is because Hello messages are only employed to distinguish between a tunnel outage and during periods of no control messages or data activity.

- **Incoming-Call-Request (ICRQ):** This control message is sent by the LAC to the LNS when an incoming call is detected. This message is the first within a three-message exchange for establishing an L2TP tunnel.

- **Incoming-Call-Reply (ICRP):** This control message, which is sent by the LNS to the LAC in direct response to an ICRQ, indicates the ICRQ was successful and that the LAC must answer the call if it has not already done so. The message must include locally assigned session ID. It can include the physical channel id and the calling number.

- **Incoming-Call-Connected (ICCN):** This control message, the last of the three-message exchange, is sent by the LAC to the LNS. It is used to indicate both that the ICRP was accepted and that the call has been answered. In addition, it indicates that the L2TP session must move to the establish state. The message must include the locally assigned session ID.

- **Outgoing-Call-Request (OCRQ):** This control message is the first of three messages exchanged by the LNS to the LAC to indicate that an outbound call from the LAC must be established. Sent by the LNS, the message must include all of the parameters necessary for the call to be placed such as session ID, minimum and maximum BPS allowed, bearer type, framing type, and the number to call.

- **Outgoing-Call-Reply (OCRP):** This control message sent by the LNS is used to acknowledge the receipt of an OCRQ message. It is the second message of a three-message exchange. It provides the assigned session ID from the LNS.

- **Outgoing-Call-Connected (OCCN):** This control message is sent by the LAC to the LNS immediately after an OCRP message is received. It is used to indicate that the result of a requested outgoing call was successful. It also provides parameters about the call, such as Connect speed (transmit and receive) and framing type.

- **Call-Disconnect-Notify (CDN):** This message can be sent by either the LAC or the LNS to request a disconnection of a specific all within the tunnel. This enables the L2TP peer to clean up resources in use by the session. A response is not necessary for this code. The L2TP peer must send the result code and the assigned session ID to be terminated.

- **WAN-Error-Notify (WEN):** This message can be sent by either the LAC or the LNS to indicate WAN error conditions. The counters are cumulative and must not be sent more than once every 60 seconds. The message must indicate the type of errors that are being detected.

▓ **Set-Link-Info (SLI):** This L2TP control message is sent by the LNS to the LAC to set PPP-negotiated options. According to the RFC, these options can change at any time during the life of the call. The LAC must be able to update its information and behavior on this active PPP session.

After reviewing the call control messages that are listed above, it should become obvious that we can categorize them into four different groups of messages.

	Message Category	Message Type
Table 8-1 L2TP control message types and categories	Tunnel Establishment	SCCRQ, SCCRP, SCCCN, StopCCN
	Incoming Connection (user established)	ICRQ, ICRP, ICCN
	Outgoing Connection (LNS established)	OCRQ, OCRP, OCCN
	Miscellaneous Messages	Hello, CDN, WEN, SLI

Although all of these messages and processes might seem like a waste of time to learn, they are very helpful to understand when problems arise with your L2TP tunnel. This will be shown in the troubleshooting section.

8.2.2 Establishing an L2TP Tunnel

In order for an L2TP session to be established between a host and a LNS, there must be an L2TP tunnel that can tunnel the PPP packets from the LAC to the LNS. Let's look at the process used to set up an L2TP Tunnel between a LAC and LNS Figure 8-3.

1. The LAC sends a *Start Control Connection Request* (SCCRQ) to the LNS.

2. The LNS sends a *Start Control Connection Reply* (SCCRP) to the LAC.

3. The LAC sends a *Start Control Connection Connected* (SCCRN) to the LNS.

Figure 8-3

Process used to
establish an
L2TP tunnel

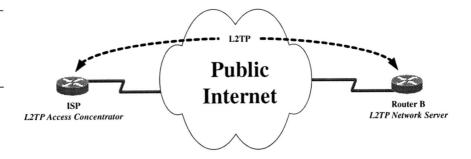

L2TP

Public Internet

ISP
L2TP Access Concentrator

Router B
L2TP Network Server

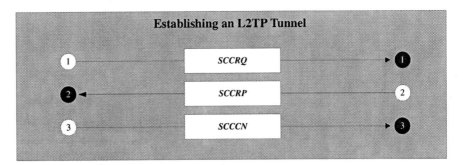

Establishing an L2TP Tunnel

1 ⟶ SCCRQ ⟶ 1

2 ⟵ SCCRP 2

3 SCCCN ⟶ 3

8.2.3 Establishing a L2TP Session

Now that we have seen how an L2TP tunnel is created, we now need to see how an L2TP session is created. We have studied various messages and how they have worked together to provide an L2TP session. Now, let's look at the process used to establish a connection as seen in Figure 8-4.

1. Host A initiates a PPP connection to the LAC through a standard analog telephone or ISDN. The LAC accepts the connection, and the data-link layer is established.

2. Next, the LAC partially authenticates Host A. The username is then used to verify if the user is a VPDN client. If the user is not a VPDN user, the user is authenticated using the local ISP's username database, and the L2TP session is established. If the username is recognized as a VPDN user, steps are taken to establish a L2TP session.

Figure 8-4

Process used to establish an L2TP session

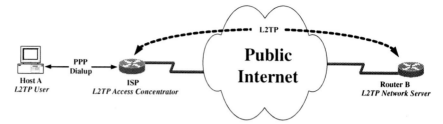

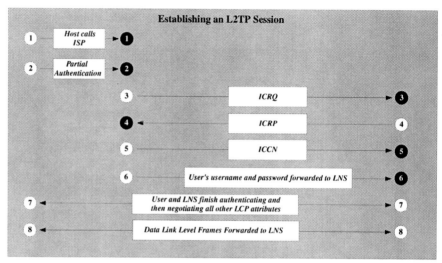

Note:

If there is no L2TP tunnel at this point, an L2TP tunnel is established between the ISP and Router B.

3. The LAC initiates a L2TP session with an ICRQ message.

4. The LNS accepts the L2TP session with an ICRP message.

5. The LAC sends a L2TP session established using the ICCN message.

6. The LAC forwards the username and password to the LNS to complete authentication.

7. The LAC will then forward all LCP negotiated options to the LNS. The LNS will then create a Virtual Access Interface cloned from a

Virtual Template Interface, at which point the user will finish authenticating with the LNS as well as all other LCP negotiated options. If the user fails to authenticate, the LNS sends a disconnect message to the LAC.

8. Data link level frames can now be passed between the LNS and the virtual interface of the home-gateway.

8.3 Cisco IOS Support for L2TP

L2TP is a relative newcomer to the VPN arena. Cisco's IOS has had support for L2F for quite a while, whereas L2TP has only recently been incorporated into Cisco' IOS. L2TP can generally be found in the "Enterprise" or "Plus" software feature set. An "s" designation within the IOS name indicates support for VPDN technologies.

L2F was Cisco's first VPDN technology. L2TP wasn't released until much later, but even then only on limited platforms. Cisco's first IOS offering L2TP support came in IOS 11.3(5)AA, but only for Cisco's 7200, AS5200, AS5300, and AS5800 series routers. The first IOS to support L2TP on the majority of Cisco's platforms including the 1600, 1700, 2500, 2600, 3600, 4000 series routers was with the release of 12.0(1)T. Cisco updated its VPDN command syntax and structure to accommodate the new VPDN protocol, L2TP, introducing a concept called VPDN groups, which will be discussed later in this chapter. The underlying structure of VPDN groups in 12.0(1)T was still very similar to the structure found in IOSes prior to 12.0(1)T.

Shortly after introducing L2TP to the 12.0T IOS train, Cisco completely overhauled the VPDN commands and structure starting with IOS 12.0(5)T. Prior to the reorganization of the VPDN commands, L2TP was implemented using the same basic command syntax and structure used to implement L2F. Because the older VPDN command syntax and structure was only released on a limited basis, we will only cover L2TP implementation specific tasks for IOS 12.0(5)T and newer.

Note:

What is the point of describing updates to you, the reader? First, this new technology is continually being worked on by Cisco to provide network engineers with an easy to follow and logical methodology for configuring their products. Unfortunately, these same developments make providing an easy to follow guide for configuring VPNs an extremely difficult task. However, by outlining the protocol specific steps you should be able to find the commands that are missing from your IOS and "fill-in the blanks" (even if Cisco changes the command structure again).

For those of you who are still unsure as to whether your IOS supports L2TP or not, we have a quick method for determining whether your IOS supports L2TP. Using the user exec command *show vpdn,* you can determine very quickly if your IOS supports L2TP. Figure 8-5 shows that Router A supports both L2TP and L2F because no L2TP or L2F tunnels are available. In Figure 8-6, we can that Router B only supports L2F. This is because when we use the command, *show vpdn*, only L2F tunnels are in the output, L2TP tunnels are missing and is thus missing from this IOS.

Figure 8-5

Cisco IOS that supports L2TP and L2F from IOS c2500-jos56i-1.120-5.T.bin

```
RouterA#show vpdn

% No active L2TP tunnels

% No active L2F tunnels
RouterA#
```

Figure 8-6

Cisco IOS that supports L2F only from IOS c2500-jos56i-1_120-9.bin

```
RouterB#show
RouterB#show vpdn
% No active L2F tunnels
RouterB#
```

Note:
Even though Cisco gave a face-lift to the commands that implemented L2TP, the commands used to show current VPDN tunnels remained the same through all of Cisco's IOSes.

Remember that L2TP is not a proprietary protocol and can be implemented using other vendor's implementations. Currently, Microsoft's Windows 2000 is the only Microsoft operating system that supports L2TP. Therefore, we will also cover how to configure L2TP on Windows 2000.

8.4 Configuring L2TP

Once we understand the changes that Cisco has made to its IOS and the command structure used to implement L2TP on a Cisco router, configuring L2TP is not a difficult task. As with all VPDN technologies, it is easier to think of L2TP in terms of dialup (such as incoming and outgoing connections). This simple analogy will help you better understand the concepts and help your retention of Cisco VPDNs.

In order to set up L2TP, we need to configure both the LAC and the LNS. From a user's perspective, L2TP can handle both incoming and outgoing connections. Because of this, it can become very confusing for the reader to understand exactly which device is handling a call for either direction. Two distinct ways are available to configure L2TP: Dial-In and Dial-Out. Each service requires that we configure the LAC and LNS for the appropriate service. In either case, the concept is the same; the direction of the phone call being placed changes. In Figure 8-7, we can see the difference between an L2TP Dial-In connection versus an L2TP Dial-Out connection.

Table 8-2 will help the reader understand which key words are used with each L2TP device during the configuration of a LAC or LNS.

Note:
L2TP Dial-Out requires the use of AAA server and is beyond the scope of this book.

Figure 8-7

Difference between L2TP Dial-In versus L2TP Dial-Out

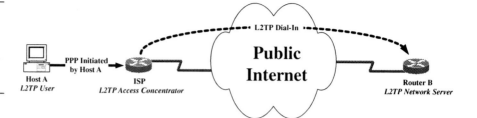

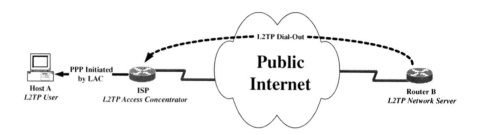

Table 8-2		**LAC Keyword**	**LNS Keyword**
L2TP Configuration keywords	L2TP Dial-In	Request Dialin	Accept Dialin
	L2TP Dial-Out	Accept Dialout	Request Dialout

The idea behind each of the keyword phrases is to describe the activity the L2TP device needs to perform from its own perspective. For example, when a user is dialing into a LAC, the LAC must request dialin service from the LNS, whereas the LNS needs to accept dialin service.

Remember that you generally implement L2TP in a single direction (that is, Dial-In or Dial-Out). However, you can configure a Cisco router to act simultaneously as any of the four different devices (LNS-Accept Dial-In, LNS-Request Dial-Out, LAC-Request Dial-In, or LAC Accept-Dialout) by using multiple VPDN groups.

Note:

In order for a Cisco router to be a LAC, it must be configured for dialup. If you are not familiar with configuring a Cisco router for dialup, review Chapter 3, which discusses dialup configurations on a Cisco router in detail.

Let's now look at the commands used to set up L2TP between a LNS and LAC for Dial-In. Keep in mind that whereas many of the high-level tasks appear to be the same task repeated, embedded within each of the tasks are different steps that are specific to configuring that L2TP device.

8.5 Configuring L2TP For Dial-In

When configuring a pair of Cisco routers to support L2TP dial in service, the end user will initiate the connection to the corporate network. When the end user dials up to the LAC, the LAC will establish physical layer attributes and perform a partial authentication (that is, it parses the user's name so that the user is associated with the correct VPDN group). The LAC will then send the connection to the LNS. The LNS server is then responsible for the rest of the data-link and network layer configuration of the end user's connection.

8.5.1 LAC Request Dial-In

An L2TP Access Concentrator is responsible for terminating the physical connection of a PPP dialup connection. Once a connection is established to the ISP's LAC, the LAC is responsible for tunneling the packets from the dialin user to the LNS. The LNS is then responsible for authenticating the user and negotiating the user's network layer attributes. Because the responsibilities of the LAC are minimal, setting one up is fairly easy even though a number of tasks need to be accomplished. To configure a LAC, we need to perform the following tasks:

- Enable VPDN
- Create VPDN group
- Configure VPDN group to Request Dial-In
- Specify VPDN protocol to use in VPDN group
- Specify method used to identify a L2TP user's LNS in VPDN group
- Specify the IP address of the LNS in VPDN group
- Specify the name the LAC will use to Identify itself to the LNS in VPAN group
- Specify the shared authentication password in VPDN group

8.5.1.1 Enable VPDN

In order to configure any VPDN technology, we must first enable it. Enabling VPDN is a simple task that is carried out using the following global configuration command:

```
Router (config)#vpdn enable
```

Until we have enabled VPDN, we cannot use any of the other VPDN commands used to configure a LAC for L2TP Dial-In. That is why it is crucial to make sure you've enabled it before attempting to use any of the other commands.

Note:

Depending upon the IOS you are running when enabling VPDN, you may get the following error: % SPD temporarily disabled. Not compatible with VPDN. Starting with IOS 11.2(5)P, Cisco added Selective Packet Discard (SPD) *to its IOS. SPD, enabled by default, allows a router during times of severe overload conditions to choose which packets to discard. Without this intelligence, a router may discard routing protocol packets, thus affecting the stability of the network. On access routers this is generally not a problem. However, this can present a major problem on core routers.*

8.5.1.2 Create VPDN Group

A VPDN group is a mechanism that enables us to organize all of the relevant VPDN commands that are associated with a VPDN peer into a single discrete component. It is this mechanism that specifies whether a

Cisco router is one of the four L2TP devices (that is, LAC-Request Dial-In, LAC-Accept Dial-Out, LNS-Accept Dial-In, and LNS-Request Dial-Out). Once a VPDN group has been configured as one of these two L2TP devices (LAC or LNS), it cannot be changed. This does not mean that a Cisco router can only be one of these two L2TP devices, but that a VPDN group can only enable a router to be a LAC or a LNS. By utilizing multiple VPDN groups, we can enable a router to be either a LAC or an LNS.

To create a VPDN group we can use the following global configuration command:

```
Router (config)#vpdn-group vpdn-group-name
```

vpdn-group-name   **WORD**   Name of the VPDN group

8.5.1.3 Configure VPDN Group to Request Dial-In

To enable a VPDN group to request dialin, we can use the following configuration command:

```
Router (config-vpdn)#request-dialin
```

Once a VPDN group has been configured for a specific L2TP device, it cannot be changed. This means that if you configure a VPDN group as a LAC, it can only accept configurations pertinent to a LAC (refer to Table 8-2). For example, if a VPN group were configured to *accept-dialout*, it would identify the group as a LAC L2TP device. The VPDN group could then also be configured for *request-dialin*, but it could not be configured for *accept-dialin* or *request-dialout*, which are configurations for LNS L2TP devices.

8.5.1.4 Specify VPDN Protocol to use in VPDN Group

Once we've created a VPDN group, we can configure the VPDN protocol that we use. Remember that L2F can be used instead of L2TP. In most instances, you will want to configure a VPDN group for L2TP unless you need to support legacy L2F devices. A VPDN group can use L2F or L2TP (remember that the L2TP control message version field uses a value of one to indicate an L2F frame, whereas a value of two indicates an L2TP frame). To specify the command to be used by a VPDN group, we can use the following command:

```
Router(config-vpdn-req-in)#protocol vpdn-protocol
```

vpdn-protocol   **12f**   Use L2F for this VPDN group

              12tp   Use L2TP for this VPDN group

8.5.1.5 Specify Method used to Identify a L2TP User's LNS

When a user dials into a LAC, the LAC needs a method to determine where to send the user's data. Remember that an ISP could have multiple L2TP customers serving multiple LNSs. Thus, they need a method to determine which LNS will be used to tunnel a user's data.

To map an incoming dial-in connection to a LAC, two methods exist. First, an L2TP user can append a domain name to the username (for example, rick@coleman.com where coleman.com is the domain name) to map the user to a LNS. Using the user's domain name, the LAC is able to look up the IP address of the user's LNS in the Cisco configuration file. The second method used to determine a user's LNS is through the *Dialed Number Information* (DNIS). The DNIS is the number that the host has dialed. For example, if we had multiple phone numbers terminating on the same Cisco Access Server, we can differentiate between users by the phone number they dialed. Then, we would provide a different service based upon the number the host dialed.

To identify the LNS using the domain name found in the username, use the following command:

```
Router(config-vpdn-req-in)#domain domain-name
```

domain-name **WORD**   Associate a user to a VPDN group using this domain
                          name

To identify the LNS using the phone number the user dialed, use the following command:

```
Router(config-vpdn-req-in)#dnis dnis-number
```

dnis-number **WORD**   The phone number that the user dialed

By using DNIS instead of a domain name, a user does not have to append the domain name to their userid. The L2TP client only needs to specify their username during authentication.

8.5.1.6 Specify the IP Address of the LNS (L2TP)

At this point, we have configured all of the required information to setup a L2TP tunnel except for the destination. The following command is used to specify the ip address of the LNS.

```
Router(config-vpdn)# initiate-to ip ip-address limit sessions
```

ip-address   *x.x.x.x*   IP address of the LNS

sessions   **0-32767**   (optional) Number of L2TP sessions allowed
through this tunnel

The optional variable *sessions* gives an ISP the ability to limit the number of L2TP sessions that can be established through a L2TP tunnel. This lets an ISP sell a predefined number of simultaneous dial in sessions at a specific *Point-of-Presence* (POP).

8.5.1.7 Specify the Name the LAC will use to Identify Itself to the LNS

In order for a tunnel to be established, the LAC and LNS need to identify each other. By forcing the LAC to identify itself (since it is initiating the tunnel), the LNS can then find the appropriate VPDN group in its configuration and send back a name that the LAC can use within its show commands. It is not important what name is used by the LNS in an L2TP Dial-In Tunnel, but it is very important that the LAC identifies itself correctly. Otherwise, the LNS will not be able to find a VPDN group to associate a tunnel with. To configure the name used to identify a LAC, use the following command:

```
Router(config-vpdn)# local name LAC-hostname
```

LAC-hostname   **WORD**   Name that will be offered by the LAC to the LNS
during tunnel establishment

8.5.7.8 Specify the Shared Authentication Password

To set up a tunnel, both the LAC and the LNS must authenticate each other using the shared password configured within the corresponding VPDN group. This is not the authentication phase that is triggered by the client during PPP negotiations. Tunnel authentication happens before client/LNS authentication occurs. If tunnel authentication fails, the dialin client/LNS authentication will not start and will only appear to the end user as a generic failure. To configure the shared password to use during Tunnel authentication, use the following VPDN group configuration command:

```
Router (config-vpdn)# l2tp tunnel password password
```

password   **WORD**   Password used by the LAC or the LNS

8.5.7.9 Example Configuration of an L2TP LAC Request Dial-In

In Figure 8-8, we can see the commands necessary to configure a Cisco router to support L2TP as a LAC supporting dialin. Don't forget that in order for this configuration to work, the router must also support some type of dial in configuration. For those of you testing your knowledge of how L2TP works, you can connect a modem to the auxiliary port and configure it for PPP, as seen in Figure 8-8. Remember, you need to configure the *async interface* to support the correct type of authentication that will be performed by the LNS. Otherwise, the LAC will not be able to parse out the domain name of the dialin user. In turn, it will not forward the connection to the LNS.

Figure 8-8

Example of a
LAC Request
Dial-In
configuration

```
!
vpdn enable
!
vpdn-group 3
 request-dialin
 protocol l2tp
 domain dwyer.com
 initiate-to ip 3.3.3.3 limit 15
 local name LocalISP
 l2tp tunnel password 0 tunnelpassword
!
interface Async1
 encapsulation ppp
 ppp authentication chap
!
```

8.5.2 LNS Accept Dial-In

An L2TP Access Concentrator is responsible for terminating the physical connection of a PPP dialup connection. Once a connection is established to the ISPs LAC, the LAC is responsible for tunneling the packets from the dialin user to the LNS. The LNS is then responsible for authenticating the user, and negotiating the user's network layer attributes. Because the responsibilities of the LAC are minimal, setting one up is a fairly easy task. To configure a LAC, we need to perform the following tasks:

- Enable VPDN
- Create VPDN group
- Configure VPDN group to accept dialin

- Specify VPDN protocol to use in VPDN group
- Specify virtual template interface in VPDN group
- Specify the name of the LAC and LNS (L2TP peer) in VPDN group
- Specify the shared authentication password in VPDN group
- Create and configure virtual template interface
- Configure usernames and passwords for dialin users

Whereas many of these tasks are similar to configuring a LAC to *request dialin*, they aren't always identical. Make sure that you always use the commands as laid out here. Do not use steps outlined from another section.

8.5.2.1 Enable VPDN

In order to configure any VPDN technology, we must first enable it. Enabling VPDN is a simple task that is carried out using the following global configuration command:

```
Router (config)#vpdn enable
```

Until we've enabled VPDN, we cannot use any of the other VPDN commands used to configure a LAC for L2TP Dial-In. That is why it is crucial to make sure you've enabled it before attempting to use any of the other commands.

Note:

Depending upon the IOS you are running when enabling VPDN, you may get the following error: % SPD temporarily disabled. *Not compatible with VPDN. Starting with IOS 11.2(5)P, Cisco added* Selective Packet Discard (SPD) *to its IOS. SPD, enabled by default, enables a router during times of severe overload conditions to choose which packets to discard. Without this intelligence, a router may discard routing protocol packets, thus affecting the stability of the network. On access routers this is generally not a problem. On core routers however, this can present a major problem.*

8.5.2.2 Create VPDN Group

A VPDN group is a mechanism that enables us to organize all of the relevant VPDN commands that are associated with a VPDN peer into a single discrete component. It is this mechanism that specifies whether a Cisco router is one of the four L2TP devices (that is, LAC-Request Dial-In, LAC-Accept Dial-Out, LNS-Accept Dial-In, and LNS-Request Dial-Out). Once a VPDN group has been configured as one of these two L2TP devices (LAC or LNS), it cannot be changed. This does not mean that a Cisco router can only be one of these two L2TP devices, but that a VPDN group can only enable a router to be a LAC or a LNS by utilizing multiple VPDN groups we can enable a router to be either a LAC or an LNS.

To create a VPDN group we can use the following global configuration command:

```
Router (config)#vpdn-group vpdn-group-name
```

vpdn-group-name   **WORD**   Name of the VPDN group

8.5.2.3 Configure VPDN Group to Accept Dialin

To enable a VPDN group to accept dialin connections, we can use the following VPDN group configuration command:

```
Router (config-vpdn)#accept-dialin
```

Once a VPDN group has been configured for a specific L2TP device (LAC or LNS), it cannot be changed. This means that if you configure a VPDN group as a LAC, it can only accept configurations pertinent to a LAC (refer to Table 8-2). For example, if a VPDN group were configured to *accept-dialout*, it would identify the group as a LAC L2TP device. The VPDN group could then also be configured for *request-dialin*, but it could not be configured to *accept-dialin* or *request-dialout*, which are configurations for LNS L2TP devices.

8.5.2.4 Specify VPDN Protocol to Use in VPDN Group

Once the VPDN group is created, we can configure the VPDN protocol that we use. Remember that L2F can be used instead of L2TP. In most instances, you will want to configure a VPDN group for L2TP unless you need to support legacy L2F devices. A VPDN group can use L2F or L2TP (remember, the L2TP control message version field uses a value of one to indicate an L2F frame, whereas a value of two indicates an L2TP frame).

To specify the command to be used by a VPDN group, we can use the following command:

```
Router(config-vpdn-acc-in)#protocol vpdn-protocol
```

| *vpdn-protocol* | l2f | Use L2F for this VPDN group |
| | l2tp | Use L2TP for this VPDN group |

8.5.2.5 Specify Virtual Template Interface

In order for an incoming L2TP session to be terminated, we must have an interface to terminate it on. This is because an L2TP data packet is actually a PPP packet with an additional header. Once the header is stripped off, the PPP packet must be acted upon. In order for the PPP packet to be acted upon, it needs an interface that can understand the PPP header data. This is the responsibility of the virtual access interface. The virtual access interface is dynamically created from the virtual template interface that we specify within the VPDN group. Once we specify the virtual template interface, we must create and configure it so that it may interpret the PPP packets.

To specify which virtual template interface should be used to create the virtual-access interface during the establishment of an L2TP session, use the following command:

```
Router(config-vpdn-acc-in)# virtual-template virtual-template-number
```

virtual-template-number   **1-25**   Number of the virtual template.

8.5.2.6 Specify the Name of the LAC and LNS (L2TP Peer)

In order for a LNS device to terminate an incoming tunnel request, it must have a VPDN group to associate with that tunnel. This is accomplished through the use of the LAC name. When a LAC wants to create a tunnel with an LNS, it sends its name to the LNS. The LNS then looks at all of its VPDN groups and finds the corresponding VPDN group to authenticate with.

Within the configuration of L2TP, you must also specify the name of the LNS. However, this name is not very functional and it is only used by the LAC during troubleshooting to verify that the correct VPDN group is being used by the LNS.

To configure the name used to identify a LAC, use the following command:

```
Router(config-vpdn)# terminate-from hostname LAC-hostname
```

LAC-hostname **WORD**   Name that will be offered by the LAC to the LNS

Once we've specified the name of an incoming connection, we must now specify the name for the LNS to identify itself to the LAC. This can be done with the following command:

```
Router(config-vpdn)# local name LNS-hostname
```

LNS-hostname **WORD**   Name that will be offered by the LNS to the LAC

8.5.2.7 Specify the Shared Authentication Password

In order for a tunnel to be set up, both the LAC and the LNS must authenticate each other using a shared password. Both the LAC and LNS must have the shared password configured within the corresponding VPDN group. This is not the authentication phase that happens by the client during PPP negotiations. Tunnel authentication happens before client/LNS authentication occurs. If tunnel authentication fails, the dial-in client/LNS authentication will never start and will appear to the end user as a generic failure. To configure the shared password to use during tunnel authentication, use the following VPDN group configuration command:

```
Router (config-vpdn)# l2tp tunnel password password
```

password   **WORD**   Password used by the LAC or the LNS

8.5.2.8 Create and Configure Virtual Template Interface

After the generic VPDN configuration for a VPDN group has been set up, we can concentrate on defining the attributes necessary for a VPDN server to operate. A LNS server needs an interface to terminate a L2TP connection. Because these connections are dynamic, we do not configure the attributes directly on a physical interface. So, if we don't configure the attributes of our tunnel on the physical interface, where are the attributes located for our VPN tunnel? Virtual access interfaces are the logical elements that terminate our L2TP tunnel. These dynamic interfaces are created when the router detects an incoming connection. As long as the connection exists, the virtual access interface does as well.

So where do these dynamic interfaces get their configuration if we cannot configure them directly? The Virtual Template Interface is a template that is used to create virtual access interfaces. This template contains all the configuration settings required to configure the virtual access interface, as seen in Figure 8-9.

Figure 8-9

Virtual template interface versus virtual access interface

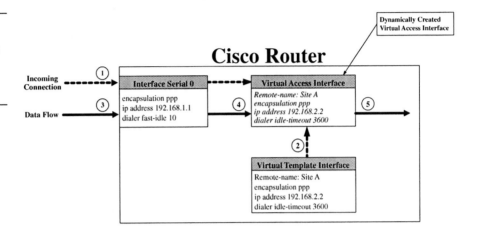

Once this virtual access interface is created, it is used during the entire VPDN session. You will notice that there is no way to modify the virtual access interface. The only way to modify your connection is to modify the virtual template interface and then reestablish your connection. When the L2TP client disconnects, the L2TP server destroys the virtual access interface created by that session.

To create a virtual template use the following command:

```
Router (config)#interface virtual-template virtual-template-number
```

virtual-template-number   **1-25**   Number of the virtual template.

Note:

On most interfaces, the encapsulation method is one of the most important elements that must be configured within an interface. However, the default encapsulation method for a virtual template interface is PPP, so there is no need to manually configure it.

Once we have created the interface, we still need to configure it with the various attributes that enable a LAC and a LNS to establish a connection. You will notice that the attributes configured on a virtual template interface are very much like an interface that needs to support PPP. This is because L2TP uses PPP for its payload and must adhere to the same type of rules bound to PPP (such as authentication, compression, network layer attributes, and so on). In Chapter 3, "Dialup over Cisco Routers," in which we covered PPP dialup, remember that four different characteristics need to be agreed upon in order for a connection to be established. When using L2TP, only two attributes need to be agreed on: authentication and compression.

When establishing a L2TP connection, the two dial peers must agree on which authentication protocol to use. To specify the authentication protocol to use during the authentication process between the dialup host and the LNS, use the following command:

```
Router (config-if)#ppp authentication authentication-protocol
```

authentication-protocol	**PAP**	Use PAP as the authentication protocol
	CHAP	Use CHAP as the authentication protocol
	MS-CHAP	Use MS-CHAP as the authentication protocol

At this point, we now need to configure all of the network layer attributes (for example, IP addressing, IPX addresses, and so on) that will be associated with an incoming connection. For more information on the commands to complete this task, refer to Chapter 3.

8.5.2.9 Configure Usernames and Passwords for Dialin Users

Because L2TP breaks up the physical layer assignments with the logical layer attributes during a PPP call, the LAC only needs to be responsible for the physical layer attributes. The LNS is responsible for the logical layer characteristic, including authentication, network layer attributes, and so on. Therefore, the LNS needs to create the username and passwords. However, if you want to use a AAA server to authenticate dialin users, you need to make sure that you configure the appropriate AAA commands found in Chapter 3. However, if you plan to authenticate dialin users locally, you can use the following global configuration command:

```
Router (config)#username username password password
```

username   **WORD**   Name used by the L2TP client
password   **WORD**   Password used by the L2TP client

Note:
Usernames and passwords are case sensitive.

8.5.2.10 Example Configuration of an L2TP LNS Accept Dial-In

In Figure 8-10, we can see the commands that are necessary to configure a Cisco router to support L2TP as a LNS supporting dialin. We can see that in this particular configuration we are supplying IP addresses to our dialup clients through the virtual template interface. Remember that the virtual template interface is only cloned to create the virtual access interface when an incoming call is detected.

Figure 8-10

Example of a LNS accept dial-in configuration

```
!
username meg@dwyer.com password 0 italy
!
vpdn enable
!
vpdn-group 2
 accept-dialin
 protocol l2tp
 virtual-template 1
 terminate-from hostname isp
 local name DwyerCorp
 l2tp tunnel password 7 tunnelpassword
!
interface Virtual-Template1
 ip unnumbered Loopback1
 peer default ip address pool dialup-pool
 ppp authentication chap
!
ip local pool dialup-pool 172.16.20.10 172.16.20.100
!
```

8.6 L2TP Client on Windows 2000

Unlike Windows 98 and Windows NT, Windows 2000 has L2TP built into the operating system. It is not an optional attribute that needs to be installed. L2TP is available with the installation of the networking component within Windows 2000, which requires a modem or NIC.

Using the *Make New Connection* wizard as seen in Figure 8-11, found in the *Network and Dialup Connections* folder, we can create a L2TP connection very easily.

Figure 8-11

Windows 2000 network and dial-up connections

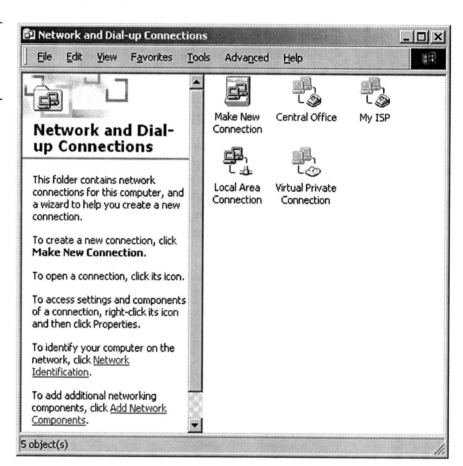

8.6.1 Creating L2TP Connection Scripts

To create a L2TP connection script use the following procedure.

1. Open **Network and Dial-Up Connections** in the control panel window.
2. Select **Make New Connection**.

Figure 8-12

Network
connection wizard

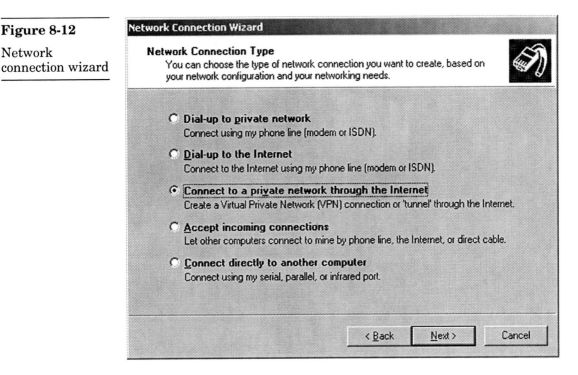

3. Select **Connect to a private network through the Internet**, as seen in Figure 8-12.

4. Select whether you want to establish the initial connection or not.

5. Enter the IP address of the L2TP server.

6. Select whether this connection is for **all users** or **only for myself**.

7. Name the L2TP Connection script and click **finish**.

Just like Windows 95 and Windows NT, we have the opportunity to modify the connection attributes. By opening the dialup script, we get a window shown in Figure 8-13.

Windows 2000 supports multiple authentication types, which can be configured under the properties of the login script. Those authentication protocols are:

- *Password Authentication Protocol* (PAP)
- *Shiva Password Authentication Protocol* (SPAP)

Figure 8-13

L2TP connection
script

- *Challenge Handshake Authentication Protocol* (CHAP)
- *Microsoft Challenge Handshake Authentication Protocol* (MS-CHAP)
- *Microsoft Challenge Handshake Authentication Protocol version 2* (MS-CHAPv2)

Keep in mind that a Cisco router will only support PAP, CHAP, and MS-CHAP for authentication protocols.

Because Windows 2000 also supports L2TP, we may find it necessary to make sure we only use L2TP. Therefore, Microsoft has given us the opportunity to specify the type of VPN protocol to use for a connection script as seen in Figure 8-14.

Figure 8-14

Specifying the
VPN protocol to
use for a
connection script

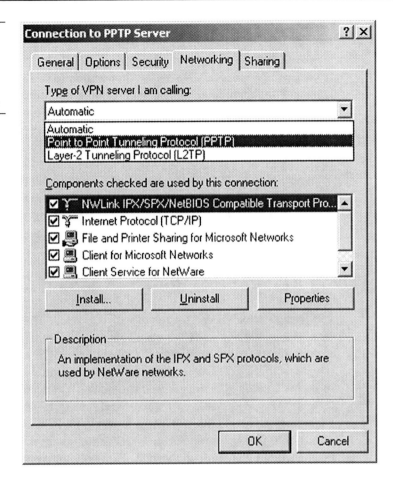

8.7 Design Considerations

8.7.1 Comparing L2F, L2TP, and PPTP

Whereas the concepts behind L2TP and PPTP are quite similar, their
underlying structures are quite different. For example, L2F, PPTP, and
L2TP provide reliable delivery of control messages. How this is done from
protocol to protocol is quite different. For example, in PPTP, the control
messages are sent using TCP, which means their reliability is defined

entirely by TCP. However, L2F and L2TP define the reliable delivery mechanisms within the protocol itself.

The mechanisms used for sending LCP and authentication information from the LAC to the LNS is another example of their differences. Both L2F and L2TP enable for the sending of LCP and authentication information when a session is being established, whereas PPTP does not have this ability. This means that the PPTP server may have to renegotiate LCP between it and the remote computer if any LCP negotiation has taken place.

Most likely the best example of L2TP inheriting traits from PPTP and not L2F is found within outgoing calls. No constructs exist within L2F to establish an outgoing call. However, both L2TP and PPTP have the ability to establish an outgoing call.

8.7.2 Upgrading IOS on Cisco Routers Running L2F

L2F has existed since the release of IOS 11.2. The command structure that was originally used to setup L2F tunnels is quite different than the command structure that is used to establish L2TP and L2F tunnels with the latest IOSes. This change in structure could leave network engineers in a bind during IOS upgrades if the newer IOS does not understand how to parse the old style commands. Fortunately for the network engineer, Cisco has given IOSes, with the newer VPDN command structure, the ability to correctly parse out these commands and convert them into a format suitable for immediate use. However, as with any upgrade, it is always best to test and confirm before deploying.

8.7.3 Where to Place an L2TP LNS

In most instances, the location of the LAC is predetermined. Either the LAC is the responsibility of the ISP, or it is the user's machine that is dialing into the corporate network. In either case, its location is already established. However, the location of the LNS is up to the network engineers designing the L2TP solution. In some instances, it may make sense to place the L2TP LNS at the edge of an organization's network, whereas in other instances it may make sense to put the L2TP device in a DMZ. It all depends upon the level of security required. In many instances, a budget for a firewall may not exist, whereas in other cases, a large enough budget for multiple firewalls will exist.

Setting up an L2TP LNS at the edge of the corporate network certainly makes its configuration very simple. We don't have to worry about any device between the LNS and the edge of the network filtering out the TCP/UDP ports that make L2TP work (except those specifically filtered on the LNS). In addition, there is no firewall that can cause connectivity problems with the L2TP peers. Therefore, we can easily make changes to the L2TP LNS without organizing the efforts with the team who runs the firewalls. Unfortunately, this location also opens the door to attackers. Whereas Cisco routers can be hardened against network attacks, they are not designed to work in a truly hostile environment (not environmentally hostile, but hostile network environments that are constantly protecting themselves due to the value of their intellectual property). Remember that the primary function of a router is to route packets; everything else is secondary.

In very large organizations, there is usually a firewall, or even several firewalls that protect intellectual property from network bandits. In this environment, your L2TP LNS can be shielded from all sorts of nasty attacks that take place on the Internet. The firewall can be configured to enable incoming connections that use TCP/UDP port 1701 and block all other connections. This minimizes the number of security holes that an attacker would be able to find on our LNS. Unfortunately, it makes our solution less flexible because any IP address changes need to be coordinated with the firewall team.

This is where an education in risk management can be very useful. Every decision that is made has distinct consequences. If you fail to understand those consequences, your choices could subsequently be flawed.

8.7.4 Mobile User Versus Telecommuter

Trying to solve the connectivity problem for mobile users and telecommuters using secure communications has historically been solved using the same solution. That is, set up an access server at the corporate network and let everyone dial in. This minimizes the exposure of corporate data to prying eyes. With the advent of many VPN protocols, these secure solutions have grown dramatically. Whereas L2TP might seem ideal for the mobile workforce, it is also ideal for the telecommuter. By enabling a telecommuter to set up a voluntary tunnel when they need to access the corporate network, they will not need to be reliant on a third party LAC, because they will be the LAC themselves! As a matter of fact, our mobile users can take advantage of voluntary tunnels using L2TP as well. With every advantage, there is always a disadvantage. In the case of a user's machine being the LAC, the disadvantage is that the user's machine will require additional software to make it operational. Fortunately, Windows 2000 already has this software built-in. The majority of other operating systems lack native L2TP functionality.

8.8 Verify L2TP Connections

No matter what technology is being used, it is always good to have tools available that will show you who is using a resource and for how long. When verifying L2TP, two elements need to be kept separate when troubleshooting. The first is the L2TP tunnel. This is the virtual connection between two VPDN peers. Using the *show vpdn tunnel* command, we can see what tunnels our VPDN device has set up. In Figure 8-15, we can see there is a single L2TP tunnel between router C and the remote host *isp*. We can also see that no current L2F tunnels on router C exist.

Figure 8-15

Output from show vpdn tunnel command

```
RouterC#show vpdn tunnel

L2TP Tunnel Information (Total tunnels=1 sessions=1)

LocID RemID Remote Name   State Remote Address Port Sessions
173   11    isp           est   192.168.10.2   1701 1

% No active L2F tunnels
RouterC#
```

The second element to look at is the L2TP session with the tunnel. This represents an end user's connection through the tunnel. In Figure 8-16, we see that meg@dwyer.com has been connected for over 24 minutes and has been using *virtual-access interface 1*.

Figure 8-16

Output from show vpdn tunnel command

```
RouterC#show vpdn session

L2TP Session Information (Total tunnels=1 sessions=1)

LocID RemID TunID Intf  Username      State Last Chg Fastswitch
236   23    173   Vi1   meg@dwyer.com est   00:24:03 enabled

% No active L2F tunnels
```

Note:

The show vpdn *command is the combination of the* show vpdn session *and* show vpdn tunnel *command.*

8.9 Troubleshooting L2TP

In this chapter, we've looked at using a Cisco router as a L2TP server. Looking at the configurations of two L2TP peers can be a difficult task at times. Because of this, it may make more sense to approach troubleshooting from the perspective of seeing how the protocol works. L2TP first creates a tunnel between two L2TP peers, at which point it then establishes a user session within the L2TP tunnel. This means we have multiple places that authentication can fail as well as unique paradigms in which routing can work.

When experiencing problems with L2TP, it may be difficult to know where to start. However, most problems can be broken down into one of three areas:

- IP/L2TP connectivity (LNS and LAC)
- L2TP tunnel setup (LAC and LNS)
- User connection (L2TP user and LNS)

By breaking down the problem into logical components, we can quickly identify where the trouble may exist.

8.9.1 IP/L2TP Connectivity (LNS and LAC)

Do the LNS and LAC have IP connectivity to each other, or more specifically, can they communicate using TCP/UDP port 1701? This is the most basic problem that needs to be resolved. Whereas this may seem to be a trivial task, putting your LNS behind a firewall can make this a difficult task, especially if the firewall is filtering ICMP echos. If your LNS is behind a firewall and you are wondering about connectivity between your two L2TP peers, ask your firewall team if they will temporarily allow ICMP echo. Usually, those who manage the firewalls will accommodate this request so they may be removed from the problem. In most cases they won't leave the firewall down for a long period of time, so make sure you conduct your tests quickly.

8.9.2 L2TP Tunnel Setup (LAC and LNS)

In order for the L2TP user and the LNS to authenticate each other, the LAC and LNS must set up an L2TP tunnel between them. Without this tunnel, there is no place for the user's PPP packets to go. Thus, having a L2TP tunnel is critical for the successful operation of L2TP. So what can go wrong with an L2TP tunnel? A number of things can go wrong when a LAC and LNS are setting up an L2TP tunnel:

- Cannot determine a user's LNS
- Misconfigured or unreachable L2TP destination configured on LAC
- Incorrect L2TP hostname configured on LNS
- Authentication fails between LAC and LNS
- VPDN protocol mismatch

Before we have an in-depth discussion regarding what can go wrong with creating an L2TP tunnel, let's look at what a correctly configured L2TP connection looks like.

In line 1 of Figure 8-17, we can see that the *State Machine* (SM) starts in an idle state. Subsequently, an incoming L2TP packet sparks the rest of the output from Figure 8-17. During the creation of this tunnel we can see the standard L2TP messages. Table 8-3 has parsed out these descriptions and line numbers for easier reading.

Now let's look to see what types of things can go wrong during the establishment of an L2TP session.

8.9.2.1 Incorrectly Specify How to Identify a User's LNS

Two methods exist that enable a LAC to determine a user's LNS. We can either use the domain name appended to the user's name, or identify the number that they call into. Identifying the incoming call's DNIS is generally only found within ISDN, so if you are using analog connections, then you will have to have use a domain name appended to the user's name. For example, when dialing into my ISP I generally use the username in my dialup networking script, but if I were dialing into a LAC, I would have to append a domain name to my username so that my username in my dialup networking script would look like **aquiggle@dwyer.com**.

Figure 8-17

Output from
debug vpdn l2x-
events during the
successful
creation of a
L2TP tunnel and
session

```
1  Tnl 15 L2TP: SM State idle
2  Tnl 15 L2TP: O SCCRQ
3  Tnl 15 L2TP: Tunnel state change from idle to wait-ctl-reply
4  Tnl 15 L2TP: SM State wait-ctl-reply
5  Tnl 15 L2TP: I SCCRP from DwyerCorp
6  Tnl 15 L2TP: Got a challenge from remote peer, DwyerCorp
7  Tnl 15 L2TP: Got a response from remote peer, DwyerCorp
8  Tnl 15 L2TP: Tunnel Authentication success
9  Tnl 15 L2TP: Tunnel state change from wait-ctl-reply to
   established
10 Tnl 15 L2TP: O SCCCN to DwyerCorp tnlid 177
11 Tnl 15 L2TP: SM State established
12 Tnl/Cl 15/27 L2TP: Session sequencing disabled
13 Tnl/Cl 15/27 L2TP: Session FS enabled
14 Tnl/Cl 15/27 L2TP: Session state change from idle to wait-for-
   tunnel
15 As1 Tnl/Cl 15/27 L2TP: Create session
16 Tnl 15 L2TP: SM State established
17 As1 Tnl/Cl 15/27 L2TP: O ICRQ to DwyerCorp 177/0
18 As1 Tnl/Cl 15/27 L2TP: Session state change from wait-for-tunnel
   to wait-reply
19 As1 Tnl/Cl 15/27 L2TP: O ICCN to DwyerCorp 177/240
20 As1 Tnl/Cl 15/27 L2TP: Session state change from wait-reply to
   established
21 %LINEPROTO-5-UPDOWN: Line protocol on Interface Async1, changed
   state to up
22 As1 Tnl/Cl 15/27 L2TP: I CDN from DwyerCorp tnl 177, cl 240
   -Traceback= 3B5D286 3B5BA30 3B5F5F4 3B5B470 3B5C07C
```

Table 8-3

Defining the
output from
Figure 8-17

Line	Keyword	Description
2	SCCRQ	The L2TP peer would like to establish an L2TP tunnel
5	SCCRP	The L2TP peer received reply from its L2TP peer
10	SCCN	The L2TP tunnel is established between the L2TP peers
17	ICRQ	The LAC is receiving an incoming call and wants to set up a L2TP session
19	ICCN	The L2TP session has successfully been established

If the domain name is misconfigured or if you are using the incorrect domain name, the LAC will not find a VPDN group to associate with the user. The LAC will then try to authenticate the user locally, which will not be successful. Keep in mind that you can configure multiple domain names within a single VPDN group as seen in Figure 8-18.

Figure 8-18

Multiple domain names configured within a single VPDN group

```
vpdn-group 4
 request-dialin
 protocol l2tp
 domain dwyer.com
 domain quiggle.com
 domain coleman.com
 initiate-to ip 192.168.100.22 limit 155
 local name LargeISP
 l2tp tunnel password 7 121A061E17090311242F
```

8.9.2.2 Misconfigured Tunnel

Although this is a rather easy attribute to resolve, it can be difficult to spot. A misconfigured tunnel can masquerade itself as several different problems. By using the *debug vpdn l2x-events* command, we can quickly determine that we've got a misconfigured tunnel. In Figure 8-19, you will see the connection starts OK (lines 1-4), but at line 5, the LAC needs to resend the *Start Connection Request* (SCCRQ). After three attempts to reach the LNS (lines 2, 5, and 7), the LAC declares the LNS to be unreachable (line 9).

Figure 8-19

Output from debug VPDN l2x-events on an LAC

```
1  Tnl 20 L2TP: SM State idle
2  Tnl 20 L2TP: O SCCRQ
3  Tnl 20 L2TP: Tunnel state change from idle to wait-ctl-reply
4  Tnl 20 L2TP: SM State wait-ctl-reply
5  Tnl 20 L2TP: O Resend SCCRQ, flg TLF, ver 2, len 128, tnl 0, cl
   0, ns 0, nr 0
6  Tnl 20 L2TP: Control channel retransmit delay set to 2 seconds
7  Tnl 20 L2TP: O Resend SCCRQ, flg TLF, ver 2, len 128, tnl 0, cl
   0, ns 0, nr 0
8  Tnl 20 L2TP: Control channel retransmit delay set to 4 seconds
9  %VPDN-5-UNREACH: L2TP LNS 4.4.4.4 is unreachable
10 Tnl 21 L2TP: Control channel retransmit delay set to 8 seconds
11 Tnl 21 L2TP: Shutdown tunnel
12 Tnl 21 L2TP: Tunnel state change from wait-ctl-reply to idle
```

So what can cause this type of behavior? In order to have a correctly configured L2TP tunnel, we must have the following things set properly:

- LAC: Correct destination address of LNS
- IP reachability between LAC and LNS
- LNS: Correct name associated with incoming L2TP session

The most obvious problems are related to basic IP problems. Do we have the right IP address? Do we have two-way communication between our LAC and LNS? At this point, your basic IP troubleshooting skill set should be used to determine the problem which could range from either a routing problem, using the wrong IP address, or simply that the LNS is down.

Another possible problem is that the LNS has an incorrect hostname configured within the VPDN group. When an L2TP tunnel is initiated from a LAC, the LAC must send the LNS a hostname. This hostname is used by the LNS to associate the incoming tunnel with a VPDN group. If the local name is configured incorrectly on the LAC, or the *terminate-from* hostname is configured incorrectly on the LNS, the tunnel will never find a home to terminate the tunnel.

To determine if this is your problem, you should be able to use the *debug vpdn l2x-errors* command on the LNS. In Figure 8-20, we can see that the LNS has never heard the name of the incoming L2TP session.

To resolve this problem, make sure that you put an entry in the correct VPDN group that belongs to that incoming L2TP session. In Figure 8-20, we would have to use the command *local name RouterE* within the appropriate VPDN group.

Figure 8-20

Output from debug vpdn l2x-errors on an LNS

```
L2X: Never heard of RouterE
L2TP: Could not find info block for RouterE
L2X: Never heard of RouterE
L2TP: Could not find info block for RouterE
L2X: Never heard of RouterE
L2TP: Could not find info block for RouterE
```

8.9.2.3 Authentication Fails Between LAC and LNS

Once we've identified the two VPDN groups that will be responsible for the L2TP tunnel (one on the LAC and one on the LNS), the two devices must authenticate each other. This is not user authentication. It is machine authentication, which verifies that the LAC and LNS are communicating with the machine with which they desire to communicate.

Tunnel authentication happens through the use of a shared secret between the two VPDN groups (LAC VPDN group and LNS VPDN group). The *l2tp tunnel password* command within a VPDN group identifies the shared secret to use for an L2TP tunnel.

In Figure 8-21, an unsuccessful tunnel authentication can be shown by using the *debug vpdn l2x-events* command. The most interesting aspect of this authentication failure is found in lines 9 and 10 where we can see what the L2TP peer expected for hash as well as what it received.

Figure 8-21

Output from
debug vpdn
l2x-events
with a tunnel
authentication
failure

```
1   Tnl 22 L2TP: SM State idle
2   Tnl 22 L2TP: O SCCRQ
3   Tnl 22 L2TP: Tunnel state change from idle to wait-ctl-reply
4   Tnl 22 L2TP: SM State wait-ctl-reply
5   Tnl 22 L2TP: I SCCRP from DwyerCorp
6   Tnl 22 L2TP: Got a challenge from remote peer, DwyerCorp
7   Tnl 22 L2TP: Got a response from remote peer, DwyerCorp
8   Tnl 22 L2TP: Tunnel Authentication fails for DwyerCorp
9   Tnl 22 L2TP: Expected 6E817461DDF62B120A80839623A7A88E
10  Tnl 22 L2TP: Got  27CC182D136E1E979AAF4495697BD1FF
11  Tnl 22 L2TP: O StopCCN to DwyerCorp tnlid 182
12  Tnl 22 L2TP: Tunnel state change from wait-ctl-reply to
    shutting-down
13  Tnl 22 L2TP: Shutdown tunnel
14  Tnl 22 L2TP: Tunnel state change from shutting-down to idle
```

8.9.2.4 VPDN Protocol Mismatch

Although this chapter mostly focuses on L2TP, it is possible that in haste or by default, the older L2F protocol is being used by one of the VPDN groups instead of L2TP. Depending upon your IOS, this may not be an issue. This issue can cause trouble for a network engineer because it is often easily overlooked. Using the *show vpdn domain* command, we can display the VPDN protocol that is being used by a particular VPDN group. This is shown in Figure 8-22.

Figure 8-22

Output from
show vpdn
domain

```
Router#show vpdn domain
Tunnel        VPDN Group
------        ----------
domain:dwyer.com 2 (L2F)
```

This may not necessarily alert you to having a problem, but it will help verify the VPDN protocol that is being used for a specific domain name.

8.9.3 User Connection (L2TP User and LNS)

Debugging user connection problems with L2TP is the same problem as troubleshooting a PPP connection on a Cisco access router. We can literally use the same commands for debugging L2TP that we can for PPP. Generally, three areas within a user connection that can cause problems for our L2TP connection are:

- Mismatched authentication protocols
- Incorrect username and password
- Incorrect network layer attributes

8.9.3.1 Mismatched Authentication Protocols

When an L2TP user authenticates against an LNS, standard PPP authentication is actually being performed. Cisco routers can support three different types of PPP authentication protocols: PAP, CHAP, and MS-CHAP. Even though PAP is rarely used because it sends a username and password in clear text, they each have unique ways of providing authentication. This means that an L2TP user, LAC, and LNS must use the same authentication protocol.

Because the LAC must do a partial authentication, the LAC's interface must support the authentication that is being used. Otherwise, it cannot interpret the user's name. Remember it is the user's name that enables the LAC to determine the correct VPDN group (and subsequently, the correct LNS to tunnel the data) to use. You cannot determine which LNS to send the connection to if you haven't at least negotiated which authentication protocol to use.

Note:

This step is not as critical if you are using the DNIS to determine the LNS.

When a connection is initially established, the first attribute negotiated is the authentication protocol that will be used between the L2TP user, the LAC, and the LNS. You should configure all three devices to use a common authentication protocol. It is especially important to use the correct authentication protocol on the LAC, because if it cannot determine which LNS to send the user, the connection will end (this is only applicable if you are using the domain name appended to a username to determine the LNS). A common symptom of this problem occurs when no output is received from the *debug ppp authentication* or *debug ppp negotiation* command on the LNS when trying to dial-in to a LAC.

To see which protocols are being negotiated, we can use either the *debug ppp authentication* or *debug ppp negotiation*. The *debug ppp authentication* command displays a subset of what the *debug ppp negotiation* command would display. However, *debug ppp negotiation* can show you the negotiation of all the protocols and not just the authentication protocols. This can be useful if we are not quite sure from which point to start.

If each device only supports a single authentication protocol during normal PPP negotiations (non-L2TP connection), there really is no negotiation. Either the two devices can authenticate or not. If either device supports multiple authentication protocols, then the two devices will negotiate a common authentication protocol, assuming one exists. However, an interesting thing happens within L2TP connections when there is an authentication protocol mismatch. For example, if the host only supports PAP, the LAC supports PAP, but the LNS only supports CHAP, the LNS will be forced to authenticate using PAP. This is because it is the LAC that actually negotiates the authentication protocol, not the LNS.

In Figure 8-23, we see the LNS requesting (line 5) to use CHAP authentication (line 7). However, we can see that in line 12, the LNS is being forced to use PAP authentication. To keep users from forcing an LNS to authenticate using an authentication protocol that you don't want to support, make sure the LAC doesn't support the authentication protocol. When selecting the authentication protocol using the interface configuration command *PpP authentication*, the first authentication protocol is a

Figure 8-23

Output from
debug PPP
negotiations on a
LNS during
forced
authentication
(output trimmed
for brevity)

```
1   Vi1 PPP: Phase is DOWN, Setup
2   %LINK-3-UPDOWN: Interface Virtual-Access1, changed state to up
3   Vi1 PPP: Treating connection as a dedicated line
4   Vi1 PPP: Phase is ESTABLISHING, Active Open
5   Vi1 LCP: O CONFREQ [Closed] id 1 len 25
6   Vi1 LCP:   ACCM 0x000A0000 (0x0206000A0000)
7   Vi1 LCP:   AuthProto CHAP (0x0305C22305)
8   Vi1 LCP:   MagicNumber 0xEF7E9A79 (0x0506EF7E9A79)
9   Vi1 LCP:   PFC (0x0702)
10  Vi1 LCP:   ACFC (0x0802)
11  Vi1 PPP: Treating connection as a dedicated line
12  Vi1 LCP: I FORCED CONFREQ len 20
13  Vi1 LCP:   ACCM 0x000A0000 (0x0206000A0000)
14  Vi1 LCP:   AuthProto PAP (0x0304C023)
15  Vi1 LCP:   MagicNumber 0x00C9011E (0x050600C9011E)
16  Vi1 LCP:   PFC (0x0702)
17  Vi1 LCP:   ACFC (0x0802)
18  Vi1 PPP: Phase is AUTHENTICATING, by this end
```

device's first choice, and the second authentication protocol is the device's
second choice and so on and so forth.

In Figure 8-24, we can see a host and LAC attempting to negotiate PPP
through the *debug ppp authentication* command.

Lines 4 and 6 show that a request was made to use MS-CHAP by the
LAC. The LAC then received an acknowledgement from the host (line 10
& 12) to use MS-CHAP. In line 17 we can see the two devices starting to
authenticate.

Figure 8-24

Output from
debug PPP
negotiations
between a LAC
and a dialup host
(output trimmed
for authentication
protocol material)

```
1   %LINK-3-UPDOWN: Interface Async1, changed state to up
2   As1 PPP: Treating connection as a dedicated line
3   As1 PPP: Phase is ESTABLISHING, Active Open
4   As1 LCP: O CONFREQ [Closed] id 36 len 25
5   As1 LCP:   ACCM 0x000A0000 (0x0206000A0000)
6   As1 LCP:   AuthProto MS-CHAP (0x0305C22380)
7   As1 LCP:   MagicNumber 0x00E6024D (0x050600E6024D)
8   As1 LCP:   PFC (0x0702)
9   As1 LCP:   ACFC (0x0802)
10  As1 LCP: I CONFACK [REQsent] id 36 len 25
11  As1 LCP:   ACCM 0x000A0000 (0x0206000A0000)
12  As1 LCP:   AuthProto MS-CHAP (0x0305C22380)
13  As1 LCP:   MagicNumber 0x00E6024D (0x050600E6024D)
14  As1 LCP:   PFC (0x0702)
15  As1 LCP:   ACFC (0x0802)
16  As1 LCP: State is Open
17  As1 PPP: Phase is AUTHENTICATING, by this end
```

8.9.3.2 Incorrect Username and Password

Once we have determined that all of the devices involved support the authentication protocol, we still need to make sure the correct username and password are being used. Using the same *debug ppp negotiations* command, we can tell if a username and password combination are being rejected. When attempting to see if an authentication was successful, we need to run the *debug ppp negotiations* command on the LNS as demonstrated in Figure 8-25.

Figure 8-25

Output from debug PPP negotiations between a LAC and a dialup host (output trimmed for authentication success material)

```
1 Vi1 PPP: Phase is AUTHENTICATING, by this end
2 Vi1 MS-CHAP: O CHALLENGE id 6 len 21 from "RouterC "
3 Vi1 MS-CHAP: I RESPONSE id 6 len 67 from "meg@dwyer.com"
4 Vi1 MS-CHAP: O SUCCESS id 6 len 4
5 Vi1 PPP: Phase is UP
```

In line 4 of Figure 8-25, we can see that the authentication was successful using MS-CHAP authentication. However, in lines 4 and 5 of Figure 8-26, we see that the user used incorrect passwords and thus authentication failed.

Figure 8-26

Output from debug PPP negotiations between a LAC and a dialup host (output trimmed for authentication failure material)

```
1 Vi1 PPP: Phase is AUTHENTICATING, by this end
2 Vi1 MS-CHAP: O CHALLENGE id 12 len 21 from "RouterC "
3 Vi1 MS-CHAP: I RESPONSE id 12 len 67 from "meg@dwyer.com"
4 Vi1 MS-CHAP: O FAILURE id 12 len 25 msg is "MD/DES compare
  failed"
5 %VPDN-6-AUTHENFAIL: L2F HGW DwyerCorp, authentication failure for
  Vi1 user meg@dwyer.com; MD/DES compare failed
6 Vi1 PPP: Phase is TERMINATING
```

If we use the *debug ppp negotiations* on the LAC instead of the LNS, we will see the name of the user, but there will be no details about the success or failure of the authentication. We should be able to know this by whether the connection is established or rejected, but a connection could easily have passed authentication only to be rejected by some other PPP attribute. In Figure 8-27, we can see the user name that is forwarded from the LAC to the LNS.

Figure 8-27

Output from debug PPP negotiations between a LAC and a dialup host (output trimmed for success/failure of the username material)

```
As1 PPP: Phase is AUTHENTICATING, by this end
As1 CHAP: O CHALLENGE id 6 len 21 from "RouterA "
As1 CHAP: I RESPONSE id 6 len 67 from "meg@dwyer.com"
As1 PPP: Phase is FORWARDING
```

8.9.3.3 Incorrect Network Layer Attributes

At times, it may be difficult to understand what attributes are being negotiated by the host and the LNS. Without a correctly configured IP address, DNS, WINS, and an IPX network number, our host may be able to dial in, but they won't be able to do anything useful. We can use the debug PPP negotiation command to find out what attributes are being negotiated.

In line 5 of Figure 8-28, we can see that the host said it had no preconfigured IP address. The IP address 172.16.20.10 was attained by the LNS in line 10 from its predefined pool of addresses. The LNS then offered the host both an IP address (line 22), a primary DNS (line 23), and a primary WINS server (line 24). By seeing what IP attributes exist in complex environments, the life of a network engineer's job becomes easier, because we know what is being offered.

Note:

All of the output from Figures 8-23 through 8-28 were generated using the same debug command. However, in order to display the material in a more readable fashion, we have cut and pasted the pertinent lines together so you can stick to a thread and see what happens. In reality, all of the output will be intertwined and difficult to read. I would recommend copying the output to a clipboard, pasting it to the word processor, and then cutting it up looking for the pertinent material. There was always a common header used through the debug output in each instance of the figures as displayed. For example, in Figure 8-24, we can see As1 LCP is the common header. In Figure 8-25, Vi1 MS-CHAP is the common header.

Figure 8-28

Output from
debug PPP
negotiations
between a LNS
and a dialup host
(output trimmed
for IP negotiation
material)

```
 1  Vi1 IPCP: O CONFREQ [Closed] id 1 len 10
 2  Vi1 IPCP:   Address 172.16.20.1 (0x0306AC101401)
 3  Vi1 IPCP: I CONFREQ [REQsent] id 8 len 40
 4  Vi1 IPCP:   CompressType VJ 15 slots CompressSlotID
    (0x0206002D0F01)
 5  Vi1 IPCP:   Address 0.0.0.0 (0x030600000000)
 6  Vi1 IPCP:   PrimaryDNS 0.0.0.0 (0x810600000000)
 7  Vi1 IPCP:   PrimaryWINS 0.0.0.0 (0x820600000000)
 8  Vi1 IPCP:   SecondaryDNS 0.0.0.0 (0x830600000000)
 9  Vi1 IPCP:   SecondaryWINS 0.0.0.0 (0x840600000000)
10  Vi1 IPCP: Pool returned 172.16.20.10
11  Vi1 IPCP: O CONFREJ [REQsent] id 8 len 22
12  Vi1 IPCP:   CompressType VJ 15 slots CompressSlotID
    (0x0206002D0F01)
13  Vi1 IPCP:   SecondaryDNS 0.0.0.0 (0x830600000000)
14  Vi1 IPCP:   SecondaryWINS 0.0.0.0 (0x840600000000)
15  Vi1 IPCP: I CONFACK [REQsent] id 1 len 10
16  Vi1 IPCP:   Address 172.16.20.1 (0x0306AC101401)
17  Vi1 IPCP: I CONFREQ [ACKrcvd] id 10 len 22
18  Vi1 IPCP:   Address 0.0.0.0 (0x030600000000)
19  Vi1 IPCP:   PrimaryDNS 0.0.0.0 (0x810600000000)
20  Vi1 IPCP:   PrimaryWINS 0.0.0.0 (0x820600000000)
21  Vi1 IPCP: O CONFNAK [ACKrcvd] id 10 len 22
22  Vi1 IPCP:   Address 172.16.20.10 (0x0306AC10140A)
23  Vi1 IPCP:   PrimaryDNS 192.168.24.42 (0x8106C0A8182A)
24  Vi1 IPCP:   PrimaryWINS 192.168.67.22 (0x8206C0A84316)
25  Vi1 IPCP: I CONFREQ [ACKrcvd] id 11 len 22
26  Vi1 IPCP:   Address 172.16.20.10 (0x0306AC10140A)
27  Vi1 IPCP:   PrimaryDNS 192.168.24.42 (0x8106C0A8182A)
28  Vi1 IPCP:   PrimaryWINS 192.168.67.22 (0x8206C0A84316)
29  Vi1 IPCP: O CONFACK [ACKrcvd] id 11 len 22
30  Vi1 IPCP:   Address 172.16.20.10 (0x0306AC10140A)
31  Vi1 IPCP:   PrimaryDNS 192.168.24.42 (0x8106C0A8182A)
32  Vi1 IPCP:   PrimaryWINS 192.168.67.22 (0x8206C0A84316)
33  Vi1 IPCP: State is Open
34  Vi1 IPCP: Install route to 172.16.20.10
35  %LINEPROTO-5-UPDOWN: Line protocol on Interface Virtual-Access1,
    changed state to up
36  Vi1 LCP: TIMEout: State Open
```

8.10 Case Studies

This section is one of the most important parts of any hands-on book. We
have shown you how to configure a router to participate in a VPN, but how
do we take a technical problem and solve it with a VPN? In each of the
three case studies to follow, we will explain five following things before
moving to configuration specific information.

1. VPN Type

2. Tunnel Type

3. When to deploy

4. Verifying our VPN

5. VPN Configurations

8.10.1 Case Study #1 - Compulsory L2TP Dial-In

VPN Type: Remote Access/Intranet VPN

Tunnel Type: Compulsory Tunnel

When to deploy: To give dial in users access to IPX based servers using an outsourced ISP.

Verifying VPN has been enabled: Remote workstation can login to NetWare server.

Note:

All links are considered to have a subnet mask of 255.255.255.0 unless otherwise specified.

Figure 8-29

Compulsory L2TP dial-in

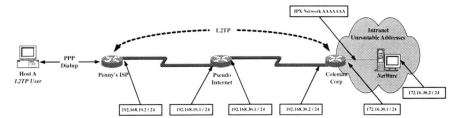

Note:

It is assumed that the reader can configure the backbone reader for simple IP address assignments and OSPF routing. If you need help, you can use the Backbone Router Configuration File from the 1st case study for guidance found in Chapter 5, GRE Tunnels with CET Encryption.

8.10.1.1 Penny's ISP Router Configuration File (LAC)

Figure 8-30

Penny's ISP
configuration file
for Case Study #1
in Chapter 8

```
1   version 12.0
2   service timestamps debug uptime
3   service timestamps log uptime
4   no service password-encryption
5   !
6   hostname PennysISP
7   !
8   enable secret 5 $1$Bsij$RL0c2HVo1na2m1GvVTT60/
9   !
10  ip subnet-zero
11  !
12  vpdn enable
13  !
14  vpdn-group 10
15  request-dialin
16   protocol l2tp
17   domain coleman.com
18  initiate-to ip 3.3.3.3
19  local name PennysISP
20  l2tp tunnel password 0 tunnelpassword
21  !
22  interface Loopback0
23  ip address 1.1.1.1 255.255.255.255
24  no ip directed-broadcast
25  !
26  interface Ethernet0
27  no ip address
28  no ip directed-broadcast
29  no ip route-cache
30  no ip mroute-cache
31  shutdown
32  !
33  interface Serial0
34  ip address 192.168.10.2 255.255.255.0
35  no ip directed-broadcast
36  no ip route-cache
37  no ip mroute-cache
38  no fair-queue
39  !
40  interface Serial1
41  no ip address
42  no ip directed-broadcast
43  no ip route-cache
44  no ip mroute-cache
45  shutdown
46  no fair-queue
47  !
48  interface Async1
49  no ip address
50  no ip directed-broadcast
51  encapsulation ppp
52  async mode interactive
53  peer default ip address pool default
54  ppp authentication ms-chap chap pap
```

Figure 8-30

Penny's ISP
Configuration file
for Case Study #1
in Chapter 8
(cont.)

```
55 !
56 router ospf 10
57 network 1.1.1.1 0.0.0.0 area 0
58 network 192.168.10.0 0.0.0.255 area 0
59 !
60 ip classless
61 !
62 line con 0
63 exec-timeout 0 0
64 transport input none
65 line aux 0
66 no exec
67 no motd-banner
68 no exec-banner
69 autoselect ppp
70 modem Dialin
71 modem autoconfigure type usr_sportster
72 transport input all
73 stopbits 1
74 speed 38400
75 flowcontrol hardware
76 line vty 0 4
77 login
78 !
79 end
```

8.10.1.2 Coleman's Corp Configuration File (LNS Router)

Figure 8-32

Coleman Corp
Configuration file
for Case Study #1
in Chapter 8

```
80  version 12.0
81  service timestamps debug uptime
82  service timestamps log uptime
83  no service password-encryption
84  !
85  hostname ColemanL2TP
86  !
87  enable secret 5 $1$f3N0$sw3ma37RCyNAWvY1Hs62h/
88  !
89  username rick@coleman.com password 0 holly
90  username bev@coleman.com password 0 kitten
91  !
92  ip subnet-zero
93  !
94  vpdn enable
95  !
96  vpdn-group 2
97  accept-dialin
98  protocol l2tp
99  virtual-template 1
100 terminate-from hostname PennysISP
101 local name ColemanCorp
102 l2tp tunnel password 0 tunnelpassword
103 !
104 ipx routing 00e0.1e3e.8476
```

Figure 8-32

Coleman Corp
Configuration file
for Case Study #1
in Chapter 8
(cont.)

```
105 async-bootp dns-server 172.16.20.21
106 async-bootp nbns-server 172.16.20.22
107 !
108 interface Loopback0
109 ip address 3.3.3.3 255.255.255.255
110 no ip directed-broadcast
111 !
112 interface Loopback1
113 ip address 172.16.20.1 255.255.255.0
114 no ip directed-broadcast
115 ipx network BBBBBBBB
116 !
117 interface Ethernet0
118 ip address 172.16.30.1 255.255.255.0
119 no ip directed-broadcast
120 no ip route-cache
121 no ip mroute-cache
122 ipx network AAAAAAAA encapsulation SAP
123 !
124 interface Virtual-Template1
125 ip unnumbered Loopback1
126 no ip directed-broadcast
127 ipx ppp-client Loopback1
128 peer default ip address pool VPDN-pool
129 ppp authentication chap pap ms-chap
130 !
131 interface Serial0
132 ip address 192.168.30.2 255.255.255.0
133 no ip directed-broadcast
134 no ip route-cache
135 no ip mroute-cache
136 no fair-queue
137 !
138 interface Serial1
139 no ip address
140 no ip directed-broadcast
141 shutdown
142 !
143 router ospf 10
144 network 3.3.3.3 0.0.0.0 area 0
145 network 192.168.30.0 0.0.0.255 area 0
146 !
147 ip local pool VPDN-pool 172.16.20.10 172.16.20.100
148 ip classless
149 no ip http server
150 !
151 line con 0
152 exec-timeout 0 0
153 transport input none
154 line aux 0
155 line vty 0 4
156 exec-timeout 0 0
157 password cisco
158 login
159 !
160 end
```

Figure 8-33

Show IP route
from Penny's ISP
for Case Study #1
in Chapter 8

```
PennysISP#show ip route
Codes: C - connected, S - static, I - IGRP, R - RIP, M - mobile, B
 - BGP
    D - EIGRP, EX - EIGRP external, O - OSPF, IA - OSPF inter area
    N1 - OSPF NSSA external type 1, N2 - OSPF NSSA external type 2
    E1 - OSPF external type 1, E2 - OSPF external type 2, E - EGP
    i - IS-IS, L1 - IS-IS level-1, L2 - IS-IS level-2, ia - IS-IS
    inter area
    * - candidate default, U - per-user static route, o - ODR
    P - periodic downloaded static route

Gateway of last resort is not set

     1.0.0.0/32 is subnetted, 1 subnets
C       1.1.1.1 is directly connected, Loopback0
     2.0.0.0/32 is subnetted, 1 subnets
O       2.2.2.2 [110/1850] via 192.168.10.1, 00:00:07, Serial0
     3.0.0.0/32 is subnetted, 1 subnets
O       3.3.3.3 [110/1850] via 192.168.10.1, 00:00:07, Serial0
O    192.168.30.0/24 [110/1849] via 192.168.10.1, 00:00:07, Serial0
     4.0.0.0/32 is subnetted, 1 subnets
O       4.4.4.4 [110/1850] via 192.168.10.1, 00:00:07, Serial0
O    192.168.110.0/24 [110/1859] via 192.168.10.1, 00:00:07, Serial0
C    192.168.10.0/24 is directly connected, Serial0
O    192.168.40.0/24 [110/1849] via 192.168.10.1, 00:00:07, Serial0
     6.0.0.0/32 is subnetted, 1 subnets
O       6.6.6.6 [110/65] via 192.168.10.1, 00:00:07, Serial0
O    192.168.20.0/24 [110/1849] via 192.168.10.1, 00:00:07, Serial0
O    192.168.2.0/24 [110/1859] via 192.168.10.1, 00:00:07, Serial0
```

8.10.1.3 Case Study Analysis

In this case study, we have shown you how to configure a L2TP LAC, and
L2TP LNS. In addition, when we study this particular case, we shall look
at two interesting things.

First, the dialup host can login to the Netware server running IPX in
the Coleman Intranet even though none of the other routers are configured to support IPX. Notice that in lines 124 through 129, we do not configure an IPX network number in the virtual interface. Instead, we have
to configure the IPX network number in the loopback 1 interface and then
associate that loopback interface with the virtual template interface. This
is exactly how it is done using normal PPP dialup. Remember that all of
the commands and idiosyncrasies that apply to PPP dialup also apply to
L2TP.

One other interesting feature of this case study (along the lines of tunneling the IPX traffic), is that we have given our dialup user an IP address

that is not routable behind the Coleman Intranet. This is perfectly acceptable because the Coleman router knows how to get to the unroutable 172.16.20.0/24 addresses even though Penny's ISP router has no path to that network, as seen in Figure 8-33. This is because the PPP packet is tunneled to the Coleman router where the PPP headers are stripped off and the packet is acted upon.

As we look at the basics of the L2TP configuration, we should note that in line 20 and 102, the shared password is being used to authenticate the L2TP tunnel. We could have used usernames and passwords to authenticate the tunnel, but using a shared password is much easier.

In order for the LAC to know which LNS to send packets to, a user must login with a domain name of coleman.com (line 17). When we look at the LNS the only two valid users are Rick and Bev (lines 89 and 90). Whereas knowing the domain name of the dial-in user was important for the LAC to find the VPDN group, the LNS must also know the local name of the LAC so that it may associate the dial-in user to a VPDN group (lines 19 and 100).

The advantage of this configuration is that we can keep our Intranet private while giving access to remote users through a public facility without the need for a either a firewall or fancy access lists that restrict traffic. Whereas this configuration isn't hacker proof, it certainly goes a long way from keeping out unwanted Internet users.

8.10.2 Case Study #2 - Compulsory L2TP Dial-In through NAT

VPN Type: Remote Access/Intranet VPN
Tunnel Type: Compulsory Tunnel
When to deploy: When network engineers are concerned about attacks on the corporate network.
Verifying VPN has been enabled: Remote workstation can ping Web server.

Note:
All links are considered to have a subnet mask of 255.255.255.0 unless otherwise specified.

Figure 8-34

Case Study #2—
Access a
departmental
intranet

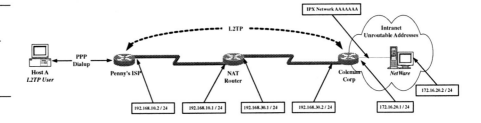

8.10.2.1 Penny's ISP Configuration file (LAC)

Figure 8-35

Penny's ISP
Configuration file
for Case Study #2
in Chapter 9

```
1   version 12.0
2   service timestamps debug uptime
3   service timestamps log uptime
4   no service password-encryption
5   !
6   hostname PennysISP
7   !
8   enable secret 5 $1$Bsij$RL0c2HVo1na2m1GvVTT60/
9   !
10  vpdn enable
11  !
12  vpdn-group 10
13  request-dialin
14   protocol l2tp
15   domain colemanresearch.com
16  initiate-to ip 192.168.20.2
17  local name PennysISP
18  l2tp tunnel password 7 044F1E080124405E080A16001D1908
19  !
20  interface Ethernet0
21  no ip address
22  shutdown
23  !
24  interface Serial0
25  ip address 192.168.10.2 255.255.255.0
26  no ip directed-broadcast
27  no ip route-cache
28  no ip mroute-cache
29  no fair-queue
30  !
31  interface Serial1
32  no ip address
33  shutdown
34  !
35  interface Async1
36  no ip address
37  no ip directed-broadcast
```

Figure 8-35

Penny's ISP
Configuration file
for Case Study #2
in Chapter 9
(cont.)

```
38 encapsulation ppp
39 async mode interactive
40 peer default ip address pool default
41 ppp authentication ms-chap chap pap
42 !
43 ip classless
44 ip route 192.168.20.0 255.255.255.0 192.168.10.1
45 no ip http server
46 !
47 line con 0
48 exec-timeout 0 0
49 transport input none
50 line aux 0
51 no exec
52 no motd-banner
53 no exec-banner
54 autoselect ppp
55 modem Dialin
56 modem autoconfigure type usr_sportster
57 transport input all
58 stopbits 1
59 speed 38400
60 flowcontrol hardware
61 line vty 0 4
62 login
63 !
64 end
```

8.10.2.2 ColemanResearch Configuration file (LNS)

Figure 8-36

ColemanResearch
Configuration file
for Case Study #2
in Chapter 9

```
65 !
66 version 12.0
67 service timestamps debug uptime
68 service timestamps log uptime
69 no service password-encryption
70 !
71 hostname ColemanResearch
72 !
73 enable secret 5 $1$f3N0$sw3ma37RCyNAWvY1Hs62h/
74 !
75 username bev@colemanresearch.com password 0 nettik
76 username rick@colemanresearch.com password 0 remmib
77 !
78 ip subnet-zero
79 !
80 vpdn enable
81 !
82 vpdn-group 2
83  accept-dialin
84  protocol l2tp
85  virtual-template 1
86  terminate-from hostname PennysISP
```

Figure 8-36

ColemanResearch
configuration file
for Case Study #2
in Chapter 9
(cont.)

```
87  local name ColemanResearch
88  l2tp tunnel password 7 105A1C170B121E1B0D17393C2B3A37
89  !
90  async-bootp dns-server 172.16.20.21
91  async-bootp nbns-server 172.16.20.22
92  !
93  interface Loopback1
94  ip address 172.16.20.1 255.255.255.0
95  no ip directed-broadcast
96  !
97  interface Ethernet0
98  ip address 172.16.30.1 255.255.255.0
99  no ip directed-broadcast
100 no ip route-cache
101 no ip mroute-cache
102 !
103 interface Virtual-Template1
104 ip unnumbered Loopback1
105 no ip directed-broadcast
106 peer default ip address pool VPDN-pool
107 ppp authentication chap ms-chap
108 !
109 interface Serial0
110 ip address 10.10.30.2 255.255.255.0
111 no ip directed-broadcast
112 no ip route-cache
113 no ip mroute-cache
114 no fair-queue
115 !
116 interface Serial1
117 no ip address
118 shutdown
119 !
120 ip local pool VPDN-pool 172.16.20.10 172.16.20.100
121 ip classless
122 ip route 0.0.0.0 0.0.0.0 10.10.30.1
123 !
124 line con 0
125 exec-timeout 0 0
126 transport input none
127 line aux 0
128 line vty 0 4
129 exec-timeout 0 0
130 password cisco
131 login
132 !
133 end
```

8.10.2.3 ColemanNat Configuration file

Figure 8-37

ColemanNat
configuration file
for Case Study #2
in Chapter 9

```
134 !
135 version 12.0
136 service timestamps debug uptime
137 service timestamps log uptime
138 no service password-encryption
139 !
140 hostname ColemanNatRtr
141 !
142 ip subnet-zero
143 !
144 interface Ethernet0
145 no ip address
146 no ip directed-broadcast
147 shutdown
148 !
149 interface Serial0
150 ip address 10.10.30.1 255.255.255.0
151 no ip directed-broadcast
152 ip nat inside
153 clockrate 2000000
154 !
155 interface Serial1
156 ip address 192.168.10.1 255.255.255.0
157 no ip directed-broadcast
158 ip nat outside
159 clockrate 2000000
160 !
161 ip nat pool OutsidePool 192.168.20.10 192.168.20.100 netmask
255.255.255.0
162 ip nat inside source list 1 pool OutsidePool
163 ip nat inside source static 10.10.30.2 192.168.20.2
164 ip classless
165 no ip http server
166 !
167 access-list 1 permit 10.10.30.0 0.0.0.255
168 !
169 !
170 line con 0
171 exec-timeout 0 0
172 transport input none
173 line aux 0
174 line vty 0 4
175 !
176 end
```

8.10.2.4 Case Study Analysis

This case study is slightly modified from the first case study. The interesting thing to note here is that we have now inserted a NAT router between the LAC and the LNS. L2TP can operate through a NAT translation with no problems.

If we look at the Figure 8-31, we now see that anyone outside of the NAT router will have a very difficult time getting to the Intranet web server. Two security components are in affect here. First, none of the routing tables have any information about the Colemanresearch network. In addition, the hosts on the outside of the NAT router cannot get through the NAT router without a preexisting translation. This makes the task of getting to the Research network a much more difficult task. Once NAT was set up, the one thing left to do in order to to enable our L2TP VPN work; was to add a static mapping for the LNS (line 164). Without the static mapping outside hosts, specifically the LAC, would not be able to contact the LNS because of the dynamic nature of NAT.

Notice that in our LAC that the async interface accepts PAP, CHAP and, MS-CHAP (line 41), whereas the LNS only supports CHAP and MS-CHAP (line107). If an L2TP client dials whose only authentication protocol is PAP, they can legitimately negotiate PAP authentication with the LAC, but force the LNS to use PAP authentication even though line 107 has specifically excluded it. To keep this from happening, it is important to only allow the authentication protocols you want to use on the LAC.

8.10.3 Case Study #3 - Compulsory L2TP Tunnel using IPSec

VPN Type: Remote Access/Intranet VPN
Tunnel Type: Compulsory Tunnel
When to deploy: This type of tunnel is useful within an enterprise network when the core network is only routing IP and you need to run IPX between the various sites. In many situations, a department within an Enterprise may be unable to access the corporate network routers, which can be very limiting.
Verifying VPN has been enabled: Remote workstation can login to NetWare server.

Note:

All links are considered to have a subnet mask of 255.255.255.0 unless otherwise specified.

Figure 8-38

Case Study #1—
Access a
departmental
Intranet

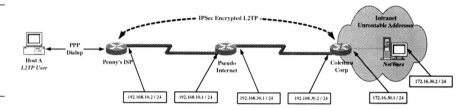

Note:

It is assumed that the reader can configure the backbone reader for simple IP address assignments and OSPF routing. If you need help, you can use the Backbone Router Configuration File found in Chapter 5, GRE with CET, which describes the 1st case study for guidance.

8.10.3.1 Penny's ISP Router Configuration File (LAC)

Figure 8-39

Penny's ISP
configuration file
for Case Study #3
in Chapter 9

```
1   version 12.0
2   service timestamps debug uptime
3   service timestamps log uptime
4   no service password-encryption
5   !
6   hostname PennysISP
7   !
8   enable secret 5 $1$Bsij$RL0c2HVo1na2m1GvVTT60/
9   !
10  vpdn enable
11  !
12  vpdn-group 10
13  request-dialin
14   protocol l2tp
15   domain coleman.com
16  initiate-to ip 192.168.30.2
17  local name PennysISP
18  l2tp tunnel password 7 044F1E080124405E080A16001D1908
```

Figure 8-39

Penny's ISP
configuration file
for Case Study #3
in Chapter 9
(cont.)

```
19 !
20 crypto isakmp policy 1
21 authentication pre-share
22 crypto isakmp key ColemanCorp address 192.168.30.2
23 !
24 crypto ipsec transform-set Dakota esp-des esp-md5-hmac
25 !
26 !
27 crypto map ColemanVPDN 10 ipsec-isakmp
28 set peer 192.168.30.2
29 set transform-set Dakota
30 match address 101
31 !
32 interface Loopback0
33 ip address 1.1.1.1 255.255.255.255
34 no ip directed-broadcast
35 !
36 interface Ethernet0
37 no ip address
38 shutdown
39 !
40 interface Serial0
41 ip address 192.168.10.2 255.255.255.0
42 no ip directed-broadcast
43 no ip route-cache
44 no ip mroute-cache
45 no fair-queue
46 crypto map ColemanVPDN
47 !
48 interface Serial1
49 no ip address
50 shutdown
51 !
52 interface Async1
53 no ip address
54 no ip directed-broadcast
55 encapsulation ppp
56 async mode interactive
57 peer default ip address pool default
58 ppp authentication ms-chap chap pap
59 !
60 router ospf 10
61 network 1.1.1.1 0.0.0.0 area 0
62 network 192.168.10.0 0.0.0.255 area 0
63 !
64 ip classless
65 no ip http server
66 !
67 access-list 101 permit ip host 192.168.10.2 host 192.168.30.2
68 !
69 line con 0
70 exec-timeout 0 0
71 transport input none
72 line aux 0
73 no exec
74 no motd-banner
75 no exec-banner
76 autoselect ppp
```

Figure 8-39

Penny's ISP
configuration file
for Case Study #3
in Chapter 9
(cont.)

```
77 modem Dialin
78 modem autoconfigure type usr_sportster
79 transport input all
80 stopbits 1
81 speed 38400
82 flowcontrol hardware
83 line vty 0 4
84 login
85 !
86 end
```

8.10.3.2 Coleman's Corp Configuration File (LNS)

Figure 8-40

Coleman
Corporation
configuration file
for Case Study #3
in Chapter 9

```
87  version 12.0
88  service timestamps debug uptime
89  service timestamps log uptime
90  no service password-encryption
91  !
92  hostname ColemanCorp
93  !
94  enable secret 5 $1$f3N0$sw3ma37RCyNAWvY1Hs62h/
95  !
96  username rick@coleman.com password 0 remmib
97  username bev@coleman.com password 0 nettik
98  !
99  vpdn enable
100 !
101 vpdn-group 2
102 accept-dialin
103  protocol l2tp
104  virtual-template 1
105 terminate-from hostname PennysISP
106 local name Coleman
107 l2tp tunnel password 7 105A1C170B121E1B0D17393C2B3A37
108 !
109 async-bootp dns-server 172.16.20.21
110 async-bootp nbns-server 172.16.20.22
111 !
112 crypto isakmp policy 1
113 authentication pre-share
114 crypto isakmp key ColemanCorp address 192.168.10.2
115 !
116 crypto ipsec transform-set Sierra esp-des esp-md5-hmac
117 !
118 crypto map ColemanVPDN 10 ipsec-isakmp
119 set peer 192.168.10.2
120 set transform-set Sierra
121 match address 101
122 !
123 interface Loopback0
124 ip address 3.3.3.3 255.255.255.255
125 no ip directed-broadcast
```

Figure 8-40

Coleman
Corporation
Configuration file
for Case Study #3
in Chapter 9
(cont.)

```
126 !
127 interface Loopback1
128 ip address 172.16.20.1 255.255.255.0
129 no ip directed-broadcast
130 !
131 interface Ethernet0
132 ip address 172.16.30.1 255.255.255.0
133 no ip directed-broadcast
134 no ip route-cache
135 no ip mroute-cache
136 !
137 interface Virtual-Template1
138 ip unnumbered Loopback1
139 no ip directed-broadcast
140 peer default ip address pool VPDN-pool
141 ppp authentication chap pap ms-chap
142 !
143 interface Serial0
144 ip address 192.168.30.2 255.255.255.0
145 no ip directed-broadcast
146 no ip route-cache
147 no ip mroute-cache
148 crypto map ColemanVPDN
149 !
150 interface Serial1
151 no ip address
152 shutdown
153 !
154 router ospf 10
155 network 3.3.3.3 0.0.0.0 area 0
156 network 192.168.30.0 0.0.0.255 area 0
157 !
158 ip local pool VPDN-pool 172.16.20.10 172.16.20.100
159 ip classless
160 no ip http server
161 !
162 access-list 101 permit ip host 192.168.30.2 host 192.168.10.2
163 !
164 !
165 line con 0
166 exec-timeout 0 0
167 transport input none
168 line aux 0
169 line vty 0 4
170 exec-timeout 0 0
171 password cisco
172 login
173 !
174 end
```

8.10.3.3 Case Study Analysis

In this case study, we used L2TP to provide the tunnel for our VPN as well as configuring IPSec to be our encryption. In this particular configuration, the VPN can provide multiprotocol support with heavy duty encryption. This can be advantageous because an attacker can not glean anything about our destination network. Encryption makes the PPP headers unavailable. It is important to note thatnothing special was done in order for these two protocols to work together (aside from their normal configurations).

8.11 Summary of L2TP

Table 8-4

Summary of L2TP features

Authentication	User authentication
Multiprotocol Support	Yes
L2TP	1701 TCP/UDP
Data Confidentiality	Yes w/IPSec
Data Integrity	Yes w/IPSec
Data Origin Authentication	Yes w/IPSec
Anti-Replay	Yes
IOS support for L2TP	11.3(5)AA (7200, AS5200, AS5300 and AS5800 only) and 12.0T
What IOS naming convention value supports L2TPs	

Table 8-5

Current RFCs related to L2TP

RFC	Title
2661	Layer Two Tunneling Protocol (L2TP)
2809	Implementation of L2TP Compulsory Tunneling via RADIUS
2867	RADIUS Accounting Modifications for Tunnel Protocol Support
2868	RADIUS Attributes for Tunnel Protocol Support
2888	Secure Remote Access with L2TP

8.12 Command Summary

8.12.1 L2TP IOS Enterprise Commands

Table 8-6

Summary of
L2TP commands

		Enable Virtual Private Dialup Networks
vpdn enable	**Global Config**	
interface virtual-template	Global Config	Create an attribute that virtual access interfaces will be created from
l2tp tunnel password	Vpdn-config	Shared key used for tunnel authentication
local name	VPDN Config Mode	Used by the VPDN device to identify itself to its VPDN peer
terminate-from hostname	VPDN Config Mode	Used by the vpdn-group to indicate the name of LNS to send back to the LAC
initiate-to ip	VPDN Config Mode	Used by the LAC to determine destination of the LNS
domain	VPDN Config Mode	Used by the LAC to determine which vpdn-group to use
request-dialin	VPDN Config Mode	Allow LAC to start incoming L2TP sessions
request-dialout	VPDN Config Mode	Allow LNS to start outgoing L2TP sessions
Accept-dialin	VPDN Config Mode	Allow LNS to accept incoming L2TP sessions
Accept-dialout	VPDN Config Mode	Allow LAC to accept outgoing L2TP sessions
ppp authentication	Interface Config mode	Specify the type of authentication used by the VPN client
vpdn-group	Global Config	Create a VPDN group which supports a VPDN protocol
accept-dialin		Allow incoming connections
protocol L2TP	VPDN Config Mode	Use L2TP within this VPDN group
show vpdn	Enable Mode	Show active VPDN connections

CHAPTER 9

PIX Firewall VPNs

In the last several chapters, we have focused on VPNs that run on Cisco routers. Although Cisco's router makes up the majority of the devices that Cisco has deployed, Cisco also has a significant presence in the firewall market with their PIX firewall. Firewalls, often called network appliances, are an organization's first line of defense against intrusion from attackers. Although firewalls are designed to protect the corporate network from intrusion, they don't necessarily protect our data once it leaves the corporate network; that is the job of the VPN.

Because firewalls generally represent the demarcation between the internal "trusted" network and the external "untrusted" network, it frequently makes sense to have a VPN connection terminate on a firewall instead of through the firewall onto another VPN enabled device, because it could give an attacker another opportunity to exploit a hole in the network. Additionally, a PIX firewall is well suited to terminate a VPN because of its capability to handle large numbers of simultaneous VPNs.

In this chapter, we will cover how to configure a PIX firewall to support IPSec and PPTP. In addition, we will show the reader some of the PIX fundamentals. This chapter should not be regarded as a chapter on configuring PIX firewalls, but as a chapter on how to configure VPNs to terminate on a PIX firewall, as well as learning some of the commands you need to know before you can set up a VPN on a PIX firewall. Because so many different aspects to configuring a PIX firewall exist, we will not go into great detail regarding the finer aspects of PIX firewall configuration. Instead, we will show you the minimum commands that will enable you to set up a PIX firewall in anticipation of a VPN.

9.1 Objectives to Be Covered in this Chapter

- Overview of PIX Firewall
- PIX firewall configuration basics
- Configuring PPTP on a PIX firewall
- Troubleshooting PPTP on a PIX firewall
- Configuring IPSec on a PIX firewall
- Troubleshooting IPSec on a PIX firewall

Note:

Although we aren't going to cover the specifics of the PIX firewall models, one of the more common surprises for those in the market for PIX firewall is the 506. Although this low-end firewall is small and fast, it is not like its modular cousins. It only has two interfaces and can only support four concurrent VPN connections. Keep this in mind when you go shopping for a PIX firewall to meet the needs of your organization.

9.2 Overview of Firewalls

For many years, the only protection that an organization could use to protect its network from the public Internet was a router. A router has many different tools available to control the flow of information between an organization's network and the public Internet.

9.2.1 Stateful Inspection

The most obvious control mechanism is through the use of *Access Control Lists* (ACL). ACLs can restrict traffic based upon three criteria:

- Source IP address
- Destination IP address
- Port number

This basic level of network security can restrict certain traffic from gaining access to the network. However, packets are filtered regardless of their context. Firewalls take this method of control one step further, by monitoring the state of a session.

Embedded within IP packets are several unique identifiers that enable a firewall to monitor each discrete conversation. By keeping track of the source IP address, destination IP address, port numbers, TCP sequencing information, and additional flags for each TCP connection associated with that particular host, a firewall can keep track of who started a conversation and enable the flow of packets based upon who starts the conversation. This is particularly useful if you want your users to access any Internet-based service, but don't want anyone from the Internet to start a conversation with your internal network. Not only can firewalls easily achieve this, but once a conversation is started between an inside peer and an outside peer, a second conversation cannot be started from the outside peer to the inside peer. This is because a firewall can keep track of each discrete conversation by understanding the state of the data stream.

9.2.2 Proxy Server

Proxy servers are another method of protecting an organization's network from the outside world. A proxy server is an application gateway that runs on top of a general-purpose *operating system* (OS) such as Unix or Windows NT. Unlike a router, which operates at Network Layer 3 of the OSI model, proxy servers work at the Application Layer of the OSI model.

These specialized applications work by enabling the user to establish a connection with the proxy server. The user is both authenticated and authorized for a particular session. The proxy server then establishes the connection for the user. This type of session flow is considered to be strong security. As with any alternative, disadvantages occur. For proxy servers two distinct disadvantages exist: performance and security of the proxy server.

A very large cost in performance with proxy servers exists, because each packet must go all the way up the OSI model to be analyzed and then sent back down the OSI model to be put on the network. To overcome these performance problems, powerful UNIX or NT machines are used as proxy servers. Unfortunately, an organization might not be able to fully make use of high-speed Internet connectivity using this architecture.

In addition, a security problem with using proxy servers exists. Because proxy servers utilize general-purpose OSs, they are vulnerable to security holes because these OSs generally focus on being open and enabling interconnectivity. In a proxy server environment, you want the proxy server to be secure. Although it is possible to shut off all the services that would normally be open on a general purpose OS, a considerable number of security holes and bugs are frequently found within these general-purpose OSs.

9.2.3 NAT

Originally designed to help solve address depletion problems, NAT is an integral component within any security paradigm. NAT makes it possible to hide the real IP address of devices on your network as well as the internal infrastructure of your network from possible attackers.

Typically when a host accesses another host located outside its local network, it sends the packet to its router. The router looks at the packet's destination, determines how to route the packet, and forwards it to the next hop according to its routing table. NAT adds an additional step to this process. Instead of forwarding the packet as is, the NAT device will replace the "inside" source IP address with an "outside" source IP address, as shown in Figure 9-1.

The router will then add an entry in its NAT table correlating the "inside" IP address with the "outside" IP address as shown in Table 9-1.

Host B receives the packet with the "outside" source address and thinks the packet came from the "outside" IP address 10.10.10.30 assigned by the NAT device. Host B will then use this "outside" IP address to communicate with Host A for the duration of their conversation. In addition, the NAT device will use that assigned IP address for any other communications with external networks.

In any organization connected to the public Internet, the number of hosts on its network simultaneously communicating with hosts external

Figure 9-1

An IP packet going round trip through a NAT gateway

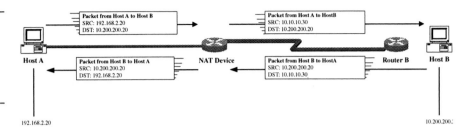

Inside IP Address	Outside IP Address
192.168.2.20	192.168.3.30

Table 9-1

NAT Table for Figure 9-1

to an organization's network is relatively low. NAT, with dynamic mappings, takes advantage of this statistical fact. If we look back at the scenario presented in Figure 9-1, we see that Table 9-1 provides a mapping of the inside addresses to the outside addresses. As time goes on, we will eventually have a table with an entry for every inside host. In order to keep the table as small as possible, we need to delete entries in the NAT table that are no longer being used. If an inside host needs to communicate with an outside host again, a new translation can be mapped.

Although it is generally possible to use a heuristic approach when terminating a session, it can cause problems. For example, if during a TCP session a NAT box detected an acknowledgement by both halves of the session that a FIN was received, it is impossible for a NAT border router to know the acknowledgment has been delivered to the destination (the packet could be dropped between the NAT border router and the destination). This makes discovering the termination of a session difficult at best. In most cases, an assumption is made that any NAT mapping that has not been active for 24 hours can be terminated. However, this is not always the case, because the idle period session timeouts vary from application to application and even within different sessions of the same applications. Therefore, according to RFC 2663, which discusses NAT terminology and considerations, session termination must be configurable. This enables network administrators the ability to adjust the timers as necessary.

Because NAT mappings are dynamic, an attacker would never be able to use the same IP address to get to a device. For those hosts that do not access the Internet, no translations ever get built, and thus always remain hidden from the rest of the Internet. In addition, if an organization were to use a single /24 network for its global NAT translations, it could hide their entire network behind a single network and not enable an attacker to determine the network infrastructure.

9.2.3.1 Port Address Translation (PAT)

Port Address Translation (PAT), frequently known as overloading, is a feature that can greatly reduce the number of public IP addresses required by a network. Normally NAT works by translating a single inside IP address to a single outside IP address (one-to-one mapping). Overloading works by translating multiple inside IP addresses to a single outside IP address (many-to-one mapping). Instead of differentiating the conversations only by IP address, it will use the IP address and the source port. This is why overloading is frequently known as PAT.

9.2.3.2 Public vs.Versus Private IP Addresses

One of the methods typically used in conjunction with NAT is the use of the private IP address space as defined by RFC 1918. In order to understand the concept of private IP addresses, we need to recall one of the basic principles of IP.

By definition, every IP address used on the public Internet is a globally unique address. This is what enables every host to directly address every other host on the public Internet. However, three blocks of IP addresses have been set aside by the IETF for use with private networks:

Class A - 10.0.0.0 - 10.255.255.255 (10/8 prefix)
Class B - 172.16.0.0 - 172.31.255.255 (172.16/12 prefix)
Class C - 192.168.0.0 - 192.168.255.255 (192.168/16 prefix)

These IP addresses are not globally unique; they can be used over and over by any organization. This reuse of IP addresses is possible because these IP addresses are not routed over the public Internet; they are for private networks only.

Combining the benefits of NAT with the private IP addresses makes our network very secure. Because the addresses are translated, an attacker cannot learn our IP address. However, even if they do find out what it is, there is no way for an attacker to get an IP packet to that network because good ISPs will filter the private address space.

Other terms used interchangeably with public IP address and private IP address are found in Table 9-2.

Table 9-2	**Public IP addresses**	**Private IP addresses**
Terms tsed to describe public versus private IP addresses	Globally unique address	Locally unique address
	Registered IP addresses	Unregistered IP addresses

At this point, we still need a valid IP address for each host on our network to connect with the public Internet.

Note:

You have probably noted that we have made extensive use of the private IP address range throughout this book. You should note that it is not necessary to use the private IP address range when setting up any of the features we discuss throughout this book. We use the private IP address range in our examples so you will not accidentally overlap with some "real" IP addresses. Whenever the use of the private IP address range makes sense, we will make sure to clarify those situations.

9.2.3.3 NAT Disadvantages

Once again, with any technology that gives us an advantage, disadvantages are bound to exist. When using NAT on a PIX firewall, two such disadvantages arise:

- Disadvantage 1—Loss of end to end connectivity. Because NAT translates the source and/or destination address of an IP packet, it becomes very difficult to trace data streams when their packet headers have been modified. This introduces another level of complexity when attempting to resolve a problem. However, the correlation to this problem is that it also makes it more difficult, but not impossible, for hackers to determine a packet's source.

- Disadvantage 2—Application may not work correctly. Any application that embeds the IP address inside the upper layer data tends to break when going through NAT. This is because the modified packet header and the IP address inside the upper layer data will be different, and the application may think an error of some sort exists.

PIX firewall NAT has been implemented to overcome this problem. By recognizing these "non-compliant" packets, NAT can break them open and change the IP address embedded in the upper layer. However, this requires NAT to understand the format of the "non-compliant" packet. This means that if NAT does not recognize the packet as one it needs to translate, that protocol will be broken. Listed in Table 9-3 is a sample list of applications that do not work using Cisco NAT and that do work with Cisco NAT.

Table 9-3 Applications that do and do not work with Cisco NAT	Applications that DO NOT work with Cisco NAT	Applications that DO work with Cisco NAT
	Routing table updates	IMCP
	DNS zone transfers	FTP
	Talk, ntalk	DNS Queries
	NetShow	CuSeeMe
	BOOTP	H.323
	SNMP	NetMeeting

9.3 Overview of PIX Firewall

Commercially available since 1994, Cisco's premier product for full firewall protection is the PIX firewall. The PIX firewall incorporates firewall services such as stateful inspection, cut-through proxy-server functionality, and optional hardware accelerated encryption, all in an integrated hardware/software platform. This combination of services rolled into a single device is why Cisco's PIX firewall has proven to be such a success.

9.3.1 Integrated Hardware/Software

By offering a complete hardware and software solution, Cisco eliminates all the potential security holes that can be introduced by using a general purpose OS. Many OSs see quarterly, if not monthly updates to keep your OS free of potential security holes. By eliminating the general-purpose OS from your firewall, you can eliminate the support required for that OS and focus on other aspects of your security solution.

9.3.2 Adaptive Security Algorithm

Cisco's *Adaptive Security Algorithm* (ASA) is a stateful approach to security. Every time a connection is established from an inside host, the PIX firewall logs all of the information about the connection into a session flow table. The table contains:

- Source IP address
- Destination IP address
- Port numbers
- TCP sequencing numbers

Using these values from the data stream between two devices, a PIX firewall creates a connection object. Subsequently, every inbound packet is checked against the ASA connection state table in memory.

All of the information stored in the connection state table is stored in a hashed format. The logic behind keeping the data stored in a hash format is that if a PIX firewall were broken into, an attacker would have to decrypt the data before it would be useful to them.

The default behavior of the ASA can be expressed with following three items:

- All outbound connections are allowed, except for those specifically denied through an access-list and some other mechanism.
- All inbound connections are denied unless a supporting connection and state in the connection table exists.
- All ICMP packets are dropped unless explicitly told to allow them through.

Let's look at Figure 9-2 for an example of what this means. Host A and Host B are both running Web servers.

1. Host A requests a Web page from Host B.
2. The PIX firewall receives the packet, gathers information about the outgoing request, enters it into the table, and forwards the packet onto Host B.
3. Host B receives the HTTP request.
4. Host B generates a response from the request and sends it to Host A.
5. The PIX firewall receives the packet, checks the information within the packet against the connection table, and allows the packet to pass.

Figure 9-2

Example of
stateful
inspection

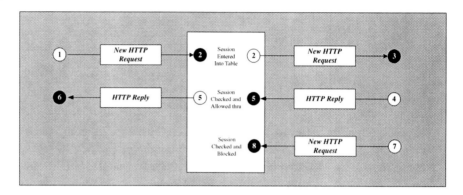

6. Host A receives the HTTP reply.

7. Host B requests a Web page from Host A.

8. The PIX firewall receives the request, checks the information within the packet against the connection table, and blocks the packet.

Notice in Figure 9-2 that all the packets in which the connection was generated from the inside are allowed through the firewall; while those packets that are initiated from the outside network get blocked.

Those familiar with UDP might wonder how a firewall can track UDP sessions because it operates in a so-called connectionless state (that is, no formal handshakes or acknowledgements). UDP filtering works by noting the source IP address, destination IP address, and port of an outbound UDP packet. The PIX firewall then expects a UDP response within a certain timeframe. Expected UDP packets (match a previously outgoing UDP packet) that arrive within the expected time frame are forwarded by the PIX firewall. Any expected UDP packet that arrives after the designated time period will be dropped by the PIX firewall.

9.3.3 Cut-Through Proxy

Cisco's new feature called cut-through proxy enables a Cisco firewall to provide proxy servers that have previously only been available to UNIX-based proxy servers. During an initial request for service, a PIX firewall with cut-through proxy can authenticate the user against a TACACS+ or RADIUS server. Once the policy is checked, the PIX firewall initiates a connection to the destination resource, subsequently monitoring the data flow between the devices.

9.3.4 Integrated VPN Option

In several of Cisco's PIX firewall solutions, you can purchase a plug-in processor card whose sole purpose is for the encryption and decryption of VPN packets. Due to the computationally intensive requirements of performing encryption, especially 3DES, it is often necessary to offload the CPU-intensive calculations to another device, which frees up the main processor for other tasks.

9.3.5 Sequence Number Randomization

Because most TCP/IP implementations use a simple additive algorithm for incrementing sequence numbers, it is very easy for an attacker to predict the next sequence number in a TCP packet, making it a trivial exercise for an attacker to hijack a session. By utilizing a randomizing algorithm for their generation, it makes the process of guessing TCP sequence numbers very complicated.

9.4 PIX Fundamentals

Cisco firewall software is very different than Cisco's IOS. Even those who consider themselves an expert at Cisco's router IOS will find it difficult to get around. You will find that you can do things in Cisco's firewall software that are not possible in Cisco's IOS. However, Cisco's IOS still has a significantly superior user interface, especially for those who are trying to learn the options available within a particular command.

This section, "PIX Fundamentals," is here to discuss the bare minimum commands that will enable a network engineer to configure a VPN on a PIX firewall from scratch. In order to accomplish this task, a reader will learn how to set up the most basic firewall. However, it is not within the scope of this book to teach the reader all of the ins and outs of PIX firewall configuration.

It is expected that anyone reading this guide already has a good understanding of Cisco IOS configurations. Thus, we will compare equivalent Cisco IOS to Cisco PIX firewall commands when appropriate. You do not necessarily have to understand Cisco IOS command structure to understand the commands here, although you will understand the commands a lot quicker if you do.

The commands that you need to know have been broken down into the following groups:

- Administrative commands
- Interface configuration commands
- NAT configuration commands
- Route commands
- Accessing inside host commands

Note:

The commands presented here are only to provide a guide for PIX firewall configuration. Because you could dedicate a whole book to PIX firewall configuration, we will not explore any of the advanced features such as DMZs, access-lists, AAA services, or hardware differences.

9.4.1 Administrative Commands

These commands do not really fall into any specific category, however without them, a PIX administrator's life could be very difficult. Most of these commands are directly from Cisco IOS, but we have included them here for your convenience.

9.4.1.1 Enable Mode

When you first start a PIX firewall, you will be in user mode (assuming no console passwords exist). Just like Cisco's IOS, you must be in enable mode to do anything but the most basic commands. To begin enable mode on a PIX firewall, you will use the same command as you would if you were on a Cisco router:

```
pixfirewall>enable
```

If no enable password set exists, you will still be prompted with a password prompt. Hit <*enter*> and you will then enter enable mode. From here, we run debugs, configure our firewall, or save the firewall configuration.

9.4.1.2 Configuring, Saving, and Erasing a PIX Firewall Configuration

In order to enter configuration mode on a PIX firewall, you need to be in enable mode. The command used to enter configuration mode is as follows:

```
pixfirewall#configure terminal
```

Note:

You can use config t *just like a normal Cisco IOS..*

Once we have configured a router, we probably want to save the configuration. This will enable the PIX firewall to boot up with the same configuration that is currently running. Failure to save a configuration after we have entered a command will enable the PIX firewall to lose the configuration changes if we reboot the firewall or experience a power outage.

```
pixfirewall(config)#write option
```

option		
	memory	Save configuration to NVRAM
	erase	Erase the saved configuration
	floppy	Save the configuration file to floppy disk
	net	Save configuration to a TFTP server

Note:

If you use the net option, you will also have to specify the IP address of the TFTP server as well as the filename being saved.

9.4.1.3 Setting PIX Enabled Mode Passwords

Setting the enable mode passwords requires that a user enter the enable mode password in order to access privileged mode. Very rarely should you ever allow a firewall not to have an enable password. To set the enable password use the following command:

```
pixfirewall(config)#enable password password
```

password   ***WORD***   Password used for enable access

9.4.1.4 Setting up Telnet Access to a PIX Firewall

By default, a PIX firewall will not allow you to telnet to it from any interface. This default behavior is good for those uninitiated with a PIX firewall. However, for more advanced administrators, you will want to have access to the PIX firewall remotely. In order to telnet from an inside interface to a PIX firewall, you must tell it which IP addresses can telnet to it. This is done through the following command for PIX IOS 5.0, 5.1, 5.2, and 5.3:

```
pixfirewall(config)#telnet ip-address net-mask inside
```

ip-address   *x.x.x.x*   Network address allowed to telnet to PIX
net-mask   *x.x.x.x*   Subnet mask used to define which addresses
                                  can telnet to PIX

Notice that you can specify an individual host using a 255.255.255.255 subnet mask; you can also specify an entire network by wisely choosing your subnet mask.

Note:

If you are running PIX software 4.4 or older, you cannot specify an interface; it is just assumed that you will be telneting from an inside interface.

Starting with PIX software 5.0, if you need access through an outside interface, you will have to set up an IPSec tunnel. Remember that when telnet passes all of your data as clear text. This means you could inadvertently pass your PIX configuration across an untrusted network and allow an attacker a view of how your firewall is set up. By setting up an IPSec tunnel, a PIX firewall will enable you to telnet through the encrypted tunnel and modify its configuration. Use the following command to allow access from an outside interface. Remember that just because you set up outside access, it will not work until you set up your IPSec tunnel.

When you telnet to the PIX firewall, it will prompt you for a password even though a password has not been set. The default telnet password for a PIX firewall is *cisco*. You can change the password using the following command:

```
pixfirewall#passwd password
```

password   **WORD**   Password used for telnet access

Do not forget to change to enable mode before trying to change the telnet password. Unlike a Cisco router, it is not necessary to be in configuration mode to set the telnet password.

9.4.2 Interface Configuration Commands

Unlike Cisco IOS, no interface configuration mode exists. All interface configuration commands are done from a global configuration mode. This can be particularly confusing if you are very comfortable with Cisco IOS and attempt to configure an interface on a PIX firewall.

Another point that can be confusing for those familiar with Cisco IOS is the naming of physical interfaces. In a Cisco router, it did not matter if you specified "Ethernet0" or "Ethernet 0" (notice the space between the last t and the zero), IOS parsed it out the same. Cisco PIX software does not take kindly to the extra space between the "t" and the zero. Therefore, make sure you remove that space when indicating a physical interface.

9.4.2.1 Nameif and Security Levels

A PIX firewall requires that all interfaces are named and a security level set before you can configure any other attributes about them. Naming an interface is often an overlooked feature that allows some modularity to a PIX firewall. By naming an interface, we, as network engineers, can better understand and grasp the security model that we are implementing. In addition, by naming an interface, we can easily change which interface does what within our configuration without changing it throughout the entire configuration. So although it might seem like a waste of time to name an interface, they come in very handy when you have to add interfaces and modify which interface does what.

A Cisco PIX firewall addresses inside and outside interfaces using a very flexible methodology. For firewalls with more than two interfaces, this is a very important concept. Because everyone is regarded as suspect, all interfaces are given a security level instead of just being designated as "inside" or "outside." The higher the security level, the more trusted the packets are from that interface. Security levels are PIX's way of determining which packets can go where. Remember that by default, all "inside" initiated conversations are allowed through a firewall; although all "outside" initiated conversations are not allowed through the firewall. By comparing security levels of an interface, you can quickly determine which direction communication can take place.

For example, let's look at Figure 9-3 in which our PIX firewall has three interfaces. Interface Ethernet 0 has a security level of 90 and has the highest security level of all three interfaces. This means that any conversations that are initiated from this interface (Host A) are allowed through Ethernet 1 (Host B) and Ethernet 2 (Host C).

Interface Ethernet 1 has a security level of 50. This means that only conversations initiated to interface Ethernet 2 are allowed through the firewall. If Host B attempts to initiate a connection to Host A, the PIX firewall will drop the packet.

Figure 9-3

Interface security levels defining levels of access

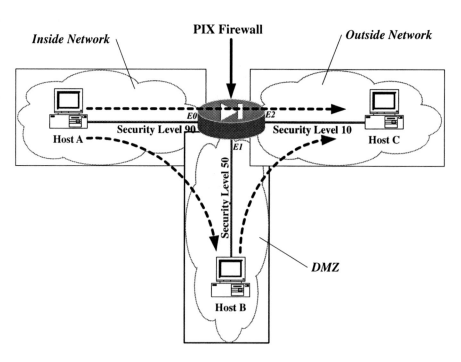

Interface Ethernet 2 has the lowest security level, 10. No conversations originated by Host C will be allowed through the PIX firewall. Either Host A or Host B must start all conversations with Host C.

Note:

If you only have two interfaces, it is then okay to think of the interfaces in terms of "inside" and "outside" interfaces. However, if you ever need to work with a PIX firewall containing more than two interfaces, you will need to be cognizant of security levels.

To name an interface, as well as set its security level, we can use the following command:

```
pixfirewall(config)#nameif interface interface-name security security-level
```

interface	ethernetX	Name this Ethernet interface
	tokenX	Name this Token Ring interface
	FDDIX	Name this FDDI interface
interface-name	WORD	Name used to describe this interface throughout the PIX configuration
security-level	0-100	Set the interface to this security level (high=more trusted)

Note:

If two interfaces are defined with the same security level, they cannot access each other.

9.4.2.2 Shut and No Shut Interface

Shutting down and enabling an interface are fairly easy concepts to understand. However, shutting down an interface is not as straightforward as you might think. To shutdown an interface, use the following command:

```
pixfirewall(config)#interface interface-name shutdown
```

interface name	ethernetX	Name this Ethernet interface
	tokenX	Name this Token Ring interface
	FDDIX	Name this FDDI interface

To enable an interface, you must specify the speed of the interface. This allows Cisco PIX IOS to enable the interface. Use the following command to enable an Ethernet interface:

```
pixfirewall(config)#interface ethernet interface-num hw-speed
```

interface-num	**X**	Number identifying the physical interface
hw-speed	**10baseT**	Set the interface to 10Mb/sec half-duplex
	10full	Set the interface to 100Mb/sec full-duplex
	100baseT	Set the interface to 100Mb/sec half-duplex
	100full	Set the interface to 100Mb/sec full-duplex

Use the following command to enable a tokenring interface:

```
pixfirewall(config)#interface token interface-num hw-speed
```

interface-num	**X**	Number identifying the physical interface
hw-speed	**4mbps**	Set the interface to 4Mb/sec
	16mbps	Set the interface to 16Mb/sec

9.4.2.3 Set IP Address

If an interface is going to participate within the network, an IP address must be assigned to the interface. This can be accomplished using the following command:

```
pixfirewall(config)#ip address interface-name ip-address subnet-mask
```

interface-name	***WORD***	Name used to describe the interface
ip-address	**x.x.x.x**	IP address to assign to interface
subnet-mask	**x.x.x.x**	Subnet mask of the IP network

9.4.3 Route Commands

Just like any device with multiple interfaces, a PIX firewall needs to know what to do with the packets it receives. Any network device with multiple interfaces can learn routes through a statically configured route or dynamically through routing protocols. Although a PIX firewall can participate in RIP networks, it is advisable to use static routes to minimize confusion.

9.4.3.1 Define Static Route

If no routers are on the inside network, then it is not necessary to configure a static route for the inside network because the PIX firewall will already know about its directly connected networks. If routers are there on the inside network, then it is important to configure a static route covering all of the networks that are on the inside network.

When deciding what static routes to set up for your external network, you will, in most instances, want to set up a default route to the outside network so that the PIX firewall knows how to handle any user's packet destined for any remote network. If your intent is to block users from accessing specific networks, then an access-control list might be an easier solution for handling this policy instead of just creating routes to the networks you want your users to use.

To configure a static route on a PIX firewall, use the following command:

```
pixfirewall(config)#route interface-name ip-address subnet-mask
```

interface-name	*WORD*	Name used to describe this interface throughout the PIX configuration
ip-address	*x.x.x.x*	Network address allowed to telnet to PIX
subnet-mask	*x.x.x.x*	Subnet mask used to define which addresses can telnet to PIX

Realize that by configuring static routes for the outside network that are network specific routes and not specifying a default route will cause the PIX firewall to drop packets that it does not know how to get to. Figure 9-4 shows us two route statements that enable a PIX firewall to route the internal address 192.168.0.0/16 to the inside network and any other addresses to the external network.

9.4.4 NAT Configuration Commands

Every PIX firewall is set up to use NAT. Although NAT is considered one of the PIX firewalls security elements, it is by no means necessary to implement it. Although NAT can break certain applications, various

Figure 9-4

Example static
route statements
for a PIX firewall

```
pixfirewall(config)#route outside 0.0.0.0 0.0.0.0 172.16.20.2
pixfirewall(config)#route inside 192.168.0.0 255.255.0.0
192.168.100.2
```

methods can be used to fix those protocols. In order to configure NAT, we
must configure three distinct elements:

- Specify the inside IP address range.
- Specify the global IP address range.
- Define the NAT translations mappings.

We shall now look at how to configure these three elements.

9.4.4.1 Define NAT's Inside Interface

The first step to configuring NAT is to define the inside IP address range.
Generally these IP addresses will be from the private IP address ranges
(RFC 1918), but they do not have to. It is important to recognize that the
IP address range associated with a particular interface has a higher security level than the outside interface. If the security level is not set correctly, then the NAT translations will not occur. To define the inside IP
address range, we can use the following command:

```
pixfirewall(config)#nat (interface-name) nat-group ip-address subnet-
mask
```

interface-name	*WORD*	Name used to describe this interface throughout the PIX configuration
nat-group	*x*	Number used to describe the nat-group (use same number for nat outside command)
ip-address	*x.x.x.x*	Network address to define inside addresses
subnet-mask	*x.x.x.x*	Subnet mask to define inside addresses

If we want to give access to all of the inside hosts without contemplat-
ing all of the possible networks we would have to allow, we can use the
command *nat (inside) 1 0.0.0.0 0.0.0.0*. Notice how this command basically
defines every IP address that can come from the inside interface should be
handled by the NAT process.

In addition, if you want to specify a group of addresses that should not participate in NAT, use the following command:

```
pixfirewall(config)#nat (inside) 0 non-nat-IP-address non-nat-subnet-mask
```

non-nat-IP-address	*x.x.x.x*	Network address to define inside addresses
non-nat-subnet-mask	*x.x.x.x*	Subnet mask to define inside addresses

9.4.4.2 Define NAT's Global Interface

When specifying the global (outside) address, a few things need to be verified before we can complete an implementation. The address range that we select for the outside interface must be routed to our outside interface from the outside network. At first glimpse, this might seem confusing; keep in mind that the external network must know where to send the IP packets associated with the global address range. If the external network routes those packets anywhere but the external interface on our PIX firewall, your access to the external network will fail; this is not because the NAT translations fail to work, but because the return IP packets never make it back to the outside interface.

Make sure that if you are connecting your outside interface to the Internet, your global addresses must be registered with InterNIC.

When specifying the address range to be associated with the global address range, use the following command:

```
pixfirewall(config)#global (interface-name) nat-group ip-address
subnet-mask
```

interface-name	**WORD**	Name used to describe this interface throughout the PIX configuration
nat-group	*x*	Number used to describe the nat-group (use same number for nat inside command)
ip-address	*x.x.x.x*	Network address to define inside addresses
subnet-mask	*x.x.x.x*	Subnet mask to define inside addresses

If instead of specifying a network range of addresses, we only specified a single ip address by omitting the subnet mask, our PIX firewall will assume that we want to perform PAT instead of NAT as shown in Figure 9-5.

Figure 9-5

Example of
configuring PAT
on a PIX firewall

```
pixfirewall(config)#global (outside) 1 192.168.200.2
```

One of the tricks that can be used is to combine both NAT and PAT on a PIX firewall for simultaneous use. This can be accomplished by specifying a network range with the global command and then specifying a single address with the global command.

This allows users to use NAT translations until the pool of NAT addresses runs out. Once the NAT pool runs out, the PIX firewall will start using PAT with the last IP address. This is useful because some functionality is lost with PAT translations; you may want to give your users a NAT translation. If your pool of NAT addresses is smaller than the number of users, it allows users to still get out even though the available address space might be very tight.

When specifying the inside addresses and global addresses, we also specified a NAT group. If our inside address and outside address are not using the same nat-group, then NAT won't work. Figure 9-6 shows us a sample configuration in which the *nat-group* is 33 for both the nat and global definitions.

Figure 9-6

Example of
configuring NAT
and PAT
simultaneously
on a PIX firewall

```
global (Outside) 33 10.10.10.5-10.10.10.25
global (Outside) 33 10.10.10.26
nat (Inside) 33 192.168.10.0 255.255.0.0
```

9.4.5 External Access to Internal Hosts

There may come a time when only allowing inside hosts to initiate a connection falls short of the particular problem we are trying to solve. For instance, if we have a Web server, we want external users to be able to access our server. If we don't make special provisions for the Web server, no one on the outside of our network will be able to connect to our Web server. This is not a particularly useful paradigm, so we need to make special provisions to allow hosts anywhere to connect to our Web server. Two elements must be configured before we can allow external users access to internal hosts:

- Static translations
- Conduits

Keep in mind that these two elements must be used together to provide access to internal resources. Let's see how they work.

9.4.5.1 Static Translations

The default behavior of a PIX firewall is to block all externally initiated requests. Thus, if we have an external host that needs to connect to our Web server through our PIX firewall, it will not work until we configure the firewall to allow external users to access our Web server. The static command is used to give external hosts access to internal resources hosts. To configure a PIX firewall to allow externally initiated requests, we can use the following command:

```
pixfirewall(config)#static (high-security-level-int-name, low-
security-level- int-name) low-security-level-ip-address high-security-
level-ip-address
```

high-security-level-int-name	***WORD***	Name of the interface with higher security level
low-security-level-int-name	***WORD***	Name of the interface with lower security level
low-security-level-ip-address	*x.x.x.x*	IP address used externally to access host
high-security-level-ip-address	*x.x.x.x*	IP address used internall to access host

9.4.5.2 Conduits

A static command without a conduit command will do nothing to allow external hosts to access our internal hosts. Although the static command is used to map a global IP address to an inside IP address, we still need to configure which protocols are allowed through. The function of the conduit statement is exactly that, to allow a protocol through the firewall. To configure a conduit statement to enable external hosts access to a single internal host, use the following command:

```
pixfirewall(config)#conduit permission protocol host global-ip-address
operator value
```

permission	**permit**	Allow protocol through firewall
	deny	Deny protocol through firewall
protocol	**TCP**	TCP Protocol (must specify port range)
	UDP	UDP Protocol (must specify port range)
	GRE	Generic Routing Encapsulation
	ICMP	Internet Control Message Protocol (ping)
	IGMP	Internet Group Message Protocol (multicast)
	EIGRP	Enhanced IGRP
	OSPF	Open Shortest Path First
global-ip-address	***x.x.x.x***	IP address used externally to access host
operator	**eq**	Equal
	gt	Greater than
	lt	Less than
	any	Any value
value	**X**	Any port number

Using these two commands in combination, we can give access through a firewall to a specific service. In Figure 9-7, we can see the commands necessary to allow external users access to the server whose internal IP address is 172.16.1.5. In addition, we have configured the conduits to allow PPTP packets to pass through (remember from Chapter 8, "L2TP," that PPTP uses TCP port 1723 for control messages and GRE packets to pass the actual data).

Note:

If you remove a conduit or a static mapping from a PIX firewall, you will also need to use the command clear xlate. *Because a PIX firewall stores all of the mappings in a table, simply removing the commands will not be enough to remove them from the table. Therefore, any removal of static mappings or conduits requires you to clear the xlate table. Keep in mind that this is not a command that should be taken lightly. You could accidentally destroy active sessions by not being specific about which xlates you want to clear.*

Figure 9-7

Example of
configuring PAT
on a PIX firewall

```
static (inside,outside) 192.168.150.25 172.16.1.5 netmask
255.255.255.255
conduit permit tcp host 192.168.150.25 eq 1723 any
conduit permit gre host 192.168.150.25 any
```

9.4.6 Troubleshoot PIX Configuration

When experiencing problems with a basic PIX configuration, we should start by looking to see if it really is a firewall configuration. Many times, a lack of understanding about how firewalls work can cause technicians to believe the problem is with the firewall. However, by using a few simple steps, we can see if the firewall is causing a problem. Troubleshooting basic PIX configurations can be broken down into three different areas:

- Allowing hosts to ping through firewall
- Verifying NAT mappings
- Verifying interface names and security levels

Using the tasks previously listed, you can resolve most firewall issues. Be sure to follow the steps as listed.

9.4.6.1 Allow Hosts to Ping Through Firewall

When troubleshooting a configuration, it may be helpful to allow the PIX firewall to enable ICMP echos through the firewall to verify connectivity. This allows you to verify that a host is reachable, as well as determine how long it will take for a packet to get to the host. Multiple ways to enable ping exist, but the quickest way is to use the command displayed in the following:

```
pixfirewall(config)#conduit permit icmp any any
```

Remember to remove this command when you are done testing.

9.4.6.2 Verify NAT Mappings

If your external host can successfully ping the inside host, then no problem with the firewall exists. However, if you cannot ping the inside device, you should start investigating your internal infrastructure, including making sure the internal host's IP address hasn't changed. By using the command *show xlate*, you can see which global IP addresses are mapped to which internal IP addresses as shown in Figure 9-8.

Figure 9-8

Example of configuring PAT on a PIX firewall

```
pixfirewall#show xlate
Global 172.16.20.100 Local 192.168.110.10 static
```

From Figure 9-8, we see that the global address 172.16.20.100 is being NATtd to 192.168.110.10.

Once you have verified the translation, you should ping both hosts from the firewall using the command:

```
pixfirewall#ping interface-name ip-address
```

Remember to use the correct interface with the associated IP address. In other words, do not try to ping an outside IP address using an internal interface and vice versa.

9.4.6.3 Verify Interface Names and Security Levels

If you cannot ping one of the destinations, check to make sure the interfaces are operational and that the routing tables of any routers have the correct routes to the destinations. In addition, you should check to make sure that the interfaces have the appropriate security levels and that corresponding conduits and static translations give two devices access to each other.

To display the names of the current interfaces security levels, we can use the following command:

```
pixfirewall#show nameif
```

In Figure 9-9, we can see the output from the *show nameif* command. We can see not only the name of the interface, but the security level that has been applied to the specific interface.

To see the current status of an interface, you can use the *show interface* command as shown in Figure 9-10.

Figure 9-9

Output from
show nameif
command

```
pixfirewall# show nameif
nameif ethernet0 outside security0
nameif ethernet1 inside security100
```

From line 2 in Figure 9-10, you can see the name of the interface and the state of the interface. Line 3 shows the hardware address, while line 4 shows us the IP address. If you are looking for physical problems, you should look between lines 7 and 12. These fields will give you a good indication as to the performance of the PIX firewall's interfaces.

Figure 9-10

Output from
show nameif
command

```
1  pixfirewall# show interface
2  interface ethernet0 "outside" is up, line protocol is up
3   Hardware is i82559 ethernet, address is 0050.54ff.b9f7
4   IP address 172.16.20.1, subnet mask 255.255.255.0
5   MTU 1500 bytes, BW 10000 Kbit half duplex
6     84209 packets input, 5061528 bytes, 0 no buffer
7     Received 52 broadcasts, 0 runts, 0 giants
8     0 input errors, 0 CRC, 0 frame, 0 overrun, 0 ignored, 0 abort
9     84201 packets output, 5406477 bytes, 0 underruns, 0 unicast
      rpf drops
10    0 output errors, 0 collisions, 0 interface resets
11    0 babbles, 0 late collisions, 7 deferred
12    3 lost carrier, 0 no carrier
13 interface ethernet1 "inside" is up, line protocol is up
14   Hardware is i82559 ethernet, address is 0050.54ff.b9f8
15   IP address 192.168.100.1, subnet mask 255.255.255.0
16   MTU 1500 bytes, BW 10000 Kbit half duplex
17    219097 packets input, 16726092 bytes, 0 no buffer
18    Received 50481 broadcasts, 0 runts, 0 giants
19    0 input errors, 0 CRC, 0 frame, 0 overrun, 0 ignored, 0 abort
20    168118 packets output, 10763131 bytes, 0 underruns, 0 unicast
      rpf drops
21    0 output errors, 1 collisions, 0 interface resets
22    0 babbles, 0 late collisions, 12 deferred
23      0 lost carrier, 0 no carrier
```

9.4.7 Section Summary

In this section, you saw a minimal set of commands that would enable you to set up a PIX firewall using NAT. However, we did not approach many of the advanced topics because an entire book could be written about PIX firewall configuration. We shall now use these basic commands to enable us to configure PPTP and IPSec on a PIX firewall.

9.5 PPTP on a PIX Firewall

Now that you have explored how to configure the basics on a PIX firewall, let's now look at how to configure PPTP on a PIX firewall. We will not cover the specifics of how a protocol works in this chapter. However, if you need more information about how PPTP works, see Chapter 7, "PPTP." This section is dedicated to configuring PPTP on a PIX firewall.

9.6 Cisco PIX Support for PPTP

Since PIX software 5.1, the Cisco PIX firewall has supported PPTP. It can be installed on the largest of PIX boxes, the PIX 535, or the smallest of PIX firewalls, the PIX 506. This new is welcomed by those who already have a PIX firewall and want to set up PPTP, but are concerned about what else they might need.

9.6.1 Configuring PPTP on a PIX Firewall

The task list when configuring PPTP on a PIX firewall might seem long, but the configurations are fairly straightforward, requiring minimal planning, as compared to IPSec. When configuring PPTP, it is much easier to think of the VPN connections much like you would an incoming dialin connection. You need to configure support for authentication (PAP, CHAP, MS-CHAP, IP address space, encryption, and so on).

In this section, we will focus on technologies that are sometimes called *Virtual Private Dialup Networks* (VPDN). VPDN refers to a VPN technology that operates almost identically to dialing into a PPP access router. Technologies that Cisco commonly refers to as VPDN are PPTP, L2F, and L2TP.

To configure a PIX firewall to support PPTP, you need to perform the following tasks:

▪ Enable VPDN.

▪ Configure VPDN group to accept PPTP dialin.

▪ Specify authentication.

▪ Specify encryption.

- IP Address pool for PPTP users.
- Create users.

Many of the commands you will see here get their heritage from PPP. This is because PPTP was designed to utilize the already well-established PPP protocol. No sense reinventing the wheel when it was PPP that the designers wanted to emulate anyway. By using the already well-established PPP protocol as a basis for PPTP, PPTP immediately had support for many of the network layer protocols that the PPP protocol had developed over its lifespan.

9.6.1.1 Enable VPDN

In order to use PPTP on a PIX firewall, you must first enable VPDN. Enabling VPDN is a simple task that is carried out using the following command:

```
pixfirewall# vpdn enable interface-name
```

interface-name	*WORD*	Name used to describe this interface throughout the PIX configuration

Although it is possible to enable VPDN on an inside interface, it might not make sense if your internal hosts already have access to all of the hosts on the corporate network. However, if you are using a PIX firewall for an internal firewall (a firewall inside the corporate network), you may want to use the inside interface. However, in most situations, you will use the outside interface for your PPTP implementation.

9.6.1.2 Configure VPDN group to Accept PPTP Dialin

One of the steps that must be done before PPTP works with a PIX firewall is to allow the PIX firewall to accept PPTP packets. Because a PIX firewall does not allow any packets from the lower-level security interface, through a higher-level security interface, you must tell the firewall to allow PPTP packets into the firewall. Although you can do this through an association of access-lists, conduits, and access-group commands, it is much easier to use a single command that has been supplied by Cisco to implicitly allow any PPTP packet into the PIX firewall:

```
pixfirewall(config)# sysopt connection permit-pptp
```

Once you have allowed incoming PPTP packet into the PIX firewall for processing, you must tell the PIX firewall to accept incoming connections. This can be accomplished using the following command:

```
pixfirewall(config)# vpdn group vpdn-group-name accept dialin pptp
```

vpdn-group-name　　**WORD**　　　　Name of the PPTP VPDN group

This allows the PIX firewall to process incoming PPTP packets destined for the PIX firewall. In essence this command is what turns our PIX firewall into a PPTP server. You now need to handle all of the connection details.

Note:

The updn group-name *enables the PIX firewall to bring all of the configuration commands together for a properly working PPTP configuration.*

9.6.1.3 Specify Authentication

When a PPTP client and PPTP server authenticate, they use the same authentication protocols that PPP dialin users use (PAP, CHAP, and MS-CHAP). For those unfamiliar with these authentication protocols, you can review their behavior in Chapter 4, "VPN Security Primer." To specify an authentication protocol, use the following command:

```
pixfirewall(config)# vpdn group vpdn-group-name ppp authentication
auth-protocol
```

vpdn-group-name	**WORD**	Name of the PPTP VPDN group
auth-protocol	**PAP**	Use PAP as the authentication protocol
	CHAP	Use CHAP as the authentication protocol
	MS-CHAP	Use MS-CHAP as the authentication protocol

Unlike a Cisco router, we cannot configure multiple authentication protocols within a single command. A PIX firewall requires that each authentication protocol be established on it's own line. Thus, if you want to support all three authentication protocols, you would have three individual authentication commands.

If you are using a AAA server, you will also need to specify whether you are using a RADIUS or a TACACS server, the IP address of the AAA server, as well as the shared key used between the PIX firewall and the AAA server. To allow a AAA server to authenticate users, use the following command:

```
pixfirewall(config)# aaa-server auth-name protocol aaa-server
```

auth-name	**WORD**	Name which will describe aaa-server attributes
aaa-server	**RADIUS**	Use RADIUS to authenticate the user
	TACACS+	Use TACACS+ to authenticate the user

To specify which AAA server to use for authentication, use the following command:

```
pixfirewall(config)# aaa-server auth-name (interface-name) host ip-
address-of-aaa-server shared-key
```

auth-name	**WORD**	Name which will describe aaa-server attributes
interface-name	**WORD**	Name of interface that will accept an inbound connection.
ip-address-of aaa-server	*x.x.x.x*	IP address of AAA server
shared-key	**WORD**	Shared key used to encrypt communications between PIX firewall and AAA server.

The last step to getting a PIX firewall to accept authentication is to associate the VPDN group with the authentication method that has be dictated by the solution. This last step ties all of the configuration commands together to provide a cohesive authentication mechanism for PPTP. If you are using local users, you can use the following command:

```
pixfirewall(config)# vpdn group vpdn-group-name client authentication
local
```

| *vpdn-group-name* | **WORD** | Name of the PPTP VPDN group |

If you are using AAA to authenticate users, you can use the following command:

```
pixfirewall(config)# vpdn group vpdn-group-name client authentication
aaa auth-name
```

| *vpdn-group-name* | **WORD** | Name of the PPTP VPDN group |
| *auth-name* | **WORD** | Name which will describe aaa-server attributes |

In Figure 9-11, you can see a sample configuration specifying CHAP authentication using an AAA server. In this sample configuration, you can see we are using tacacs for our AAA server, which is located at 192.168.12.99. In addition, we will use CHAP authentication only.

Figure 9-11

Sample AAA configuration for PPTP on a PIX firewall

```
aaa-server PPTPAuth protocol tacacs+
aaa-server PPTPAuth (outside) host 192.168.12.99 tacacssharedkey
vpdn group 33 client authentication aaa PPTPAuth
vpdn group 33 ppp authentication chap
```

9.6.1.4 Specify Encryption

Some network engineers will only be interested in using PPTP as a multiprotocol transport over an IP backbone. However, if you have taken the time to implement a firewall, you will most likely want to implement encryption. Implementing encryption is done using the following command:

```
pixfirewall(config)# vpdn group vpdn-group-name ppp encryption mppe
encryption-option
```

vpdn-group-name	**WORD**	Name of the PPTP VPDN group
encryption-option	**40**	Allow client to negotiate 40-bit encryption
	128	Allow client to negotiate 128-bit encryption
	Auto	Allow client to negotiate 40-bit or 128-bit encryption
	Require	Require client to use either encryption (use with 40 or 128 option)

If you are going to use MPPE, you must use MS-CHAP authentication.

Note:

If you want to implement Microsoft's 128-bit encryption, you will need to have a 3DES license.

9.6.1.5 IP Address Pool for PPTP Users

At this point, you have configured all of the options that make PPTP functional, but that is not everything that makes your PPTP solution work. You still need to have IP address space for incoming connections to receive. The command to allocate IP addresses to an incoming PPTP connection is as follows:

```
pixfirewall(config)# ip local pool address-pool-name first-ip-address
last-ip-address
```

address-pool-name	***WORD***	Name for this IP address pool block
first-ip-address	***a.b.c.d***	First ip address in the block of IP addresses
last-ip-address	***a.b.c.d***	Last ip address in the block of IP addresses

Keep in mind that this will not work unless the IP address assigned is on the same subnet as the inside interface of the PIX firewall.

Having only an IP address and no other attributes makes using TCP/IP difficult at best. Therefore, you also need to give your PPTP client other TCP/IP related information such as a DNS server and a WINS server. Using the following can give your PPTP user a DNS or WINS server.

```
pixfirewall(config)# vpdn group vpdn-group-name client configuration
ip-attribute ip-address
```

vpdn-group-name	***WORD***	Name of the PPTP VPDN group
ip-attribute	**dns**	Set DNS server for PPTP client to use
	wins	Set WINS server for PPTP client to use
ip-address	***a.b.c.d***	Ip address of the server specified

In most instances, we will use the private address space as dictated in RFC 1918 to assign our IP address pool. More importantly, as network engineers, we need to make sure that the inside IP address space gets routed back to the inside interface on a PIX firewall. Otherwise, packets will go out, but never come back to the PIX firewall. If no other routers are on the inside interface of our PIX firewall, this should not be a problem because local hosts will point their default gateway at the PIX firewall's internal IP address. If routers are behind the inside interface, we need to make sure we configure a static route for the internal network on the PIX firewall to the inside routers.

Once we have defined the IP address space to use, we need to tie it in with the VPDN group hosting the PPTP session. This command is as follows:

```
pixfirewall(config)# vpdn group vpdn-group-name client configuration
address local address-pool-name
```

address-pool-name	***WORD***	Name for this IP address pool block
auth-name	***WORD***	Name which will describe aaa-server attributes vpdn group 1 client configuration address local pptp-pool

9.6.1.6 Create Users

The last step in configuring PPTP on a PIX firewall is to create the usernames and passwords that incoming PPTP connections will be authenticated against. If we are using an AAA-server, we do not need to configure local users because PPTP users will be authenticated against the centralized AAA-server.

To locally configure a username and password on a PIX firewall, use the following command:

```
pixfirewall(config)#vpdn username username password password
```

username	***WORD***	Name that a PPTP user will use to authenticate
password	***WORD***	Password that a PPTP user will use to authenticate

9.6.2 Troubleshoot PPTP Connections

Troubleshooting a PPTP connection on a PIX firewall is not nearly as easy as it is on a Cisco router. This is because quite a few more debug commands are available on a Cisco router than a PIX firewall. This does not mean debugging a connection is impossible; it means we have to pay attention to the details. Where a Cisco router would tell us that a user did not authenticate because the passwords did not match, we need to figure it out based upon the sequence of events that happen. The steps involved when troubleshooting a PPTP connection are the same regardless of whether we are troubleshooting it on a PIX firewall or a Cisco router. There are three areas to focus on when troubleshooting a PPTP connection:

▓ User account

▓ Authentication protocol

▓ Encryption

We will now focus on troubleshooting the elements previously listed. However, all of these tips are predicated on the fact that our PPTP client can ping the PPTP server (or at least have IP reachability with ports TCP port 1723 and IP port 47).

9.6.2.1 User Account

In most instances, it should become obvious that a user account and password do not match when attempting to authenticate a PPTP connection, because the PPTP client will tell you that your username and password was incorrect. Unfortunately, there is no way to determine on a PIX router that a user failed to authenticate, unless you are using AAA for your username database. In the event that you are using AAA, we can use the command *debug ppp uauth* to view the success or failure of a connection.

9.6.2.2 Authentication Protocol

Resolving mismatched authentication protocols can be very difficult when using a PIX firewall as a PPTP server because the PPTP client's machine will not tell you that it couldn't negotiate an authentication protocol; neither will the PIX firewall. The PPTP client might give you a cryptic error such as "PPP negotiation is not converging." That should be your clue that LCP negotiations are failing. From Chapter 3, "Dailup over Cisco Routers," we discussed that LCP is comprised of four protocols: authentication, compression, multilink, and callback. Of these four protocols, authentication should stand out as a protocol that will cause connection failure.

Note:

For a more complete description of LCP negotiations, see Chapter 3.

If you are running one or two authentication protocols, a quick method to test whether it is an authentication protocol mismatch is to enable all three authentication protocols and see if the PPTP client can connect. This will not cover 100 percent of the cases (a PPTP client could be running EAP or SPAP), but it certainly will cover most of them.

9.6.2.3 Encryption

Within the PPTP protocol, it is not a requirement to do encryption. If you are using a PIX firewall, then you will most likely be using encryption due to your security requirements. Realize that failure to negotiate encryption terminates the connection.

Problems with encryption stem from two different areas:

▓ Globally

▓ Encryption mismatch between client and server

In order to use MPPE, you must have activated DES on your PIX firewall. For all firewalls, a DES activation key is free; it is just a matter of activating it. Standard DES is what is used for MPPE's 40-bit encryption. If you plan on using 128-bit DES encryption, you must have a 3DES activation key, which is not free.

If DES is enabled on your PIX firewall and you think the problem might be related to negotiating encryption, turn encryption off and see if you can negotiate a connection with the PPTP server.

Failure to negotiate encryption results in a disconnection. Because both the PPTP client and PPTP server will indicate very little about why the connection was rejected, troubleshooting an encryption problem can be difficult. The quickest method to eliminate encryption from the realm of problems is to remove it from both the client and server. Then see if you can still establish a connection. Be careful using this method as it might have unattended consequences to those users who are still connected.

9.7 Cisco PIX Firewall Software Support for IPSec

Since PIX software 5.0, the Cisco PIX firewall has supported IPSec. Because the same PIX firewall software can be installed on the largest of PIX boxes, the PIX 535 or the smallest of PIX firewalls, the PIX 506 commands are the same. In addition, there are not any different feature sets or different software trains with PIX software like there is with Cisco IOS software. This is welcomed news to those who already have a PIX firewall and want to set up IPSec, but are concerned about what else they might need. The only item that a network engineer might be concerned about is if you have a requirement to run 3DES. A 3DES license is not free and you will have to contact your local sales office to get a 3DES activation key.

9.8 Configuring IPSec on a PIX Firewall

We are now to the last section in this chapter in which we explore how to configure IPSec on a PIX firewall. Just like the section on PPTP, we are not going to cover the specifics of how IPSec works in this chapter. This section in this chapter is dedicated to configuring IPSec on a PIX firewall. We will assume you already know about *Internet Security Association and Key Management Protocol* (ISAKMP), the *Authentication Header* (AH) protocol, the *Encapsulating Security Protocol* (ESP), transform sets, and all of the elements that make up IPSec. However, if you need more information about how IPSec works, see Chapter 6, "IPSec."

The task list when configuring IPSec on a PIX firewall can seem very daunting at first. However, by breaking it up into components, you will find the tasks more manageable. One of the advantages of configuring IPSec on a PIX firewall over a Cisco router is that the commands rarely change from one version of software to another, unlike Cisco IOS, which frequently changes the commands used to configure IOS.

To configure a PIX firewall to support IPSec, we need to perform the following tasks:

- Allow IPSec packets through the firewall.
- Configure the transform set.

    * Specify ESP.
    * Specify the AH protocol.

- Create and configure crypto maps.

    * Specify the VPN peer.
    * Specify the data stream to encrypt.
    * Specify the transform set.

- Configure key management.
- Apply a crypto map to the interface.

This list of tasks should look very familiar from when we configured IPSec on a Cisco router in Chapter 6. The only difference is in the commands used to configure IPSec.

9.8.1 Allow IPSec Packets Through the Firewall

One of the steps that must be done before IPSec works with a PIX firewall is to allow IPSec packets inside the PIX Firewall. Because a PIX firewall does not enable any packets from the outside interface, we must tell the firewall to allow IPSec packets into the Firewall. Although you can do this through a conglomeration of access-lists, conduit statements, and access-group commands, it is much easier to use the single command that has been supplied by Cisco to implicitly enable any PPTP packet:

```
pixfirewall(config)# sysopt connection permit-ipsec
```

This is one of the few steps required when configuring IPSec on a PIX firewall; it has no equivalent on a Cisco router.

9.8.2 Configure the Transform Set

Transform sets are used to define the IPSec encryption policies. They can represent a combination of AH protocols or ESP protocols that are used during the negotiation of a security association. When configuring a transform set, two elements can be configured:

▓ ESP (multiples per transform set)

▓ AH Protocol (single encryption per transform set)

As we saw in Chapter 6, IPSec can operate in one of two modes: transport and tunnel mode. When configuring a Cisco router, we had the option of specifying the mode of the IPSec VPN, but we have no way to configure the mode on a PIX firewall. If we cannot configure it, which mode does it operate? A PIX firewall operates by default in tunnel mode and not transport mode.

During ISAKMP security association negotiations, both peers search for a transform that each of them support, as shown in Figure 9-12.

If the two IPSec peers fail to find a common set of ISAKMP protocols, the IKE security association negotiation will fail.

When configuring AH and ESP to be used by a transform set, each of the protocols are listed on the same configuration line as the name of the transform set. The format of the command is as follows:

Figure 9-12

Negotiation of
ISAKMP
protocols to use
for IPSec

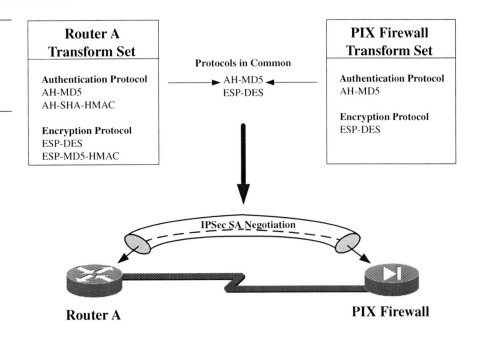

Router A Transform Set
Authentication Protocol AH-MD5 AH-SHA-HMAC
Encryption Protocol ESP-DES ESP-MD5-HMAC

Protocols in Common
AH-MD5
ESP-DES

PIX Firewall Transform Set
Authentication Protocol AH-MD5
Encryption Protocol ESP-DES

IPSec SA Negotiation

Router A

PIX Firewall

```
pixfirewall(config)# crypto ipsec transform-set transform-name
protocol1 protocol 2 protocol3
```

transform-name	**WORD**	Name of the transform set.
protocol	**ah-md5-hmac**	Use AH-HMAC-MD5 for authentication.
	ah-sha-hmac	Use AH-HMAC-SHA transform for authentication.
	esp-des	Use ESP transform using DES cipher (56 bits).
	esp-md5-hmac	Use ESP transform using HMAC-MD5 authentication.
	esp-null	Use ESP transform without cipher.
	esp-sha-hmac	Use ESP transform using HMAC-SHA authentication.

When specifying which protocols to use, you can only choose one AH
protocol, one ESP (encryption) protocol, and one ESP (authentication) protocol. Table 9-4 shows us in which category each of the various transform
types are found.

Table 9-4	Transform Type	Protocol
Categorization of ESP and AH protocols	AH	ah-md5-hmac
		ah-sha-hmac
	ESP (encryption)	esp-des
		esp-3des
		esp-null
	ESP (authentication)	esp-md5-hmac
		esp-sha-hmac

9.8.3 Configuring Crypto Maps

Crypto maps are logical devices that define all of the configuration-specific information about how to apply encryption. Within the generic crypto map you can have multiple crypto map entries. Each crypto map entry specifies a crypto map that falls under the umbrella of the generic crypto map (this will make more sense a bit later when you see that in order to create a crypto map you must specify a sequence number, even though we never created a crypto map umbrella for it to fall under). By giving us the ability to create multiple crypto map entries, we can define parameters for different IPSec peers.

Because IPSec is such a flexible and extensible protocol, it can be configured in multiple ways. Figure 9-13 shows the various types of crypto maps that can be configured.

Each leaf (end node) represents unique attributes that must be configured regarding that crypto map. We are going to focus on the crypto maps that are predominantly used today.

The first type of crypto map we will concentrate on is a crypto map in which the encryption and authentication keys are manually configured. When IPSec was first introduced and ISAKMP was still in its infancy, many engineers used manually configured crypto maps. It was the only way to guarantee interoperability between vendors.

As time went along, ISAKMP become more mature. Now, the bulk of IPSec configurations use ISAKMP pre-shares. The main reason ISAKMP pre-share installations greatly outnumber ISAKMP RSA installations is due to the cost of the infrastructure. PKI infrastructures are expensive,

Figure 9-13

Different types of
crypto maps

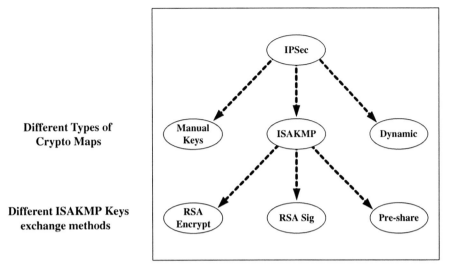

Different Types of
Crypto Maps

Different ISAKMP Keys
exchange methods

time-consuming, and cumbersome to build, while ISAKMP pre-shares can
be set up in a matter of hours.

The type of crypto map you select will depend upon the VPN you are
deploying (compulsory or voluntary) and how you approach key management for your VPN. The two different types of crypto maps that we will
focus on for the rest of the chapter are

▨ Crypto maps with manually configured keys

▨ Configuring crypto maps using ISAKMP pre-share

9.8.3.1 Crypto Maps—Manual IPSec SAs versus ISAKMP SAs

When determining the task list for configuring IPSec, we need to look at
the type of key management that will be performed. We can either manually configure the encryption and authentication keys that will be used for
the security association, or we can use ISAKMP to negotiate the encryption and keys. The advantage of using ISAKMP over manually configuring the encryption is that you can negotiate the type of encryption and
authentication algorithms to be used, thus giving your configuration flexibility. In addition, you do not have to manually enter the key into your
configuration, which, depending on the length of the keys, can be error-
prone.

In order to create a working crypto map, we must perform the following six tasks:

- Create a crypto map entry.
- Specify the data stream to encrypt.
- Specify the peer router.
- Specify the transform set to use (the encryption and authentication algorithms to use).
- Configure key management.
- Apply the crypto map to an interface.

We will now look at the steps involved with creating crypto maps for the two different types of crypto maps utilizing the six steps. Although all of the steps need to be performed on every crypto map, the commands and protocols used to accomplish that task are not always the same. Make sure you follow the steps within a single crypto map methodology (such as crypto maps with manually configured keys or crypto maps using ISAKMP).

9.8.4 Configuring Crypto Maps with Manually Configured Keys

Crypto maps that do not use ISAKMP are probably the easiest crypto maps to configure, but not because they have the fewest number of commands used to support them; no negotiation can be done, and you always know how your crypto map is configured. In order to support manual crypto maps, you must reach an agreement with your IPSec peer as to the type of encryption, authentication algorithms, and keys that will be used prior to configuring your crypto maps.

9.8.4.1 Create a Crypto Map Entry

When creating a crypto map, three things must be identified: the name of the crypto map, the sequence number, and the type of key management that will be used with the tunnel. The command used to create a crypto map for use with manual keys is as follows:

```
pixfirewall(config)#crypto map name-of-map sequence-number ipsec-
manual
```

name-of-map	***WORD***	Name for the crypto map.
sequence-number	**0-65535**	Unique number identifying destination-specific information for the remote VPN peer.

Because a crypto map can only be applied to a single interface, we need a method to identify different IPSec peers. This is accomplished by the priority used to identify a crypto map entry.

9.8.4.2 Specify the Data Stream to Encrypt

When configuring a crypto map, we must use an extended access-list to define traffic that should be encrypted by the IPSec peer. Extended access-lists offer a high degree of flexibility by filtering a data stream based on the session-layer protocol, source address, destination address, and application port number. Extended access-lists are identified in a PIX firewall as those access-lists whose number is between 100 and 199. Once the access-list has been created, we can associate it to a crypto map using the following global configuration mode command:

```
pixfirewall(config)#crypto map name-of-map sequence-number match
address access-list
```

name-of-map	*WORD*	Name for the crypto map.
sequence-number	**0-65535**	Unique number identifying destination-specific information for the remote VPN peer.
access-list	**100-199**	Extended access-list to use to identify the data stream to encrypt.

9.8.4.3 Specify the Peer Router

A crypto map must be associated to a unique VPN peer. Although you can have two IPSec peers using the same crypto map, it is a bad idea from an operational perspective because it will get confusing very quickly. To specify the IPSec peer, we can use the following command:

```
pixfirewall(config)#crypto map name-of-map sequence-number set peer
VPN-ip-address
```

name-of-map	*WORD*	Name for the crypto map.
sequence-number	**0-65535**	Unique number identifying destination-specific information for the remote VPN peer.
VPN-ip-address	*x.x.x.x*	IP address of the VPN peer.

When specifying the VPN peer IP address, it must be the IP address that has the crypto map applied to on the remote end, which will generally be the outside interface. If you pick a different IP address, your IPSec SA negotiations will fail.

9.8.4.4 Specify the Transform Set

Remember that the transform set identifies the encryption/authentication protocols that will be used. Thus, it is here that we will determine which algorithms are used for encryption and authentication. To specify the transform set, a crypto map should use the following command:

```
pixfirewall(config)#crypto map name-of-map sequence-number set
transform-set transform-set-name
```

name-of-map	***WORD***	Name for the crypto map.
sequence-number	**0-65535**	Unique number identifying destination-specific information for the remote VPN peer.
transform-set-name	***WORD***	Name of existing transform set.

Only a single transform set can be used within a crypto map entry (denoted by the sequence number). However, you can specify multiple crypto map entries within a crypto map.

9.8.4.5 Specify Keys

Because we will be using a manual crypto map, we need to configure the keys used by ESP and AH protocols by hand. Four different components must be specified when manually configuring the keys between two VPN peers:

- ESP encryption key or an AH encryption key
- Inbound traffic key or outbound traffic key
- *Security Parameters Index* (SPI)
- The key

Because we can have multiple encryption entries within our crypto map, we must make sure that we have defined that type of encryption/authentication within our transform set and that our IPSec peer is using the same key with the same encryption/authentication within their transform set. We also need to remember that the outbound key for one IPSec peer is the inbound key for the other IPSec peer. To protect ourselves from replay attacks, we can use the SPI to identify the starting sequence number associated with our data streams. Once again, the starting value of the inbound key on one IPSec peer is the starting value of the outbound key on the other IPSec peer.

When configuring an ESP key, we must configure both the inbound and outbound keys. The inbound and outbound keys do not need to match, but they must be the inverse of your IPSec peer. The command used to configure an ESP key is as follows:

```
pixfirewall(config)#crypto map name-of-map sequence-number set
session-key direction esp SPI cipher cipher-key authenticator auth-key
```

name-of-map	**WORD**	Name for the crypto map.
sequence-number	**0-65535**	Unique number identifying destination-specific information for the remote VPN peer.
direction	**inbound**	Decrypt packets using this key.
	outbound	Encrypt packets using this key.
SPI	**256-4294967295**	Starting sequence number to use for SPI.
cipher-key	**WORD**	The key in hexadecimal format (without leading 0x).
auth-key	**WORD**	The key in hexadecimal format (without leading 0x).

Because ESP can do authentication and encryption, we need the capability to configure both the encryption key and the authentication key.

Configuring the AH key is almost identical to configuring an ESP key. The important aspect when manually configuring keys is to make sure that your IPSec peer keys match. If you are using the same key for inbound and outbound, then this is not a problem. If you use different keys for inbound and outbound traffic, you need to make sure that the outbound key from one PIX firewall uses the same key on inbound traffic on its IPSec peer and vice versa.

The command used to configure an AH key is as follows:

```
pixfirewall(config)#crypto map name-of-map sequence-number set
session-key direction ah SPI auth-key
```

name-of-map	**WORD**	Name for the crypto map.
sequence-number	**0-65535**	Unique number identifying destination-specific information for the remote VPN peer.
direction	**inbound**	Decrypt packets using this key.
	outbound	Encrypt packets using this key.
SPI	**256-4294967295**	Starting sequence number to use for SPI.
auth-key	**WORD**	The key in hexadecimal format (without leading 0x).

One of the most commonly missed subjects is key length. Each encryption algorithm has its own minimum key length for each encrypting or decrypting a data stream. Unfortunately, if you use the wrong key length, the PIX software will not inform you of your mistake. If you use a key that does not meet the minimum key length requirement, then your encryption algorithms will not work correctly. The encryption algorithms will not fail; they will attempt to encrypt but fail, and it will appear to you (at least on the surface) that your keys do not match. The minimum key lengths for each algorithm are displayed in Table 9-5. You will probably use longer key lengths when actually deploying it, but if you are testing your configuration, you can easily fall into this trap.

Table 9-5	Algorithm	Minimum Length (in bits)
Minimum key lengths for each encryption algorithm	DES	16 hexadecimal digits
	MD5	32 hexadecimal digits
	SHA	40 hexadecimal digits

9.8.4.6 Apply Crypto Map to an Interface

Now that we have created our crypto map and specified all the parameters associated with the crypto map, we need to apply the crypto map to an interface. The crypto map should only be applied to the lower-level security interface. To apply a crypto map to an lower-level security interface, use the following command:

```
pixfirewall(config)#crypto map name-of-map interface name-of-outside-
interface
```

name-of-map	***WORD***	Name for the previously created crypto map.
name-of-outside-interface	***WORD***	Name of the interface with the lower security level.

9.8.4.7 Example of Two PIX Firewalls with Manual Configured Keys

Let's now take a look at everything we have learned and see what the relevant combination of commands looks like from two VPN peers. In Figures 9-14 and 9-15, you can see the necessary commands needed to configure two IPSec VPN peers to communicate and manually configure the keys.

Figure 9-14

Example of PIX
configuring a
manual mode
IPSec

```
hostname pixfirewalla
nameif ethernet0 inside security0
nameif ethernet1 outside security100
interface ethernet0 100full
interface ethernet1 100full
mtu outside 1500
mtu inside 1500
ip address outside 192.168.10.10 255.255.255.0
ip address inside 172.16.30.3 255.255.255.0
sysopt connection permit-ipsec
access-list 101 permit ip 172.16.30.0 255.255.255.0 10.10.10.0
255.255.255.0
crypto ipsec transform-set testset esp-des
crypto map test 20 ipsec-isakmp
crypto map test 20 match address 101
crypto map test 20 set peer 192.168.30.10
crypto map test 20 set transform-set testset
crypto map test interface outside
crypto map test 20 set session-key inbound esp 300 cipher
1010101010101010
crypto map test 20 set session-key outbound esp 300 cipher
abcdabcdabcdabcd
nat (inside) 0 access-list 101
```

Figure 9-15

Example of a PIX
configuring a
manual mode
IPSec

```
hostname pixfirewallc
nameif ethernet0 inside security0
nameif ethernet1 outside security100
interface ethernet0 100full
interface ethernet1 100full
mtu outside 1500
mtu inside 1500
ip address outside 192.168.30.10 255.255.255.0
ip address inside 10.10.10.1 255.255.255.0
sysopt connection permit-ipsec
access-list 105 permit ip 10.10.10.0 255.255.255.0 172.16.30.0
255.255.255.0
crypto ipsec transform-set testset esp-des
crypto map test 50 ipsec-manual
crypto map test 50 match address 105
crypto map test 50 set peer 192.168.10.10
crypto map test 50 set transform-set testset
crypto map test interface outside
crypto map test 50 set session-key inbound esp 300 cipher
abcdabcdabcdabcd
crypto map test 50 set session-key outbound esp 300 cipher
1010101010101010
nat (inside) 0 access-list 105
```

9.8.5 Configuring Crypto Maps Using ISAKMP Pre-share

Now that we have seen how to configure a crypto map without ISAKMP (manual configuration), let's look at how to configure a crypto map that utilizes ISAKMP for key exchanges. Crypto maps that utilize ISAKMP have more steps that must be completed to get a working IPSec VPN. However, it eliminates the possibility of entering an incorrect key. In addition, it provides for a more flexible environment because IPSec peers can negotiate the settings they will use for the new security associations. The steps used to create a crypto map that use ISAKMP are very similar to the commands in which we manually specified the keys, but more steps are involved because we still need to configure ISAKMP, which will exchange keys for us.

9.8.5.1 Create a Crypto Map Entry

When creating a crypto map, three things must be identified: the name of the crypto map, the sequence number, and the type of key management that will be used with the tunnel. The configuration command used is as follows:

```
pixfirewall(config)#crypto map name-of-map sequence-number ipsec-
isakmp
```

name-of-map	***WORD***	Name for the crypto map.
sequence-number	**0-65535**	Unique number identifying destination-specific information for the remote VPN peer.

Because a crypto map can only be applied to a single interface, we need a method to identify different VPN peers. This is accomplished by the priority used to identify a crypto map entry.

9.8.5.2 Specify the Data Stream to Encrypt

When configuring a crypto map, we must use an extended access-list to define traffic that should be encrypted by the VPN peer. Extended access-lists offer a high degree of flexibility by filtering a data stream based on the session-layer protocol, source address, destination address, and application port number. Extended access-lists are identified in a PIX firewall as those access-lists whose number is between 100 and 199. Once the access-list has been created, we can associate it to a crypto map using the following global configuration mode command:

```
pixfirewall(config)#crypto map name-of-map sequence-number match
address access-list
```

name-of-map	*WORD*	Name for the crypto map.
sequence-number	0-65535	Unique number identifying destination-specific information for the remote VPN peer.
access-list	100-199	Extended access-list to use to identify the data stream to encrypt.

9.8.5.3 Specify the Peer Router

A crypto map must be associated to a unique VPN peer. Although you can have two VPN peers using the same crypto map, from an operational perspective it is a bad idea because it will get confusing very quickly. To specify the VPN peer, we can use the following command:

```
pixfirewall(config)#crypto map name-of-map sequence-number set peer
VPN-ip-address
```

name-of-map	*WORD*	Name for the crypto map.
sequence-number	0-65535	Unique number identifying destination-specific information for the remote VPN peer.
VPN-ip-address	*x.x.x.x*	IP address of the VPN peer.

When specifying the VPN peer IP address, this must be the IP address that has the crypto map applied on the remote end. If you pick a different IP address, your IPSec SA negotiations will fail.

9.8.5.4 Specify the Transform Set

Remember that the transform set identifies the encryption/authentication protocols that will be used. Thus, it is here that we will determine which algorithms are used for encryption and authentication. To specify the transform set, a crypto map should use:

```
pixfirewall(config)#crypto map name-of-map sequence-number set
transform-set transform-set-name
```

name-of-map	*WORD*	Name for the crypto map.
sequence-number	0-65535	Unique number identifying destination-specific information for the remote VPN peer.
transform-set-name	*WORD*	Name of existing transform set.

Only a single transform set can be used within a crypto map entry (denoted by the sequence number). However, you can specify multiple crypto map entries within a crypto map.

9.8.5.5 Configure ISAKMP

Just like IPSec's encryption algorithms, ISAKMP also needs to have a key in order to create a SA so that IPSec can securely negotiate the parameters of an IPSec SA. This means that we need another key. We can use either a pre-existing key to set up the ISAKMP SA or we can use a CA server to provide us with a key. In any event, the following items need to be configured in order for ISAKMP to work:

- Enable ISAKMP.
- Create an ISAKMP policy.
- Specify the encryption algorithm.
- Specify the hash algorithm.
- Specify the ISAKMP policy to use keys (RSA or pre-share).
- Configure pre-share keys for an ISAKMP policy.
- Specify *Diffie-Hellman* (DH) group.
- Specify the security assocation lifetime.

Enable ISAKMP   To enable ISAKMP, you can use the following global configuration command:

```
pixfirewall(config)#isakmp enable name-of-outside-interface
```

name-of-outside-interface   **WORD**   Name of the interface with the lower security level.

Create ISAKMP Policy   An ISAKMP policy defines the security parameters that will be defined during the ISAKMP SA negotiation. It defines the encryption mechanisms that will be used during ISAKMP SA negotiations. By default, 56-bit DES-CBC will be used during the negotiation of ISAKMP. However, two other options must be configured within an ISAKMP policy as well as two optional attributes (see Table 9-6).

When two peers begin the ISAKMP process, they first exchange all their ISAKMP policies. The peers, starting with their own highest value policy, start working their way down the list of their remote peers policy looking for a match. If the local peer cannot find a policy that matches its

	Security Mechanism	Required/Optional	Option
Table 9-6	Hash	Required	sha
			md5
Options to be configured in an ISAKMP policy	Authentication	Required	rsa-sig
			rsa-encr
			pre-share
	DH Group	Optional	1 (768 bit)
			2 (1024 bit)
	Lifetime	Optional	Seconds

highest priority policy, the local peer will then look to its own second highest value policy, continuing on the search until it has exhausted its own list of ISAKMP policies. If the peers cannot find a mutually agreeable policy, the peers then refuse negotiation, and ISAKMP will fail; ultimately IPSec will not be established.

Unlike Cisco IOS, in which we created a policy and then configured it similar to an interface, a PIX firewall requires you to configure each of the ISAKMP attributes, making sure you specify the number of the policy you are configuring. Thus, in the end, you have one less command to enter because you do not have to manually create the policy.

Specify Encryption Algorithm   Two different encryption algorithms can be used within an ISAKMP SA: DES and Triple DES. If your PIX firewall does not have Triple DES enabled, then you really only have one encryption option for your ISAKMP SA. To specify the encryption algorithm to use for ISAKMP, use the following command:

```
pixfirewall(config)# isakmp policy policy-number encryption
encryption-protocol
```

policy-number	1-65534	Priority identifier.
encryption-protocol	**DES**	Use DES encryption.
	3DES	Use Triple DES encryption.

Specify Hash Algorithm To specify the hash algorithm used within an ISAKMP policy, use the following command:

```
pixfirewall(config)# isakmp policy policy-number encryption
encryption-protocol
```

policy-number	**1-65534**	Priority identifier.
encryption-protocol	**DES**	Use DES encryption.
	3DES	Use Triple DES encryption.

Specify ISAKMP Policy to Use Keys (RSA or Pre-share) When setting up authentication within an ISAKMP policy on a Cisco PIX firewall, two different protocols can be used to encrypt the ISAKMP SA, which will be used for IPSec negotiations. It is important to understand their distinction when implementing IPSec with ISAKMP because using each one has non-trivial ramifications. The two different protocols that can be used are as follows:

- **Pre-share:** Just like any symmetric encryption, both parties must know the key. This is useful for small environments in which the number of peers are small, because we do not need to use a CA server.

- **RSA signature**: In order to utilize this protocol, you must already have a CA server in which you can exchange public keys. By utilizing a CA server, you can considerably improve the scalability of an IPSec network.

To define the authentication protocol that will be used during ISAKMP negotiations, we can use the following command:

```
pixfirewall(config)# isakmp policy policy-number authentication auth-
protocol
```

policy-number	**1-65534**	Priority identifier.
auth-protocol	**pre-share**	Use a pre-shared key.
	rsa-sig	Use RSA signature.

Note:

A Cisco router has three different protocols that can be used for ISAKMP authentication. The missing protocol is RSA encryption, which can provide nonrepudiation. In this chapter, we are only going to focus on pre-share ISAKMP policies.

Configure Pre-share Keys for an ISAKMP Policy   Two possible types of keys can be used when configuring ISAKMP: pre-share and RSA keys. RSA keys can be configured to use a CA server, or you can manually configure RSA keys, whereas a pre-share enables the use of an agreed-upon key for encryption. You cannot use a pre-share key in combination with an RSA key for an ISAKMP encryption. You can, however, use a pre-share for one ISAKMP policy and an RSA key encryption within another policy. If you choose to use a pre-shared key for authentication, you must the following command on both ISAKMP peers:

```
pixfirewall(config)#isakmp key key address ISAKMP-peer-ip-address
```

key	*WORD*	Key to be used for encryption.
ISAKMP-peer-ip-address	*x.x.x.x*	IP address of the ISAKMP peer.

For each of your ISAKMP peers, you must configure an independent pre-share identifying the key to be used by the router (you do not need to use a different key; you only need to identify other ISAKMP peers). It is easy to see in a large environment where security is of extreme importance that using a pre-shared key is not a recommended solution.

Specify DH group (Perfect Forward Secrecy)   *Perfect Forward Secrecy* (PFS) is a method of providing an extra level of protection. If you are utilizing PFS, it ensures that your IPSec SA key was not derived from any previous secret. If someone were to break one of the keys used during encryption, and you were not using PFS, it is hypothetically possible to compromise additional keys. However, PFS makes certain that an attacker would have to break each IPSec SA individually. The cost of this advantage is time, because during an ISAKMP SA negotiation, an extra DH exchange has to take place.

```
pixfirewall(config)#isakmp policy policy-number set pfs group
```

policy-number	**1-65534**	Priority identifier.
group	**group1**	Use a 768-bit key for DH when utilizing PFS.
	group2	Use a 1024-bit key for DH when utilizing PFS.

Specify the Security Assocation Lifetime   When IPSec security associations are negotiated, the security-association lifetime parameter is one of the parameters that is negotiated. This variable indicates how much time or data must pass before a new security association is negotiated. By default, Cisco only enables an ISAKMP SA to age to 86,400 seconds (one day) with no limit on the amount of traffic that can pass through the ISAKMP SA; an IPSec SA can last for only 3,600 seconds before expiring or transporting 4,500 Mbs.

These limits may be reasonable for standard IPSec installations, but some always require a different policy. To configure the security association lifetime on an IPSec SA, use the following command:

```
pixfirewall(config)# isakmp policy policy-number lifetime num-of-
seconds
```

policy-number	**1-65534**	Priority identifier.
num-of-seconds	**120-86400**	Security association duration in seconds.

9.8.5.6 Apply Crypto Map to an Interface

Now that we have created our crypto map and specified all of the parameters associated with the crypto map, we need to apply the crypto map to an interface. The crypto map should only be applied to the outside interface. To apply a crypto map to an outside interface, use the following command:

```
pixfirewall(config)#crypto map name-of-map interface name-of-outside-
interface
```

name-of-map	**WORD**	Name for the previously created crypto map.
name-of-outside-interface	**WORD**	Name of the interface with the lower security level.

9.8.5.7 Example Configuration of two PIX Firewalls Using IPSec ISAKMP Pre-share

In Figure 9-16 and 9-17, we can see the configurations necessary to make IPSec between two PIX firewalls utilizing ISAKMP for key management.

9.8.6 Troubleshoot IPSec

Troubleshooting an IPSec configuration can prove to be a difficult task, especially when multiple tunnels are terminating on our PIX Firewall. This is because a lot of variables could have problems. Unlike debugging PPTP problems, the tools Cisco has given us to debug IPSec are much better.

Figure 9-16

Example of PIX firewall A utilizing ISAKMP pre-share

```
hostname pixfirewalla
nameif ethernet0 inside security0
nameif ethernet1 outside security100
interface ethernet0 100full
interface ethernet1 100full
mtu outside 1500
mtu inside 1500
ip address outside 192.168.10.10 255.255.255.0
ip address inside 172.16.30.3 255.255.255.0
sysopt connection permit-ipsec
access-list 101 permit ip 172.16.30.0 255.255.255.0 10.10.10.0
255.255.255.0
crypto ipsec transform-set testset esp-des
crypto map testmap 20 ipsec-isakmp
crypto map testmap 20 match address 101
crypto map testmap 20 set peer 192.168.30.10
crypto map testmap 20 set transform-set testset
crypto map testmap interface outside
isakmp enable outside
isakmp key Testpassword address 192.168.30.10 netmask
255.255.255.255
isakmp policy 30 authentication pre-share
isakmp policy 30 encryption des
isakmp policy 30 hash md5
isakmp policy 30 group 1
isakmp policy 30 lifetime 8500
nat (inside) 0 access-list 101
```

Figure 9-17

Example of PIX firewall C utilizing ISAKMP pre-share

```
hostname pixfirewallc
nameif ethernet0 inside security0
nameif ethernet1 outside security100
interface ethernet0 100full
interface ethernet1 100full
mtu outside 1500
mtu inside 1500
ip address outside 192.168.30.10 255.255.255.0
ip address inside 10.10.10.1 255.255.255.0
sysopt connection permit-ipsec
access-list 105 permit ip 10.10.10.0 255.255.255.0 172.16.30.0
255.255.255.0
crypto ipsec transform-set testset esp-des
crypto map testmap 50 ipsec-isakmp
crypto map testmap 50 match address 105
crypto map testmap 50 set peer 192.168.10.10
crypto map testmap 50 set transform-set testset
crypto map testmap interface outside
isakmp enable outside
isakmp key Testpassword address 192.168.10.10 netmask
255.255.255.255
isakmp policy 60 authentication pre-share
isakmp policy 60 encryption des
isakmp policy 60 hash md5
isakmp policy 60 group 1
isakmp policy 60 lifetime 8500
nat (inside) 0 access-list 105
```

When experiencing problems with an IPSec session, it may be difficult to know where to start. However, you can break these problems down into one of three areas:

- ISAKMP negotiations
- IPSec negotiations
- Identify the data stream to encrypt

By focusing on where problems can occur, we can see where the problems are or are not based upon the symptoms that we are seeing. We will not address troubleshooting problems that stem from incorrectly identifying the data stream as this is simply an access-list problem. The other two can be more difficult to determine.

9.8.6.1 ISAKMP Negotiations

In any IPSec session utilizing ISAKMP, two negotiations have to take place. ISAKMP is the first negotiation that takes place; then, IPSec negotiates a connection within the secure ISAKMP SA. Therefore, if you do not have any idea where to start looking, start with the ISAKMP negotiation. If that is not successful, your ISAKMP peers will not move on to IPSec SA negotiations. In Figure 9-18, we can see the output from *debug crypto isakmp* during an ISAKMP SA negotiation.

In line 1, we can see that the local peer made a request to its ISAKMP peer. Starting in line 9 of Figure 9-18, we can see the PIX firewall evaluating the different policies its ISAKMP peer has offered. In this particular policy, line 9 shows us that the authentication algorithm will be AH_SHA, while the encryption algorithm will be DES (line 20). The most important line in Figure 9-18 is line 27, in which the PIX firewall is telling us it found an acceptable ISAKMP policy. Starting in line 39 we can see the creation of the ISAKMP SAs and their associated lifetimes. Once the ISAKMP SAs have been created, the two IPSec peers can then start negotiating the IPSec SAs inside the ISAKMP SA.

In this captured debug, only a single policy is being exchanged and evaluated between the two ISAKMP peers. If there had been more policies, you would have seen each and every policy be evaluated within the debug output.

9.8.6.2 IPSec Negotiations

If you are having difficulties establishing an IPSec SA, one of the most informative commands you can use is the *debug crypto ipsec* command.

Figure 9-18

Output from the
*debug crypto
isakmp* during
ISAKMP
negotiations on a
PIX firewall

```
 1  crypto_isakmp_process_block: src 172.16.21.2, dest 172.16.20.1
 2  OAK_QM exchange
 3  oakley_process_quick_mode:
 4  OAK_QM_IDLE
 5  ISAKMP (0): processing SA payload. message ID = -1353578758
 6
 7  ISAKMP : Checking IPSec proposal 1
 8
 9  ISAKMP: transform 1, AH_SHA
10  ISAKMP:    attributes in transform:
11  ISAKMP:       encaps is 1
12  ISAKMP:       SA life type in seconds
13  ISAKMP:       SA life duration (basic) of 3600
14  ISAKMP:       SA life type in kilobytes
15  ISAKMP:       SA life duration (VPI) of  0x0 0x46 0x50 0x0
16  ISAKMP:       authenticator is HMAC-SHA
17  ISAKMP (0): atts are acceptable.
18  ISAKMP : Checking IPSec proposal 1
19
20  ISAKMP: transform 1, ESP_DES
21  ISAKMP:    attributes in transform:
22  ISAKMP:       encaps is 1
23  ISAKMP:       SA life type in seconds
24  ISAKMP:       SA life duration (basic) of 3600
25  ISAKMP:       SA life type in kilobytes
26  ISAKMP:       SA life duration (VPI) of  0x0 0x46 0x50 0x0
27  ISAKMP (0): atts are acceptable.
28  ISAKMP (0): processing NONCE payload. message ID = -1353578758
29
30  ISAKMP (0): processing ID payload. message ID = -1353578758
31  ISAKMP (0): ID_IPV4_ADDR_SUBNET src 10.10.10.0/255.255.255.0
                 prot 0 port 0
32  ISAKMP (0): processing ID payload. message ID = -1353578758
33  ISAKMP (0): ID_IPV4_ADDR_SUBNET dst 192.168.100.0/255.255.255.0
                 prot 0
    port 0
34  return status is IKMP_NO_ERROR
35  crypto_isakmp_process_block: src 172.16.21.2, dest 172.16.20.1
36  OAK_QM exchange
37  oakley_process_quick_mode:
38  OAK_QM_AUTH_AWAIT
39  ISAKMP (0): Creating IPSec SAs
40          inbound SA from     172.16.21.2 to      172.16.20.1
            (proxy      41 10.10.10.0 to    192.168.100.0)
42          has spi -1626443867 and conn_id 8 and flags 4
43          lifetime of 3600 seconds
44          lifetime of 4608000 kilobytes
45          outbound SA from      172.16.20.1 to      172.16.21.2
            (proxy
46  192.168.100.0 to      10.10.10.0)
47          has spi 427631892 and conn_id 7 and flags 4
48          lifetime of 3600 seconds
49          lifetime of 4608000 kilobytes
50  ISAKMP (0): Creating IPSec SAs
51          inbound SA from      172.16.21.2 to      172.16.20.1
            (proxy
52  10.10.10.0 to   192.168.100.0)
53          has spi -476584578 and conn_id 6 and flags 4
```

Figure 9-18

Output from the *debug crypto isakmp* during ISAKMP negotiations on a PIX firewall (cont.)

```
54          lifetime of 3600 seconds
55          lifetime of 4608000 kilobytes
56          outbound SA from     172.16.20.1 to     172.16.21.2
            (proxy    57 192.168.100.0 to      10.10.10.0)
58          has spi 143985938 and conn_id 5 and flags 4
59          lifetime of 3600 seconds
60          lifetime of 4608000 kilobytes
61 return status is IKMP_NO_ERROR
```

This debug does not provide any useful information until the router attempts to negotiate an IPSec SA, which does not happen until after the ISAKMP SAs are negotiated. In Figure 9-19, we can see the output generated from a debug command during an IPSec negotiation.

In lines 1 through 7 in Figure 9-19, we can request for an IPSec authentication SA (line 5). Then in lines 8 through 14, we can see the request for an IPSec encryption SA (line 12). Then in lines 29 through 56, we see four different IPSec SAs. Lines 29 through 35 show us the AH SA being initialized, while lines 36 through 42 show us the outgoing AH SA being initialized. Starting on line 43, we see the incoming ESP SA being initialized, while lines 50 through 56 show us the outgoing ESP SA being initialized. As we can see from this output, each SA has a maximum lifetime duration as well as a maximum amount of data that can be put through the connection before expiring the SA.

9.9 PIX Firewall Case Studies

9.9.1 Case Study #1—Terminating PPTP on a PIX Firewall

VPN Type: Intranet VPN

Tunnel Type: Voluntary tunnel

When to deploy: This type of tunnel is useful within an enterprise network when the core network is only routing IP and you need to run IPX between the various sites. Using the Internet as your backbone, you can tunnel IPX securely across the Internet.

Figure 9-19

Output from the *debug crypto ipsec* command during an IPSec SA negotiation PIX firewall

```
1   IPSEC(validate_proposal_request): proposal part #1,
2      (key eng. msg.) dest= 172.16.20.1, src= 172.16.21.2,
3      dest_proxy= 192.168.100.0/255.255.255.0/0/0 (type=4),
4      src_proxy= 10.10.10.0/255.255.255.0/0/0 (type=4),
5      protocol= AH, transform= ah-sha-hmac ,
6      lifedur= 0s and 0kb,
7      spi= 0x0(0), conn_id= 0, keysize= 0, flags= 0x4
8   IPSEC(validate_proposal_request): proposal part #2,
9      (key eng. msg.) dest= 172.16.20.1, src= 172.16.21.2,
10     dest_proxy= 192.168.100.0/255.255.255.0/0/0 (type=4),
11     src_proxy= 10.10.10.0/255.255.255.0/0/0 (type=4),
12     protocol= ESP, transform= esp-des ,
13     lifedur= 0s and 0kb,
14     spi= 0x0(0), conn_id= 0, keysize= 0, flags= 0x4
15  IPSEC(key_engine): got a queue event...
16  IPSEC(spi_response): getting spi 0x2361063f(593561151) for SA
17         from        172.16.21.2 to        172.16.20.1 for prot 2
18  IPSEC(spi_response): getting spi 0x91ff5731(2449430321) for SA
19         from        172.16.21.2 to        172.16.20.1 for prot 3
20  IPSEC(map_alloc_entry): allocating entry 5
21
22  IPSEC(map_alloc_entry): allocating entry 6
23
24  IPSEC(map_alloc_entry): allocating entry 7
25
26  IPSEC(map_alloc_entry): allocating entry 8
27
28  IPSEC(key_engine): got a queue event...
29  IPSEC(initialize_sas): ,
30     (key eng. msg.) dest= 172.16.20.1, src= 172.16.21.2,
31     dest_proxy= 192.168.100.0/255.255.255.0/0/0 (type=4),
32     src_proxy= 10.10.10.0/255.255.255.0/0/0 (type=4),
33     protocol= AH, transform= ah-sha-hmac ,
34     lifedur= 3600s and 4608000kb,
35     spi= 0x2361063f(593561151), conn_id= 5, keysize= 0, flags=
           0x4
36  IPSEC(initialize_sas): ,
37     (key eng. msg.) src= 172.16.20.1, dest= 172.16.21.2,
38     src_proxy= 192.168.100.0/255.255.255.0/0/0 (type=4),
39     dest_proxy= 10.10.10.0/255.255.255.0/0/0 (type=4),
40     protocol= AH, transform= ah-sha-hmac ,
41     lifedur= 3600s and 4608000kb,
42     spi= 0x1f1a003f(521797695), conn_id= 6, keysize= 0, flags=
           0x4
43  IPSEC(initialize_sas): ,
44     (key eng. msg.) dest= 172.16.20.1, src= 172.16.21.2,
45     dest_proxy= 192.168.100.0/255.255.255.0/0/0 (type=4),
46     src_proxy= 10.10.10.0/255.255.255.0/0/0 (type=4),
47     protocol= ESP, transform= esp-des ,
48     lifedur= 3600s and 4608000kb,
49     spi= 0x91ff5731(2449430321), conn_id= 7, keysize= 0, flags=
           0x4
50  IPSEC(initialize_sas): ,
51     (key eng. msg.) src= 172.16.20.1, dest= 172.16.21.2,
52     src_proxy= 192.168.100.0/255.255.255.0/0/0 (type=4),
53     dest_proxy= 10.10.10.0/255.255.255.0/0/0 (type=4),
54     protocol= ESP, transform= esp-des ,
55     lifedur= 3600s and 4608000kb,
56     spi= 0x36400e5(56885477), conn_id= 8, keysize= 0, flags= 0x4
```

Figure 9-20

Case Study #1—
terminating
PPTP on a PIX
firewall

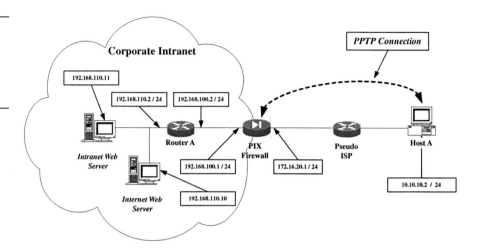

Verifying VPN has been enabled: The remote workstation can connect to an intranet Web server and ping the Internet Web server.

Note:

All links are considered to have a subnet mask of 255.255.255.0 unless otherwise specified

9.9.1.1 PPTP PIX Firewall Configuration File

Figure 9-21

PIX PPTP
firewall
configuration file

```
1   PIX Version 5.1(2)
2   nameif ethernet0 outside security0
3   nameif ethernet1 inside security100
4   enable password 2KFQnbNIdI.2KYOU encrypted
5   passwd 2KFQnbNIdI.2KYOU encrypted
6   hostname PIXPPTPServer
7   access-list 101 permit ip 192.168.100.0 255.255.255.0
    192.168.100.0 255.255.255.0
8   interface ethernet0 10baset
9   interface ethernet1 10baset
10  mtu outside 1500
11  mtu inside 1500
12  ip address outside 172.16.20.1 255.255.255.0
13  ip address inside 192.168.100.1 255.255.255.0
14  ip local pool pptp-pool 192.168.100.10-192.168.100.20
15  global (outside) 1 172.16.20.5-172.16.20.25
16  nat (inside) 0 access-list 101
17  nat (inside) 1 192.168.110.0 255.255.0.0 0 0
18  static (inside,outside) 172.16.20.100 192.168.110.10 netmask
    255.255.255.255
19  conduit permit tcp host 172.16.20.100 eq www any
20  route outside 0.0.0.0 0.0.0.0 172.16.20.2 1
21  route inside 192.168.0.0 255.255.0.0 192.168.100.2 1
22  sysopt connection permit-pptp
23  telnet 192.168.110.10 255.255.255.255 inside
24  vpdn group 33 accept dialin pptp
25  vpdn group 33 ppp authentication mschap
26  vpdn group 33 ppp encryption mppe 40 required
27  vpdn group 33 client configuration address local pptp-pool
28  vpdn group 33 client authentication local
29  vpdn username meg password italy
30  vpdn enable outside
31  Cryptochecksum:f21a4485443b47d4eb868397873a3e4e
```

9.9.1.2 Router A Configuration File

Figure 9-22

Router A
configuration file

```
32 version 12.0
33 service timestamps debug uptime
34 service timestamps log uptime
35 no service password-encryption
36 !
37 hostname RouterA
38 !
39 interface Ethernet0
40  ip address 192.168.100.2 255.255.255.0
41  no ip directed-broadcast
42  no ip route-cache
43 !
44 interface Ethernet1
45  ip address 192.168.110.1 255.255.255.0
46  no ip directed-broadcast
47  no ip route-cache
48 !
49 interface Serial0
50  no ip address
51  shutdown
52 !
53 interface Serial1
54  no ip address
55  shutdown
56 !
57 router ospf 10
58  redistribute static metric 10 subnets
59  network 192.168.110.0 0.0.0.255 area 0
60  network 192.168.100.0 0.0.0.255 area 0
61  default-information originate always metric-type 1
62 !
63 ip route 0.0.0.0 0.0.0.0 192.168.100.1
64 !
65 line con 0
66  exec-timeout 0 0
67  transport input none
68 line aux 0
69 line vty 0 4
70 !
71 end
```

9.9.1.3 Case Study Analysis

In this case study, we have configured a PIX firewall to act as a PPTP server with a single router behind the firewall on the corporate intranet (Router A). As we start to look at the config file for the PIX firewall the first thing that we see related to PPTP is the address pool on line 14. This is the address pool that the PIX firewall will pull from for incoming PPTP connections. Once a PPTP client gets a connection, they can tunnel their packet to the outside interface. Once the GRE header is stripped off, it still has to go through the PIX firewall's engine. In this particular case, we do not want to run it through *Network Address Translation* (NAT) because the packet already has an inside address. To keep from translating this packet, lines 7 and 16 have been set up to instruct the PIX firewall not to translate those packets.

As we start to scrutinize the details of this configuration, we can see that external devices can get to the Internet Web server because of the static command and conduit (lines 18 and 19). Notice, though, that although they can connect to the Web server through port 80, they cannot ping it, nor can they access the Intranet Web server. However, once a PPTP user connects to the PIX firewall, they can connect to either the intranet Web server or Internet Web server. In addition, they can easily ping either server, because their ICMP echoes are not being processed by the PPTP server; the GRE packets are being processed and put on the corporate network.

So what happens to your PPTP user when he or she connects to the corporate intranet and does a DNS lookup? If the DNS server is on the corporate network, then the DNS response must return the local IP address 192.168.110.10. However, if the DNS server is outside of the firewall, which IP address should be returned to the DNS query? The DNS query must respond with the Web server's global IP address: 172.16.20.100. This is what will enable external hosts to resolve the IP address to a global routable address. But how can a DNS server know when to respond with which address? DNS servers do not know which address to respond with. It is NAT that resolves this problem. Even though the IP address is embedded within the actual payload, NAT has the capability to fix protocols that embed the IP address in the actual payload. When NAT sees the DNS response from the inside DNS server to an external host, it breaks open the packet, looks at the IP address in the response, and checks against its static mappings to see if there is a match. Once NAT finds that internal IP address, it sticks the real IP address into the DNS response and sends the packet to the DNS client.

Looking at line 26, we can see that 40-bit MPPE is required for connecting to our PPTP server. In order to use MPPE, we also need to use MS-CHAP authentication (line 25) only. We can't use PAP or CHAP when utilizing MPPE.

The advantage of this configuration is that for sites that already have a PIX firewall deployed, PPTP can easily be added to the configuration without significantly impacting the security of the corporate network. This is particularly advantageous for organizations that are heavily invested in Microsoft Windows OSs.

9.9.2 Case Study #2—IPSec on a PIX Firewall to a Cisco Router

VPN Type: Intranet VPN
Tunnel Type: Compulsory tunnel
When to deploy: This type of tunnel is useful for creating secure communications between two networks connected to the Internet.

Note:

All links are considered to have a subnet mask of 255.255.255.0 unless otherwise specified.

Figure 9-23

Case Study #2—
IPSec on a PIX
firewall to a Cisco
router

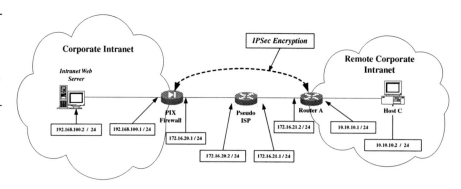

9.9.2.1 IPSec PIX Firewall Configuration File

Figure 9-24

PIX IPSEC
firewall
configuration file

```
1   PIX Version 5.1(2)
2   nameif ethernet0 outside security0
3   nameif ethernet1 inside security100
4   enable password 2KFQnbNIdI.2KYOU encrypted
5   passwd 2KFQnbNIdI.2KYOU encrypted
6   hostname PIXPPTPServer
7   access-list ipsec permit ip 192.168.100.0 255.255.255.0
    10.10.10.0
      255.255.255.0
8   interface ethernet0 10baset
9   interface ethernet1 10baset
10  mtu outside 1500
11  mtu inside 1500
12  ip address outside 172.16.20.1 255.255.255.0
13  ip address inside 192.168.100.1 255.255.255.0
14  arp timeout 14400
15  global (outside) 1 172.16.20.5-172.16.20.25
16  nat (inside) 0 access-list ipsec
17  nat (inside) 1 192.168.100.0 255.255.0.0 0 0
18  route outside 0.0.0.0 0.0.0.0 172.16.20.2 1
19  route inside 192.168.0.0 255.255.0.0 192.168.100.2 1
20  sysopt connection permit-ipsec
21  crypto ipsec transform-set IntranetVPN ah-sha-hmac esp-des
22  crypto map Intranet 33 ipsec-isakmp
23  crypto map Intranet 33 match address ipsec
24  crypto map Intranet 33 set peer 172.16.21.2
25  crypto map Intranet 33 set transform-set IntranetVPN
26  crypto map Intranet interface outside
27  isakmp enable outside
28  isakmp key venice address 172.16.21.2 netmask 255.255.255.255
29  isakmp identity hostname
30  isakmp policy 21 authentication pre-share
31  isakmp policy 21 encryption des
32  isakmp policy 21 hash md5
33  isakmp policy 21 group 2
34  isakmp policy 21 lifetime 86400
35  Cryptochecksum:eb5a41f526a5446d88c0324
```

9.9.2.2 Router A Configuration File

Figure 9-25

Router A IPSec
configuration file

```
36 version 12.0
37 no service pad
38 service timestamps debug uptime
39 service timestamps log uptime
40 no service password-encryption
41 !
42 hostname RouterA
43 !
44 crypto isakmp policy 100
45   hash md5
46   authentication pre-share
47   group 2
48 crypto isakmp key venice address 172.16.20.1
49 !
50 crypto ipsec transform-set IntranetVPN ah-sha-hmac esp-des
51 !
52 crypto map CorporateNet 20 ipsec-isakmp
53   set peer 172.16.20.1
54   set transform-set IntranetVPN
55   match address 101
56 !
57 interface Ethernet1/0
58   ip address 10.10.10.1 255.255.255.0
59   no ip directed-broadcast
60   no ip route-cache
61   ip ospf interface-retry 0
62   no ip mroute-cache
63 !
64 interface Serial2/0
65   ip address 172.16.21.2 255.255.255.0
66   no ip directed-broadcast
67   no ip route-cache
68   no ip mroute-cache
69   crypto map CorporateNet
70 !
71 router ospf 10
72   network 10.10.10.0 0.0.0.255 area 0
73   network 172.16.21.0 0.0.0.255 area 0
74 !
75 ip classless
76 ip route 0.0.0.0 0.0.0.0 172.16.21.1
77 !
78 access-list 101 permit ip 10.10.10.0 0.0.0.255 192.168.100.0
   0.0.0.255
79 !
80 line con 0
81   exec-timeout 0 0
82   transport input none
83 line aux 0
84 line vty 0 4
85   login
86 !
87 end
```

9.9.2.3 Pseudo Internet Router Configuration File

Figure 9-26

Pseudo Internet
router
configuration file

```
88   version 12.0
89   service timestamps debug uptime
90   service timestamps log uptime
91   no service password-encryption
92   !
93   hostname PseudoInternet
94   !
95   interface Ethernet0
96    ip address 172.16.20.2 255.255.255.0
97    no ip directed-broadcast
98    no ip route-cache
99   !
100  interface Serial0
101   ip address 172.16.21.1 255.255.255.0
102   no ip route-cache
103  !
104  interface Serial1
105   no ip address
106   no ip directed-broadcast
107   shutdown
108  !
109  router ospf 10
110   passive-interface Ethernet0
111   network 172.16.20.0 0.0.0.255 area 0
112   network 172.16.21.0 0.0.0.255 area 0
113  !
114  line con 0
115   exec-timeout 0 0
116   transport input none
117  line aux 0
118  line vty 0 4
119  !
120  end
```

9.9.2.4 Pseudo Internet Router Routing Table

Figure 9-27

Pseudo Internet router routing table

```
121 PseudoInternet#show ip route
122 Codes: C - connected, S - static, I - IGRP, R - RIP, M -
    mobile, B - BGP
123 D - EIGRP, EX - EIGRP external, O - OSPF, IA - OSPF inter area
124 N1 - OSPF NSSA external type 1, N2 - OSPF NSSA external type 2
125 E1 - OSPF external type 1, E2 - OSPF external type 2, E - EGP
126 i - IS-IS, L1 - IS-IS level-1, L2 - IS-IS level-2, ia - IS-IS
    inter area
127 * - candidate default, U - per-user static route, o - ODR
128 P - periodic downloaded static route
129
130 Gateway of last resort is not set
131
132      172.16.0.0/24 is subnetted, 2 subnets
133 C       172.16.20.0 is directly connected, Ethernet0
134 C       172.16.21.0 is directly connected, Serial0
135      10.0.0.0/24 is subnetted, 1 subnets
136 O       10.10.10.0 [110/74] via 172.16.21.2, 01:09:17, Serial0
```

9.9.2.5 Case Study Analysis

In this case study, we have configured a PIX firewall to act as an IPSec peer with a Cisco router. We have done this to show the differences and similarities between the configurations.

At first glimpse we can see some quick similarities, such as ISAKMP policies and crypto maps. The first problematic component of our solution is ISAKMP. If we do not successfully negotiate a policy, we will not be able to set up the ISAKMP SAs that subsequently enable the IPSec SAs to be negotiated. When looking at the PIX ISAKMP configuration (lines 27–34), we can see that the configuration is quite different than the Cisco router's ISAKMP configuration (lines 44–48). Keep in mind that these policies both specify the exact same attributes.

Let's take a quick look at how we have defined the data stream to be encrypted. At this point we should realize the command syntax is slightly irregular from Cisco IOS, but we should be able to recognize what is going on with the configuration. More importantly, it is the definition of the data streams that is important, as well as how each router handled it.

Let's start by recognizing that even though we did not specify tunnel mode for our IPSec packets, it was on by default. This means that every packet that gets encrypted by the crypto map automatically encrypts the header and inserts the source and destination of the two IPSec peers.

Once the remote IPSec peer receives the IPSec packet, it strips off the header and puts it on the network. This means that our pseudo-router does not need to have any knowledge of the networks behind our IPSec peers, as we can see in Figure 9-23.

A closer look at the data stream that was defined to be encrypted is the actual IP addresses from the corporate network and not the NATed addresses. In order to keep the PIX firewall from translating those addresses, we need to use the commands in lines 7 and 16. The combination of those two lines excludes our packets from being run through the proverbial NAT mill. Interestingly enough, because NAT/PAT can break certain applications, we can use IPSec in tunnel mode to give corporate devices a direct communication path to each other that will enable them to operate, even though they use NAT to communicate with the rest of the world. The secret is that the packets actually bypass NAT and thus don't get corrupted.

The last thing to look at on the PIX firewall is line 26. When applying a crypto map to an interface on a PIX firewall, it must be defined on the outside interface (the interface with the lower security level). Failure to install the crypto map on an outside interface will cause your VPN not to work.

APPENDIX A

VPN Protocol Comparison

	GRE	CET	IPSec	PPTP	L2TP
Machine Authentication	No	Yes	Yes	No	Yes
User Authentication	No	No	No	Yes	Yes
Multiprotocol Support	Yes	N/A	No	Yes	Yes
IP Protocol Number	47	N/A	50–ESP, 51–AH	47	N/A
UDP Port Number	N/A	N/A	500–IKE	N/A	1701
TCP Port Number	1723	N/A	N/A	1723	1701
Data Confidentiality	No	Yes	Yes	Yes	No
Data Integrity	No	No	Yes	Yes	No
Data Origin Authentication	No	No	Yes	Yes	No
Anti-Replay	No	No	Yes	Yes	Yes
IOS Support	10.0 and later	11.2 and later	11.3T and later	12.0(5)XE and later	12.0T and later
IOS Name Value Supports VPN Technology	N/A	40 or 56	56i	s	s
IOS Name Value Supports VPN w/Strong Encryption	N/A	N/A	k2	k2	N/A

APPENDIX B

Command Summary

Table B-1	Command	Config Mode	Function
Tunnel commands	**interface tunnel** *tunnel-number*	Global Config	Creates a tunnel interface or changes to a previously created tunnel
	tunnel mode gre ip	Tunnel Interface	Specifies the tunnel to operate in point-to-point mode
	tunnel mode gre multipoint	Tunnel Interface	Specifies the tunnel that will operate in multipoint mode
	tunnel source *source-ip*	Tunnel Interface	Specifies the source IP address to use for the tunnel
	tunnel destination **tunnel destination** *destination-ip*	Tunnel Interface	Specifies the destination IP address to use for the tunnel
	tunnel key *key-number*	Tunnel Interface	Configure key for the multipoint tunnel
	ip nhrp network-id *network-number*	Tunnel Interface	Specifies the network ID of the NHRP network
	ip nhrp nhs VPN- *ip-address*	Tunnel Interface	Specifies the next hop server the NHRP device should use

continues

Table B-1	Command	Config Mode	Function
Tunnel Commands (cont.)	**ip nhrp map** *real-ip-address VPN-ip-address*	Tunnel Interface	Manually maps an NHRP address to a NBMA address
	show interface tunnel	User/Enable	Shows the status of the current tunnel
	show ip nhrp	User/Enable	Shows the current NHRP mappings
	show ip nhrp traffic	User/Enable	Shows traffic over the NHRP network

Table B-2

CET IOS 11.3 enterprise commands

Command	Config Mode	Function
crypto gen-signature-keys *crypto-engine-name {slot}*	Global Config	Generates public/private key pair
crypto engine accelerator	Global Config	Enables VPN module for crypto engine on Cisco 1700 series router
show crypto mypubkey	User/Enable	Displays your public key
crypto key-exchange passive	Global Config	Specifies that a router goes into passive mode during a key exchange
crypto key-exchange *VPN-peer-ip-address crypto-engine*	Global Config	Specifies that a router contact a VPN peer at the IP address to exchange keys
crypto algorithm 40-bit-des *cfb-type*	Global Config	Enables a 40-bit cryptography algorithm globally
crypto algorithm des ***cfb-type***	Global Config	Enables a 56-bit cryptography algorithm globally
show crypto algorithms	User/Enable	Shows all the current enabled algorithms
crypto *crypto-map-name sequence-number*	Global Config	Creates a crypto map or enters a previously created crypto map
set peer *crypto-engine-name*	Crypto Map Config	Defines the peer you will exchange encrypted data with in this crypto map
match address *access-list*	Crypto Map Config	Defines the data stream that should be encrypted
set algorithm *encrypt-algorithm cfb-type*	Crypto Map Config	Defines the encryption algorithm to be used by the crypto map
crypto map *crypto-map-name*	Interface Config	Applies the crypto map to an interface
crypto key-timeout *timeout*	Crypto Map Config	Specifies the length of time to use before expiring an encrypted connection
crypto pregen-dh-pairs *number-of-pairs*	Crypto Map Config	Specifies the number of DH numbers that can be pregenerated
show crypto connections	User/Enable	Shows the active encryption sessions
show crypto engine connections	User/Enable	Shows active and disabled encryption sessions

Table B-3

CET IOS 11.3T and 12.0 Enterprise Commands

Command	Config Mode	Function
crypto key generate dss *crypto-engine-name [slot]*	Global	Generates public/private key pair
crypto engine accelerator	Global	Enables VPN module for crypto engine on Cisco 1700 series router
show crypto key mypubkey dss	User/Enable	Displays your public key
crypto key exchange dss passive	Global Config	Specifies a router to go into passive mode during a key exchange
crypto key exchange dss *VPN-peer-ip-address crypto-engine*	Global Config	Specifies that a router contact a VPN peer at the IP address to exchange keys
crypto cisco algorithm 40-bit-des *cfb-type*	Global Config	Enables a 40-bit cryptography algorithm globally
crypto cisco algorithm *cfb-type*	Global Config	Enables a 56-bit cryptography algorithm globally
show crypto algorithms	User/Enable	Shows all the current enabled algorithms
crypto *crypto-map-name sequence-number*	Crypto Map Config	Creates a crypto map or enters a previously created crypto map
set peer *crypto-engine-name*	Crypto Map Config	Defines the peer you will exchange encrypted data with in this crypto map
match address *access-list*		Defines the data stream that should be encrypted
set algorithm *encrypt-algorithm cfb-type*	Crypto Map Config	Defines the encryption algorithm to used by the crypto map
crypto map *crypto-map-name*	Interface Config Mode	Applies the crypto map to an interface
crypto cisco key-timeout *timeout*	Crypto Map Config	Specifies the length of time to use before expiring an encrypted connection
crypto pregen-dh-pairs *number-of-pairs*	Crypto Map Config	Specifies the number of DH numbers that can be pregenerated
show crypto map	User/Enable	Shows the active encryption sessions
show crypto engine connections	User/Enable	Shows active and disabled encryption sessions

Table B-4

IPSec IOS enterprise commands

Command	Config Mode	Function
crypto ipsec transform-set *transform-name protocol1 protocol 2 protocol3*	Global Config	Defines the encryption algorithms used with crypto maps
mode *mode-of-operation*	Transform-set Config	Defines the mode (transport or tunnel) of a transform set
crypto map *name-of-map sequence-number* **ipsec-manual**	Global Config	Brings all the components together for encryption (algorithms, interfaces, and so on)
match address *access-list*	Crypto Map Config	Specifies an access list to define the data stream to encrypt
set peer *VPN-ip-address*	Crypto Map Config	Defines the IP address of your remote VPN peer
set transform-set *transform-set-name*	Crypto Map Config	Applies the preexisting transform set to a crypto map
set security-association *direction* **esp** *SPI protocol key*	Crypto Map Config	Defines the key to use for ESP (IOS 11.3 manual mode only)
set security-association *direction* **ah** *SPI key*	Crypto Map Config	Defines the key to use for AH (IOS 11.3 manual mode only)
set session-key *direction* **esp** *SPI protocol key*	Crypto Map Config	Defines the key to use for ESP (IOS 12.0 and 12.1 manual mode only)
set session-key *direction* **ah** *SPI key*	Crypto Map Config	Defines the key to use for AH (IOS 12.0 and 12.1 manual mode only)
crypto map *name-of-map*	Interface Configuration	Apply crypto map to an interface
crypto ipsec enable	Global Config	Enables IPSEC
crypto isakmp policy *policy-number*	ISAKMP Policy Config	Enables ISAKMP
hash *hash-protocol*	ISAKMP Policy Config	Defines the hash to use during ISAKMP negotiations
authentication *auth-protocol*	ISAKMP Policy Config	Defines the password to use during ISAKMP negotiations (non-PKI, CA server implementation)

continues

Table B-4	Command	Config Mode	Function
IPSec IOS enterprise commands (cont.)	**crypto isakmp key** *key* **address** *ISAKMP-peer-ip-address I*	Global Config	The key to use during ISAKMP negotiations (non-PKI, CA server implementation)
	crypto key generate rsa *option*	Global Config	Generates public/private keys to use in a PKI infrastrucure
	crypto isakmp identity *isakmp-identity*	Global Config	Name to use in a PKI infrastructure
	crypto key pubkey-chain rsa	Global Config	Defines other VPN peers' public keys if you are using RSA encryption
	named-key *isakmp-identity option*	Public Key Chain	Defines remote peer's ISAKMP identity
	crypto key generate rsa *option*	Global Config	Generates RSA keys
	crypto ca identity *name*	Global Config	The name you use to identify yourself to a PKI infrastructure
	enrollment url *url*	CA identity	Used to enroll in a PKI
	enrollement mode ra	CA identity	Used to enroll in a PKI
	query url *url*	CA identity	Used to enroll in a PKI
	crypto ca authenticate *name*	Global Config	Authenticates your CA server and verifies that you know whom you are talking to
	crypto ca enroll *name*	Global Config	
	crypto dynamic-map *name-of-map sequence-number*	Global Config	Crypto map for voluntary tunnels
	set security-association lifetime seconds *num-of-seconds*	Crypto Map Config	Defines the number of seconds that require an SA to expire
	set security-association lifetime kilobytes *num-of-bytes*	Crypto Map Config	Defines the number of bytes that require an SA to expire
	set pfs *group*	Crypto Map Config	Attribute for added security

continues

Table B-4

IPSec IOS
enterprise
commands (cont.)

Command	Config Mode	Function
show crypto map	Enable	Shows current crypto maps available
show crypto ipsec sa	Enable	Shows active IPSec SAs
show crypto isakmp policy	Enable	Shows ISAKMP policies available
debug crypto isakmp	Enable	Debugs the ISAKMP SA negotiation
debug crypto ipsec	Enable	Debugs the IPSec SA negotiation

Table B-5

PPTP IOS
enterprise
commands

Command	Config Mode	Function
vpdn enable	Global Config	Enables VPDNs
interface virtual-template *virtual-template-number*	Global Config	Creates an attribute that virtual access interfaces will be created from
ppp authentication *authentication-protocol*	Interface Config	Specifies the type of authentication used by the VPN client
ppp encrypt mppe *num-encryption—bits use-of-enncryption-option*	Interface Config	Specifies encryption requirements
vpdn-group *vpdn-group-name*	Global Config	Creates a VPDN group that supports a VPDN protocol
accept-dialin	VPDN Config	Enables incoming connections
protocol pptp	VPDN Config	Uses PPTP within this VPDN group
virtual-template *virtual-template-interface*	VPDN Accept-Dialin Config	Defines a virtual interface to use for VPDN group
username *username* **password** *password*	Global Config	Create local PPTP users
show vpdn	Enable	Shows active VPDN connections

Table B-6

L2TP IOS
enterprise
commands

Command	Config Mode	Function
vpdn enable	Global Config	Enables VPDNs
interface virtual-template	Global Config	Creates an attribute that virtual access interfaces will be created from
l2tp tunnel password *password*	Vpdn-config	A shared key used for tunnel authentication
local name	VPDN Config	Used by the VPDN device to identify itself to its VPDN peer
terminate-from hostname *LAC-hostname*	VPDN Config	Used by the VPDN group to indicate the name of the LNS to send back to the LAC
initiate-to ip *ip-address* **limit** *sessions*	VPDN Config	Used by the LAC to determine the destination of the LNS
domain	VPDN Config	Used by the LAC to determine which VPDN group to use
request-dialin	VPDN Config	Enables LAC to start incoming L2TP sessions
request-dialout	VPDN Config	Enables LNS to start outgoing L2TP sessions
accept-dialin	VPDN Config	Enables LNS to accept incoming L2TP sessions
accept-dialout	VPDN Config	Enables LAC to accept outgoing L2TP sessions
local name *LAC-hostname*	VPDN Config	Defines the name LAC will use to identify itself to the LNS
ppp authentication	Interface Config	Specifies the type of authentication used by the VPN client
vpdn-group *vpdn-group-name*	Global Config	Creates a VPDN group that supports a VPDN protocol
accept-dialin		Enables incoming connections
protocol *vpdn-protocol*	VPDN Config	Uses L2TP within this VPDN group
username *username* **password** *password*	Global Config	Creates local PPTP users
domain *domain-name*	VPDN Request-Dialin Config	Defines the domain name to use on LAC to determine which VPDN group to use for the L2TP user
show vpdn	Enable	Shows active VPDN connections

Table B-7

PIX firewall basic commands

Command	Config Mode	Function
enable	Configuration	Enters enable mode
configure terminal	Configuration	Enters configuration model from the terminal
enable password *password*	Configuration	Sets the enable password
telnet *ip-address net-mask* **inside**	Configuration	Defines the IP addresses that can Telnet to a PIX firewall
passwd *password*	Configuration	Defines Telnet password
nameif *interface interface-name* **security** *security-level*	Configuration	Names and assigns a security level to an interface
interface *interface-name* **shutdown**	Configuration	Shuts down an interface
ip address *interface-name ip-address subnet-mask*	Configuration	Sets an IP address on an interface
route *interface-name ip-address subnet-mask*	Configuration	Defines static routes
nat (*interface-name*) *nat-group ip-address subnet-mask*	Configuration	Defines an inside interface and address
global (*interface-name*) *nat-group ip-address subnet-mask*	Configuration	Defines an outside interface and address
static (***trusted-interface-name, untrusted-interface-name***) ***global-ip-address internal-ip-address***	Configuration	Defines outside to inside static NAT mappings
conduit *permission protocol* host *global-ip-address operator value*	Configuration	All specific protocols from the outside to inside
show xlate	Configuration	Shows the current translations

Table B-8

PIX PPTP
commands

Command	Config Mode	Function
vpdn enable	Configuration	Enables VPDN technologies
sysopt connection permit-pptp	Configuration	Enables PPTP from the outside interface to the inside interface
vpdn group vpdn-group-name ppp authentication *auth-protocol*	Configuration	Defines the PPTP authentication protocol
aaa-server auth-name **protocol** aaa-server	Configuration	Defines the AAA server (RADIUS/TACACS)
aaa-server auth-name (*interface-name*) **host** *ip-addres-of-aaa-server*	Configuration	Defines the location of the AAA server
vpdn group *vpdn-group-name* **client authentication local**	Configuration	Defines the PPTP users on the PIX box
vpdn group *vpdn-group-name* **client authentication aaa** *auth-name*	Configuration	Uses AAA to authenticate PPTP users
vpdn group *vpdn-group-name* **ppp encryption mppe** *encryption-option*	Configuration	Specifies encryption algorithms
ip local pool *address-pool-name first-ip-address last-ip-address*	Configuration	Defines the IP address pool
vpdn group *vpdn-group-name* **client configuration address local**	Configuration	An associate pool of addresses for use with PPTP users
vpdn group *vpdn-group-name* **client configuration** *ip-attribute ip-address*	Configuration	Specify additional IP attributes
vpdn username *username* **password** *password*	Configuration	Defines local users
debug ppp uauth	Enable	Debugs ppp negotiations

Command	Config Mode	Function
Table B-9		
PIX firewall IPSec commands		
sysopt connection permit-ipsec	Configuration	Enables IPSec from the outside interface to the inside interface
crypto ipsec transform-set *transform-name protocol1 protocol 2 protocol3*	Configuration	Defines the IPSec transform set
crypto map *name-of-map sequence-number* **ipsec-manual**	Configuration	Creates the manual IPSec crypto map
crypto map *name-of-map sequence-number* **match address** *access-list*	Configuration	Defines the traffic to encrypt
crypto map *name-of-map sequence-number* **set peer** *VPN-ip-address*	Configuration	Specifies the IPSec peer router
crypto map *name-of-map sequence-number* **set transform-***set transform-set-name*	Configuration	Specifies which transform set to use
crypto map *name-of-map sequence-number* **set session-key** *direction* **esp** *SPI* **cipher** *cipher-key* **authenticator** *auth-key*	Configuration	Defines encryption keys
crypto map *name-of-map sequence-number* **set session-key** *direction* **ah** *SPI auth-key*	Configuration	Define authentication keys
crypto map *name-of-map* **interface** *name-of-outside-interface*	Configuration	Applies a crypto map to an interface
isakmp enable *name-of-outside-interface*	Configuration	Enables ISAKMP
isakmp policy *policy-number*	Configuration	Creates the ISAKMP policy
isakmp policy *policy-number* **encryption** *encryption-protocol*	Configuration	Defines the encryption policy

continues

Command	Config Mode	Function
Table B-9		
PIX firewall IPSec commands (cont.)		
isakmp policy *policy-number* **encryption** *encryption-protocol*	Configuration	Defines the hash used in an algorithm
isakmp policy *policy-number* **authentication** *auth-protocol*	Configuration	Specifies the type of key to use
isakmp key *key* **address** *ISAKMP-peer-ip-address*	Configuration	Configures the pre-share key for the ISAKMP policy
isakmp policy *policy-number* **set pfs** *group*	Configuration	Specifies the DH group
isakmp policy *policy-number* **lifetime** *num-of-seconds*	Configuration	Specifies the SA lifetimes
debug crypto isakmp	Enable	Debugs the ISAKMP negotiations
debug crypto ipsec	Enable	Debugs the IPSec negotiations

Cisco 2000, 2500, 3000, 4000, and 7000 Series Routers Password Recovery

In order for this password recovery method to work, your Cisco router must have a ROM of 10.0 or later.

1. Using a rolled cable, connect a COM port on your PC to the console port on your Cisco router.

2. Hit <enter> several times until you are in user mode.

3. Router>**show version.** Make note of the configuration register as shown in Figure C-1.

4. Reboot the Cisco router.

5. Within 30 seconds after the router is powered up, hit the **ctrl-break**. The router will respond, as shown in Figure C-2. If you wait too long, the Cisco router will not register the key sequence.

6. >**o/r 0x42**

   This command instructs the router to boot from flash and skip the configuration file.

Figure C-1

Output from the
Show Version
command

```
TestRouter>show version
Cisco Internetwork Operating System Software
IOS (tm) 2500 Software (C2500-IS56-L), Version 12.0(8), RELEASE
SOFTWARE (fc1)
Copyright (c) 1986-1999 by cisco Systems, Inc.
Compiled Mon 29-Nov-99 17:32 by kpma
Image text-base: 0x0303F638, data-base: 0x00001000

ROM: System Bootstrap, Version 4.14(9.1), SOFTWARE

TestRouter uptime is 2 minutes
System restarted by power-on
System image file is "flash:c2500-is56-1_120-8.bin"

cisco 2500 (68030) processor (revision D) with 16384K/2048K bytes
of memory.
Processor board ID 01739404, with hardware revision 00000000
Bridging software.
X.25 software, Version 3.0.0.
1 Ethernet/IEEE 802.3 interface(s)
2 Serial network interface(s)
32K bytes of non-volatile configuration memory.
8192K bytes of processor board System flash (Read ONLY)

Configuration register is 0x2102
```

Figure C-2

Output during a
reboot in which
Ctrl-Break has
been executed

```
System Bootstrap, Version 11.0(10c), SOFTWARE
Copyright (c) 1986-1996 by cisco Systems
2500 processor with 6144 Kbytes of main memory

Abort at 0x1098B26 (PC)
>
```

7. **>i**

   This command instructs the router to reboot boot from flash.

8. When prompted, answer **no** to the setup questions. This keeps it from running through Cisco's auto-configuration wizard.

9. Router>**ena**

   This enables you to enter enable mode. No enable password can be used at this point because it has been bypassed.

Note:

If you want to view the password, you can use the show config command. However, if the enable password is encrypted, you will not be able to view it.

---

10. Router#**configure memory**

This copies the configuration file in *Non-Volatile Random Access Memory* (NVRAM) into memory. Because you are already in enable mode, you have effectively bypassed the enable password. If you fail to do this step, then when you save your changes in step 15, you will overwrite NVRAM with an generic configuration file (except for the password).

11. Router#**configure terminal**

Enter the global configuration mode.

12. Router(config)#**enable secret *password***

This command sets the enable secret password.

13. Router#**config-register *config-register-value***

Use the value found in step 3. Typically, this will be 0x2102, but it could be a different value.

14. Router(config)#**exit**

Exit global configuration mode.

15. Router#**write memory**

Save the configuration file with your new enable password into NVRAM.

16. Router#**reload**

If you have followed the previous steps, this reboots the router with only the enable password changed.

Cisco 3600, 4500, 4700, 7200, and 7500 Series Routers Password Recovery

1. Using a rolled cable, connect a COM port on your PC to the console port on your Cisco router.

2. Hit <enter> several times until you are in user mode.

3. Router>**show version**

   Make note of the configuration register, as shown in Figure C-3.

4. Reboot the Cisco router.

5. Within 30 seconds after the router is powered up, hit the **ctrl-break**. The router will respond, as shown in Figure C-4. If you wait too long, the Cisco router will not register the key sequence.

Figure C-3

Output from the show version command

```
TestRouter#show version
Cisco Internetwork Operating System Software
IOS (tm) 3600 Software (C3640-IS-M), Version 12.0(3)T3,  RELEASE
SOFTWARE (fc1)
Copyright (c) 1986-1999 by cisco Systems, Inc.
Compiled Thu 15-Apr-99 21:46 by kpma
Image text-base: 0x600088F0, data-base: 0x60AD6000

ROM: System Bootstrap, Version 11.1(19)AA, EARLY DEPLOYMENT RELEASE
SOFTWARE (fc1)

TestRouter uptime is 13 minutes
System restarted by power-on
System image file is "slot0:c3640-is-mz_120-3_T3.bin"

cisco 3640 (R4700) processor (revision 0x00) with 28672K/4096K
bytes of memory.
Processor board ID 10705813
R4700 CPU at 100Mhz, Implementation 33, Rev 1.0
MICA-6DM Firmware: CP ver 2310 - 6/3/1998, SP ver 2310 - 6/3/1998.
Bridging software.
X.25 software, Version 3.0.0.
Basic Rate ISDN software, Version 1.1.
1 Ethernet/IEEE 802.3 interface(s)
4 ISDN Basic Rate interface(s)
12 terminal line(s)
Integrated NT1's for 4 ISDN Basic Rate interfaces
DRAM configuration is 64 bits wide with parity disabled.
125K bytes of non-volatile configuration memory.
4096K bytes of processor board System flash (Read/Write)
8192K bytes of processor board PCMCIA Slot0 flash (Read/Write)

Configuration register is 0x2102
```

Figure C-4

Output during a reboot in which ctrl-break has been executed

```
System Bootstrap, Version 11.1(19)AA, EARLY DEPLOYMENT RELEASE
SOFTWARE (fc1)
Copyright (c) 1998 by cisco Systems, Inc.
C3600 processor with 32768 Kbytes of main memory
Main memory is configured to 64 bit mode with parity disabled


monitor: command "boot" aborted due to user interrupt
rommon 1 >
```

6. **>confreg 0x42**

   This command instructs the router to boot from flash and skip the configuration file.

7. **>reset**

   This command instructs the router to reboot boot.

8. When prompted, answer **no** to the setup questions.

   This keeps from running through Cisco's auto-configuration wizard.

9. Router>**ena**

   This enables you to enter enable mode. No enable password can be used at this point because it has been bypassed.

Note:

If you want to view the password, you can use the show config command. However, if the enable password is encrypted, you will not be able to view it.

---

10. Router#**configure memory**

    This copies the configuration file in NVRAM into memory. Because you are already in enable mode, you have effectively bypassed the enable password. If you fail to do this step, then when you save your changes in step 15, you will overwrite NVRAM with an generic configuration file (except for the password).

11. Router#**configure terminal**

    Enter the global configuration mode.

12. Router(config)#**enable secret *password***

    This command sets the enable secret password.

13. Router(config)#**config-register *config-register-value***

    Use the value found in step 3. Typically, this will be 0x2102, but it could be a different value.

14. Router(config)#**exit**

    Exit global configuration mode.

15. Router#**write memory**

    Save the configuration file with your new enable password into NVRAM.

16. Router#**reload**

    If you have followed the previous steps, this reboots the router with only the enable password changed.

Glossary

Accounting Accounting is the process of determining who is using what resource.

AIM The Advanced Integration Module is used to offload data compression and decompression from the main *central processing unit* (CPU).

Algorithm A procedure that defines a mathematical method used to solve a specific problem. It consists of a well-defined set of rules and/or processes.

ANSI The American National Standards Institute, an organization that publishes and endorses standards for various industries.

ANSI X9.17 The ANSI standard for secret key exchange using the *Data Encryption Standard* (DES) algorithm.

Anti-replay A security feature found in *virtual private network* (VPN) protocols that detects when a message has been received more than once. This type of restriction is used to prevent messages being replayed by an attacker.

Asymmetric algorithm A cryptographic algorithm that uses two different keys for encryption and decryption. Most often associated with public key algorithms.

Authentication The process by which an individual is identified through either something they have, something they know, or both.

Authentication Header (AH) An *IP Security* (IPSec) header that is used to verify that the contents of a packet have not been modified.

Authorization Authorization is the process of determining which services an individual is allowed to access.

AUX The AUX port is the auxiliary port on a Cisco router. This is not to be used a second console port, but as an asynchronous port.

Bandwidth Bandwidth describes how much data can be sent through a network medium. The ability to send larger amounts of data is described as having lots of bandwidth.

Baud A measurement used to describe the number of changes per second, sometimes confused with bit rate.

B-channel Bearer channel used for the transmission of data. Typically, it has 64Kbps of bandwidth available.

BECN Backward Explicit Congestion Notification. A bit used in a Frame Relay packet to indicate that packets going the other direction are experiencing congestion through the Frame Relay cloud.

Bit rate The rate at which bits are sent over a communications link.

Block cipher A cipher that encrypts data in fixed sized blocks.

BRI The Basic Rate Interface is composed of two B-channels and one D-channel. It is typically used for voice, video, and data.

Brute force cracking The process of trying to recover a key by trying all possible combinations.

Callback A process in which a host-initiated dialup session calls an access server to set up the callback, and then the access server disconnects and calls the client back.

CD Carrier Detect, which is used to indicate when there is or is not a connection to the *plain old telephone service* (POTS).

CDP The Cisco Discovery Protocol, a subnetwork access layer protocol used by Cisco devices to discover their neighbors.

Certificate A cryptographically signed object that contains an identity and a public key associated with this identity.

Certification Authority (CA) A third-party entity that is responsible for issuing and revoking certificates. Each device that has its own certificate and public key of the CA can authenticate every other device within a given CA's domain.

CHAP Challenge Handshake Authentication Protocol, a secure authentication protocol.

Checksum A tool used to verify the integrity of a message. Its value is computed using a checksum algorithm.

Cipher   A crypto algorithm that converts data between plaintext and ciphertext.

Cipher block chaining (CBC)   A block cipher mode that combines the previous block of ciphertext with the current block of plaintext before encrypting it.

Cipher feedback (CFB)   A block cipher mode that feeds previously encrypted ciphertext through the block cipher to generate the key that encrypts the next block of ciphertext.

Ciphertext   Data that has been encrypted.

Compression   A process in which data is run through an algorithm in an attempt to reduce the size of the data.

Computer Emergency Response Team (CERT)   An organization that collects and distributes information on computer security incidents and software problems.

CON   The CON port is the console port on a Cisco router.

confidentiality   The ability to ensure that information is kept private between intended parties.

Cracking   The process of overcoming a security measure, or an attempt to recover the value of a key (shared or public).

CRC   The Cyclical Redundancy Check is used to determine if there are any errors detected within a frame.

Cryptanalysis   The process of trying to recover crypto keys or plaintext associated with a crypto system.

Cryptography   Mechanisms used to create ciphertext from plaintext, by using algorithms that are hard to reverse without some secret knowledge.

Crypto map   A Cisco IOS software configuration entity that performs two primary functions: it defines the data flows that need to be encrypted and defines the policies of that encrypted traffic.

CTS   Clear To Send, which tells the *data terminal equipment* (DTE) device that the *data circuit-terminating equipment* (DCE) device is ready to receive data.

CTY   Also known as the console port. *See* CON.

Custom queuing   Method of reserving the specific amount of bandwidth (percentage wise) used by a queue.

Data confidentiality   Method in which protected data is manipulated so that no attacker can read it without the appropriate keys.

Data Encryption Standard (DES)   Block cipher that is vulnerable to attack by well-funded adversaries.

Data integrity   Data integrity mechanisms that enable the recipient to verify that the data has not been modified in transit.

Data origin authentication   A security service where the receiver can verify that protected data could have originated only from the sender. This service requires a data integrity service plus a key distribution mechanism where a secret key is shared only between the sender and receiver.

DCE   Data circuit-terminating equipment, which provides a physical connection to the network. In addition, it provides the clocking on the WAN link.

Differential cryptanalysis   Technique for attacking a cipher by feeding it plaintext and watching for patterns in the ciphertext.

Diffie-Hellman (DH)   Public key crypto algorithm that generates a shared secret between two entities through a public medium.

Digital   The use of a 1 (high) or 0 (low) to represent information.

Digital Signature Standard (DSS)   Digital signature algorithm developed by the *National Security Agency* (NSA) and endorsed by the *National Institute of Standards and Technology* (NIST).

DNIS   The number that a host dials as reported to the NSA by the Telco switch.

Domain name   The Domain Name Service (DNS) protocol that translates between textual names and numerical IP addresses.

DSR   Data Send Ready, which indicates the data circuit-terminating equipment (DCE) device is ready to function. This is not used with modems.

DTE   Data terminal equipment, which provides a physical connection to a Wide Area Network (WAN) but does not provide the clocking on the WAN link.

DTR   Data Terminal Ready, which is used to indicate that the *data circuit-terminating equipment* (DCE) device is ready to send and receive data.

E1   ISDN PRI circuit available only in Europe. It has 30 B-channels and one D-channel.

EIA/TIA   Electronics Industry Association/Telecommunications Industry Association, a standards organization that establishes standards for cabling.

EIGRP   The Enhanced Interior Gateway Routing Protocol is a Cisco proprietary distance vector protocol.

Electronic codebook (ECB)   Block cipher mode that consists of simply applying the cipher to blocks of data in sequence, one block at a time.

Encapsulating Security Payload (ESP) *IP Security* (IPSec) header that encrypts the contents of an IP packet.

ESF Extended Super Framing is a framing protocol used for *Integrated Services Digital Network* (ISDN) *Primary Rate Interface* (PRI) connections.

FECN Forward Explicit Congestion Notification, a bit used in a Frame Relay packet to indicate that it experienced congestion through the Frame Relay cloud.

FDDI The Fiber Distributed Data Interface is a 100Mbs dual ring, token-passing network using fiber optic cable.

Firewall A device installed at the point where external entities enter a site and is used to control the type of networking traffic that flows in and out.

Flowcontrol A method of starting and stopping the transmission of data. It can be implemented through hardware or software.

Forgery Data whose purpose is to mislead the recipient into believing the item and its contents were produced by someone other than the actual author.

Frame Relay A newer packet switched network that uses virtual circuits to create a path to the remote site.

Frequency The number of times a cycle repeats itself within a given amount of time.

GRD An acronym standing for Ground, a reference voltage used for other voltages.

HDLC The High-Level Data Link Control is a bit-oriented synchronous data link layer protocol. HDLC is an encapsulation method that uses frame characters and checksums.

Header compression A compression type that compresses only the header in order to increase the efficiency of protocols like Telnet and X-windows.

Hijacking An attack in which the attacker takes over a live connection between two entities so that the attacker can masquerade as one of the entities.

HMAC A mechanism for message authentication using cryptographic hashes such as SHA and MD5.

I/O Input/output. A system address used by the computer to access devices such as disk drivers, serial ports, or printer ports.

IGRP The Interior Gateway Routing Protocol is a Cisco proprietary distance vector protocol.

Integrity The ability to ensure that information is not modified except by people who are explicitly intended to modify it.

International Data Encryption Algorithm (IDEA) Block cipher developed in Switzerland and used in *pretty good privacy* (PGP).

Internet Address and Numbering Authority (IANA) An organization that assigns host addresses and other numeric constants used in the Internet.

Internet Engineering Task Force (IETF) An organization that establishes and maintains Internet protocol standards.

Internet Key Exchange (IKE) The key management protocol for IPSec based on the *Internet Security Association Key Management Protocol* (ISAKMP) and tailored for typical.

Internet Security Association Key Management Protocol (ISAKMP) The key management application protocol for *IP Security* (IPSec) that has been endorsed by the *Internet Engineering Task Force* (IETF) as a required part of any complete IPSec implementation. Used to create a secure tunnel in which to exchange IPSec keys.

Interrupt *See* IRQ.

Intranet A private network, usually within an organization, that uses Internet protocols but is not connected directly to the global Internet.

IPSec An acronym for IP Security, this is a protocol developed for encrypting data at the IP layer instead of layer 6, as specified in the *Open Systems Interconnection* (OSI) model.

IRQ Interrupt Request Line. This enables a hardware device in a computer to indicate that it needs attention. Fifteen IRQs are available in any computer.

ISDN The Integrated Services Digital Network is a digital network that enables the transmission of voice, data, and video over a circuit switched network.

ITU The International Telecommunications Union develops international telecommunication standards.

Key A value used to encrypt or decrypt information in a distinctive way.

Key distribution center (KDC) Used in Kerberos-based systems, it is a device that provides secret keys to hosts to encrypt traffic.

Kflex56 A proprietary 56K modem modulation method.

L2F Layer Two forwarding is a Cisco proprietary protocol used for tunneling protocols inside of the *Transmission Control Protocol/Internet Protocol* (TCP/IP).

L2TP   The Layer Two tunneling protocol is an Internet standard for tunneling protocols inside of the *Transmission Control Protocol / Internet Protocol* (TCP/IP).

L2TP access concentrator (LAC)   A Layer Two tunneling protocol (L2TP) device that establishes a data link layer connection with the host and tunnels its data to a L2TP network server (LNS).

L2TP network server (LNS)   A *Layer Two tunneling protocol* (L2TP) device that terminates incoming *Virtual Private Dialup Networking* (VPDN) connections from the *L2TP access concentrator* (LAC).

LAN   Local Area Network.

Latency   The amount of time between transmitting a packet and the reception of that packet across a network.

LCP   The Link Control Protocol. It negotiates authentication, callback, compression, and multilinks between the host and access server.

LED   Light Emitting Diode.

Link compression   Compression type that compresses the entire packet. Typically used with point-to-point connections like dedicated connections or an *Integrated Services Digital Network* (ISDN).

Lossless   A compression scheme that does not allow for any loss of information when uncompressed.

Lossy   A compression scheme that allows for a loss of information when uncompressed.

Man in Middle (MIM)   An attack against the *public key exchange* (PKE) in which the attacker substitutes his own public key for the requested public key.

Message Digest #5 (MD5)   A one-way hash algorithm that is used in crypto applications such as authentication.

MNP   The Microcom Networking Protocol is a protocol created by Microcom for error correction and error detection.

Modem   A device that converts digital signals into analog signals for transmission over the public telephone network.

Modulate   The process of converting digital signals to an analog signal.

MPPC   Microsoft Point-to-Point Compression. A compression method developed by Microsoft used on dial-up links for use with Windows machines. It is defined by RFC 2118.

Multilink PPP   The aggregation of multiple links into a single logical WAN connection.

Multiplex Identifier (MID)   The logical number associated to a specific user's *Layer Two tunneling protocol / Layer Two forwarding* (L2TP/L2F) session.

National Institute of Standards and Technology (NIST)   U.S. government agency that establishes national standards.

National Security Agency (NSA)   U.S. government agency responsible for intercepting foreign communications for intelligence reasons and for developing crypto systems to protect U. S. government communications.

NCP   Network Control Protocol, used to negotiate network layer protocol attributes for use with a dialup session.

NRN   NetWare Remote Node, an encapsulation method used over dialup links by NetWare Connect.

Nyquist theorem   A theorem that states you can reconstruct an analog signal by sampling two times the highest frequency to be reconstuctured.

Ohms   A measurement of electrical resistance.

One-way hash   Hash function for which it is extremely difficult to construct two blocks of data that yield exactly the same hash result. Ideally, it should require a brute force search to find two data blocks that yield the same result.

OSI   Open Systems Interconnection that describes a model for which network communication takes place.

output feedback (OFB)   Block cipher mode in which the cipher is used to generate the key stream.

PAD   Packet Assembler/Disassembler. It is responsible for connecting asynchronous terminals to an X.25 network.

PAP   Password Authentication Protocol, the simplest authentication protocol.

Payload compression   Compression type that only compresses the body of the packet, because the header is still required in order to correctly deliver the packet. It is typically used with Wide Area Network (WAN) services such as Frame Relay and X.25.

PCM   Pulse Code Modulation enables telcos to convert analog transmissions to digital for superior communication.

Perimeter   Boundary between an intranet (organizations network) and an outside network.

Perfect Forward Secrecy (PFS)   PFS ensures that a given *IP Security* (IPSec) *Security Association's* (SA) key was not derived from any other secret (like some other keys).

Plaintext   Message that has not been encrypted, or data that was decrypted from ciphertext.

Plug-and-Play   A hardware and software specification that enables a plug-and-play computer to define the system resources any plug-and-play-compliant device uses.

Point-to-Point Tunneling Protocol (PPTP)   An IP tunneling protocol based upon the *Point-to-Point Protocol* (PPP), designed to encapsulate *Internetwork Packet Exchange* (IPX) and AppleTalk within IP for transmission across IP-based networks.

POTS   Plain Old Telephone System.

PPP   The Point-to-Point Protocol is an encapsulation method used over asynchronous connections.

Predictor   Link compression protocol that utilizes the Lempel-Ziv encoding method and is used on *Wide Area Network* (WAN) links. It is more central processing unit-intensive but less memory-intensive.

PRI   Primary Rate Interface. It consists of 23 B-channels in the U.S. (T1) and 30 B-channels in Europe (E1).

Priority queuing   Method of queuing that enables the priority of high queues at the exclusion of other queues.

Private key   Key used in public key crypto that belongs to an individual entity and must be kept secret.

PSE   Packet Switching Exchange. It defines the cloud in a X.25 and Frame Relay network.

Public key   Key used in public key crypto that belongs to an individual entity and is distributed publicly. By using the public key to encrypt a message, only the key's owner can decrypt using his private key.

Public key algorithm   An asymmetric algorithm that uses a pair of keys, a public key and private key, for encryption and decryption.

PVC   Permanent Virtual Circuit. One of two types of virtual circuits in X.25 and Frame Relay networks. Once established, the connection remains until disrupted by power outage, *Wide Area Network* (WAN) outage, or human intervention.

RADIUS   Remote Access Dial-In User Service. It is used for centralized authentication and various other accounting, authorization processes.

Repeaters   A device that reconditions a signal and passes it onto the next segment. It works at the physical layer of the Open Standards Interface (OSI) model.

RIP   The Routing Information Protocol is a routing protocol that is not used very much because of its limited scalability and bandwidth usage.

Rivest Cipher #2 (RC2)   A block cipher sold by RSA Data Security, Inc. RC2 used with a 40-bit crypto key was treated as lightweight crypto under older U. S. crypto export rules.

Rivest Cipher #4 (RC4)   A stream cipher that is widely used in commercial products. RC4 with a 40-bit key provides exportable lightweight crypto for use with Web browsers.

Rivest, Shamir, Adelman (RSA)   Public key crypto system that can encrypt or decrypt data and also apply or verify a digital signature.

Rolled adapter   An adapter in which pins 3 and 4 are reversed inside the adapter that interfaces a cable and a *data terminal equipment* (DTE) or *data circuit-terminating equipment* (DCE) device.

Rolled cable   A wire in which pins 3 and 4 are reversed inside the cable that connects two devices (DTE or DCE).

RTS   A signal sent by the sender indicating it is ready to send data.

RxD   Receive data.

SAP   Service Advertisement Protocol. It is used to advertise *Internetwork Packet Exchange* (IPX)-related services.

Secret key   Crypto key that is used in symmetric algorithms.

Security Association (SA)   An instance of security policy and keying material applied to a data flow. Both the *Internet Key Exchange* (IKE) protocol and *IP Security* (IPSec) use SAs, although for different reasons. A set of SAs is needed for a protected data stream, one per direction per protocol.

Shim   A component inserted at a well-known interface between two other components.

SLIP   The Serial Line Internet Protocol was originally developed for use with Berkeley Unix for transmission over slow dialup connections.

SONET   A Synchronous Optical Network is a high-speed network designed to run on optical fiber at speeds up to 2.5Gbps.

STAC   A link compression protocol that utilizes the Lempel-Ziv encoding method. It is more *central processing unit* (CPU)-intensive but less memory-intensive.

Stopbits   A signal that indicates the end of a datagram.

Stream cipher   Cipher that operates on a continuous data stream.

Superconductors   A substance that has extremely low electrical resistance typically at very low temperatures.

SVC   Switched Virtual Circuit, one of two types of virtual circuits in x.25 and Frame Relay networks. They can be established on demand and torn down when no longer needed. Similar to *Dial on Demand Routing* (DDR).

Symmetric algorithm   Crypto algorithm that uses the same crypto key for encrypting and decrypting. Also called a secret key algorithm.

T1 T1s transmit data in a DS-1 format at 1.544 Mbps.

T3 T3s transmit data in a DS-3 format at 45.736 Mbps.

TACACS Terminal Access Controller Access Control System. Proprietary software used for centralized authentication and various other accounting, authorization processes.

TDM Time Division Multiplexing.

TE1 A device that complies with an *Integrated Services Digital Network* (ISDN) network.

TE2 A device that does not comply with an *Integrated Services Digital Network* (ISDN) network.

Telnet A character-oriented terminal traffic protocol.

Terminal Adapter A device used to connect non-*Integrated Services Digital Network* (ISDN) equipment to an ISDN network.

Transform-set A transform describes a security protocol (AH or ESP) with its corresponding algorithms.

Transport mode *Enhanced Service Provider* (ESP) mode that encrypts the data contents of a packet and leaves the original IP addresses in plaintext.

Triple DES (3DES) Cipher that applies the DES cipher three times with either two or three different *Data Encryption Standard* (DES) keys.

TTY Asynchronous line in a Cisco access server.

Tunneling The encapsulation of complete datagrams within other datagrams. Frequently used to transmit non-IP protocols across IP networks.

Tunnel mode Enhanced Service Provider (ESP) mode that encrypts an entire IP packet including the IP header.

TxD Transmit Data.

UART The Universal Asynchronous Receiver/Transmitter is responsible for the sending and receiving of data on a serial port.

V.35 A standard from *International Telegraph and Telephone Consultative Committee* (CCITT) describing data transmission.

VC *See* virtual circuit.

Virtual circuit End-to-end significance defines the channel used between two routers for a specific set of protocols.

Virtual private network (VPN) A private network built on a public network. Hosts within the private network use encryption to communicate with other hosts.

Virtual Private Dialup Networking (VPDN) A system that enables the separation of the physical call with the logical call, giving the appearance that the host dialed directly into the remote network (logical) even though they have dialed into a local Internet service provider ISP (physical).

Virtual profiles The dynamic creation application of attributes that pertain to an individual.

VTY Telnet line.

WAN Wide Area Network.

Weighted Fair Queuing Method of queuing that enables all conversations equal access to a *Wide Area Network* (WAN).

x2 Proprietary 56K protocol.

APPENDIX E

Bibliography

Bates, J. Regis, and Donald Gregory. *Voice and Data Communications Handbook*. New York, NY: McGraw Hill, 2000.

Brown, Steven. *Implementing Virtual Private Networks*. New York, NY: McGraw Hill, 1999.

Caputo, Robert. *Cisco Packetized Voice and Data Integration*. New York, NY: McGraw Hill, 1999.

CCIE Fundamentals: Network Design and Case Studies. Indianapolis, IN: Cisco Press, 1999.

Cheswick, William, and Steven Bellovin. *Firewalls and Internet Security: Repelling the Wily Hacker*. New York, NY: Addison Wesley, 2000.

Cisco IOS Dial Solutions. Indianapolis, IN: Cisco Press, 1998.

Cisco IOS Network Security. Indianapolis, IN: Cisco Press, 1998.

Coulibaly, Mack. *Cisco IOS Releases: The Complete Reference*. Indianapolis, IN: Cisco Press, 2000.

Dhawan, Chander. *Remote Access Networks*. New York, NY: McGraw Hill, 1998.

Downes, Kevin, Merilee Ford, H. Kim Lew, Steve Spanier, and Tim Stevenson. *Internetworking Technologies Handbook*. Indianapolis, IN: Cisco Press, 1998.

Fisher, Paul. *Cisco Routers for ISDN*. New York, NY: McGraw Hill, 1999.

Held, Gilbert. *Understanding Data Communications*. Indianapolis, IN: SAMS Publishing, 1996.

———. *Voice and Data Internetworking*. New York, NY: McGraw Hill, 2000.

Huston, Geoff. *Internet Performance Survival Guide: QoS Strategies for Multiservice*. New York, NY: Wiley, 1998.

Kaeo, Merike. *Designing Network Security*. Indianapolis, IN: Cisco Press, 1999.

Kessler, Gary C., and Peter V. Southwick. *ISDN: Concepts, Facilities, and Services*. New York, NY: McGraw Hill, 1998.

Kosiur, Dave. *Building and Managing Virtual Private Networks*. New York, NY: Wiley, 1998.

Lee, Donald. *Enhanced IP Services for Cisco Networks*. Indianapolis, IN: Cisco Press, 1999.

McDysan, Dave. *VPN Applications Guide*. New York, NY: Wiley, 1998.

Norton, Peter, and Mike Stockman. *Peter Norton's Network Security Fundamentals*. Indianapolis, IN: SAMS Publishing, 2000.

Oppenheimer, Priscilla. *Top-Down Network Design*. Indianapolis, IN: Cisco Press, 1999.

Perlmutter, Bruce, and Jonathan Zarkower. *Virtual Private Networking: A View from the Trenches*. Upper Saddle River, NJ: Prentice Hall, 2000.

Quiggle, Adam. *Building Cisco Remote Access Networks*. New York, NY: McGraw Hill, 2000.

Scott, Charlie, and Paul Wolfe. Mike Erwin. *Virtual Private Networks, 2nd Edition*. Sebastopol, CA: O'Reilly & Associates, 1998.

Shea, Richard. *L2TP: Implementation and Operation*. Reading, MA: Addison-Wesley, 2000.

Shinder, Debra Littlejohn, Thomas W. Shinder, and Syngress staff. *Managing Windows 2000 Network Services*. Rockland, MA: Syngress Media Inc, 2000.

Shinder, Thomas W., Stace Cunningham, D. Lynn White, Garrick Olsen, and Syngress staff. *Configuring Windows 2000 Server Security*. Rockland, MA: Syngress Media Inc, 1999.

Stallings, William. *Cryptography and Network Security: Principles and Practice*. Upper Saddle River, NJ: Prentice Hall, 1999.

Velte, Toby J., Amy Hanson, and Anthony T. Velte. *Cisco Internetworking with Windows NT and 2000*. New York, NY: McGraw Hill.

Index

Symbols

A

INTERNATIONAL CONTACT INFORMATION

AUSTRALIA
McGraw-Hill Book Company Australia Pty. Ltd.
TEL +61-2-9417-9899
FAX +61-2-9417-5687
http://www.mcgraw-hill.com.au
books-it_sydney@mcgraw-hill.com

CANADA
McGraw-Hill Ryerson Ltd.
TEL +905-430-5000
FAX +905-430-5020
http://www.mcgrawhill.ca

**GREECE, MIDDLE EAST,
NORTHERN AFRICA**
McGraw-Hill Hellas
TEL +30-1-656-0990-3-4
FAX +30-1-654-5525

MEXICO (Also serving Latin America)
McGraw-Hill Interamericana Editores S.A. de C.V.
TEL +525-117-1583
FAX +525-117-1589
http://www.mcgraw-hill.com.mx
fernando_castellanos@mcgraw-hill.com

SINGAPORE (Serving Asia)
McGraw-Hill Book Company
TEL +65-863-1580
FAX +65-862-3354
http://www.mcgraw-hill.com.sg
mghasia@mcgraw-hill.com

SOUTH AFRICA
McGraw-Hill South Africa
TEL +27-11-622-7512
FAX +27-11-622-9045
robyn_swanepoel@mcgraw-hill.com

**UNITED KINGDOM & EUROPE
(Excluding Southern Europe)**
McGraw-Hill Publishing Company
TEL +44-1-628-502500
FAX +44-1-628-770224
http://www.mcgraw-hill.co.uk
computing_neurope@mcgraw-hill.com

ALL OTHER INQUIRIES Contact:
Osborne/McGraw-Hill
TEL +1-510-549-6600
FAX +1-510-883-7600
http://www.osborne.com
omg_international@mcgraw-hill.com

Leading the Pack for Cisco® Solutions...

The McGraw-Hill Technical Expert Series

Having the right information at your fingertips is crucial when you're in the networking trenches. McGraw-Hill Technical Expert books are written by seasoned networking pros, offering you detailed, step-by-step instruction—plus hundreds of tips and techniques.

Cisco Router Handbook, Second Edition
GEORGE SACKETT
0-07-212756-2
$70.00

Cisco TCP/IP Professional Reference
CHRIS LEWIS
0-07-212557-8
$55.00

Remote Access for Cisco Networks
BILL BURTON
0-07-135200-7
$55.00

Available at bookstores everywhere!

OSBORNE
www.osborne.com

LaVergne, TN USA
18 March 2010
176435LV00003B/38/A